P9-DYY-515

The Good High School

WITHDRAWN

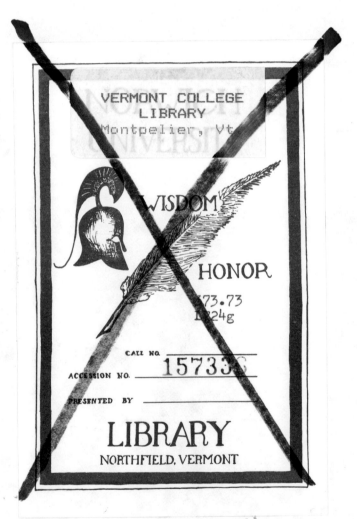

VERMONT COLLEGE
LIBRARY
Montpelier, Vt

WISDOM

HONOR

73.73
1324g

CALL NO.

157336

ACCESSION NO.

PRESENTED BY

LIBRARY
NORTHFIELD, VERMONT

WITHDRAWN

Please remember that this is a library book,
and that it belongs only temporarily to each
person who uses it. Be considerate. Do
not write in this, or any, library book.

THE GOOD
HIGH SCHOOL

Portraits of Character
and Culture

SARA LAWRENCE LIGHTFOOT

WITHDRAWN

Basic Books, Inc., Publishers   *New York*

Library of Congress Cataloging in Publication Data

Lightfoot, Sara Lawrence.
  The good high school.

  Bibliography: p. 387
  Includes index.
  1. High schools—United States—Case studies.
2. Education, Secondary—United States—Case studies.
I. Title.
LA222.L53   1983   373.73   83-70772
ISBN 0-465-02693-1

Copyright © 1983 by Basic Books, Inc.
Printed in the United States of America
Designed by Vincent Torre
10 9 8 7 6 5 4 3 2 1

This book is for my
Mother and Father,
Margaret and Charles Lawrence,
whose love, courage, and grace
I deeply cherish

CONTENTS

vii

Contents

ACKNOWLEDGMENTS

I want to begin by thanking the students, teachers, principals, and headmasters of the six schools portrayed in this book. In every case they generously welcomed me, patiently and thoughtfully responded to my questions, and gracefully tolerated my intrusions. They were brave in allowing me to observe and scrutinize their work, and their special blend of confidence and self-criticism is part of what makes their schools good. I am indebted to them all and admire their stamina, resilience, and good will.

This work has deeply personal roots, partly derived from my experiences as the subject of drawings, paintings, sculpture, and photography. As the artist's subject, I learned important lessons that greatly influenced my work as a social observer, a drawer of lives. I thank Paula Lawrence Wehmiller, Susan Sirris Wexler, Jane Beveridge, Marion Cuthbert, Christine Gwinn, Anthy Doxiadis Tripp, and Roger Gregoire for their artistic vision and empathetic regard; for teaching me about the creative, imaginative, and interpretive dimensions of portraiture. Mostly I thank them for the positive self-regard that I gained from being at the center of their benign and discerning gaze.

The more immediate origins of this book grew from intellectual encounters with colleagues and friends. Stephen Graubard, the inspired editor of *Daedalus*, convened and orchestrated the seminar that spawned the idea of high school portraits. I am thankful for his wisdom, enthusiasm, and critical judgment. The conversations among my colleagues in the *Daedalus* seminar, and the written pieces they produced in that jour-

Acknowledgments

nal, were important in shaping many of the ideas and perspectives found in this book. The chapters on George Washington Carver High School, Highland Park High School, and St. Paul's School were originally published in the Fall 1981 issue of *Daedalus*. The chapter on Brookline High School was funded by the Carnegie Foundation for the Advancement of Teaching as part of their major Study on the American High School. I am grateful for their support and extend special thanks to Vito Perrone, who coordinated the case study portion of the Carnegie project with a deft hand and great insight.

At various phases of my work I was assisted by three graduate students at Harvard. Linda Terrill Chapman spent several days in the field with me at Brookline High School. She was a perceptive observer, a systematic reporter, and a wonderful documenter of adolescent voices. In their reviews of the literature, Susan Templeton and Belle Zars were careful readers, thoughtful analysts, and enthusiastic critics of my work. Betty Barnes typed the bulk of this manuscript. I appreciate her dedication. Nancy Fjeldheim organized members of her staff in manuscript production, responding in crisis with a clear head, great efficiency, and professionalism. Jane Isay, editor extraordinaire, came into the picture at the perfect moment; carefully and wisely pushing me to the limits, asking the piercing questions that opened channels of thought, and offering her special brand of tough love. Thank you to Judith Greissman for graciously and enthusiastically shepherding the manuscript through its final stages. Theresa Craig, the project editor, deserves high praise for being beautifully organized and thoroughly unflappable.

Finally, how can I thank my family for their endurance, good humor, and love. Our daughter, Tolani, arrived a year into this three-year effort. Her presence brought a wonderful, vital spirit into our lives that became a welcome source of perspective and distraction for her mother. My days of writing were spiced with Tolani's visits. She brought laughter, play, and warm hugs that would fuel me until the next visit. Pam Frey, her resourceful and loving nanny, offered me peace of mind. I knew, that in her care, Tolani would be safe and sound. And Orlando Brown Lightfoot, my husband, provided the solace and support that only he can give me. I will always be thankful for his gentle patience, his wise counsel, his unswerving honesty, and his love.

The Good High School

157336

Origins: Art and Science

Several years ago an artist painted my portrait. Twice a week, for several weeks, I posed for the portrait. I would arrive early in the morning, climb the three flights to her garret studio, change into my beautifully embroidered Afghani dress and shimmering golden earrings, and stand motionless for an hour. It was difficult, wearing work trying to hold my pose, with arms hanging long and loose and hands clasped softly. At first the stance would feel natural, then I would lose my ease. My arms would stiffen, my fingers would press each other until the red showed through my brown skin, and my jaw would grow tight. The painter would notice the slow stiffening of my body and she would offer a break, sometimes a cup of tea. But we would soon return to the task and she would encourage me to relax and think good thoughts. Finally, the artist discovered the words that would produce the expression she wanted. "Think of how you would like your children to remember you," she said earnestly. Still not thirty and not yet a mother, I found the request overly sentimental, and almost incomprehensible. I did, however, try to produce a look that conveyed goodness, nurturance, care, and understanding.

The portrait passed through several phases and my image was transformed in front of my eyes. The transformations were all unsettling; even when the emerging image offered a prettier, more likable portrayal. With a sensitive eye, a meticulous brush, and enduring patience the artist painted me "from the inside out"; the skeleton sketched in before the bulky frame; the body contours drawn before the layers of clothing. I did not see the final product until months after its completion when my husband and I quickly bought the piece fearing it would be sold, and I would be hanging in someone else's living room.

When I saw it I was shocked, disappointed, and awed all in the same moment. I had the odd sensation that the portrait did not look like me, and yet it captured my essence. I quibbled about the eyes looking empty, the mouth being tight and severe, the expression being overly serious. I had not thought of myself as high-waisted, nor did I recognize the yellowish cast to my brown skin. The woman in the portrait looked more mature and static than I felt. "She's thirty years my senior," I complained to myself. I was relieved when friends saw the painting and commented on how much younger I looked in person and how the artist had not captured my vitality and spirit. Although many of the details of this representation seemed wrong, the whole was deeply familiar. She was not quite me as I saw myself, but she told me about parts of myself that I never would have noticed or admitted. More important, I had the eerie sensation that she anticipated my future and echoed my past. I could look at her and see my ancestors, and yes, see myself as my children would see me. In these troubling features there was an ageless quality. Time moved backward and forward through this still and silent woman.

When my husband brought the large canvas home he leaned it up against the wall and gave it a sharp and skeptical look. His first comment, "It's not you." His second, "It's a family portrait. . . . all of you women are in her." Both his observations seemed right to me. I did not see Sara alone (such a singular vision forced me to complain about the details, to deny my imperfections, to flinch at the signs of aging and vulnerability), but I did see my mother Margaret, my sister Paula, my grandmothers Lettie and Mary Elizabeth—women who have had a profound influence on my life, women who have shaped my vision of myself, women who have known me "from the inside out." And when my mother Margaret saw the portrait for the first time, she stood in the doorway of the dining room where it hung, her arms loosely hanging, her hands lightly clasped, her head slightly tilted, and her gaze maternal. A look of recognition swept over her face and tears shot to the corners of her eyes. "That's a picture of me," she said with wonder. And at that moment her posture and aspect made her look remarkably like the woman in the picture. The artist had caught my attempt to look maternal, a replica of the motherly eyes that had protected me all of my growing up years.

This family portrait was not the first portrait done of me. It was certainly the largest and most elaborate, but I had been sketched, painted, carved, even rendered in glass before this experience—each time learning something new about myself, or about the artistic process; each time watching myself evolve with that strange combination of shock and recognition.

The summer of my eighth birthday, my family was visited by a seventy year-old Black woman, a professor of sociology, an old and dear friend. A woman of warmth and dignity, she always seemed to have secret treasures hidden under her smooth exterior. On this visit, she brought charcoals and a sketch pad. Midafternoon, with the sun high in the sky, she asked me to sit for her in the rock garden behind our house. I chose a medium-sized boulder, perched myself upon it in an awkward, presentable pose, and tried to keep absolutely still. This suddenly static image disturbed the artist, who asked me to talk to her and feel comfortable about moving. She could never capture me, she explained, if I became statue-like. Movement was part of my being.

Her well-worn, strong, and knowing hands moved quickly and confidently across the paper. She seemed totally relaxed and unselfconscious; her fingers a smooth extension of the charcoal. Her deep calm soothed me and made me feel relaxed. But what I remember most clearly was the wonderful, glowing sensation I got from being attended to so fully. There were no distractions. I was the only one in her gaze. My image filled her eyes, and the sound of the chalk stroking the paper was palpable. The audible senses translated to tactile ones. After the warmth of this human encounter, the artistic product was almost forgettable. I do not recall whether I liked the portrait or not. I do remember feeling that there were no lines, only fuzzy impressions, and that I was rendered in motion, on the move. This fast-working artist whipped the page out of her sketch pad after less than an hour and gave it to me with one admonition: "Always remember you're beautiful," she said firmly.

The adult and child experiences of being an artist's subject were different in many ways. One quick and impressionistic, the other painstaking and laborious; one sitting on a big rock in the middle of my mother's pansies and impatiens, the other standing on a raised platform in an artist's studio; one with the midafternoon sun shining on my face interrupted by shifting tree shadows, the other with the subtle, well-placed track lights poised to offer consistent effects; one with me shifting, talking, and gesturing, and the other with me stationary and posed. But the experiences also taught me some of the same lessons—that portraits capture essence: the spirit, tempo, and movement of the young girl; the history and family of the grown woman. That portraits tell you about parts of yourself about which you are unaware, or to which you haven't attended. That portraits reflect a compelling paradox, of a moment in time and of timelessness. That portraits make the subjects feel "seen" in a way they have never felt seen before, fully attended to, wrapped up in an empathetic gaze. That an essential ingredient of creating a portrait is the process of human interaction. Artists must not view the subject as object, but as a person of myriad dimensions. Whether the artist sees the body stiffening and offers the woman a cup of tea, or tells the young girl that she does not have to be still like a statue, there is a recognition of the humanity and vulnerability of the subject. The artist's gaze is discerning as it searches for the essence, relentless as it tries to move past the surface images. But in finding the underside, in piercing the cover, in discovering the unseen, the artist offers a critical *and* generous perspective—one that is both tough and giving.

I recognize, of course, that portraits do not always capture these myriad human dimensions, nor do the encounters between artist and subject always have these empathetic, piercing qualities; but my experiences with the medium and the process influenced my work as a social observer and recorder of human encounter and experience. As a social scientist I wanted to develop a form of inquiry that would embrace many of the descriptive, aesthetic, and experiential dimensions that I had known as the artist's subject; that would combine science and art; that would be concerned with composition and design as well as description; that would depict motion and stopped time, history, and anticipated future.

I also wanted to enter into relationships with my "subjects" that had the qualities of empathetic regard, full and critical attention, and a discerning gaze. The encounters, carefully developed, would allow me to reveal the underside, the rough edges, the dimensions that often go unrecognized by the subjects themselves. I hoped to create portraits that would inspire shock and recognition in the subjects, and new understandings and insights in the viewers/readers. I am not an artist. My medium is not visual. My concern became then how I would translate the lines and shapes into written images and representations.

The portraits in this book are not drawn, they are written. They do not present images of a posed person, but descriptions of high schools inhabited by hundreds and thousands of people. In these six portraits, I seek to capture the culture of these schools, their essential features, their generic character, the values that define their curricular goals and institutional structures, and their individual styles and rituals. I also try to trace the connections between individual and institution—how the inhabitants create the school's culture and how they are shaped by it; how individual personality and style influence the collective character of the school. On each canvas, in broad strokes, I sketch the backdrop. The shapes and figures are more carefully and distinctly drawn, and attention is paid to design and composition. Using another artistic metaphor, for each portrait the stage is set, the props are arranged, the characters are presented, and the plot develops. Individual faces and voices are rendered in order to tell a broader story about the institutional culture. The details are selected to depict and display general phenomena about people and place. I tell the stories, paint the portrait—"from the inside out."

It is only in retrospect that I recognize the origins of my interest in portraiture derive partly from early experiences as the subject of an artist's brush. The aesthetic, interpersonal experiences of being sketched, painted, and carved had a profound effect on my views of myself, the artists, and the medium; and convinced me of the power of the form for artist, subject, and audience. Then my more recent intellectual experiences brought sharper focus to this work. Three years ago I casually entered a scholars' seminar expecting rare moments of pleasure and insight, as well as the more common experiences of deliberation, even boredom. However, I emerged from the seminar with new designs for research and writing, new thoughts about the forms of inquiry best suited to my style and temperament, and with new understandings of schools as cultural windows.

Stephen Graubard, the inspired editor of *Daedalus: The Journal of the Academy of Arts and Sciences*, was the major protagonist. Wanting to develop an issue on secondary schools, he gathered together leading scholars whose work centered on the history, policies, and practices of schools; the philosophies and goals shaping school curricula; the state of the art in pedagogy; and the developmental phenomena associated with adolescence. The disciplines of history, sociology, psychology, economics, and political science were well represented. As with all of the many groups Graubard deftly assembles, it was an illustrious panel of scholars whose diverse and passionate interests promised a lively exchange.

Although dominated by academics, the seminar also included practitioners in the field—people who primarily saw themselves as activists, whose perspectives were more immediate, subjective, pragmatic, and uncompromising than their academic colleagues. The practitioners were also considered leaders in their field with exemplary records as thoughtful, purposeful, and skilled superintendents, school administrators, teachers, and counselors. They came from broad geographic areas, represented different constituencies, and possessed a variety of styles and approaches that matched their daily work challenges. Even though the seminar offered the rare opportunity for formal and informal conversations between theorists and activists, the tone and substance of the discussions were dominated by the academics, who were more used to the carefully fashioned intellectual discourse.

A secondary imbalance in the seminar group reflected the administrators' dominance over the teachers and counselors. Not only were their numbers greater, but their voices were clearer and louder. They were more practiced in voicing proclamations, defending and rationalizing their positions, and engaging in public forums with other adults. The lost voices, therefore, were from those closest to the educational process, to the daily life of schools. With no students present and the token representation of teachers, one would have predicted a conversation full of abstractions and assumptions, largely shaped by intellectual understandings rather than emotional responses. From the top administrators, one could have anticipated bureaucratic language filled with the rhetoric of efficiency, cost-effectiveness, management style, and organizational behavior.

To some extent the stereotypes held firm and the anticipated differences in language, style, and thought patterns were reinforced. But there were memorable occasions when roles were switched; when the practitioners became the idealists, and the academics spoke like pragmatists; when the practitioners talked in abstractions and the academics referred to "real life." One of the superintendents, for example, had a subtle, smooth, charismatic style that mesmerized listeners. His messages were full of optimism, hope, and courage. They were inspirational lessons designed to move people beyond the constraints of reality, not embedded in management rhetoric or bounded by fiscal resources. If one had entered the room blindfolded it would have been difficult to identify his role or his perspective. Without the benefit of a label he sounded like a combination philosopher, spiritualist, and psychologist. These varied identities and surprisingly hybrid views of seminar members enlivened the discussion, and helped to erode the boundaries between academics and school people.

A third imbalance, less vividly recognizable, was between the "publics" and the "privates." Although the *Daedalus* seminar had been generously sponsored by St. Paul's School, an elite private school in New Hampshire, I recall a definite tilting toward public school issues. Of course, the great proportion of our country's young people attend public schools, and the greatest educational dilemmas and deprivations lie in the public arena. But the common assumption that the private schools were thriving and flourishing was unsettling, and was experienced by some members as a disregard for the great variations in success and resources among them. This asymmetry between academics and practitioners, between administrators and frontline people, and between publics and privates was neither surprising nor dysfunctional to the discussion. After all, *Daedalus* was not seeking a democratic forum of representative voices. It wanted the tough thinking of intellectuals inspired by the realism of activists, and it wanted the focus of conversation primarily on the most widespread, universal problems and prospects facing adolescent school children.

The seminar met several times over a two-year period, beginning with general, far-reaching discussions about the state of American secondary schooling, the pressing dilemmas it faces, the differences between past and present, the developmental issues of contemporary adolescents, and moving to more focused exchanges about what questions should be investigated in depth. After we had met together a few times, we began to hear echoes of earlier conversations and recognize redundancies and blind spots. As with any collection of academics, people brought to the discussion table their pet frameworks for viewing the world. Often attached to disciplinary backgrounds, these frameworks both clarified and distorted our views of life in secondary schools. The multiple lenses that we looked through offered different, often opposing, views of reality, but it was difficult for each of us to shift windows on the scene, to consider contrary perspectives. This is not an unusual phenomenon of intellectual debate. The various theories and observations are often the inspiration for lively exchanges and collective enlightenment. But the rigid declaration of views and perspectives, and the rehearsing of abstractions, can take the discussion further and further away from the reality that is being considered.

As the conversation swirled around me and as I participated in my share of obfuscation I began, along with others, to recognize the paradoxical exchange of elegant abstraction and dissonance with "reality." Or to put it more strongly, the seesaw effect of theorizing and wrong-headedness. As the frustrations increased, it became apparent to many of us that we needed more information about the culture of secondary schools and the daily experiences of the people who inhabit them, that we needed descriptions of life in schools that conveyed pictures of them, and that these portrayals needed to be relatively unencumbered by theoretical frames or rigid perspectives. The vivid descriptions could provide current material from which to work—road maps, texts of cultures that seemed distant from our abstractions.

Interestingly, it was hoped that these reality-based pictures would act as a counterbalance to a second tendency in the discussion, the temptation to speak autobiographically. In searching for "relevant" material we often found ourselves referring to our own experiences in schools or to those of our children. There were great sweeps in the conversation

9

from highly abstract descriptions of secondary schooling to vivid, charged anecdotal references. Both extremes seemed inadequate—the first guided by distant assumptions, and the second shaped by retrospection and passion.

The third tendency in our discussions was again related to a liability common to social scientists: the tendency to focus on what is wrong rather than search for what is right, to describe pathology rather than health. It seemed easy for us to recite all of the problems teachers and students confront and create in secondary schools—the truancy and dropout rates, the vandalism, the alcohol and drug addiction, the illiteracy of graduates, the teacher "burnout," the undisciplined curriculum, the rigid tracking, the racial warfare, on and on—but it seemed difficult, even awkward, to find the goodness and talk about the successes. There were some contrapuntal tendencies, scholars who pointed to contemporary achievements—a historian who saw great strides in the success rate of secondary schools as a mechanism of democratization; a sociologist who claimed that many of those issues that academics regard as persistent, irreconcilable dilemmas of education are not perceived as such by practicing teachers, who resolve them in the immediacy of practice. But the strong themes of conversation were distressingly pessimistic.

Certainly, a prominent tradition of social science inquiry has been the uncovering of malignancies and the search for their cures. This has been particularly true for researchers studying schools. The negative regard of schools and the documentation of their failure are shaped by profound feelings of dissatisfaction and disappointment among scholars and lay people. Schools have not fulfilled our great expectations. They have not produced a civilized, literate populace; they have not eliminated deep inequalities; they have not encouraged creativity, innovation, or social change. The list of their inadequacies and failures are endless.[1] The great expectations remain unmet while the origins of the expectations continue to be largely unexamined. Surely some of the complaints reflect minimal requirements and are clearly warranted, and others serve as important goals towards which school people can strive. But still other expectations hang on, impossible in their idealism, and distort efforts to improve schools.[2] In recent years scholars who study schools have become increasingly aware of this tendency towards negativism, the pessimistic thrust of a large body of research, and have begun to ask a different series of questions. The inquiry begins by examining what works, identifying good schools, asking what is right, here, and whether it is replicable, transportable, to other environs.[3]

Stephen Graubard sought to respond to the three persistent temptations that plagued our conversations: the tendency toward theoretical abstraction, toward autobiography, and toward negativism. Not seeking to rectify these common academic vulnerabilities, but searching for a way to counterbalance the tendencies, he asked three members of the seminar to do life drawings of real schools in action. Robert Coles of Harvard University, Philip Jackson of the University of Chicago, and I became the seminar's representatives in "the field." Each of us had had extensive experience in social observation, an intense and long interest in the lives of schools, and a burning curiosity about the contemporary scene of adolescents and high schools. We also had enormous admiration for one another's work, respected the great differences in our orientations and styles, and were eager to collaborate on a project together.

Three schools were chosen by Graubard with the help of colleagues and school people throughout the country who were knowledgeable about the educational landscape. First, we searched for goodness—exemplary schools that might tell us something about the myriad definitions of educational success and how it is achieved. Second, we wanted diversity among the secondary schools—diversity of philosophies, resources, populations, and type. And third, we were eager to have geographic representation. Our selection was not scientific. No random sample was taken, no large-scale opinion surveys were sent out in order to identify good schools. They were chosen because of their reputation among school people, the high opinion of them shared by their inhabitants and surrounding communities, and because they offered easy and generous entry.

St. Paul's School, the major sponsor of the *Daedalus* project, was an obvious and immediate choice for representing elite, private schools. Celebrating its 125th anniversary, this seemed a ripe, ceremonial occasion for ritual *and* scrutiny. Believing that St. Paul's should do more than focus inward, William Oates, the Rector, had suggested to Graubard that this was a fine opportunity to look more broadly at secondary education in general. Despite the fact that St. Paul's provided the resources for the *Daedalus* project, Oates was convincing in his wish that his school be regarded with an honest and critical eye. He was not seeking a puff piece or a public relations story when he agreed that we should visit, but an unencumbered, rich description by practiced observers—an outsider's perspective.

George Washington Carver High School in Atlanta, Georgia, is a public school with a lower-class Black population. Long known as the dumping ground of Atlanta schools, it has recently made a dramatic turnaround under the charismatic leadership of a new Black principal. The school's recovery has been watched closely and firmly supported by

Alonzo Crim, Atlanta's smooth and forceful superintendent of schools. The connections to Carver High were almost as immediate as the St. Paul's entree. Crim was a contributing member of the *Daedalus* seminar and kindly offered Carver as an example of inspired, inner-city education. At the other end of the spectrum from the privileged, confident culture of St. Paul's, Carver seemed an interesting and provocative contrast.

Highland Park High School, the third chosen, is in a suburban, upper middle-class community northwest of Chicago. With a large Jewish population, it has a reputation as an exclusive enclave dominated by aggressive, bright, and ambitious students. The school's homogeneous image of achievement and success does not match the diverse and complicated reality inside. With the prevailing themes of ambition, success, and stress, Highland Park represented a third cultural window—one that was neither comfortable in its abundance, like St. Paul's, nor struggling with problems of inequality and low status, like Carver. St. Paul's, the elite academy; Carver, the dynamic inner city school; and Highland Park, the prestigious upper middle-class suburban school, do not represent the great variety of schools in this country. But seminar members thought that they reflected the extremes of the broad range of educational options available in this society, diverse geographic regions, and striking differences in student and teacher populations, and were, therefore, useful settings for our inquiry.

Just as the choice of the three schools was not accomplished scientifically, so too were the form and methods of inquiry used by each of us not classically designed. In order to take full advantage of the diverse perspectives of the three observers, we decided not to define rigid a priori research agendas or consult with one another about our plan of action. We were to produce three distinctly individual documents, not collaborative pieces. It was decided that each of us would separately visit each school for three or four days, observe, and write without conversation or interaction. After collecting descriptive data on the schools we were to create pieces that captured their lives, rhythms, and rituals. No other methodological boundaries or strategies were stipulated in advance of our visits.

The observers agreed that such fast and intuitive work could never be characterized as classical, systematic research; that we would inevitably be taking great risks of interpretation; and that our written pieces would reveal at least as much about the authors as they did about the school settings. We were not doing the carefully documented, longitudinal work of ethnographers, although we were interested in many of the same qualitative and interpretive phenomena. We were not creating holistic case studies that would capture multi-dimensional contexts and intersecting processes, although we wanted to describe schools as cultural organizations and uncover the implicit values that guided their structures and decision making. As a matter of fact, before embarking on this adventure, it was easier to know what we would *not* be able to accomplish in a few days (even with our practiced eyes, years of experience in schools, and great curiosity) than it was to know what we might be able to produce.

I suggested we call our pieces "portraits" because I thought it would allow us a measure of freedom from the traditions and constraints of disciplined research methods, and because I hoped that our work would be defined by aesthetic, as well as empirical and analytic, dimensions.[4] I doubt that my two observer colleagues necessarily shared these goals of scientific and artistic integration. Perhaps they did not even feel inhibited by their long years of research training and the usual commitments of tough skepticism, standards of reliability, the dogged pursuit of evidence, and very-close-to-the-vest interpretations. After all, part of the adventure of this exercise was the unshared assumptions and individual goals each of us took to the field.

Ironically, I discovered that rather than being a burden, my research training supported and enhanced the development of this emerging form of inquiry. The rapid-fire work of portraiture used many of the same strategies and techniques that I had used in the longitudinal ethnographic research of my earlier studies. The systematic, detailed observational work that had been part of my prior long-term research helped me document the subtle exchanges and behavioral details that were so important to the larger picture. And the thematic in-depth interviews that have been central to data gathering in my previous work guided the quality of my interactions with respondents, and helped me know the scope and boundaries of a useful conversation.[5]

Not only were the techniques of observation, interviewing, and ethnographic description similar to my earlier research experiences, but the values and assumptions that have shaped my work also held firm with the creation of portraits. For example, I visited the schools with a commitment to holistic, complex, contextual descriptions of reality; with a belief that environments and processes should be examined from the outsider's more distant perspective and the insider's immediate, subjective view; that the truth lies in the integration of various perspectives rather than in the choice of one as dominant and "objective"; that I must always listen for the deviant voice as an important version of the truth (and as a useful indicator of what the culture or social group defines as normal), not disregard it as outside of the central pattern. I also believe, as did those artists who painted me, that portraits—and research—should be critical *and* generous, allowing subjects to reveal their many dimensions and strengths, but also attempting to pierce through the smooth and correct veneers. Given these empirical tendencies and value positions, it is not surprising that the portraits I have written move from the inside out, search out unspoken (often unrecognized) institutional and interpersonnel conflicts, listen for minority voices and deviant views, and seek to capture the essences, rather than the visible symbols, of school life.

It is in this conscious expression of *personal* intellectual and value positions that one sees some of the differences between "pure" research and portraiture.[6] In the former, the investigator behaves in a counterintuitive manner, always the consummate skeptic. He or she tries not to let personal inclinations shape the inquiry. Portraiture, on the other hand, permits these same inclinations to flourish, admits the shaping hand of the artist, and is less concerned with anticipated problems of replication.[7] Working quickly and at great risk, the social scientist who writes the portrait is more of a "creator" than the "pure" research colleague. The portraitist rapidly selects themes that emerge as central to the landscape and vigorously pursues those themes in an attempt to establish their prevalence and centrality.[8] The pace is accelerated, choices are quickly made about the avenues to pursue, and much is left out—either unnoticed and unrecorded, or consciously excluded.

Even though the observer is more conscious of defining the canvas and shaping the connections among central themes, portraits seek to capture the insiders' views of what is important. Paradoxically, the observer is aware of offering shape to the portrait, and at the same time is aware of being shaped by the context. In my visits to schools, I did not enter with preconceived notions of key themes or a specific list of predetermined questions but tried to learn early what the inhabitants regarded as central issues.[9] Sometimes teachers', administrators', and students' concerns were easily identifiable because they were spoken of by large numbers of people or pointed to by respondents who were the best informed by virture of their roles or positions. In St. Paul's, for instance, everyone made reference to the shaping and determining influences of history, the power and certainty of tradition, and the comforts they provide. The Rector spoke of it as he bid farewell to the Seniors and their parents on graduation day. Many of the students enjoyed the rituals, ceremony, and clarity attached to the historical traditions of daily chapel. Dressed in the modern casual garb of L. L. Bean and Calvin Klein, they crowded into assigned seats at morning chapel and experienced feelings of community and enlightenment in the Gothic structure. Certainty, abundance, and history permitted creativity and risk-taking, dramatically expressed in the pedagogy, classroom processes and curricula developed by teachers. It is not that there was no one who resisted the historical imperative or struggled against the classical, unquestioned institutional forms. Certainly there were voices who offered criticism and resistance. Yet even their hushed rage and muted frustration confirmed the strength of the phenomenon of rootedness and tradition.

At George Washington Carver in Atlanta, there was an equally strong and identifiable contrary theme. The principal, with his passion, force, and energy, was fighting against historical imperatives and trying to forge a new image. Everything he did was calculated to undo old perceptions, reverse entrenched habits, and inculcate new behavioral and attitudinal forms. The new image and the proud rhetoric preceded the resistant institutional changes which lagged behind. Immediately, an observer could recognize these themes. They were shouted out by inspirational signs prominently displayed in the hall; they were part of a slick slide show on Carver the principal wanted me to watch *before* I visited the real place; they were part of the harangue a loving and angry teacher gave to the graduating seniors when he feared they would not live up to the image of correctness, civility, and poise at the graduation ceremony.

Sometimes the repetitive refrains, the persistent themes, were not voiced as forcefully and clearly as they were at Carver and St. Paul's, but I found that they emerged at all of the schools I visited and became the central dimensions of the portraits. It is in finding the connections between these themes that the observer begins to give shape to the portrait. In Highland Park, for example, teachers, students, administrators, and counselors spoke about the .tough competition, rigid hierarchies, and enormous stress experienced by students. There were obviously different perspectives concerning these phenomena. The more successful and rewarded students were less critical of the brutal competition, but they always feared losing their lofty status and worried about slipping down the steep pyramid. The low status, non-achieving students were more likely to be critical of the competition, seek rewards outside of school, and find ways of punishing the achievers. The broad range of students in the middle often felt lost and without identity or voice. The creative and analytic task of portraiture lies in exploring and describing these competing and dissonant perspectives, searching for their connections to other phenomena, and selecting the primary pieces of the story line for display.

One searches for coherence, for bringing order to phenomena that people may experience as chaotic or unrelated. The search has the qualities of an investigation. It is determined, uncompromising, and increasingly focused. All of one's senses are used to try to decipher what is important and the quality of things. Decisions are made about what must be left out in order to pursue what one thinks are central and critical properties. The piecing together of the portrait has elements of puzzle building and quilt making. How does one fit the jagged, uneven pieces together? When the pieces are in place, what designs appear? A tapestry emerges, a textured piece with shapes and colors that create moments of interest and emphasis. Detailed stories are told in order to illuminate more general phenomena; a subtle nuance of voice or posture reveals a critical attitude. What evolves is a piece of writing that conveys the tone, style and tempo of the school environment as well as its more static structures and behavioral processes. Words are chosen that try to create sensations and evoke visions for the reader. It is a palpable form, highly textured—what Jerome Bruner has referred to as "life writing."

In my visits to schools, I was continually overwhelmed by people's openness and generosity. Most seemed to welcome the opportunity to talk about themselves, the school, and the quality of their work. I was always very explicit about my purposes and role, and my honesty seemed to enhance people's willingness to speak candidly. Because of the accelerated pace of my work, there was less time for the elaborate rituals of entry used by most ethnographers. Conversations and interactions tended to be very intense and focused. Almost everyone I interviewed and many whom I observed thanked me for the opportunity to explore their thoughts, voice their ideas, and "learn what I think." Some were embarrassed by unleashed feelings that seemed to explode from them during our conversations. Said one tearful man quietly, "I trust that you will be careful with what I said . . . guard my hurt." A thoughtful young woman echoed the feelings I had had when I was the subject of an artist's work—the palpable sensation of complete and focused attention. "When you look at me so directly and listen to me so intensely I feel what I used to feel when my mother brushed my hair in the evenings," she said with surprise and poignancy.

Even though many expressed feelings of trust and personal connection to me, these exchanges were not designed to be friendly conversations or therapeutic interactions. Occasionally, there were moments of playfulness or catharsis. But for the most part, the exchanges were information gathering sessions with parameters and depth defined by the respondent and by my insistent, often tough, probes. During almost every interview I took long and detailed notes, usually trying to record the exact wording of the respondents. Observations of classes, sports events, play rehearsals, and teacher meetings were written in great detail as I documented verbal exchanges, tempo and mood shifts, as well as my impressionistic responses to what I was seeing. When spontaneous interactions occurred that did not permit an immediate record, or on the rare occasions when a person seemed uncomfortable with my note taking, I would find a place to write my recollections as soon as time would permit. After full days, and often evenings of observation, I would leave the field with pages and pages of detailed narratives. Once home, I would plow through the notes, filling in the blanks and clarifying confusions while my memory was still fresh. This initial perusal helped me identify the emerging themes and decide on a plan of action for the next day. My verbatim notes became the text for the interpretive, summary pieces I would compose as the day's final effort.

The observational records and interview material were supported by a thorough analysis of the school's written documents. During and after data collection I would review the published and unpublished written material in order to get a sense of how the school wanted to be perceived; how it sought to characterize activities and events; and who seemed to be the leading public figures, the most popular symbolic images. I analyzed, therefore, current and past school newspapers, yearbooks, and student literary and poetry collections. The school catalogues were closely reviewed in order to document curricular structure and substance, and to be able to contrast the advertised content with the processes I had observed. Finally, I was given access to unpublished reports on racial and ethnic distributions; on attendance, truancy, and disciplinary records; on college attendance rates and post-graduate vocational choices; and on departmental evaluations and faculty committee decisions. All of these written records served as important sources of information, perspective, and contrast with the descriptive data I collected.

The portraits emerged more slowly and deliberately than the gathering of data. In preparation for writing I would read my daily records and summaries several times over, often taking notes on my notes and offering tentative hypotheses and interpretations. When there were apparent contradictions, I would search for the roots of the dissonance. When I began to find persistent repetitions and elaborations of similar ideas, I would underscore them and find traces of the central themes in other contexts. Slowly the skeleton of the story would begin to emerge, filled in over time by detailed evidence, subtle description, and multiple perspectives. At this point the task would shift from one of searching for evidence and distilling themes to one of composition and aesthetic form, from finding the plot to telling the story. During this transition from empiricism to aesthetics I took great care not to distort the material, not to get seduced by the story's momentum or let a character take on fictional proportions. In my effort to remain faithful to the descriptive data, I would frequently return to my original notes, offer several examples of a single phenomenon, and make extravagant use of direct quotations.

The three initial pieces on St. Paul's, Carver, and Highland Park were followed by three more expansive and complicated portraits on Milton Academy, John F. Kennedy High School, and Brookline High School. Inspired by my early experiences, I was eager to explore further the methods of social science portraiture and learn more about the culture of high schools. The second wave of schools were chosen to parallel the resources, populations, and structures of the original three. That is, I selected an elite academy, an inner city school, and a suburban school, all recognized as exemplary, all receptive to my observations and scrutiny. In order to make data collection easier and more efficient, the second round of schools were all located in the Northeast, in relative proximity to one another. I relinquished geographic variety in an effort to spend more time in each place. For instance, Brookline High, a school of extraordinary reputation and enormous variety, is located in a suburb of Boston. Less than ten miles away from home and work, I was able to spend more than three times as many days in the field than I had at St. Paul's, Carver, or Highland Park. My observations at Milton Academy and Kennedy High, though not as extensive, also exceeded my first round of visits by several days. The expanded time frame allowed me to explore methodological questions of pace, tempo, and validity as well as compose portraits of greater complexity and depth. In this second round of portraits I was still intent upon conveying the life and immediacy of the school cultures, but I also wanted to probe issues in greater depth, have more time to follow intriguing leads, and find a clearer balance between the coherent story and the jagged inconsistencies.

Not only did I spend more days in the field when I visited Brookline, Kennedy, and Milton Academy; I also found that my growing experience in the strategies of portraiture made my visits more productive and efficient. I learned more comfortable and articulate ways of expressing the purposes and goals of my work; I grew more easy with adolescents and their styles and modes of expression; and I became more adept and detailed in my note taking. As my techniques became increasingly systematic and my style more adaptive, I also found it easier to take the interpersonal and interpretive risks that are often necessary in such highly personal work. It was not unusual, for example, for me to express ranges of emotion and affect in order to gain a better sense of a respondent's perspectives or feelings. Some exchanges were purposefully confrontational, others were supportive and receptive. But rarely did I proceed through the course of a day with a flat consistency and evenness in my approaches to various people or situations. With increased experience in the genre of portraiture, therefore, I became more disciplined and systematic on the one hand, and more eclectic and risk-taking on the other.[10] The longer portraits reflect somewhat longer stays in the field, greater experience in the method, and more confidence in using myself as interpreter.

In some sense, the second wave of portraits resemble the more painstaking, deliberate approach of the painter who carefully fashioned my adult image "from the inside out." The first wave of portraits, more like sketches in their length and contours, are reminiscent of the charcoal drawing done of me at eight in my mother's rock garden. Ironically, the quick, intuitive, earlier pieces render a more coherent, distilled portrayal. With greater penetration in the school settings, the later portraits evolved as more complicated pieces which tend to present contrasting perspectives and several angles on events and people. These pieces move closer to the often fragmented, complex quality of life in these settings, and they inevitably lose the coherence and certainty of the earlier portraits. In his essay on "Thick Description," in the *Interpretation of Culture*, Clifford Geertz writes about this intriguing phenomenon of the inverse relations between coherence and in-depth knowledge. As we get closer and closer to understanding the culture of a social group, the anatomy of an institution, we recognize the inevitable inconsistencies and dissonant themes. Smooth coherence fades into jagged incoherence as we grow less certain of a single story and discover the myriad tales to be told.[11]

The data for these portraits were collected over a period of three years. My first visit, to St. Paul's School, was in the winter of 1979, and my final visit, to Kennedy High School, took place in the fall of 1982. Although I made every effort to treat each school separately and not let my experiences at one influence my perceptions of another, I am certain that the order of my visits must have had some impact on my work in each setting. For example, the abundance and splendor of St. Paul's must have, to some extent, shaped my perception of deprivation and poverty during my next visit at Carver; just as the subtlety and understated expression of authority at the first school probably exaggerated my views of the charismatic, dramatic display of power at the second. My third visit, in the late fall of 1980, was to Highland Park. The second wave of observations at Brookline, Milton Academy, and Kennedy took place in fall,

1981; spring, 1982; and fall, 1982, respectively. In every case I collected the data in uninterrupted, consecutive days, believing that I would gain a much richer picture from total immersion in the schools than I would from intermittent visits. In fact, I found that the opportunity to live in these settings for several days, the chance to return immediately to unfinished business or unsolved puzzles the following day, and to enter into the field without distraction or interruption was a great benefit to my work. Description, interpretation, and analysis could proceed in tandem as I worked daily on the retrieval and review of my field notes. And each portrait was completely crafted before I moved on to data collection in the next school.

Although there were two distinct phases of data collection that produced three "sketches" followed by three "portraits" of high schools, this volume is not organized to conform to the chronology of visits, but to school types. It begins with urban school portraits, first looking at George Washington Carver High in Atlanta, then at John F. Kennedy High School. Located in Riverdale, one of the most scenic and affluent neighborhoods in New York, Kennedy draws its population from as far away as West Harlem and the Inwood section of upper Manhattan. Each morning two thousand Black and Hispanic students travel for more than an hour on the Broadway subway to get to Kennedy. They are joined by an upper middle-class, largely Jewish group from affluent sections of Riverdale; working-class Irish; and newly middle-class Blacks and Browns from Riverdale's flatlands and valley. Built ten years ago, Kennedy offers the compelling story of urban school pioneering—the brave and determined attempts to build a stable, pluralistic community; the balancing of forces between school-based autonomy and connection to the wider city and state bureaucracies; the negotiating of tensions between the school and the nearby community.

The suburban high schools, Highland Park and Brookline, are presented next. With a rich and proud history as an excellent school, for the past fifteen years Brookline has been experiencing the shock waves of change. Once a relatively elite, upper middle-class enclave, it has now become a school with a diverse racial, ethnic, and social class mix. Once a school that focused primarily on preparing students for prestigious colleges and universities, it now has a more diversified, eclectic curriculum designed to appeal to a broader range of students. Once referred to exclusively as an example of the best in "suburban" education, now many administrators and faculty consciously call Brookline an "urban" school. Not only has there been a significant transformation in the student population at Brookline; there are also bold attempts to rearrange and restructure power and decision making in the school. The new headmaster brought a different ideological stance towards responsibility and power at all levels of the school structure. With shifts in authority networks, decision-making bodies, and patterns of interaction among student groups, Brookline High is a wonderful example of an institution evolving a balance between a sturdy and abundant history and deliberate efforts at change.

The third section, on elite schools, includes the portraits of St. Paul's School and Milton Academy. Although steeped in history and prestige, life at Milton does not have the smooth certainty and preciousness of St. Paul's. Less than an hour's drive from Boston, the city backdrop is a much-used metaphor for Milton's attempts to combine the asylum and safety of an elite private school with the dynamic cosmopolitanism of city life. A portion of the day students arrive on the subway from Boston and "they bring the city with them." Their presence is an expression of the school's "intercourse with the wider world." Milton is proud of its windows that look out on the wider, more diversified scene; but it also practices a highly committed brand of education that to some extent underscores the boundaries between school and society. Some call it "tender loving care," others refer to it as "holistic medicine." Whatever its name, Milton has had a historic commitment to "humanistic" education that survives today. This educational philosophy values the individual, attends to the social and psychological as well as the intellectual dimensions of students, and views education as a great, uncertain adventure. The humanism of the pedagogical process at Milton combines with a purposefully decentralized authority structure to produce a highly fragile, dynamic and questioning school culture.

Throughout the text, I use the real names of the high schools I studied and the real names of their headmasters and principals. The rest of the cast of characters are given pseudonyms. The use of real names marks a significant departure from the classic traditions of social science. Usually pseudonyms are given to people and places in order to disguise their identities and assure some measure of anonymity. The practice of identifying the schools and their leaders by name was the form originally used in the *Daedalus* pieces. The journal's editor and school administrators decided that the identities of schools were a compelling part of the narratives, but that the less public figures (who had not entered into the original publication agreements) deserved some protection from public display. My decision to use the actual names of these high schools, therefore, was partly based on my wish to keep the forms consistent through-out the volume. But more important, I wanted to use this opportunity to honor the schools and make their work more widely visible.

Admittedly, the high schools portrayed in this book had an unusual degree of self-confidence, saw themselves as healthy and resilient institutions, and were relatively unthreatened by public scrutiny. Some school leaders believed that teachers, administrators, and parents in other schools might learn something from their stories. Others saw the study as an excellent opportunity for self-scrutiny and institutional diagnosis. It is easy, of course, to agree to disclosure when you anticipate that the praise will be consistently laudatory. However, these portraits are far from eulo-gistic proclamations. They are admiring and highly critical, and it was in the schools' tolerance for tough scrutiny that I saw the first evidence of their organizational strength and goodness.

Not only did I want to honor these schools, applaud their efforts and acclaim their successes; I also recognized that it was important for readers to be able to place these high schools in context—visualize the terrain, the community, the neighborhood streets, and the people. As a form that is partly shaped by aesthetic considerations, portraiture is to some extent a visual medium, full of powerful imagery. If I were to mask details of context or provide misleading descriptors, for example, I would begin to compromise the portrait. If I merely chose to change the institutions' names, without making any other contextual transformations, the schools would be immediately identifiable to all those who were either knowl-edgeable or curious. The decision to use the high schools' and leaders' real names, therefore, reflected the school people's generosity and confi-dence, my wish to publicly applaud their efforts, and my decision to portray the settings in vivid, exacting detail.

This book offers a rare view of human experience in each of these high schools. It is an important angle for social scientists who have tended to use methods of analysis that have precluded the perspectives and voices of the schools' inhabitants.[12] It is a critical lens for teachers and administrators who rarely have the opportunity to see their schools "whole" because in the immediacy of practice they must inevitably take on the narrow view connected to their roles. In these portraits they can see themselves (or people with similar habits, inclinations, and values with whom they can identify) in relation to a broader frame; as individ-uals within a complex network of personalities, social groups, structures, and cultures. It is also an intriguing view for parents of adolescents, or prospective adolescents, who are often excluded from high school life because of unwelcoming bureaucratic procedures, or their own attempts to keep the clear boundaries between home and school, or because their offspring are typically silent on the subject of school life.

Not only does this book offer a penetrating look inside high schools, it also explores the goodness of these schools. Purposefully, I chose to study good schools—schools that were described as good by faculty, students, parents, and communities; that had distinct reputations as fine institutions with clearly articulated goals and identities.[13] My descriptions of good high schools were, of course, shaped by my views on institutional goodness—a broader, more generous perspective than the one commonly used in the literature on "effective" schools. My first assumption about goodness was that it is not a static or absolute quality that can be quickly measured by a single indicator of success or effectiveness.[14] I do not see goodness as a reducible quality that is simply reflected in achievement scores, numbers of graduates attending college, literacy rates, or attendance records. I view each of these outcomes as significant indicators of some level of success in schools. And I view these as potent, shorthand signs of workable schools, but each taken separately, or even added together, does not equal goodness in schools. "Goodness" is a much more complicated notion that refers to what some social scientists describe as the school's "ethos," not discrete additive elements.[15] It refers to the mixture of parts that produce a whole. The whole includes people, structures, relationships, ideology, goals, intellectual substance, motivation, and will. It includes measurable indices such as attendance records, truancy rates, vandalism to property, percentages going on to college. But it also encompasses less tangible, more elusive qualities that can only be discerned through close, vivid description, through subtle nuances, through detailed narratives that reveal the sustaining values of an institution. It is important to know, for example, *how* the attendance officer seduces truant adolescents back to school—his strategies of persuasion, cajoling, and rewarding—not just the attendance records. Likewise, it is important to know whether students experience the caring, individualized attention of "humanistic" education, not merely be aware of the ideological rhetoric voiced by faculty and administrators.[16]

In recognizing goodness as a quality that refers to the complex whole, we also see it as situationally determined, not abstracted from context. In the search for goodness, it is essential to look within the particular setting that offers unique constraints, inhibitions, and opportunities for its expression. We have little understanding of how to interpret a behavior, an attitude, a value unless we see it embedded in a context and have some idea of the history and evolution of the ideals and norms of that setting.[17] From the more explicit physical dimensions of the school's ecology to the more interpretive dimensions of individual styles, group norms, and the organization's collective assumptions, it is important to regard goodness as a quality of institutional life expressed in context. This is not to say that some elements of goodness are not transportable or reproducible in other settings. But I do mean to say that the interpretation of goodness is only possible in context, and that the attempt to transpose "the goods" to other settings requires an awareness of the ecology and dynamics of the original context.

In these portraits, then, goodness is seen as a holistic dimension whose interpretation requires an embeddedness in the context. Through these portraits, one also recognizes that goodness is imperfect and changing. One of the persistent problems with social scientists' pursuit of effective schools, or their critiques of poor schools, is that they often view them as static and judge them against standards of perfection. Typically, their methods of inquiry are ahistorical and do not allow for an evolutionary view. A snapshot is taken at a moment in time and judgments are made about the success or worth of the school. But schools are changing institutions (despite the anachronistic caste that often plagues their public image) and recognitions of their goodness should reflect these transformations. For instance, we would think very differently about one school that got stuck in habits of mediocrity and a second school that exhibited similar habits but had travelled from chaotic, terrible beginnings, emerged into mediocrity, and was working towards improvement and change. Our perspective on the second school would recognize the changes over time, consciousness about weaknesses, the motivation to act, and the vision of future goals. Here goodness not only reflects the current workings of the institution but also how far it has come and where it is headed. The concern with evidence of institutional transformation is also linked with a definition of goodness that permits imperfection. The assumption is that no school will ever achieve perfection. It is inconceivable that any institution would ever establish an equilibrium that satisfied all of its inhabitants, where values closely matched behaviors, where there was no tension between tradition and change. Even the most impressive schools show striking moments of vulnerability, inconsistency, and awkwardness. It is not the absence of weakness that marks a good school, but how a school attends to the weakness. As a matter of fact, we will discover through these portraits that one of the qualities of good schools is their recognition and articulation of imperfection. Weakness, made visible, can be confronted directly and worked with over time. Goodness in schools, therefore, anticipates change and imperfection, and the former usually ushers in the disorientation and imbalance of the latter.

In offering this more generous, less absolutist vision of goodness I am in no way trying to compromise standards of excellence in education. Rather I am seeking to formulate a view that recognizes the myriad ways in which goodness gets expressed in various settings; that admits imperfection as an inevitable ingredient of goodness and refers instead to the inhabitants' handling of perceived weaknesses; that looks backward and forward to institutional change and the staged quality of goodness; that reveals goodness as a holistic concept, a complex mixture of variables whose expression can only be recognized through a detailed narrative of institutional and interpersonal processes.[18]

The final chapter of this book is an examination of the ways goodness was expressed in these six high schools. Despite their unique stories, there are themes that emerge in all of the settings, often in different forms and with different levels of success and purposiveness. One could not possibly generalize to the broad universe of high schools from these six cases. But the interpretive, in-depth analyses in this volume uncover compelling organizational themes worthy of further disciplined study.

In each of these schools we find intriguing and important lessons about educational goodness. We discover that good high schools reveal a sustained and visible ideological stance that guards them against powerful and shifting societal intrusions; that what is often perceived as solitary leadership in schools is fueled by partnerships and alliances with intimate, trusted associates. We discover that the qualities traditionally identified as female—nurturance, receptivity, responsiveness to relationships and context—are critical to the expression of a non-caricatured masculine leadership. Good leaders redefine the classic male domain of high school principals. We also discover that good high schools offer teachers the opportunity for autonomous expression, a wide angle on organizational participation and responsibility, and a degree of protection from the distorted social stereotypes that plague their profession.

In good high schools students are treated with fearless and empathetic attention by adults. Teachers know individual students well and are knowledgeable about adolescence as a developmental period. Their comfort with adolescents is expressed in the subtleties of humor and in the teachers' interpretation of and response to acts of deviance. Good schools exhibit coherent and sturdy authority structures which give support and legitimacy to the individual disciplinary gestures of teachers. Although adults and adolescents in high schools tend to focus a great deal of their attention on the social and psychological dimensions of the environment, good schools are also preoccupied with the rationale, coherence, and integrity of their academic curriculum. These intellectual considerations are often focused on resolving the perceived tensions between equity among student groups and the quality of academic pursuits.

Finally, the students in good high schools feel visible and accountable. They balance the pulls of peer group association against the constraints of adult requirements. And they embrace the tensions between the utilitarian promises of schooling and the playful adventures of learning. Each of these good schools portrayed in this book imperfectly display these themes. The final chapter is rich with vivid and textured examples of how these themes get expressed through personality, structures, interactions, ideology, habits, rituals, and symbols.

PART ONE

URBAN PORTRAITS

I

George Washington Carver High School

Charismatic Leadership: Building Bridges to a Wider World

AT THE TOP

When Dr. Hogans, the principal of Carver, speaks of "The Boss," he is referring to Dr. Alonzo Crim, the superintendent of the Atlanta Public Schools. Hogans speaks of him with great respect and deference. He warns a beleaguered music teacher about a last-minute change of plans in the graduation ceremonies, an early morning "request" from Crim. "The Boss absolutely wants the band to play at the graduation on Sunday. So you know that means we'll have to change our plans and get instruments down to the Civic Center. . . . This is critical. . . . What can I do to make this happen?" The negotiations with the central office for more buses, extra rehearsals, and the program readjustments are made within ten minutes of Crim's call. Hogans is relieved to have quickly extinguished "another brush fire," and the young music teacher goes off looking dazed and overwhelmed. The system's hierarchies are clear, the chain of command vivid. Although not visibly present, Crim is a guiding force at George Washington Carver High School. His vision for Atlanta Public Schools is woven into the everyday life of Carver.

Alonzo Crim is a smooth, urbane, articulate man who is proud of the work he is doing in Atlanta. He exudes thoughtfulness, focus, and excitement when he talks about the challenges of urban education. Superintendent of Atlanta for seven years, Crim plans to stay for one more term of four years so that he will be able to see the culmination of many of his efforts. Before coming to Atlanta, he was a superintendent in Compton, California, a largely Black system of 45,000 students. When he enrolled in the Administrative Careers Program at Harvard's School of Education, Crim had not intended to become a superintendent. He had expected to return to being a principal at Wendell Phillips High, a big-city, all-Black school on the South Side of Chicago. But at Harvard, Crim's advisor, Harold Hunt, quickly recognized his student's potential and gently but persistently encouraged him to consider superintending positions. When Crim would return discouraged from job interviews that Hunt had engineered, his mentor would offer generous support and sound advice. With each venture out into the world, Crim became less awkward and more self-assured. His style ten years later is meticulously professional, practiced, and smooth. There are no traces of the early vulnerabilities and uncertainties. He seems to meet the inevitable crises with a clear head and a firm hand.

His experiences at Wendell Phillips still serve him well. They help him identify with the teachers and administrators who work on the front line. He fully recognizes the social and economic barriers that school people face as they try to motivate and teach poor and minority children. He vividly recalls his first year as principal in Chicago when he had to welcome 3,200 students, socialize 85 novice teachers, and structure the school day around five lunch periods in a cramped cafeteria. Fights and skirmishes would flare up like brush fires around the school. Crim worked to change the school from a violent atmosphere dominated by adolescents to a livable environment run by adults.

He brings this direct experience to his work as the superintendent of Atlanta. When he recounts the challenges ahead, he speaks with passion and precision in the same voice. He is both optimistic and piercingly realistic. "My intention," says Crim, "is to provide a good education for poor, urban Blacks . . . . and for that I make no apologies." When Kenneth Clark and other old-time integrationists say he is misdirected in his efforts, Crim is filled with impatience and frustration. Why spend money and energy on an unrealistic goal? He sees his challenge as difficult, but clear: to provide quality education for the city's poor and minority children. There are 75,000 pupils in Atlanta's public schools; 54,000 are Title I students. Of the 121 schools in the system, only three are non-Title I schools. Ninety percent of the school system is Black. Crim reels off the statistics with ease.

His guarded optimism in the face of the harsh realities grows out of his childhood experiences. Born and reared on Chicago's West Side, Crim was a lonely survivor. Out of a class of about forty in which he began elementary school, only five finished high school, and only Crim went on to finish college. He cites the human casualties of his childhood as a way of giving perspective to the present. Today in Atlanta, 54 percent of the high school graduates go on to some form of higher education. Of the remaining 46 percent, 37 percent have secured jobs before they leave high school.

There are other signs of promise and success. In Atlanta, the schools' walls are not covered with graffiti, attendance is high, and there is minimal violence. Says Crim, "I think that the lack of violence is related to school size. Violence grows out of urban anonymity." Most of Atlanta's schools are comparatively small and there are explicit attempts to see faces in the crowd. In these signs of progress, Crim sees evidence of health and cause for hope. "We are now in the position to do something great. I get so tired of hearing folks say bad things about urban schools. . . . Next week I'll be asking the school board for the budget for a full day of kindergarten. I can expand here at a time when other systems are barely staying afloat." His job is part of a long mission, and a very serious one. It is almost as if Crim feels grateful for being "the chosen one," saved from the west side of Chicago. He owes it to himself, his people, and future generations of city children to increase the survival rate, even to help a few thrive.

Three years ago, Crim was getting ready to close Carver High School. It was an ugly reminder of the deterioration, chaos, and unrest that plagues many big-city schools. When the community got wind of Crim's intention to close the school, they rose up to defend it. "It's not much, but it is ours!" Hogans, an energetic, ambitious young principal of a nearby elementary school, was chosen to save Carver from total demise. Crim sensed that Hogans was capable of filling the void and thought he might take Carver on as a personal challenge. "He is a diamond in the rough, a jock who made good. . . . He's a man who learns and grows every day." In just a few years, Hogans has transformed Carver. He has used every ounce of his energy and spirit to turn the place around and Crim is proud of his efforts. "He has gotten the kids to listen. . . . He has disrupted the inertia."

THE OTHER SIDE OF THE TRACKS

George Washington Carver Comprehensive High School is in the southeastern section of Atlanta, the poorest area of the city. No matter what route you take from downtown Atlanta, you must cross the tracks in order to get to Carver. On the fifteen-minute journey from downtown, the scenery changes dramatically. Downtown Atlanta, with its bold new high-rises and shiny edifices, symbolizes the hope and transformation of an emerging southern metropolis. In contrast, southeast Atlanta looks gray and shabby. Fast-food joints, gas stations, small grocery stores, and low-cost housing line the main streets.

Carver High looks like a small college campus. An old gothic-looking structure bought from Clark College several years ago sits at the top of the hill and serves as the administration building. It is surrounded by several buildings—a modern concrete structure that houses the science and math departments; a building for gym, music, and the ROTC program; a long, two-story, brick building that houses the vocational education shops; a greenhouse; an auto-mechanics shop; other assorted small structures; and playing fields. In all, the campus has eight buildings on sixty-eight acres. A short distance away you can see the borders of the Carver Homes, the public housing projects where most of the Carver students live (75 percent of the students at Carver come from the Carver Homes, the remaining 25 percent are transfers from the twenty-two other high schools throughout the city). Built around World War II, row upon row of these simple, brick, two-level structures form an enclosed community. The low dwellings do not resemble the high-rise public housing of other major cities, but the sense of hopelessness and boundaries is just as apparent and the statistics are hauntingly similar. The median income for families in the Carver Homes is $3,700; 80 percent of the families are headed by single parents, and a higher percentage are on welfare.

The student enrollment at Carver High School has fluctuated, but seems to have stabilized at 890. As with all public high schools in Atlanta, Carver goes from eighth through twelfth grades. The five-year grade span is most vivid and visible with the boys. The young eighth-graders appear vulnerable and childlike in contrast to the tall, bearded senior boys who seem to have suddenly shot into manhood. Except for one white boy who had been bounced from several other schools and finally found a comfortable home at Carver, the students are all Black. The teaching staff is predominantly Black with a small sprinkling of White faces. The white teachers are so thoroughly interspersed into the faculty that everyone I ask finds it hard to say exactly how many there are. None of the seventy-five teachers on Carver's full-time staff live in the community. They travel several miles each morning from the more affluent middle-class sections of Atlanta and its suburbs. One teacher, who lives in a subdivision twelve miles away, is incredulous when I ask him whether he lives close by. "I can't imagine living close by . . . leaving the school, driving down the hill, and being home . . . my head couldn't take it." A little uncertain about how his remarks might be taken, he counters, "But none of the teachers look down on the kids even though they live in much classier neighborhoods, because the kids are sensitive and they would pick it up." The head guidance counselor of the school feels very connected to the community even though she, too, lives miles away. "I really take my job as servant to the community very seriously. . . . That phone is one of the best things we have. Not only this one on my desk but that one at home. I let kids know because a lot of parents work during the day. A lot of them can't make parent meetings. They can't come up here during the day so I let them know that my phone at home is open to them at any time. Because they hold the key to these kids, and you have to let parents know that, too."

A DIAMOND IN THE ROUGH

Despite the grim statistics and relentless poverty that appears unchanged in the Carver community, the high school has undergone a major transformation in the last four years. Everyone speaks of the time before and after the arrival of Dr. Hogans. Norris Hogans, a dark-skinned Black man in his late forties, has been a catalyst of change. A former football player, Hogans is powerful in stature and character. He dominates the school. Hogans is a man of great energy. He walks about the campus in perpetual motion, looking severe and determined, always carrying his walkie-talkie. Hogans does not want to be out of touch with any corner of his sphere. Through the walkie-talkie he barks orders and makes inquiries. His requests sound like commands. There is an immediacy about him, an unwillingness to wait or be held back.

Everyone agrees Hogans is powerful. Some view his power as the positive charisma and dynamic force required to turn an institution around and move it in a new direction. These enthusiasts recognize his abrupt, sometimes offensive style, but claim that his determined temperament is necessary to move things forward. They willingly submit to his autocratic decisions because they view his institutional goals as worthy and laudable. Hogans's detractors, on the other hand, tend to keep their complaints to themselves, forming a covert gossip ring and passively resisting his attempts to make changes by preserving their own inertia. Many of these resistant faculty have been at Carver for twenty-five or thirty years and are threatened by the changes that Hogans has forced on them. They were used to a more laissez-faire administrative policy that permitted more faculty autonomy. Some claim that these old-guard faculty were used to "sitting on their butts and not doing anything . . . and Hogans made them clean up their act." Although there must be a variety of responses to Hogans's leadership, he seems to be a person that people feel strongly about one way or the other. He is despised or revered. He is not a neutral figure but one who demands response and reaction from those around him.

Even those who applaud his great work speak of feeling threatened and submissive in his presence. His decisions are ultimate and non-negotiable, and his commands are sometimes delivered with a callous disregard for the feelings of the person to whom he is talking. Only a very few people seem to escape these assaults. They compose the "inner circle" that surrounds and supports Hogans, offering guidance and assistance, even private criticism. His closest colleague, friend, and confidant is Mr. James, the tall, slender, and impeccable vice-principal who Hogans brought with him to Carver. His visibility is high around campus as he maintains order and discipline, puts out "the brush fires," and serves as principal surrogate when Hogans is not around. He, too, carries a walkie-talkie and seems to be wired directly to Hogans. They are a pair, read each other's minds, and have a kind of intimacy that reflects a deep trust between them. Hogans is clearly the big boss, but James is his totally committed right-hand man. He takes care of the mundane, everyday, nitty-gritty details that elude Hogans, who is dealing with the larger picture. James's style is very similar to that of his boss. He is disciplined, autocratic, and uncompromising. Both men have an exuberant side and lively humor that appears privately and during after-school hours. Their laughter, storytelling, and ribbing behind the scenes seems to fuel them for the toughness that shapes their public image.

Joining in some of the backstage intimacy and fun is Ms. Powell, the registrar, and Mr. Thomas, a department head. Both are deeply committed to and protective of Hogans. They work very hard on his behalf and form a critical support system. Powell and Thomas see his weak and vulnerable side, and are privy to his mistakes and occasional poor judgment. Says Mr. Thomas, "I help 'Doc' out. Many times I've gotten him out of some tough jams." With great femininity and certainty, Ms. Powell provides a kind of disciplined attention to details. She is the recorder at important meetings, drafts letters for Hogan that require a subtle touch, and draws up the schedule of events for each day—all tasks that are not officially part of her job. She is valued by Hogans for her organizational talents, her hard work, and her candor. She lets him know gently and sweetly when he's off base and probably has more power than most realize. Underneath her soft exterior is a strong will, a keen intelligence, and a sturdy spirit.

Hogans's ultimate and uncompromising power is not without focus or reason. Certainly his temperamental tendencies appear to be authoritarian, and he has a large measure of personal ambition. But more important, he believes that he will only be able to realize his goals for Carver if he runs a tight ship. Discipline and authority have become the key to gaining control of a change process. His commitment is powerful and genuine. He believes that schools are transforming institutions that offer Black children the chance to participate meaningfully and productively in society. Schools must provide the discipline, the safety, and the resources that these students are not getting at home. And school must demand something from them. "I think we don't expect enough from our students. We seem to be content if they score two years below grade level." But before they can learn, Hogans believes they must be strictly disciplined and mannerly. A chaotic school setting and a permissive atmosphere can only lead to ruin and failure. So there is a preoccupation with rules and regulations at Carver. Radios and basketballs are confiscated by the vice-principal, boys can't wear caps or walk around with Afro-combs stuck in the back of their hair, and girls are not allowed to wear rollers in their hair. Visible conformity, obedience, and a dignified presence are critical concerns.

In fact, the mood on campus is one of order and decorum. There is not the edge of fear or the potential of violence that one often experiences going into large urban high schools. Bathrooms are free of graffiti, hallways are swept and kept clean, and students express pride in the restored campus. Students gathered in groups do not appear ominous and threatening, but well behaved and friendly. Throughout my visit students were mannerly and receptive. They were curious about my reasons for being there, and, when approached, were eager to tell their stories. The students' controlled demeanor is reinforced by their well-scrubbed appearance and their stylish and colorful dress. The external images seem to convey emerging feelings of self-esteem and hopes for moving up and out of poverty and ghetto life.

The discipline and control of students, however, does not appear to lead to a deeply engrained passivity. In response to questions about their lives at Carver, students are candid and critical. Some are even vociferous. They do not seem to fear the repercussions of being outspoken.

Terrence Tubman, a student leader, describes himself as a "fiery person." He is adamant about the overly oppressive rules at Carver which leave little room for exuberance and expression. For example, he complains about the callous abuse of authority Hogans showed when he abruptly disbanded the popular Friday afternoon student pep rallies:

"If it's on a Friday, nobody really wants to keep working Friday anyway. So, I couldn't see why we couldn't get a chance to release a little steam. But we had them cut to two and we just barely got four in during the whole year. I suggested, 'Why don't we have one every other week?' 'Uh, we'll see.' No definite answer. So it was just like at Hogans's whim. That's what it was. Whenever he felt like we should have a pep session, we'd have one. And he didn't see that this meant an awful lot to the students. This is something that they look forward to on Friday and I can see it because it's not every day they get a chance to release, you know, get down and holler. Even then we have restrictions on the pep sessions which I can't understand. When you come to a pep session, you come to act crazy and have a good time. Yet, we had to act a certain way at the pep session. I thought that was totally ridiculous and I've been to some fantastic pep sessions at other schools."

Although Terrence feels that students are disenfranchised and powerless, he thinks they are less silenced than teachers. He sees the grim passivity of teachers who are afraid to speak out:

"Teachers are very uptight. I say this with freeness because I see the teachers and talk with them. I have been granted the opportunity to really get behind the scenes to see what's going on. They're kind of scared. They see things they don't like but they are scared to say them because they don't want to get transferred. I feel that maybe you don't want to buck the ways, but if something's not right you got to speak out about it. That's probably one of the reasons why I'm a thorn because I don't mind saying this isn't cool and that isn't cool. But the teachers, they get paid and Hogans is the boss and you can't rock the boat. They're really getting uptight because a lot of them are forced to do an extra amount of work and they can't really concentrate on the student. This is an uptight situation."

The timid behavior that Terrence sees in teachers' responses to superior authority are not mimicked in students' interactions with teachers. For the most part, the relationships between students and teachers do not seem to be shaped by threat and fear. Even when I saw teachers becoming frustrated and overwhelmed in class, I never saw them deal abusively with students. Some seemed to have the patience of Job as students made insistent and noisy demands. Some seemed to disregard the turmoil and turn off at points when students were overly aggressive and disruptive. Still others, in the face of impending chaos, became more demanding and insistent upon a good performance and obedience from students. But I saw no evidence of careless punishment or unleashed anger on the part of the teachers. Rather, I saw the opposite—a genuine concern for their charges, a dedication to their work, and a commitment to broad institutional ideals.

On a hot, steamy morning, the seniors are rehearsing for the graduation exercises in the school gym. The job of orchestrating this extravaganza belongs to Mr. Thomas, the head of the English Department, who is excited about the theme and format of the occasion. Rather than the traditional graduation speeches, Thomas has designed a complex series of skits that display Carver's commitment to work, careers, and employment. In small groups on the stage, students enact scenes from the different vocations they have learned at Carver—dry cleaning, tailoring, nursing, auto mechanics, and horticulture—while student commentators offer the accompanying descriptions. The speakers, who have all memorized their speeches, stand rigidly, voicing their well-practiced and flowery prose. Thomas insists upon perfection as he makes the seniors practice their parts over and over again. When the speakers' lines come out dull and over-rehearsed, Thomas bursts forth dramatically and harshly admonishes them, "You are not projecting and I feel no life in it. . . . I feel you are very jittery. . . . I'm totally dissatisfied. . . . When you walked up there you didn't have enough *class*. You need class!" Thomas's message is uncompromising. He wants and expects an excellent performance. But underneath his vigorous and grueling demands, there is a theme of respect and caring. "If I didn't love you like I do, I wouldn't do this. . . . I wouldn't come down so hard on you. I'm not going to lighten up until you get it right. It must be perfect. I won't stand for less. And I won't stand for any negative attitudes. There is no time for that."

A sense of order and structure and an atmosphere of caring and concern would seem to be prerequisites of a successful and productive education, but not the full and necessary ingredients. These prerequisites do not easily or inevitably lead to academic excellence or inspired teaching and learning. In many of the classrooms I visited, very little of substance was happening educationally. Teachers were caught up in procedural directives and students appeared disinterested, turned off, or mildly disruptive. The institution has begun to emerge as stable and secure, but attention to the intellectual development and growth of students will require a different kind of focus, new pedagogical skills, and a profound change in faculty views of student capabilities. This most difficult challenge is connected, I think, to the perceptions faculty hold of student futures and the place and station that students are expected to take as adults in the world beyond school.

Mr. Parrot, a slow-talking, slight man with a deep Southern accent, teaches a social science course to juniors and seniors. The late-afternoon class is depleted by the absence of the seniors, who have gone off to rehearse for graduation. Five students, who have all straggled in well after the bell, are scattered throughout the large, well-equipped classroom. One has her head on the desk and is nodding off to sleep; another girl is chewing gum vigorously and leafing through a magazine; a third student stares straight ahead with glazed eyes. These three never respond to the teacher's questions and remain glumly silent during the class discussion. Two boys, Lowry and Richard, sit right under the teacher's nose and spend most of the class period being noisy and disruptive. Mr. Parrot hopes for other students to arrive, but finally decides to begin the class about twenty minutes after the bell. His opening remarks sound formal. He seems to be addressing his comments to more than the few people present. Standing behind a podium at the front of the room, he says, "Young people, let me have your attention quickly." Lowry and Richard quiet down momentarily, but the others appear to ignore his announcement of the final exam. "The exam is something I give to help you, not hurt you. Say if Carolyn got a D or an F on the final, I would not hold that against her because she has gotten mostly Bs all year. . . . I tend to go on progression. If you start out bad and finish good, I take that into consideration." Another ten minutes are consumed as the two vociferous boys ask distracting questions about the examination. Now thirty minutes into the period, Mr. Parrot takes his place at the overhead projector and begins the topic for the day: "social distance." Out of left field, Lowry asks, "Has anyone ever broken the sound barrier?" The teacher tries to ignore the question and proceed with his explanation of social distance, saying that when people approach one another in Spanish culture, "two feet is far away . . . to us it is close." Richard, intrigued by Parrot's comments, offers his understanding of social distance. "I heard of a guy who killed a guy because he stepped on his feet." The teacher is pleased that someone is with him and rewards Richard's contribution. "Very good. That's what we mean by social distance." The rest of the class consists of disjointed and chaotic exchanges between the strongwilled teacher and two relentless students. In the fragmented conversation, sociological terminology is hurled around and terms like "propaganda," "mass communication," and "public opinion" are given dubious definitions. When I talk to Mr. Parrot after class, he is undiscouraged. Enthusiastically, he says, "This is the best school I've worked in. . . . The administration is great, the principal and vice-principal are as thick as thieves, and that helps. . . . And I think most people care about the children and work hard."

Although there are glimmers of more lively and skillful teaching going on at Carver and evidence of some sophisticated work done by a few students in biology, graphic arts, and literature, for example, the academic program seems to lag far behind the vocational training that is offered in the more than thirty shops at the school. Perhaps one reason that the shop training appears to be more successful and well-focused is that teachers and students feel minimal ambivalence about what they are doing. Highly skilled technicians are clearly and systematically transmitting their knowledge to the next generation of workers. Mr. Ward, the instructor of the dry-cleaning shop, has been at Carver for over thirty years. He teaches what he knows best to over eighty students majoring in dry-cleaning. The appreciative and responsive learners can see the connections between the skills they are learning and jobs in the real world. And Mr. Ward is teaching something he feels proud of and values. His heart soars when students learn to do the job with exactness, thoroughness, and punctuality. These skills, translated to values concerning work and life, fit with Mr. Ward's notion of where his students will find themselves in the future. There is, then, an economy of effort, a promise of some return for one's work, and a lack of ambivalence in the minds of shop teachers.

This clarity of vision and purpose is reinforced by a strong history. For the one thing that seems continuous about this rapidly changing environment is the training for vocations. In times past, perhaps the shops were less well-equipped and more run-down, but the educational efforts led toward the same explicit goals—to teach poor, outcast Black students to become responsible workers, to move children from lives of poverty and chaos to futures of disciplined, steady, hard work. Historically, if these goals were met, teachers felt successful and rewarded.

But Hogans's vision for the school is far more ambitious and much less clearly focused. It is not that he looks down upon or devalues technical training, but that he wants a more comprehensive and sophisticated education for Carver students. As a matter of fact, he is intolerant of people who emphasize academics to the exclusion of shop training, and feels that realists and pragmatists must recognize the value of technicians. "After all, most plumbers get paid a lot more than teachers," he says. But in redesigning the school's curriculum, Hogans wants to create more options and more choices for expanded futures. He wants to open more doors in business, industry, and academia. Hogans's vision of a "comprehensive" high school (which includes the three realms of general, vocational, and academic training) is shaped by his wish to change and broaden the institutional processes and goals. But almost inevitably the broader horizons are not clearly defined; there are dispersion of effort, less clearly focused goals, and ambivalence in the hearts of many. The academic side of life seems undeveloped and embryonic at the same time the vocational training feels rooted in history and clearly drawn.

SHAPING A NEW IMAGE

Part of the struggle for a broader, more lofty definition reflects Carver's attempt to regain status. Its image as the city's dumping ground lingers on and casts a dark shadow on the new and enlightened attempts at change. Sometimes one gets a feeling that more efforts are going toward redefining the image than facing the reality. In fact, teachers in the other city high schools still continue to use Carver as a threat: "If you don't act right, we'll send you to Carver." Carver teachers are sometimes asked by their upwardly striving, middle-class friends why they have chosen to work with "those dumb kids over there," and other schools continue to dump their "bad kids" onto Carver's rolls. (This year, when it was discovered that many of the students from outside the district had been transferred to Carver because other schools could no longer handle them, Hogans transferred them out and the school size dropped from 1200 to 850.) Carver will no longer willingly accept outcasts from other schools and knows that their presence will prolong the negative images.

Despite his attempts to shape a new image, Hogans still seems to enjoy Carver's location "on the other side of the tracks." But his own continuous allusions to Carver's low status are heard as humorous self-deprecatory gestures—a way to get the upper hand on visitors who may feel uncomfortable venturing from one side of the tracks to the other, and a way to express his commitment to working in this community. At the same time he makes reference to Carver's poverty and lowly image, he fights to change it. With all his energy, he battles to turn the school around. I think he would be extremely satisfied if he managed to do the unthinkable—make the dumping ground into a place of excellence and productivity, a place that could be selective, a place where students would clamor to be admitted.

The promotional material on Carver begins to convey the new image. The first thing I am shown when I come to Carver is a slide tape that was originally prepared for a presentation on educational innovation given by Hogans at the National Academy of Science. It is a slick effort at public relations. In the slides, Carver looks like a snazzy college campus buzzing with activities, students are pictured as well-scrubbed and ambitious, and explicit connections are made between the world of business and profit and the curriculum and culture of the school. The language is flowery, even pretentious. As with most promotional attempts it expresses the optimistic ideal, not the reality. It conveys a sense that life at Carver is intense and productive, when it sometimes appears as unfocused and wasteful. Most pointedly, the vision and energy of Hogans shines through this slide tape—his orchestration of the myriad realms that constitute Carver, his imagination and ingenuity in building partnerships between business and education, and his ability to convince others of the worth of it all. Hogans is a very sophisticated entrepreneur, a packager of ideas, and this slide tape is one of his public expressions of image making.

There are many who complain that Hogans devotes far too much time creating images and expanding his empire and feel that his efforts are mostly designed to gain public attention and applause. In fact, he is already beginning to become something of a national figure, traveling around the country hoping to sell his ideas and spread his "model" of a comprehensive education. Recently, he appeared with Crim before a Congressional subcommittee and told the audience that he "did not come to ask for money but for a commitment to the challenges ahead." And he is planning a trip to Portland, then maybe to parts of Texas, to consult with school administrators on their educational plans.

Hogans clearly enjoys the exposure and the attention. It appeals to the extrovert that dominates his character. But he also seems to think of his role at Carver as largely external. He has an ambitious vision and he expects that the resources for executing his plan will be found in the connections he creates with sources of power and influence far beyond the poor Black community. So much of his energy and intellect is spent making and sustaining these connections, moving outward and away from Carver.

As they watch Hogans go off to wheel and deal, some Carver people feel neglected, left behind, and deeply envious. Students complain of his invisibility and his seeming disregard for their need for attention. For weeks they try to see him for an appointment, only to have their meeting cancelled for more important priorities. A senior angrily spoke of Hogans's disregard for students:

"I had to run him down to the office to get him and even then he's so busy I can barely get a word in edgewise to him, and if it's not that, there's somebody in his office at all times when I can't get in there. And I say, well, let me schedule an appointment so maybe I can come. And every time I come in, he's hopping to Washington or another place. Half the students on this campus can't even relate to him. It's not like he goes in with the students and tries to talk with each one. You get the feeling he's kind of way back, distant. I mean, he's just in the office and that's it. That's the way I feel about the administration. I feel that they have set themselves apart. If a student don't like it, they got to leave."

Occasionally, Hogans is abruptly reminded of his inattention to the internal life of Carver.

In a faculty meeting of department heads and program administrators, Hogans interrupts the largely bureaucratic proceedings by saying, "I want to share a personal problem with you." His tone immediately becomes softer and his face shows more concern. The day before, Hogans had been visited by Sylvia Brown, a seventeen year-old student at Carver. Sylvia's mother died several years before. Her eighty-two year-old father became disgusted with her adolescent ways and threw her out of the house eight months ago. In the meeting, the normally fast-moving Hogans pauses to contemplate Sylvia's story. "Sylvia kind of slipped through our fingers while all of this was going on. . . . Sylvia's a basically good girl. This is not a discipline problem. This is a counseling problem. . . . We spend far too much time on administrative and staff problems and too little on the well-being of individual students." Hogans concludes by expressing his own feelings of guilt. "The worst part about it was she said she had tried to see me for a week. I really caved in when I heard that."

A few faculty express these same feelings of neglect. They regard Hogans's promotional activities as efforts at self-promotion and self-aggrandizement. But most recognize the inevitable trade-offs of having a principal who is willing to track down resources and broaden horizons. They accept his neglect of the daily operations of school in exchange for the benefits of his external activities. Without his strong political acumen and his energetic search for finances, they know that Carver would have fewer resources with which to work and that school life would be less abundant.

One of the potential casualties of model building and the packaging of ideas is that more attention is paid to selling than producing; that before the ideas have been adequately formed, tested, and refined, there are attempts to disseminate them abroad. (One of the tensions that must plague Hogans is his realization of the discrepancies between image and reality at Carver, and the unfinished state of his operations there. He is eager, even impatient, to "close the gap" and move toward a smoother stability.) Carver is certainly not alone in its imperfections. Any social institution, particularly if it is growing and evolving, copes with weaknesses and rough edges. But Carver's imperfections are made more visible by contrast with the projected, idealized images being portrayed to the wider public. It seems to fall short only in relation to the public relations picture, not if one views its tortuous history or the difficult realities that shape its present. One is, in fact, exceedingly impressed with what has been accomplished at Carver if one looks back a few years.

When Hogans was assigned to Carver and told to report there the next day, he sat up all night and drank a whole case of beer. Hogans had been principal of the elementary school right down the hill from Carver and was well aware of the chaos and deterioration that existed there. And for years, he had heard Carver identified as the "dumping ground" of the Atlanta school system. So it was with dread that Hogans approached his new assignment. His trepidation was also mixed with a sense of challenge and promise. This seemed a good place to test his imagination, his energy, and his commitment to poor Black children. He also recognized that if he were successful, he would be recognized as a great educator, as one who had the magic key to the complex problems facing urban education.

On his first day at Carver, Hogans faced a curious and skeptical faculty. It was also a depleted and discouraged faculty that needed renewal, energy, and direction from their new leader. For several years, they had existed under a laissez faire, weary administration; a principal who was chronically ill and who let things erode and deteriorate around him. Teachers were used to a great deal of autonomy, little interdependence, and almost no sense of cohesion in the staff. Hogans's first response to the aimlessness and laziness that he perceived was "to show them who was in charge." He started the first faculty meeting with fighting words: "You are either part of the team or you are not." Tough standards of behavior and decorum were stressed with his new faculty; rules and regulations were consistently and rigorously enforced. Hogans began with a heavy hand and an autocratic style—an orientation that matched his temperament, but also one that he believed would re-establish order and control in an environment that had lost all sense of direction and stability.

The physical environment matched the deteriorating human spirit. "Roaches were running around like cats. . . . There was dirt and filth everywhere. . . . The band instruments were all broken up. . . . Athletic trophies were falling out of the broken glass cabinets!" Hogans says incredulously, "I can't believe no one stood up and screamed about it!" Climbing out of the rubbish took optimism, perseverance, and hard work, all qualities that Hogans seems to possess in good measure. But in order to get people to conform to the imposed structure, Hogans also used limits and threats. No deviations or improvisations were tolerated by the new principal. Some almost suffocated in this claustrophobic atmosphere that allowed little room for self-expression and professional autonomy. Others welcomed the imposed order, the new sense of collectivity, and the big-daddy, paternalistic image of a take-charge principal.

Hogans believes that faculty found the transition more difficult than

43

the students did. Four years later, some faculty are "dragging their feet" and resisting his direction. He recognizes that in general adults are more set in their ways and less malleable than adolescents, but he uses similar strategies for molding their behavior. Strict obedience and absolute conformity are required of both groups. Privileges and rewards are withheld when teachers or students do not follow orders. A teacher who has not followed the standard procedures for signing out for off campus is given no chance to defend himself. Hogans responds immediately and angrily: "That person is going to be docked. Hit them in the pocketbook. . . . When teachers are irresponsible, the kids always get the short end of the stick."

Hogans recognizes that a preoccupation with discipline will not shape good teachers or inspire faculty commitment, although he does feel that order is a precondition for educational progress. He knows that faculty need to be energized and shored up. They grow stale after years of teaching and need periodic in-service training that offers new approaches and ideas. Hogans sees a need for this kind of external stimulation of experienced staff as well as the need for some "new blood" on the faculty. He wants to rid the faculty of the lingering lethargy that he perceives as inhibiting to student success in school. But behind his call for increased energy and commitment seems to be the budding realization that inspired teaching cannot be enforced—that the creativity and productivity of teachers must be generated from within, and requires the complex and subtle mixture of inputs from students and teachers. It is that elusive combination of psychic and intellectual forces that continues to be beyond the reach of Hogans.

He does make meaningful attempts to provide sustenance and nourishment for needy teachers. How can teachers give to students when they themselves feel hungry? Hogans speaks proudly of the daily expression of nourishment. "I feed the faculty a hot breakfast every morning . . . grits, eggs, bacon . . . the whole thing." Additionally, the faculty are not required to patrol the halls or stay for afternoon meetings. All faculty meetings take place between 8:00 and 8:30 in the morning, and there is only one full faculty meeting per month. Hogans insists that these meetings be organized and efficient. "We don't have busy-work meetings. We can't waste our time on nothing." Although he recognizes the difficult challenges they face, Hogans sees his faculty as a privileged and respected group that gets its fair share of benefits. He wonders out loud why some continue to be complaining and recalcitrant and has no sympathy for those who do not make an energetic contribution.

44

THE SPIRAL, THE HUB OF ALL ACTIVITY

The promotional slide tape on Carver describes the school as "the spiral, the hub of all activity." The forces at Carver are centrifugal. As it spins around in energetic activity, it tends to move away from center. The school's orientation is outwards and into the wider community. As a matter of fact, a description of the internal organism of Carver would offer a very narrow view of the nature of this complex, far-reaching institution. It is the multiple networks that are attached to Carver that account for its unique character.

The dominant connection seems to be with the world of work and industry. Many programs establish the alliance between work and schooling, making them often inseparable. The vast majority of students say they have come to Carver in order to learn salable skills and gain an entree into the work world. Education is viewed as pragmatic and oriented towards the economic "slots" in industry, business, and the service occupations.

A primary program that establishes the direct connections between work and schooling is the Work-Study Program. Approximately 150 juniors and seniors are involved in this program that places them in skilled jobs throughout the city of Atlanta. Half of their day is spent at Carver and half in positions at banks, hospitals, offices, service stations, and fast-food establishments. Students are paid from $3.15 to $4.85 an hour and allowed to pocket all the money they make. This is a highly selective program whose status and image have been primarily generated by Ms. Gertrude Taylor, an energetic woman committed to shaping her students into dedicated, disciplined careerists.

Before coming to Carver four years ago, Ms. Taylor had worked as an executive secretary, office manager, accountant, and proposal writer. One afternoon while taking shorthand and typing for Dr. Benjamin Mays, the president of the Atlanta Board of Education, he presented her with a challenge that she could not resist. "Would you be interested in training young people for jobs?" Dr. Mays asked in soft, but persuasive tones. Admiration and respect for Dr. Mays as well as her wish to "make a contribution to the lives of young Black students" made her hesitate for only a moment before saying she would do it. Within three days, she had a teaching position at Carver.

Her love for her work and her belief in what she does is immediately obvious. With enthusiasm and pride, she recounts her many successes with students, her shaping of their skills over several years, and her rigorous selection process. Ms. Taylor's approach to students is respectful and demanding. A student coming in late to school is reprimanded for his casual laziness, warned that his behavior will never earn him a position in the Work-Study Program, and firmly prodded to shape up. Her manner is strong, imposing, and uncompromising, but the message is one of deep care and understanding. Part of her caring comes from knowing her students very well. Beginning with their eighth-grade entrance into the school, she watches them carefully and tests their potential as responsible workers.

> "I try to learn about my students . . . the total student—the make-up, the attitudes, the way the student thinks, the ability, et cetera. But there are other characteristics that I must learn . . . the habits, the temperament of the student."

Along with observing students herself, Ms. Taylor consults with others who know them well.

> "I work closely with homeroom teachers, classroom teachers, and especially with the registrar and counselors. . . . Along with the information I pick up there, I call the homes and go into the neighborhood. . . . This is my perspective. I'm looking into the future. I tell the parent the advantage of putting the student out in the world of work early. . . . They can use this as a reference. This is experience. It looks good on the resume. It helps when the student goes to college. . . . I keep close contact with the parents."

Once Ms. Taylor has gathered all of the information on "the whole child," she begins the subtle process of matching students with the work settings. She must be concerned with responding to the needs of the employers, the skills and temperament of the students, and establishing a "track record" that will assure the stability of "work slots." For a slot in the "Coin and Currency" department at the Federal Reserve Bank, Ms. Taylor searched for a student who was "very pleasant and highly honest." For a job at General Motors that required balancing the skills of accounting, data processing, computer programming, and record keeping, Ms. Taylor found a young woman with a "calm temperament who would not get flustered" by all the demands being made of her. Occasionally, a match between student and job does not work out.

> "Now I have had to take students out of jobs and move them from slot to slot because the student was unhappy. I just did that the other day. A young lady was very unhappy. Mr. Jordan at the Federal Labor Department is a lovely person. But Mr. Jordan has been there twenty-five years and this young lady is one of those hyperactive types. She's a good worker but she

has some attitudes that just didn't work. And *she* detected that. And she came to me and expressed some sort of dissatisfaction."

Clearly, Ms. Taylor thinks of herself as part entrepreneur ("I sell my program"), part psychologist ("I have to find out what deeply motivates these students"), and part technical trainer ("They must feel confident in these basic office skills before we send them out into the world of work"). She actively seeks to combine the environments of work, school, and family as she guides and shapes students for career positions. In the process of molding students, Ms. Taylor becomes deeply involved with them, convinced and determined that they can be successful, and links her ambitions for the program with their best efforts.

The Work-Study Program culminates in an extravagant ritualistic event called Free Enterprise Day. Students who have successfully completed the program receive generous acclaim as they parade on stage and tell the audience about their work accomplishments and future career objectives. It is a carefully staged and dramatic presentation of the value of discipline, perseverance, punctuality, and civility for rising in the world of work. It is a public event that symbolizes Carver's new image. Vocational education no longer has to be linked with tough and menial work for people of low status, but can be seen as training for jobs of choice, skill, and honor. On the cover of the program for Free Enterprise Day there is a workman's hand "laying the foundation to success." The bricks of the pyramid being constructed are labeled "business," "community," and "education," and the major inscription reads: "What a youngster becomes later in life is a direct result of what that youngster is exposed to early in life."

The architects of the new Carver believe in the principles of democracy, free enterprise, and capitalism. Their images are classically mainstream. They communicate to students their belief in the fairness and rationality of "the system"—a system that they believe will respond to the hard work, determination, and calculated risks of individual will. At Carver, however, there is a slight variation in the traditional view of capitalist enterprise. It is a common minority perspective. There is the realistic perception that Blacks, particularly poor Blacks, have for generations been disenfranchised, powerless, and excluded from society's resources and bounty. The experience of exclusion and oppression has led some to fight for their meager share of the American pie, but has led many more to withdraw from the race, to assume it is rigged and refuse to run. The new ideology of Carver conveys a double message and conflicting imagery. It says that Blacks have been treated unfairly, but that

47

the system is basically fair. In order to overcome the profound injustices, Carver students need to learn how to successfully negotiate the system, must refuse to become discouraged by the barriers that they will face, and must become exemplary models of discipline and civility. Carver opens the first window to this wider world of entrepreneuring and profit. It offers a taste of what lies beyond the ghetto walls. School people hope that these frequent trips to the other side of the tracks will inspire a belief in the system and a commitment to the fight for inclusion in the mainstream.

These trips across ghetto boundaries are institutionalized as part of the Explorers Program begun by Hogans three years ago. Every tenth-grader at Carver becomes a member of the Explorers Program, an adaptation of the Explorer Scouts, "designed to provide an initial linkage to the world of work." Each month, students are bused downtown amidst the shiny glass high-rises to visit the major businesses and agencies of Atlanta, to explore how they function, and to receive orientations to the careers they offer. The public relations material on the program claims that students gain "an awareness of vocation, accurate images of work life, awareness of the full range of job settings and opportunities available, motivation for learning, increased access to job opportunities, and a broad base for vocational and career decision making." It is unlikely that any single program could accomplish all of these lofty goals. But many point to the Explorers Program as critical to the new purposes and direction of Carver. Tenth-graders all receive clean, white Explorer jackets, and it becomes an important collective experience for them. Perhaps the immersion into the work world is made less threatening because students "explore" the new environments as a group, and do not have to worry about being individually inadequate or awkward. The hope is that this initial exposure to business and industry in the tenth grade will not only lift the sights of Carver students, but also help them make more informed curricular and vocational decisions in the eleventh and twelfth grades. The 1980 graduating class was the first group to experience the Explorers Program at Carver, and Hogans claims that compared to their predecessors he sees striking differences in the graduates' understanding of the work world, their career choices, their determination, and their dedication to achievement.

The Explorers Program was Hogans's brainchild. In characteristic fashion he raised money, made connections, and convinced the Boy Scouts of America that an entire class of students—both boys and girls—could, by virtue of their student status, join the program. But Carver Explorers do not leave the city for hikes and camping in the woods. Their explorations carry them to the urban, industrial turf of business and banking. They are not learning survival skills for outdoor jungles but the calculating skills of entry and industry. But a central theme prevails that is rooted in the Boy Scout tradition: scouting is supposed to make strong men out of undisciplined boys. Likewise, the Explorers Program stresses honor, honesty, and rigor—all critical pieces of the new school image.

Most of the doors to the business world could not be opened without David Tanner, the man Superintendent Crim describes as "the second most important person" to Carver's turnaround and a man whom Hogans describes as a father figure. A more apt description might be one of a godfather, because the father image implies a kind of judgment and generational competition which is not evident in Tanner's relationship to Hogans. Rather, their fifteen-year relationship is marked by enormous generosity, trust, and intimacy. They are an odd couple. Tanner is the privileged, smooth, cosmopolitan banker with broad connections and a humanitarian spirit. Hogans is the rough-edged, ambitious, and resourceful Black man with big plans for himself and his people. Tanner admires Hogans's unleashed energy and aggressiveness. Hogans is appreciative of the prosperous and genteel style of Tanner. It is out of their mutual admiration and trust that Carver has been conceived and shaped. They are the architects, the visionaries, the builders playing interdependent roles.

David Tanner is the vice-president for community affairs for a major trust company in Atlanta. His office sits on the eleventh floor of a tall glass and metal structure that rises twenty-five stories into the Atlanta skyline. The floors are plushly carpeted, and the atmosphere is one of efficiency and polish. There is a sprinkling of Black faces among the secretarial staff, but the bank seems strikingly white after spending some time at Carver. Tanner's office is comfortable, not opulent.

Contemplative and slow to speak, Tanner talks about his mission in a way that is almost religious. But he speaks with humility, minimizing his part in the building of Carver, and giving Hogans most of the credit. "I am a behind-the-scenes person. . . . I coordinate the relationship with the business community." His commitment to Carver grew out of his long, personal attachment to Hogans, but also his increasing concern for the deterioration of urban communities. "We seem to have forgotten to tell the young people of today that with opportunity comes responsibility." Tanner fears the lack of commitment and industry in today's youth, and worries that their irresponsibility will lead to societal chaos and violence. The repercussions will fall hardest on poor and minority communities. Tanner assesses the task of restructuring society as an integration of efforts from the political, economic, social, and spiritual realms. But he is clear about the boundaries of his own involvement. "I am fortunate," says Tanner, "that the bank allows me to do the work which I most want to do. . . . I have been in foundation work for over twenty years, and I continue to believe in the philosophy of my mentor, who is now ninety-three years old—search out and identify strong, indigenous people and support them in their work . . . and that is what I'm doing with Norris."

Tanner's philosophy sounds very general and full of platitudes, but his actions are highly specific, focused, and calculated. Behind that generous and smooth veneer of a southern gentleman, one senses a tough-minded and savvy operator. Most of his backstage activity has been focused on establishing ties between the business community and Carver. The monthly visits for tenth-graders in the Explorers Program are largely arranged by Tanner. For years he has been a prominent member of the Inter-Agency Council, a coalition of public schools, private enterprise, higher education, and social agencies that comes together each month for collective learning, problem solving, and action. Recently, he has been involved in beginning the Carver Corporation, a group whose efforts are designed to respond to the economic, social, and health needs of young, unwed mothers living in the Carver Homes.

Tanner's most visible moment came recently when he was master of ceremonies at this year's Free Enterprise Day. Yet even on this occasion, he was reluctant to take center stage. He feels ineffective working directly with the Carver students and thinks he must be perceived as distant and irrelevant by them. He points to the persuasive powers of a Black woman newscaster who was the keynote speaker on the same program. "She was absolutely magnificent . . . . She told them things they would never hear if they came from me."

Although they move in different spheres, Hogans and Tanner share the same view of the complex interdependence of social institutions in our society. They are constantly seeking connections to new sources of influence and building networks that will draw in more resources to Carver. Hogans claims that more revenue flows from these independent connections than comes from the school system's budgetary allocations.

Carver's relationships to business and industry seem most prominent, but connections to other institutions are being slowly shaped and clarified. One such connection is to four prosperous churches that form the Ecumenical Council. The council was Tanner's inspiration. It grew out of his concern for the increasing separation between the sacred and the secular in this society, and his sense that churches were not taking a responsible social role in community life. Tanner worried about the complacency and introversion of the affluent parishes in Atlanta that were content to worship on Sundays, but never move beyond Christian rhetoric. A member of an upper-class, predominantly white Presbyterian church, Tanner began conversations with three other prominent parishes in an attempt to combine forces to participate in social action. After much persuasion and groundwork, another Presbyterian, an Episcopal, and a Lutheran church (all affluent, three White and one Black) joined together to create the Ecumenical Council. Guided by Tanner's determination and strategy, they decided to focus their resources on the Carver Homes and offer support in the form of an active ministry in that community. Collectively, the churches raised money to send Black divinity students into the Carver community to live and work. Says Tanner realistically, "They are not there to save souls . . . just to help in any way they can."

The divinity students are joined by a "circuit rider," a minister who also works in the Carver Homes and travels among the four churches on Sundays, bringing the messages of urban distress to the congregations. Tanner calls him an "urban translator" and clearly recognizes the mutual ignorance and threat that prevail between rich and poor, Black and White. The parishioners need to hear the word and be reminded of the separations, just as the Carver folks need their support and resources. As Tanner talks about organizing these churches for action, he speaks with the same calculated purpose that characterizes his business acumen. Clearly, his spiritual life is inseparable from his business interests. Many of the same people who inhabit Atlanta's corporate offices are found in these church pews. With this in mind, Tanner persuaded Hogans to join his all-white Presbyterian parish. He knew that Hogans's presence at church would be a visible reminder of the church's commitment to Carver. Perhaps more importantly, he wanted to further encourage Hogans's ascent into the circles of influence and power in Atlanta.

The beautiful, gleaming edifices in which Tanner and Hogans worship every Sunday are far away from the modest Black churches that surround the Carver Homes. Dotting the landscape, these small buildings are closed all week long. Their ministers can only afford to open the churches on Sunday. The other six days of the week, they are off making a living in real estate, teaching, dry-cleaning—jobs that will subsidize their almost voluntary status as ministers of poor churches. The closed church doors don't only symbolize their other commitments, but also what some identify as a negligent, condescending attitude of the churches towards people in the Carver Homes. Over the past few decades, distance and hostility have grown between the closed churches and the needy community. It is with this legacy of skepticism and distrust that the urban ministers, sponsored by the rich white churches, entered the Carver community almost four years ago.

They came to live and work in the poorest community in Atlanta. The Carver Homes crowd 5,400 people into 990 apartments. The two-story, brick buildings lined up along nine streets were built twenty-five years ago as public housing. They do not appear as ominous and isolating as the high-rise public housing of Chicago or New York. There is something more humane about the scale of these buildings. There are stoops and porches to sit on and more possibility for neighborly contact. Yet the people here are just as poor and just as imprisoned by poverty and discrimination. What might have once been planted lawns and greenery has long since turned to gray, beaten-down dirt, and there are no sidewalks for people to walk on from house to house. Through the eyes of a Northeasterner, the Carver Homes look semi-rural, even though they are part of a big-city problem.

Velma King, an articulate, forceful young woman, and one of the three original divinity students to come and live in the Carver Homes, told of their long struggles for community acceptance, their battles with bureaucrats, and their ambivalent relationships with the sponsoring churches. King is direct and uncompromising as she tells her story: "Even in attempting to be good, I have to be me." Her certainty, strength, and wisdom make her seem older than her twenty-eight years. When she decided to take on the urban ministry assignment, her father encouraged the new venture. "You send off special rays that will help people . . . and you need to experience the pain of poverty," he said.

Round, brown-skinned, and simply dressed, there is no visible evidence that King is a minister. She says, "It is so easy to hide behind a clerical uniform. Let what I am come from what you see me doing." Her "community ministry" in the Carver Homes has been related to her struggle to become "one of the people," not separate from or above them in status. She has purposely not become an ordained minister because she is suspicious of organized religion and "very critical of the people who work with social systems." Her inclinations to work outside the system have only been reinforced and strengthened by her increasing identification with community folk.

King arrived at the Carver Homes with two male colleagues, both Black. Of West African origin, Cyrus Lungu brought his wife and children with him and maintained close contact with St. Bede's, the prosperous

Black Episcopal church that joined in sponsoring their ministry. On Sunday mornings people in the Carver Homes could turn on their televisions and see Lungu administering the sacraments to his wealthy, well-heeled, St. Bede's parishioners. This bourgeois connection stirred suspicion in the Carver people, who tested his commitment by slashing his tires and robbing his home. They sensed in him an arrogance derived from his upper middle-class life in West Africa and the cultural misunderstandings that grew out of their different origins. It was also difficult for Lungu to balance the needs of his family with the heavy demands of his ministry. Leroy Green, a young, dapper, single man, was tested in another way. Rumors grew up around him as people interpreted his smooth style as the behavior of a police plant. One day when he came home, he found his apartment broken into, all of his furniture and clothes taken, and his ordination certificate torn up in a neat pile on the floor. Velma King faced a more subtle kind of community exclusion and skepticism. Most of the dominant forces in the community were women, and they worried that this new woman minister would draw some of the power and influence away from them. King's womanly presence was not muted by ministerial garb or manners. She came on like a neighbor ("I wanted to be recognized as their friend"), and this more modest approach increased their wariness of her.

For all three ministers, their first year was a difficult and trying time. During this period of great suspicion, they chose to begin their ministry by offering a visible, pragmatic, and much-needed service—emergency medical transportation from the Carver Homes to nearby hospitals during the times of the day when it was virtually impossible to get hospitals to respond to their cries for help. It was a year of slowly growing trust as the ministers tried to stay visible and responsive to people's needs and began to shape a different image of a religious presence. They began to erode the once severe separations that had existed between church and community.

Even though Tanner and Hogans had been central in developing and sponsoring the urban ministry at Carver, during the first year there was no attempt to build alliances with Carver High School. As a matter of fact, the ministers learned to be generally suspect of all the established institutions that served the community. For example, they soon recognized the importance of confidentiality and the dangers of providing any information to the social service agencies that probed for their secrets. "We are successful because we don't have a tattletale system." Their identification with the community and their persistent advocacy stance often put them in positions of conflict with other "care givers," but they knew that a breach of friendship and trust would destroy years of labor and commitment. Alliances with the community have also been shaped by the passage of time. Over the three years of the urban ministry, the management of the Carver Homes has changed at least six times and the staffs of the other social agencies serving the community are in constant flux. In the midst of this shifting scene, the most stable force has been the community ministry.

In its second year, the ministers established a central office in one of the Carver Homes apartments, and each one took responsibility for developing a new program direction. King carved out the services for senior citizens and children, Lungu worked with alcoholics, and Green formed liaisons between the community and the schools. Because of Hogans's membership in one of the sponsoring churches and his genuine support of the urban ministry, the connections to Carver were easily made. The other surrounding schools were not receptive to Green's initiations. Says King, "There seems to be lots of rivalry and territorial jealousies among these schools." Green was given an office at Carver, and he spent much of his time counseling students with problems, working with their families, and providing support to teachers. The crises and problems that he confronted were severe and often unrelated to schoolwork—issues of sexual assault and harassment of teenage girls, child abuse and neglect, murder, homosexual promiscuity. In the third year of the ministry, many services have been expanded and strengthened. Green and Lungu have left the Carver Homes to pursue more traditional pastoral roles, and Velma King has been joined by another young, Black, woman divinity student. The work within Carver High School is less visible, but the ministry is more embedded in community life, and the urban pastors continue to be a source of solace and support for Carver students and their families.

The school is merely the hub of Carver's fast-spinning wheel. The spokes that whirl around the center are attached to businesses, universities, churches, health facilities, and community agencies. Hogans and Tanner work to coordinate the complex relationships among the myriad supporting enterprises. The impact of the business connections are most clearly visible at Carver. The Word-Study Program, the Explorers Program, and the other student apprenticeships are vital, well-established, and meaningful to students' lives at Carver. Less clearly drawn are the connections to academia. For instance, the contributions of university resources are not evident in Carver's academic program, which appears to need revitalization, new ideas, and clearer goals. The urban ministry suffers the same invisibility and disconnection. No one is currently responsible for maintaining close connections and negotiating the realms of families, community, and school. Although the effects of these weaker linkages may be indirect and less visible, it is not clear that they should be imitative of the sturdier networks to business and industry. One of the many challenges facing Carver will be in finding the balance between its centripetal and centrifugal forces.

II

John F. Kennedy
High School

Balancing Forces: Creating a Pluralistic Community

THERE ARE MANY WAYS UP

When New Yorkers think of Riverdale in the Bronx, they usually envision its scenic beauty, affluence, and civilized inhabitants. Some people say it has the most spectacular natural terrain of any city neighborhood; that it is one of the last remaining "livable" urban communities where families can thrive in relative safety. Over the bridge from Upper Manhattan, Riverdale is viewed as sedate, pretty, and clean. Even though Riverdale is in the Bronx, people are likely to explain to a stranger that, "It's really not the Bronx, even though it's located here." They are eager to distinguish Riverdale from the rest of the Bronx which has turned Black, Brown, and poor faster than any other borough in New York. Riverdale's precious image is a far cry from the harsh, dangerous streets of the South Bronx. The image of abundance and civility refers to the people who live in the hills of Riverdale.

Some of the more prosperous residents live on "Millionaire's Row" in large sumptuous houses with manicured gardens and lush green lawns. They enjoy a secluded and rarefied existence. Many more hill dwellers live in huge, high-rise apartment buildings that have recently been converted to co-ops and condominiums. In the last few years, prices of "units" in these buildings have soared. One advertises two-bedroom co-ops beginning at $125,000. The buildings are guarded by uniformed, respectful doormen and elaborate security systems. The front halls, often mirrored to give a feeling of enlarged space, are decorated with large artificial plants and shiny chrome furniture. Many buildings have their own small parks for families with young children, and outdoor pools for swimming during the warm months.

The apartments tend to be small, but the views offer a wide angle on the beautiful scenes below. From some pictures windows you can see the majestic Palisades on the other side of the Hudson River, from others you can spot the silver shimmer of the George Washington Bridge, and from still others you can watch the Circle Line tour boat sailing slowly around Manhattan island. The tiny decks that protrude from almost every apartment are crowded with lawn furniture, barbecues, and carefully tended windowboxes. Many residents claim that even though they may not have much space, they can embrace the beauty that extends for miles. "Sometimes I feel like I own this view. Those rocky ledges across the river are mine," exudes the contented wife of a retired businessman.

The inhabitants of the hill tend to describe themselves as upper middle-class, although many find that the recent surge of inflation has deprived them of some of their most precious worldly pleasures. Families must choose between a trip to the Bahamas during the winter months and a series of Broadway theater tickets, and the high cost of college tuitions has caused many to be burdened by enormous loans. Residents recognize their common affluence, but tend to describe their enclave as "cosmopolitan." "There is a wonderful mixture of people from all over the world," says a mother who appreciates her child's exposure to "all kinds of people." A young teacher who recently "spent every cent of her savings" to buy a co-op, says that half of her building is Japanese. "The big Japanese companies buy up the units and shuffle their executives in and out." Despite the claim of heterogeneity, the overwhelming proportion of hill residents is Jewish, and people in the valley below bluntly attach "Jewish" to the habits and style of their more affluent neighbors.

As you drive down the winding hills of Riverdale into the valley below, the landscape shifts from the orange and yellow colors of fall to the gray concrete of city streets. You are in the valley of Riverdale when you turn up 230th Street towards John F. Kennedy High School. The texture and pace of life are transformed. The traffic becomes congested, the sidewalks crowded, and the noise level increases. Five or six gas stations, their neon signs blaring, come into view. Fast-food joints, drug stores, dry-cleaning establishments, laundromats, and corner grocery stores line the streets.

Off this major thoroughfare there is another distinctive Riverdale neighborhood rarely included in the prosperous community image. In Kingsbridge, a largely Irish Catholic enclave, the small brick houses tend to be one- and two-family dwellings. The houses are older and more worn than the shiny high-rises on the hill, but most are lovingly cared for. They nestle close to the ground with little space between neighbors. Chain link fences and friendly hedges mark the boundaries between the small plots. Among the single-family dwellings there are also older, solidly built apartment buildings of several stories where many families have lived for several decades. Kingsbridge is a tightly knit, blue-collar neighborhood that is described by outsiders as "tough," "parochial," and "defensive." "They are meat and potatoes people—real homey plain folks," says a more sympathetic observer.

In the last few years, upwardly mobile, recently middle-class Black and Hispanic families have moved to Kingsbridge from the South Bronx, looking for better schools, safer streets, and a more comfortable existence. Their numbers are not yet substantial, but their presence feels threatening to the Kingsbridge old-timers, who value their "privacy" and "like-mindedness."

Just off 230th Street, Terrace Avenue leads you to one of the main entrances of John F. Kennedy High School. Road bumpers have been installed along Terrace Avenue in order to discourage students from drag racing their cars up this strip. Looming directly ahead is a large, eight-story, concrete and brick structure. Built in 1971, the school appears ageless and non-descript at first glance. It is distinguished only by its mammoth size, a hulking grayish structure. The doors are heavy and metal, making it seem unwelcoming and impenetrable.

Once inside, energetic human activity and a crescendo of voices bring the building to life. A friendly security guard, dressed in regular street clothes, inquires casually about my destination and writes out a visitor's card for me. As I try to follow his abbreviated directions I feel lost in the swarm of students moving through the halls. Bodies are pressed close. For a moment my feet are lifted from the floor by the crowd's momentum as we move en masse up the escalator.

There are 5,300 students in Kennedy High School, and during the changeovers between classes close to 4,000 students crowd onto the escalators that rise two floors at a time. On each step of the moving stairs there are three, sometimes four, students packed together. When the escalator reaches a floor, hundreds of people get stacked up as they try to make the swing on to the next escalator. Along the walls above the escalators are colorful murals drawn by Kennedy art students. Painted signs direct you to various offices and activity centers in the building. Other murals offer words of encouragement—cheering students on in their pursuit of "educational excellence." The most prominent message, shouted in bold colors, says "Catch the Kennedy Spirit." The inspirational, lively drawings sharply contrast with the dull institutional grays and greens that dominate the building's walls and ceilings.

Since I have never been in a school of this large a scale and never seen an escalator in a school building, my first associations are of rising from underground at a subway station, or traveling upwards in a big department store. Although I feel vaguely displaced and uneasy, everyone else seems to be totally used to the body crunch and unconcerned about the crowded conditions. I see no pushing and shoving or gestures of impatience even though the momentum of the crowds often throws people against one another. A short, vivacious girl with a head full of tight curls and a ready smile may have noticed my disorientation and turns around to me as we reach the next landing. "There are many ways up," she says cryptically, and then inquires, "Why don't you take the teachers' elevator?" Her first comment, probably meant to convey modes of transportation to the upper floors, echoes through my head for the rest of my visit to Kennedy High. It seems an apt metaphor for the rising expectations and goals of Kennedy's teachers and students; a first sign of the optimistic, spirited references that pervade the language of the school's inhabitants.

In fact, there are three ways to go up and down at Kennedy. The escalators are by far the most crowded conveyance, but students can also ride elevators or climb the stairs. The most sedate way for adults to travel is via the teachers' elevator, which requires the use of a special key. Frequently, the escalators stop working and convert easily into steep, treacherous stairs. Although the building is huge, it is not difficult to negotiate because of its logical, straightforward arrangement. Explains one helpful student, "You know, it's like a big city, but easy to find your way around . . . you just got to get a few basic landmarks down." I discover he is right and quickly learn that the English and social studies departments are on the seventh and eighth floors; the sixth floor has the science department laboratories and classrooms; the fifth floor (better known as the "Fiesta Floor") houses the foreign language department; the fourth floor all of the administrative offices; the math and business areas are on the second and third floors; and the first floor is a sprawling space that includes the auditorium, library, music department, boys' and girls' gyms, and the industrial arts shops. Art is the only department that is not neatly placed in an identifiable area of the school. Its classrooms are scattered on various floors throughout the building.

Although the floor plan of Kennedy is not hard to decipher, even a superficial tour of the building requires a few hours. On my first afternoon at the school, the principal wanted to give me a brief orientation and walked with me from top to bottom, stopping occasionally to peer into classrooms, meet various faculty members, and chat with students. In two hours we managed to see a lot, but we came nowhere close to finishing the tour. On the first floor alone, we saw a beginners' modern dance class of over thirty girls housed in a small studio that had been constructed by industrial art students. Some touches were still unfinished, but with the shiny wood floor, dance bars lining the walls, and full-length mirrors, it almost resembled a professional studio. In a small classroom down the hall, thirty-five students sat intently cradling guitars in their arms, awkwardly fingering them. The music teacher, dressed in a checkered cotton shirt and blue jeans, stood at the board pointing to notes on a scale, urging her students to concentration and precision. When we peeked in the door, she did not miss a beat as she invited us in. "Come and listen to the hard work of these brand new players," she said confidently. The sounds of thirty-five novice players fumbling for notes ranged from tentatively soft to excruciatingly loud, but the students appeared undaunted. At one point the players' attention began to lag and the teacher admonished them. "Don't get lazy. You have to work." In the auditorium, on the same floor, several students sat in small groups talking quietly with one another. Behind closed curtains we could hear the sound of an exercise class being conducted on the stage. For several periods during the day, classes are held on the auditorium stage because there is no other available space in the building. Referring to the open doors of the auditorium, the worn, slightly tattered look of the chairs, and the comfortable, unsupervised presence of several students, the principal explained, "I like auditoriums to be used, lived-in places. You know, in a lot of schools they are locked up tight and only opened for special events. They look prettier than ours, but I am not interested in maintaining a show place." Around the corner, the library has a similarly used appearance and the librarian explains, "We introduce the library to students in an active way." With 22,000 volumes, 140 journal subscriptions, and a very large collection of media kits, the library seems adequately stocked. However, "The exciting part of this work," claims one of the three librarians, "is finding ways of making kids feel comfortable in places like this."

On our way out of the building, we pass by a coed beginners' gymnastics class in the girls' gym. There are at least forty students in the class, distributed in groups around various activities. Some students seem idle and bored as they have to wait their turn on the tumbling mats, the parallel bars, or the uneven parallel bars, but many are actively engaged in coaching one another and the tone is quiet and comfortable. It is only when the teacher approaches us to introduce himself that I recognize his presence. He seems undisturbed by the huge class and broad range of talents and skills among the students, and focuses instead on his expectation of student cooperation and collaboration. The tour takes us by many other classrooms, shops, and studios, and my initial, overwhelming impression is of a very crowded and comfortable environment where teachers appear active and unthreatened, and students seem to be engaged. "That's a given," says the principal on our whistle-stop tour. "If you have problems with discipline, you will not be a teacher in this school. These kids are good kids."

From the dark interior of the building, we move outside to a bright sunny day and I am surprised by the grandeur before me. Before I can take in the scene, the principal points to a large, elaborate mural on the back wall of the building, painted and designed by students. The bright red, imposing letters "J. F. K." are surrounded by images of sports figures in action. "Isn't that just lovely!" he beams. "Those kids do great work." Sprawling in front of us is a huge athletic complex and behind it the Harlem River, the beautiful golden hills of Upper Manhattan, and the George Washington Bridge in the distance. (As if by cue the Circle Line boat, touring around Manhattan island, comes into view around the river's bend.)

Built five years ago, the two-million dollar athletic facility includes eight tennis courts; a baseball diamond; and a football field of astroturf (costing $450,000 to build), surrounded by a six-lane track. At any time during the day, you can look out and see three or four physical education classes spread out across the great field, actively exercising. When we arrive on this early October afternoon, the hot sun is beating down on a girls' soccer class in one corner of the field, a boys' football class in another area, and a group of coed joggers circling the track.

Although the principal enjoys showing me the extravagant facility and assures me that it is unique among New York City high schools, he is quick to say that the physical plant taken alone does not create a good athletic program. He points to the extraordinary efforts of the recently departed head of the physical education department, who in five years built a strong and dedicated faculty and developed a comprehensive curriculum. Everyone mourns his departure to a swanky, affluent suburban high school, but they hail his creative organizational efforts at Kennedy. Several students, all non-athletes, tell me that the best department in the school is physical education. Says one, "It offers an incredible variety of courses." Says another, "It's not macho. You don't have to be a big shot jock to get some attention." The principal admires the work of his former athletic head by reciting the impressive city-wide championships—five last year and eight in the past two years, and several semifinal matches lost by Kennedy in the last rounds.

LEADERSHIP AND COMMITMENT: A FAIR EXCHANGE

Several times a day, Principal Robert Mastruzzi glances out of his office window at the action on the athletic fields. From his fourth-floor office, at different times he can see bicyclists racing around the six-lane track, long- distance runners taking a slower pace, and city kids learning the rudiments of tennis. From faraway he can identify the teachers working with the various groups of students. "That is Johnson. I know his stance." The Kennedy football coach is preparing his team for their biggest rival, De Witt Clinton High School. He inquires of Mastruzzi, jokingly, "Is it true that you have been peering through binoculars from your window? Are you giving away our secrets to them?" Mustruzzi laughs, "You know I wouldn't do that." His place at the window is well known. Standing there with him is not so much like seeing a baron surveying his estate (although there is definitely a paternal pride), but more like watching an enthusiastic cheerleader. He seems to root for the sweating, driving athletes, for the city championships. But his encouragement has a much broader base: he watches the runners and jumpers and cheers for all of the students, for generations of Kennedy students.

One of the first stories Mastruzzi tells me is about Kennedy's hosting of New York State's Special Olympics last year. From all over the state, thousands of handicapped athletes and their escorts arrived to compete against each other in the Olympic Games. For eighteen months, Mastruzzi and his staff planned and worked on this gala event. Although the races were the central event, there were also extravagant satellite events—a big parade, an evening of disco dancing, a fireworks display over the river, and games organized for participants who were not competing. Terrace Avenue, the street leading up to the school, was temporarily renamed with a street sign that read "Special Olympics." Hundreds of students, teachers, and parents volunteered their services; the event was extensively covered by the local media; and politicians and celebrities came to offer support and gain visibility. The film students at Kennedy documented the happenings through film and video, producing an inspiring short that brought tears to the eyes of faculty viewers when they saw it several months later. As he recounts the details, Mastruzzi beams with pride. He admits to liking the public relations and the community service aspects and feels glad that Kennedy has the facilities to accommodate an event of this great magnitude. But his passion seems to be reserved for the kids as he reminds me of the Special Olympics motto "You are all winners." "I believe that is true for all the kids here at Kennedy," he says forcefully. "Each year I tell the faculty to increase their expectations of students. You ask for more and you get more."

The football coach at Kennedy pretended to worry about his principal passing on secrets to De Witt Clinton because he knew Mastruzzi had once taught at the rival school and is friendly with Clinton's coach. Before coming to John F. Kennedy High School as principal, Bob Mastruzzi had been assistant principal for administration at Benjamin Franklin High School; and sometime before that, a physical education teacher at De Witt Clinton. It is not hard to imagine that Mastruzzi followed the path from coach to principal. Not only does he seem to have a special identification with his old department, he also exudes a kind of strong physicality that goes with the coach stereotype and his talk is laced with sports metaphors.

A man in his fifties, Mastruzzi stands at about five feet seven inches tall but appears to be much taller. He has a youthful, muscular look underneath a balding head and quick energy that keeps him on the move. Impeccably dressed, Mastruzzi appears at school each day in carefully matched color combinations. His ties are wide and lively, his short sleeve shirts are rolled up twice at his upper arm, and he wears a subtle gold chain bracelet. Although his individual features do not strike me as classically attractive, several women describe him as "very handsome." It is probably not his physical attributes that make him appear tall or handsome, but his energy, his confidence, and his vitality. He is described by his colleagues, one and all, as "dynamic," "charismatic," and "charming," and they speak about his forcefulness and power.

Some observers claim that Mastruzzi's compelling style is "culturally based." Born and raised in a first generation working-class Italian family, Mastruzzi has the grand gestures, passion, and sentimentality of his Mediterranean origins. One of his ardent admirers calls him "touchy" (in the sense of being a toucher), and says that his care in warmly reaching out to faculty and students with a hand of reassurance and affection has an "enormous impact" on the tone of the school. "He is very physical, very demonstrative and it affects all of us. Even the kids hold hands in friendship and support . . . it's amazing." Another teacher, who recognizes Mastruzzi's warmth, also traces it to his Italian roots, and says it mixes with the largely Spanish student body to produce a "wonderfully vibrant" ethos. She tells the story of Sophia, a Spanish speaking tenth-grader, who had recently arrived from Mexico and felt lonely and lost in the midst of the new and strange environment. The teacher asked a bilingual Puerto Rican student to introduce the new girl around, "and immediately she put her arms around Sophia and made her feel safe and welcome. Within a week, Sophia went from fear and tears to smiles." Another faculty member of Italian origins smiles when he says, "Bob's not Italian, you know, he's Sicilian and that is very different . . . good, but different."

Although Mastruzzi had climbed far from his modest beginnings, he still remains close to his childhood turf. He grew up in a predominantly Italian-American community in the Bronx and attended Christopher Columbus High, the neighborhood public school. Christopher Columbus is still seventy percent Italian and is one of two schools in the borough that has not "turned" minority. Now Mastruzzi and his family live in one of the string of suburbs in Westchester County, but he still seems to feel a deep connection to the Bronx. He knows its streets, its politics, and its neighborhoods intimately and has a keen perception of the great changes and subtle shifts that have occurred in the community during the last few decades. One of the first impressions I get of Bob Mastruzzi, therefore, is that he feels at home, comfortable in, and knowledgeable about the wider community surrounding Kennedy. More strikingly, he seems to approach his work with a sense of mission derived from memories of childhood and family, and a belief in public schooling as the primary avenue of achievement and success. With great feeling he says, "I believe in public schools . . . I think they face enormous challenges, but they must exist. We have to make them work."

When Bob Mastruzzi arrived at Kennedy in April 1971, the final touches of the building were still not complete. As he sat in an empty office, walls were being painted and carpets were being laid around him.

Used to being "the number two man," his principalship at Kennedy represented an enormous challenge. Not only was he going to test his wings as a leader, but he was inaugurating a brand new school. He was not encumbered by the long history and old traditions of an established institution, but neither could he feel the cushion of time and the safety of well-worn habits. His first task was to articulate, for himself, an "educational philosophy," a substantive vision that would guide and shape his administrative decisions. He remembers, "I was used to following the lead of the top man and now I had to construct my own plan." In his search for ideas, he visited many other high schools that "were doing things a little differently." His wish to be innovative was also influenced by the liberal, progressive rhetoric of the late sixties and early seventies that emphasized individual choice and "relevant courses."

When school opened the following September, Mastruzzi spearheaded an ambitious curriculum designed around a quarter system. Students could choose from an enormous array of electives; courses were designed to match the faddish wishes of adolescents; and material was crammed into a few short, intense weeks. "At first the kids loved it," recalls Mastruzzi. They were seduced by feelings of power and adventure. However, the individual freedom soon turned to chaos. "There was utter confusion, greater inefficiency, and unbelievable administrative hassle." In addition, "a lot of the courses had no substance. They were Mickey Mouse courses and our kids were being cheated," admits Mastruzzi. After two years of experimentation, Mastruzzi searched his soul and decided to streamline the curriculum and return to the traditional arrangement of semesters. He wanted to develop a core curriculum that reflected the essential building blocks of learning, "basic, substantive, no frills, all real." He lamented his earlier misapprehensions, his wish to be innovative and progressive, and sought to undo the havoc by a clear and decisive mandate. He was so sure of his decision that he took action alone, without the consultation of his colleagues. "It was the first time I had made an arbitrary decision. This is *very* uncharacteristic of me . . . but I didn't care about the outcry of teachers, parents, or kids . . . and after about six months, we began to see real improvements in the academic program." Mastruzzi recounts the story of his first administrative blunder without defensiveness. In retrospect he does seem amazed by his earlier naiveté and by his tentativeness, which seems to contrast sharply with his present certainty. It is not accidental that he begins by referring to problems of curricular design, because he believes those educational issues should always be at the center of his administrative concerns.

Even though the first years at Kennedy were marked by a directionless proliferation of courses, old-timers remember the "good old days" nostalgically. Sheila Ackerman, Mastruzzi's dedicated and gracious secretary, says proudly that she has been at Kennedy "since its inception . . . and being here from the beginning gives you a real sense of responsibility and connection." She too remembers working among the carpenters and electricians as they completed the new structure, and the feelings of joining in a pioneer effort. The building of a new school was an exciting adventure that took the coordinated efforts of many. The traditional roles and boundaries were blurred as people pitched in to ready Kennedy for its opening. Several faculty and staff, who have been there since the opening day, refer to the intimacy and optimism that characterized the first year. With less than two thousand students and a small, energetic faculty "rattling around" in a brand new school, "it felt like a country club . . . very swanky and elegant." But more important than the polished and roomy edifice, were the feelings of closeness among the faculty. "We were like a family then, very close," says a young woman who believes that much of the "family spirit" still survives today even though the school has grown very big.

The small scale of the school in its opening year had permitted intimacy among faculty and students, but the newness also offered opportunities for renewed energy and optimism. Many teachers arrived with the hope that they would be breaking new ground and would meet new professional challenges. "With a new slate, I thought I might be able to see my imprint," said a twenty-year veteran of New York City schools. A bright young teacher had become totally disenchanted with teaching after two years in a neighboring high school. She came to Kennedy because she "wanted to give teaching one last shot." With bitterness still in her voice, she described her earlier experiences. "After graduating from Lehman College I took my first job. I hated it. The principal had been a colonel in the army and ran his school like a military operation. It was a very uptight place with no room for growth. I wanted out. Then I heard about the Kennedy opening and I heard very positive things about Bob Mastruzzi. I thought there might be room for growth and creativity in my teaching. Kennedy represented a hope, a vision for me."

Principal Mastruzzi capitalized on the hopes for revitalization that accompany institution building by aggressive recruitment of his key staff. Having spent all of his professional years in New York City public schools, he knew the terrain, had developed important networks, and had a good sense of the reputations of his colleagues. He went after people with impressive and enduring track records and "charmed" them into coming to Kennedy. In New York City, department chairpersons are given the label of Assistant Principals (A.P.'s). Mastruzzi searched out his A.P.'s very carefully, looking for people with solid ideas and leadership skills. One A.P. recalled her first meeting with Mastruzzi as "captivating." "My first impression of him is a lasting one. He was a human being who knew how to relate and listen. He really cared. Our interview was Friday afternoon and I was hired the following Monday. I've never regretted that impulsive decision." Another A.P., who had held the same position in another high school, responded to Kennedy's beckon because he "simply could not resist Mastruzzi. . . . He has an amazing quality of being able to get the most out of you. It is impossible to say 'no' to him. I work ten times as hard here as I have anywhere . . . and I have now discovered why I do . . . because I know Bob would do anything for me. . . . He gives of his full heart."

Not all of Mastruzzi's choices created such happy matches. I heard about one A.P. who never committed himself to his work at Kennedy, "always had one foot out the door," and another who relates poorly to the faculty who work in his department. There are also stories about a difficult and demanding A.P. whose personal qualities are "almost unbearable," but whose ideas, creativity, and energy are extraordinary assets for the school. Yet overwhelmingly, the voices of Mastruzzi's key staff sing his praises and exclaim great loyalty for him. Over and over again, superlatives are used. "He is the greatest human being I've ever known," exclaims one. "I feel a tremendous sense of pride, almost a rah-rah spirit, and I attribute that to Bob," exults another. A third speaks about Mastruzzi's "irreplaceable" qualities, "If that man were to leave this school and you were to come back three or four months later, you'd see a very different situation. The man is a great person, knowledgeable, wise, an extremely good administrator, and a beautiful supervisor of A.P.'s. I would say he enjoys the total loyalty of his cabinet and ninety-eight percent loyalty from the faculty. . . . The man's got charisma!"

Almost everyone points to the personal qualities of Mastruzzi when they are asked to identify the origins of goodness at Kennedy. His "spirit emanates" throughout the school, says one teacher with almost religious fervor. He is "the life blood of this organism," she continues as she switches to a medical metaphor. What is fascinating about Mastruzzi's bigger-than-life role and imagery is that his self-conception is based on very different views of his power and style. Listening to his admirers, one might at first imagine that Mastruzzi's seductions are too powerful to resist; that he reigns through mysterious, other-worldly attractions; that he is a guru of sorts. But listening to Mastruzzi's perceptions of his leadership role, one is struck by his notions of participation and collaboration.

He does not view himself as high on a pedestal, but as down in the trenches inspiring, cajoling, and encouraging people to "do their best and give their most." He rarely refers to the edicts and commands that he issues from his lofty station, but often to the listening, responding, and negotiating that are part of his everyday interactions. His charisma seems to derive less from his otherworldly qualities than from his very human qualities—his great ability to empathize and identify with others. When I ask Mastruzzi about his views on school leadership, he immediately refers to the collaborative dimensions of the principal's job. "First of all, I have a great concern for the quality of human relationships. I try to find ways of getting people involved in the process, using their strengths and assets. My big word is *participation*. I want to have as many people as possible join in deciding and acting. They must become responsible to something larger than themselves. If there is one fault some people say I have, it is that I try to involve too many people, and it is sometimes inefficient. But I'm willing to tolerate the inefficiency because in the end, people will feel more connected, more committed and pulled into the process."

Mastruzzi's strong and decisive views at first appear contrary to others' idealizations of him. But on closer examination, his words are echoed by the perspectives of faculty and students. Their loyalty does not seem to be an expression of idol worship, but a reflection of their connection to a communal process. When people refer to "feelings of connection," they often talk about the autonomy and independence that Mastruzzi permits and encourages. "He allows us scope, the space to develop our own thing," says one A.P. Another points to the way that Mastruzzi protects his faculty from "the arbitrary regulations of the central authority. . . . He serves as a buffer between outside and inside. If it weren't for him, we'd feel more constrained. We have a great deal of freedom here." Some observers believe Mastruzzi is able to encourage autonomy among his faculty because of his own deeply rooted self-confidence. "He is the most secure principal I have ever known. He likes to see strength, not weakness, in the people who work for him," says a relatively new faculty member who believes there is a "fair exchange" between the freedom the faculty enjoy and the commitment that Mastruzzi expects.

One enthusiast claims that Mastruzzi not only encourages faculty creativity and autonomy, but he also allows people the room to make mistakes. He is "forgiving" and believes that people often learn from repairing the damage they have created. The coordinator of student affairs, Pamela Gino, recounts the disastrous story of the first rock concert she organized for students at Kennedy. She had expected a couple of hundred students and eight hundred showed up, many high on alcohol and marijuana. "A lot of those kids think you can't listen to rock unless you're high. Booze and rock go together." Not expecting the great number of students, nor their inebriation, Gino had not planned for adequate security; and it became a chaotic, treacherous evening. "After it all, I felt a tremendous letdown, a real sense of failure," remembers Gino. "But I also had learned a lot about how to plan for that kind of event. I knew I could do it better given a second chance." Mastruzzi greeted her request for a second chance with healthy skepticism and a battery of critical questions, but he allowed her to try again. The second rock concert was a "great success. . . . He's a generous man. He sees failure as an opportunity for change," beams Gino.

Just as Mastruzzi identifies his potential source of weakness as his unending attempts to be inclusive, to encourage all voices to be heard; so too do others point to the inefficiencies and ambiguities that this causes. But most do not identify the weakness as a problem of "participation" taken to its extreme; rather, they see it as Mastruzzi's difficulty in saying "no" to people. One sympathetic colleague, who sees many of the same traits in himself, justifies the weakness by saying, "There is something in Mastruzzi which won't let you say 'no' to him. Part of that is our expectation that he won't say 'no' to us. I think that's fair." Others identify it as his single "tragic flaw." Says a close associate, "If Bob has one fault, it is his inability to say 'no,' to act quickly and decisively when he sees something wrong." One critic believes that Mastruzzi is "smart and calculating," and always wants to be seen as "the good guy. . . . Saying no would tarnish that image."

An interesting analysis of Mastruzzi's ability to maintain his affirmative stance and still be ultimately effective, refers to his close partnership with Arnold Herzog. Mastruzzi and Herzog have been friends and colleagues for most of their professional lives and they share a rare and productive companionship. Before coming to Kennedy they both worked at Benjamin Franklin High School: Mastruzzi as A.P. for administration (in charge of bureaucratic details and regulations), and Herzog as A.P. for guidance (in charge of the counselling program). When Mastruzzi was offered the principalship of Kennedy, Herzog was his immediate, intuitive choice for A.P. for Administration. He chose him not only because of his comprehensive knowledge of the city system and its numerous regulations, and their deep trust and friendship; but also because he knew Herzog had important, contrasting temperamental tendencies that would combine well with his. Their partnership would work because in many ways they were opposites. Both Mastruzzi and Herzog are admired by their colleagues, but everyone speaks of their differences. Bob is confident, unruffled, and charming, and Arnie is described as "abrasive, flamboyant, and overbearing." Even as people shake their heads at Herzog's exaggerated toughness, they recognize "the good heart underneath" and see his harshness as a necessary quality of his role. Says a Herzog admirer: "He does all the dirty work. He makes a lot of decisions and wields a lot of power, but he is greatly misunderstood. He's seen by many as a tough head-chopper, but he *has* to be. The position demands that." Another person says that everyone recognizes the distinction between Herzog's role requirements and his personal style. She points to his office and says it is always crowded with kids even though he does not need to see them in his official capacity. "The kids love him. . . . You know, this year he agreed to advise the cheerleaders because we couldn't get anyone else to do it." A few observers, however, view Herzog's toughness as the necessary foil for Mastruzzi's supportiveness. One is "bad guy" for the other's "good guy." "When Mastruzzi says 'yes,' he depends on Herzog to say 'no.' They complement each other completely," says a sharp observer. "Bob could not be seen as good if Arnie wasn't seen as bad."

Mastruzzi appreciates their different styles and approaches and admires his colleague's competence. He tolerates Herzog's ranting and raving with patience, understanding, and maybe a hint of enjoyment. To see them together is to witness the theatrical excitations of Herzog and the calm listening of Mastruzzi, knowing each expects and understands the other's response. Although the principal recognizes the temperamental partnership he shares with Herzog, he tends to point to their differences by saying, "Arnie is an administrator and I think of myself as an educator." He views the former as a narrower, largely bureaucratic role where the emphasis is on organizational details, rules, and regulations. Mastruzzi's focus as an educator, on the other hand, is with the learning and development of people. He seeks to establish an environment that will encourage teachers and students to thrive, and he does not want to become overly preoccupied with the detailed management of that environment. The educational core must always be kept at the forefront and the relationships among people must always be viewed as the vital dimension of the process.

When I ask Mastruzzi to define the criteria of an outstanding high school principal, he launches into an organized and articulate response without pause. He seems to have considered the elements of good leadership many times before. His responses are not facile or pat, but they are certainly premeditated. As he lists the ingredients of effective leadership, he points to the select few principals in New York's system whom he considers "extraordinary" and uses them as prime examples. There are one hundred high schools in New York, eighteen in the Bronx, but few of their principals deserve Mastruzzi's highest praise. As the principal with the most seniority in the Bronx, he has seen many of his colleagues come and go, and believes that the top position requires a complex combination of intellectual skills, psychological capacities, and emotional commitments. His list has six explicit ingredients:

First, being a good leader requires a "tremendous sense of dedication . . . you don't even consider the dimension of time. You do everything you can, without limit, to do what's best for the kids and the school."

Second, a principal must be "humanistic . . . . There is not a biased bone in his body. He looks at a kid and sees a person, not his ethnicity, his race, or his class. He connects with the person, without prejudice."

Third, a good leader must be "knowledgeable." Mastruzzi speaks here of a knowledge gained through experience *and* reflection on experience. "He must have gone through the rigorous training of teaching and being an assistant principal . . . he must have had time to develop a sound educational and administrative philosophy. . . . He must have a vision, a game plan . . . but always be ready to alter the plan when conditions change."

Fourth, the leader must have intelligence, "an intelligence that is quick and intuitive."

Fifth, good principals must have a "strong physical presence." Mastruzzi assures me he is not referring to the superficial cover of a Hollywood star or a fashion model, but to qualities that run much deeper. "He or she must be able to command respect, to control a group . . . have a kind of dynamism and charisma." You can usually spot this self-confidence by observing others' reactions. "When he or she talks, people stop and listen . . . like the E. F. Hutton commercial on TV."

Finally, an effective leader must be a very "flexible person, open to compromise and suggestion. When issues get tough and hairy, a leader has to be able to appreciate the other person's point of view, put himself in the other's place." This empathetic regard sometimes leads to a surprising "meeting of the minds and no one has to feel he has lost."

Although Mastruzzi's list of leadership qualities paints an image of a bigger-than-life figure with extraordinary qualities and talents, he views the role as within the purview of dedicated and committed mortals. Most of the skills can be learned through long experience and patient practice. Even the more subtle temperamental qualities, he believes, can be developed through undefensive self-criticism. Mastruzzi begins by referring to the general dimensions of a good high school principal. He ends up describing himself. This does not seem to be a purposeful, self-congratulatory gesture. It is not so much an autobiographical statement as it is an echo of the countless ways he has been described by faculty, staff, and students at Kennedy.

URBAN OASIS

Robert Mastruzzi's belief in the unbiased, colorblind stance of a good leader combines with his pride in the rich mixture of students at Kennedy High. Because students are drawn from a wide geographic area, the school population does not closely reflect the surrounding Riverdale neighborhood. In contrast to the Riverdale population, Kennedy is blacker, browner, and poorer. There is a sharp contrast between the complexions and lifestyles of people inside and outside of the school. Kennedy is a zoned high school and attracts students from as far away as West Harlem in Manhattan. When Mastruzzi describes the mélange of students he begins by reciting the racial and ethnic percentages: 40 percent Hispanic, 35 percent Black, 23 percent white, and 2 percent Asian. But those distributions do not begin to convey the heterogeneity at Kennedy. It is also a school that draws students from a range Mastruzzi describes as "the wealthiest of families to the most poverty-stricken, from the very rich to the indigent." Even though Riverdale is one of the more affluent communities in New York, Kennedy is designated as a Title I school. With 5,300 students in the school, about 3,000 of them are eligible to receive free lunches.

The poorest students at Kennedy travel the farthest distance to get to school. Most are Black and Hispanic and they board the Broadway subway in west central Harlem and arrive (2,000 strong) a few blocks from the school after more than an hour's ride. Another group of working and middle-class white and Hispanic students travel from the Inwood section of northern Manhattan. Their trip is shorter and they can continue to feel connected to their neighborhood by looking out the school windows at the Inwood hills in the distance. The largely blue-collar, Irish-American population from the Kingsbridge lowlands walk to school or take city buses. They are joined by a sprinkling of upwardly mobile middle-class Blacks and Hispanics, who are new arrivals to the neighborhood from other parts of the Bronx. The children of privilege descend the hills of Riverdale to come to Kennedy. With a largely Jewish population, Riverdale's upper middle-class families often have other attractive educational options. The very wealthiest neighbors usually choose to enroll their children in Riverdale Country Day, Fieldston, or other prestigious private schools. Others hope that their sons and daughters will pass the tough entrance examinations for the Bronx High School of Science, which is ten minutes away from Kennedy but light years away in prestige and reputation. However, the admissions standards of the Bronx High School of

Science and the elite private schools permit only a small percentage to escape the public school option. Those students whose parents cannot afford private school tuitions or who were denied entry to the more competitive schools come to Kennedy reluctantly, some with fears of big-city schools, a few with prejudice towards the racial and social class mixtures, and others with feelings of failure and defeat in being excluded from more privileged circles. Then there are some affluent families in the Riverdale hills who "believe in public schools" and are relieved that Kennedy is a viable and attractive school that allows them to match their ideological commitments with personal practice.

Despite the reluctance of some of Kennedy High's close neighbors, the great majority of students focus on the attractions and benefits of the school. They come gladly and feel proud to be attending one of "the best schools in the city." A photographic exhibit displayed just outside the principal's office shows black-and-white images of city scenes. The photographs, taken by students, reveal the subtle beauty in city scenes that are normally viewed as dangerous or grotesque. A back alley, photographed in deep shadows, is captured as a place of hiding and privacy, rather than being shown as menacing or threatening. The student exhibit is titled "Urban Oasis." For many students, particularly those traveling from long distances, Kennedy is an oasis; a place of safety and protection from the dangers and chaos of the big city. One of the guidance counselors tells me about a waif of a girl who travels an hour and forty minutes each way to come to Kennedy. Without a winter coat and no money to buy the glasses she needs to see the blackboard clearly, the girl has never missed a day of school. An A.P. points to high schools surrounding Kennedy that are half empty because they are not able to attract students. "They stand empty while we are overflowing with kids who are hungry for a decent education . . . some kids pass by two schools when they come to Kennedy." Principal Mastruzzi is aware of the numbers of students who lie, cheat, and give false addresses in order to be admitted to Kennedy. Many of them could be tracked down and sent away, but Mastruzzi admires their determination and good taste. "How can you say 'no' to a kid who really wants to be here?" he asks rhetorically. A bright-eyed Hispanic boy, who admits to me that he "lied his way in," says, "Listen, I vote with my feet. I come 'cause this is a good place, man." Not everyone is as enthusiastic about the school or makes extraordinary efforts to come. "There are hundreds of kids who never get here, some we don't even know about," admits the attendance officer. There are others who arrive each day and go through the motions without complaint, but also without generous praise for the place. But every student I spoke to at least

73

admitted that "if you have to go to school, you might as well go here."

One of the great attractions of Kennedy for students and faculty is the safety and discipline of the environment. Compared to the violence and chaos that characterize many big-city schools, Kennedy feels like a calm and productive environment. More impressive than the feelings of comfort is the recognition that the environment is truly and confidently pluralistic, that there is calm among groups that are often at odds in other settings. The visual mélange of color is unusual—black, white, brown, and yellow in all shapes and sizes. And the distinctions that people seem to attend to are not the gross and obvious ones, but more subtle differentiations. Hardly anyone I spoke to referred to Black/White differences, but several pointed to the distinctions between the Koreans and the Chinese, or between the Dominicans and the Puerto Ricans. Everyone seemed proud of the rich diversity. A veteran faculty member used to "warfare" in other schools in which he has taught exclaimed, "Isn't it beautiful the way everyone gets along!" Before coming to Kennedy, a senior whose family lives in the Riverdale hills, had heard rumors that the school was a "tough place with lots of gangs." He has discovered just the opposite. "I don't even think there are definable cliques, and I haven't seen a fight since I came here." Another student from West Harlem exudes, "It's like the United Nations, all kinds of people." One perceptive and soft-spoken Asian boy claims that most students "hang out with their own kind," but feel perfectly comfortable "mixing with other kids. . . . But that's only natural," he counters immediately. "That's human nature."

Pamela Gino, coordinator of student affairs, and a lively, gregarious woman in her early thirties, watches interactions among students very closely. She says simply, "There are very easy, natural relationships among the ethnic and racial groups. It is an *unimportant* matter. You just don't feel it." The only minor disturbances in the calm waters reflect highly specific perceptions of subgroups of students who she claims "tend to label themselves." For example, many see the "Riverdale Jewish kids as spoiled, ungrateful, indulged, and entitled." The Dominicans are viewed by their peers as "wild, menacing street kids." The Russians and Albanians are perceived as "volatile, emotional, excitable, and driven." And the Chinese students are seen as "closed and inbred. . . . The Chinese Club wanted to put up signs in Chinese so that no one else would be able to understand, even though the Club is supposed to be open to anyone who wants to join." But these vivid characterizations rarely lead to hostility or dispute. "They just make life interesting. They give the school character," claims Gino. The rarity of intergroup conflict is reflected in old-timers' remembrances of a single event that occurred several years ago, a "trivial" dispute that now causes people to laugh in disbelief. The Dominicans and Koreans began fighting over a name-calling incident. It seems that a Korean student had referred to a Dominican as "Puerto Rican," and in retaliation the Dominican had called the Korean student "Chinese." What began as a personal exchange briefly erupted into a heated fracas—but was squelched immediately.

Other adults who deal closely with the psychological, social, and academic dimensions of the Kennedy students observe the unusually positive feelings among racial and ethnic groups, but also can point to the distinctive and "colorful" qualities of some. The A.P. of guidance, who is referred to by some as "the heart" of the school, has a reputation as a gifted clinician who works equally well with all kinds of students. He believes that any clinician worth his salt should be able to cross the boundaries of class, race, and ethnicity and see the person underneath. "You see color at first, but once you get to work there is no difference." His words are tentative as he tries to express his complicated mixture of feelings. Origins and roots are important, but they often disguise universal human dilemmas. A good clinician, he believes, must reach beyond the initial boundaries to shared dimensions of human behavior. "I hope I'm better at doing it than talking about it," he says with a hesitant smile. As he probes his views on cultural differences, he discovers that the newest arrivals, the strangers to our society, have the most distinctive and vivid traits. Color and ethnicity are less important determinants of difference than the degree of assimilation and adaptation a group has made to contemporary American norms. "I see no difference in the Black and White students," says the guidance A.P. confidently. "The Hispanic kids, who are new here, seem more lively, real expressive. . . . The Russian kids are incredibly demanding and pushy. They yell loud and clear . . . maybe they were inhibited and repressed in the old country and they have grown used to fighting for everything. . . . Our school may contribute to their aggression because we listen. . . . They know they can get a response from us, so they take advantage of that."

A close colleague, who is also clinically trained, points to social class, not race, as the powerful differentiating variable. When he describes social class differences he seems to be referring to degrees of motivation and industry expressed by students and their families. He sees a stark contrast between the upper middle-class Jewish students and the newly middle-class Blacks. "The rich Riverdale kids are the saddest group of all—no drive, no optimism, too complacent." The seriousness, dedication, and shine of the middle-class Blacks remind him of his own Brooklyn upbringing in a working-class Jewish family. "To these Black kids, the value of education has become as important as it was when I was a kid. Like it or not, I had to go to school and achieve . . . even though my parents never finished high school and my grandparents were illiterate."

It is fascinating that the images of the different racial and ethnic groups at Kennedy do not seem to emerge as hardened caricatures. Different people offer different characterizations and most reveal the subtleties of observation and scrutiny, rather than the automatic responses of prejudice. It is also interesting that some claim that they see no differences, while others dwell on the detailed contrasts among groups. For some, therefore, Kennedy is special because people are "colorblind." For others, the school is extraordinary in its rich and diverse plurality. "It's so much better than flat assimilation," says an eager young teacher.

But whether people deny or underscore group differences, everyone seems to recognize and appreciate the harmony among students at Kennedy. There are several theories for why Kennedy is harmonious when other big city schools with similar populations are threatened by racial conflict. Mastruzzi, who relishes the mix ("I look out and see the pepper and salt and the amber in between. It's wonderful!"), claims that the harmony reflects the "humanitarian philosophy" of the school. Students feel they are being treated fairly and respectfully by their teachers and they respond in kind to one another. It is when students experience institutional inequalities or prejudicial attention from teachers that they form rigid and exclusive groups among themselves. "I don't know what racial tension is," claims Mastruzzi. "If a Black and White kid are fighting, we see two kids fighting—not race—and we deal with it that way. . . . I venture to say it is experienced by the kids that way." Several faculty and students point to Mastruzzi as the "perfect model" principal for attaining the goal of racial harmony. "He doesn't draw back from you," says a dark-skinned Black boy who claims that his junior high school teachers were often repelled by and afraid of students of darker hue. "They'd never touch you. Sometimes I felt like I was diseased. . . . But I've seen Mastruzzi reach out to all kinds of kids." The principal's powerful example makes it difficult for others to express their fears or distaste towards certain groups. "Mastruzzi is not just asking for tolerance among groups," claims an ardent admirer, "he's asking for respect and friendship."

Pamela Gino offers another explanation for the "natural" relationships among racial and ethnic groups at Kennedy. First, she points to the demographic stability of the school. When Kennedy opened ten years ago, there were roughly the same proportions of Hispanics, Blacks, and Whites. No one needs to feel threatened by the exodus of one group and the take over of another. Territories have never emerged. "There is a balance . . . no real minority." She predicts that a noticeable shift toward imbalance would inevitably lead to conflict among groups. Second, she claims that the school's support of group affiliation has increased positive intergroup relationships. "Assimilation is not the goal and we say that in a lot of ways." A large proportion of the extracurricular clubs at Kennedy, for example, are "ethnic clubs." There are Korean, Chinese, Christian, Jewish, Hispanic, Caribbean, and Korean/Christian clubs ("not to be confused with the Christian or the Korean clubs"). "Pride," a club for Black students, was disbanded this year because no one was willing to volunteer as the advisor. Most of these clubs draw only a small percentage of students, but they serve as "home base" for those who need to feel part of an identifiable subgroup, and they symbolize a preference for diversity rather than sameness. By far, the Korean and Chinese clubs have the largest membership. With the smallest populations in the school and "tendencies towards exclusivity," their clubs make them feel less isolated and more confident in becoming part of the school community. According to the student coordinator, then, ethnic balance and group identification are essential ingredients of a good heterogeneity.

Gladys Jackson, the A.P. of foreign languages, a graceful and wise, middle-aged Black woman, is even more pointed in her views of cultural pluralism as basic to intergroup harmony. She believes that nothing should be lost, repressed, or denied when a student enters a new cultural setting. He should be encouraged to hold on to his rich past and embellish those roots with new experiences. She strongly believes that the bicultural person is the privileged one with more perspectives, choices, and options than his one-dimensional counterpart. "I am eager not to have kids lose what was once theirs," she says with quiet passion. Such a loss would not be good for the child or healthy for the school's culture. The harmony at Kennedy, she feels, springs from the support students feel for "being themselves. . . . The image of the all-American kid is all of us!"

Jackson came to Kennedy when it opened in 1972. Although she was attracted by the promises and hopes of a new school and the "humanitarian" spirit of Mastruzzi, she was also running from an alternative school in Queens that she was "happy to leave." For fourteen years, she had been a guidance counselor committed to non-traditional approaches to education, to individualized instruction, to more open and equal relationships between teachers and students. But when the freedom and expression of the progressive philosophies turned to chaos and irresponsibility among the students, Jackson knew it was time to leave. When her students came to school stoned on drugs; when she saw her first LSD trip, and "was horrified beyond belief"; she knew it was time to pursue other options. After the distortions of "liberal" education, Jackson was ready for a more structured, traditional school. She also was eager to leave the guidance counselling role and return to the curricular and pedagogical challenges of teaching. But she wanted to continue to express her commitments to "diversity among students"; to "responding to the 'whole child'"; to reinforcing the "individual strengths and capacities" of her pupils. In her initial interview with Mastruzzi, Gladys Jackson felt they shared a common philosophical vision, and she was eager to take on a leadership role in a department whose explicit purpose it was to celebrate cultural diversity.

With thirty-four faculty members (seventeen from foreign countries), the foreign language department inhabits the fifth floor of Kennedy. Called the "Fiesta Floor" by most insiders, its name reflects the special warmth and vibrancy that infuses interactions among students and faculty there. Several people point me towards the Fiesta Floor when they want to convey "how our school treats society's strangers," or when they want to establish "the character and passion of Kennedy," or when they wish to show me "the most motivated kids in the whole school." It is on the fifth floor that one feels the most vivid expression of cultural differences.

First, one is struck by the auditory display of languages. The predominant language is Spanish, but other tongues are also heard: Russian, Albanian, Chinese, Vietnamese, French, and so on. Most of the fifth floor students have adapted to the American teenage uniforms of designer jeans, classy sneakers, fancy decorated T-shirts, and down jackets. However, many reveal vestiges of their origins. Some of the Hispanic girls, for example, seem glamorous in their fitted skirts, high-heeled shoes, lace blouses, and bright red lipstick. In contrast, the Chinese boys are low-key and understated with their monochromatic dress. But it is in style, gesture, and nuance, more than dress, that a visitor to the fifth floor feels a striking contrast with the more usual American adolescent images.

The Fiesta Floor is not famous for its regular foreign language program, although the training is competent and the offerings diverse. Kennedy offers Spanish to 75 percent of the students enrolled in foreign language instruction, French to 15 percent, and Italian to 7 percent. There is one Latin course taught by a vigorous and rigorous Italian man at 8:00 in the morning, and there is a fledgling Hebrew class with eleven students whose parents pressured the school to keep the course alive. Up until two years ago, German was also taught but the decline in enrollments and the retirement of the German teacher combined to eliminate the course from the language curriculum. Yet what distinguishes the fifth floor are its programs for non-English speaking students. It is the new arrivals, the eager immigrants, who give the Fiesta Floor its special flavor. Peering into the open doors of classrooms, the students' faces are intense as they listen. Many sit on the edges of their chairs, as if they are literally stretching to understand and reaching for the moon. It is rare that one sees such clear motivation, such visible willfulness. Everyone who teaches these newcomers comments on their civility, drive, and earnestness.

At Kennedy, the English as a Second Language (ESL) Program is taught in Spanish to 800 students. With funding from Title I and Title VII (the Bilingual Education Act), the ESL program must conform to a string of regulations from the federal government that are constantly being rewritten and revised. In addition, the ESL program receives funds from tax-levied monies collected by the city, and finally, the Aspira Consent Decree mandates specific approaches to language training. All of these sources provide a complicated array of offerings for the non-English speaking student. An ESL coordinator, who works under Jackson, seeks to keep abreast of the frequent changes in the law, acts as the primary interpreter of mandates, and translates the regulations into the realistic choices available to Kennedy students. For the most part, Jackson supports the "spirit" of the law, even though the shifting letter of it is a constant source of frustration. She strongly supports the prevailing paradox: that students should become bicultural and hold on to their cultural origins at the same time they should be moved quickly into the mainstream. "The ESL is a transitional program, not a maintenance program," she says with no ambivalence.

To achieve this transition, students move through four levels of the ESL Program (Beginning, Intermediate, Advanced, and Transitional). There are ESL classes in science, math, and social studies. Along with the federally funded courses, ESL students take tax levied courses in music, language arts, fine arts, and business and office practice. Recently, an innovative writing skills course has been created for Transition level students. The brainchild of Ellen Hyman, a dedicated and able teacher, Writing Skills is designed to make students more comfortable with the expressive and descriptive dimensions of English. Using creative pedagogical strategies and curricular ideas, the course builds on the premise that language facility provides reinforcement for self-knowledge and self-confidence. Each class begins with five minutes of journal writing. Both teacher and students join in this activity and students are asked to write about "topics that are relevant" to their lives, such as "Describe your next-door neighbor." Or "We don't have enough holidays. Invent one and tell why and when we celebrate it." Or "Pretend you cut class yesterday. Write an outrageous excuse to your teacher." In responding to these questions, students are encouraged to be spontaneous, truthful, and personal. The journals are not corrected for grammar or spelling, and if the student judges the content to be too personal for the teacher to read, she may fold the page for privacy.

Ms. Hyman, a quietly attractive woman, has a soft, soothing voice and a generous smile. Although there are thirty-two students in the class (twenty-eight Hispanics, three Asians, and one Russian), the intimacy and comfortable exchanges make the group feel much smaller. Students are attentive, but relaxed. They often speak out spontaneously without raising their hands and the dialogue is laced with laughter, but never does the organization, momentum, or focus of the class break down. The lesson centers on increasing the sensory word vocabulary of the students. It follows a series of lessons on learning how to describe "physical details" and precedes a segment on learning "emotional details." The sequence is designed to augment the expressive range of students; offer them more ways of discerning and describing events, people, and feelings.

As part of the lesson on sensory details, Ms. Hyman takes out a small bag of potato chips and says, "After today no more food, I promise." With slight melodrama, she holds the bag up and demonstrates. "I have here an ordinary brand of potato chips." The students laugh enthusiastically, as they appreciate the reference to television commercials. "Let's see if we can describe potato chips using sensory details. . . . Juan, how would you describe by *sight* this potato chip?" "It is brown, round, yellow, with a brown burn spot on it," responds Juan. "Maria touch it, feel it . . . what can you tell me about the feel?" Maria reaches for the chip and describes it as "a little hard, rough . . . I can feel the grains of salt." From the back of the room Roberto calls out, "Hey, over here, I'll try the taste." The class erupts in laughter as the teacher responds to Roberto's offer. The class quiets immediately when Ms. Hyman says, "Listen, boys and girls," and in the silence breaks a single potato chip. "Crunch," says one volunteer; "snap," says another as they try to match the correct word to the sound.

Up at the blackboard, the teacher writes three words on the board and demonstrates their meaning by crushing a potato chip in her hand, letting the pieces fall to the floor, and by shaking the bag. Together they identify "crunchy" (to crush noisily), "crumble" (to break into little pieces), and "rustle" (one thing rubbing softly against the other). Then they figure out which sense (sight, sound, touch, or taste) allows one to make those distinctions. Once they have written the words and meanings in their notebooks, the teacher asks them to repeat the words out loud. Their choral effort is vigorous. As they speak the words with a Spanish lilt, their voices begin to capture the sights and sounds of the potato chip demonstration. The lesson concludes with dramatic exchanges between Ms. Hyman and her rapt students as they collectively develop meanings for "mouthwatering" (something looks so delicious it makes you hungry), "thundering" (what word do you recognize in thundering—take it from there), "screeching" (two cars approach one another—they put on their brakes and swerve away quickly), and "thirst-quenching" (picture yourself on a very hot day—you'd do anything for a cold drink).

The class closes with a brief review of what they have covered and an exclamation and big smile from Juan: "The more you see, the more you feel, the more you write!" The homework assignment is greeted with good-natured groans. With the sound of the bell, students immediately return to Spanish; the tempo is accelerated, expressive gestures reappear, and they feel at home. A dark-skinned, shiny-haired girl approaches me and is surprised when I do not understand her Spanish. A friend nearby translates: "Ms. Hyman is great. She gives us a gift."

The fifth-floor faculty feels fairly confident about the coherence and structure of the ESL curriculum. They admit that the challenge and difficulties of the program appear during the transitional phases. When students must move from the protective environment of the Fiesta Floor to the general high school classrooms, they often feel overwhelmed by the changes. All of the department A.P.'s I spoke with identified "the transition" as a vulnerable spot in their curriculum. The A.P. of English, who speaks four or five languages fluently, believes that the greatest challenge ahead will be the curricular integration of ESL and regular classes. For several years he has watched the casualties of "mainstreaming" and believes that all departments need to provide for a smoother transition. He has worked "hand in glove" with Foreign Languages and believes that the close, cooperative relationship between departments is essential.

In a recent effort to build bridges for students, a member of the English department has developed a course called "Intensive English Skills for the Foreign," which is designed to focus on the structure and grammar of English. The teacher, an enthusiastic grammarian, is fascinated by the connections between language and thought and manages to convey to students the dynamic, communicative aspects of language. He exclaims to me, "I love language. I find it fascinating. It's so interesting to think of ways in which language determines how we think. There are no tenses in Chinese, for instance. Can you imagine what a different view of time they must have!" In two sections (one dominated by Spanish-speaking students, the other by Chinese, Korean, Vietnamese, and Russian students), the teacher displays the structure and function of language through active class participation. As he offers alternative modes of expression, he seems to be opening doors for his students, whose responses range from intense listening to exuberant participation. The teacher paces back and forth as he points to verbs written on the board. "Not only can you say, 'He should *walk*,' you can say 'He should be *walking*' . . . and guess what? There is a third alternative—'He should *have been walking.'"* With each revelation, the students join in repeating the word, some laughing with amazement by the time the third possibility is presented.

This course, in its early experimental phases, seems to be responding to the problems of transition faced by many students when they leave the Fiesta Floor. But the A.P. of English points to the difficulties he will face in expanding this effort, which presently serves only forty-five students. First, there are few faculty who have the talent, dedication, and interest in language required to teach this course. At the very least, other teachers would have to be retrained and retooled as grammarians. Second, the pedagogy requires that classes be relatively small. With twenty students in each class rather than thirty-five, the course gets a disproportionate share of resources. If the department decided to offer several sections of the course, the staff time would have to be taken from other important areas and the A.P. of English would face the tough battles of resource allocation within the school.

Some other faculty members seem less interested in finding curricular resolutions to the transitional difficulties foreign students face and are more concerned about the limitations imposed upon teachers assigned to ESL transition classes. A social studies teacher with almost two decades of experience and "an enormous commitment" to her work, complained that the language barriers inevitably constrict interesting dialogue and make teaching "boring." She pointed to her colleagues who enjoy teaching ESL classes and claimed their pleasure comes from the combination of "docility and motivation" the students offer, not from the "real learning" that should be going on. Her colleague, who also recognizes the problems of curricular standards faced in transitional classes, believes those are balanced against the "cultural understandings" that flow from the rich variety of students learning together. In his "bridge class" in global history there are two Palestinians, four Haitians, twelve Dominicans, one San Salvadorian, four Koreans, three Vietnamese, two Chinese, and one student from Bangladesh. Although it does not resemble a traditional history course, the students' origins define rich reservoirs of exploration and examination that would not be available in a thoroughly assimilated, homogeneous group.

Although there are differing views on the quality and substance of learning in transition courses, most faculty agree that the bridges are difficult to build and that large numbers of students fall into the chasm between two worlds. Paradoxically, the great success stories told at Kennedy often refer to students who arrived at school with no proficiency in English and went on to win the most prestigious academic prizes. Gladys

Jackson loves to tell these stories as evidence of the intense motivation of foreign students, the rigor and dedication of her faculty, and the open doors of Kennedy. She tells about the stellar careers of a Vietnamese boy who arrived in the country a year and a half ago and was recently offered a full scholarship to study mathematics at Cal. Tech., and a Russian boy who became the school's valedictorian after two years in the country and went on to study at M.I.T. Three years ago, a Dominican boy delivered the valedictory address. Speaking in English and without notes, he stood as a symbol of "the best of Kennedy and the best of America. . . . Mastruzzi had tears in his eyes as he listened to this kid speak," recalls Jackson. The individual stories of achievement are amazing, but the A.P. of foreign languages wants to leave me with even more captivating evidence. "Last year, seven out of the top ten students graduating had been in the ESL program. The year before, we saw the same statistics . . . the secret is motivation. With all their hearts, these kids want to succeed and they believe it can happen through education."

For many, the ESL program at Kennedy stands as a symbol of the school's best attempts at inclusion. Through ESL, the school represents the Statue of Liberty reaching out to incorporate society's new arrivals and offer them the best opportunities. Some observers, however, believe that the real symbol of Kennedy's humanitarian tendencies lies not in how the strangers are treated, but in the ways the school resists societal imperatives. "It's relatively easy to offer special attention to the folks from foreign shores. It's much more difficult to be as generous with regular kids who are less privileged," says one faculty member who believes that Kennedy is special in its "non-hierarchical" arrangements. In most high schools, he points out, the "tracks" directly correspond to the social stratification in the wider society. "Poor kids, Black kids, are always on the bottom. Rich kids are on the top. There are no surprises." In Kennedy, the correspondence is not erased, but it is purposefully challenged.

Everyone admits that there is homogenous grouping at Kennedy, and that once assignments are made there is little movement among levels. But the majority point to the ways in which Kennedy is different from most high schools in trying to resist stereotypic assumptions about different groups of students. Only one teacher I spoke to claimed that the three levels (Remedial, Average, and Honors) are actually "tracks" mirroring social class designations in the wider society. "The Riverdale kids from the hill are in the Honors courses, the Kingsbridge kids are in the 'on level' courses, and the Black and Brown kids from Harlem are stuck at the bottom." An upper middle-class student from Riverdale, who "missed getting into Bronx High School of Science by two points," echoed the teacher's observations with a sense of relief. "Even though Kennedy is a mixed bag, our classes separate the wheat from the chaff. . . . In most of my Honors classes, the kids are white. They're the better students. . . . They deserve to learn at a higher level." But for the most part, the observations and rhetoric of students and faculty point to the ways in which Kennedy seeks to undo the "social pyramid" while still recognizing differences in ability and achievement among students. "You see, usually the pyramid is totally based on social class and racial dimensions. We say that the pyramid's okay, but we base it on ability and disregard social class," explains one teacher. "I think that is both educationally sound and ethical!"

Throughout my visit, I was continually struck by the mixtures of students in classes. Although I could not be sure of their social class origins, the visual display of students showed unusual combinations of racial and ethnic groups. Certainly Black and Brown students predominate at the lowest levels, and proportionately more White students appear in advanced classes. But the pleasant surprise comes in seeing the more than token representation of minorities in Honors courses and their active participation in those classes. In no classrooms did I see segregation by seating patterns. Even when students chose their seats, they tended to arrange themselves in ways that did not reflect group affiliation. Even with my antennae poised to pick up the discriminatory behavior of teachers, I never saw evidence of biased or prejudicial responses to students, and not once did minority or majority students complain of subtle abuses I might not have seen.

In an advanced Honors English course, entitled "Creative Man," most of the almost forty students were White; but there were seven Blacks, five Hispanics, and three Asians sprinkled throughout the classroom. A sophomore Honors course in English showed even more balanced proportions of students. Eleven of the twenty-eight students were White, seven were Hispanic, seven Black, and two Asian. By far the most energetic and talkative student was Anthony, a dark-skinned Black boy. After him the student responses seemed to be equally distributed among the class. By the end of the hour, everyone had spoken either by his own initiation, or because the teacher had deftly managed to spread the opportunities around by calling on the silent ones and offering the immediate rewards of praise. When I asked her whether her efforts at inclusion of *all* students were purposeful, the teacher spoke about the need for teachers to model unbiased behavior. "There is no tension among the various groups in our school," she said matter of factly, "and it is because students don't perceive anyone as being against any group. After all, prejudice, classism, racism are not intrinsic. . . . They are defense mechanisms that arise when people feel threatened, and this environment doesn't cause people to feel worried or defensive."

In the Law Program, a special Honors specialization in the social science department, the ethnic and racial groups were equally represented with a third each of Hispanics, Whites, and Blacks. With almost forty students, the forceful and intense teacher orchestrated a wide-ranging, sometimes chaotic, discussion on the origins and purposes of law in society. Although he encouraged the participation of more than two-thirds of the class, his questions were tough and probing, and he offered discriminating, judgmental responses to student contributions. To a White girl with a long mane of blond hair, he said, "You are having a problem in expressing yourself. Think about it further." To a large Black boy in the front row he prodded, "Can you illuminate the point you raised earlier? I think it may be vital to our understanding of the issues." To a brooding Hispanic boy who accused his teacher of forcing him into a position he did not want to take, he exclaimed emphatically, "No, I'm not trying to get you to say something. I'm trying to get you to convey your point of view. *Your* point of view. Now what do *you* think?" In each of these high-powered, advanced courses teachers seemed to believe in the capacities and potential of all their students and pushed them to think hard and talk clearly. There seemed to be no distinctions made among groups of students. All were treated as if they were expected to perform. The teachers would remark on individual differences among students, but rarely take notice of group characteristics. Said one, "I get tough with Frank because he's smart and lazy. I want him to work harder. He gets mad at me for landing on him. But I don't view his laziness as a quality of Black people and he doesn't think I'm picking on him because he's Black."

Within classrooms, students appear to be treated with unusual fairness. Their individual dimensions are noticed and responded to by teachers, while their group identification seems to fade away. Although students within classrooms seem to receive evenly distributed and unbiased attention, the differences between the levels of instruction at Kennedy are vivid. Honors students have a dramatically different school experience than the Remedial students. Faculty describe the contrasts as the difference "between night and day, black and white, not even in the same ball park." Mastruzzi speaks proudly of the range of abilities and the school's attempts to "meet students where they are." At one point he worries that I am only getting a chance to observe the high level courses and says, "You have to see the Remedial kids—see how the teachers give them the same energy, effort and respect." Mastruzzi seems just as enthusiastic about the wide range of student abilities as he is about the great sweep of social classes represented or the mixtures of racial and ethnic groups at Kennedy.

Even though most of the faculty to whom I talked did not speak in degrading or disrespectful terms about teaching the "low level" students, they did not support Mastruzzi's claim that their work with all students inspired in them the same energy and excitement. Almost all of the teachers I spoke with admitted a preference for "the bright kids." A.P.'s, recognizing these preferences, have to carefully plot the assignment of courses so that no one gets a disproportionate share of the Remedial courses. The requirement of course rotation is written into the regulations of the teachers' union contract. The A.P. must distribute "the desirables" among his various faculty members; and "desirables" include a reference to high ability and "upper-termers."

There are a few teachers, however, who find it more interesting to develop courses and pedagogical approaches that will appeal to and energize the less capable students. "That's the real challenge," claims an energetic pedagogue. "It's easy and boring to teach bright and ambitious kids. It's hard and exciting to light the fire in the kids who have been turned off." A science teacher, known for his persistent optimism and creativity, has developed electives that are purposefully designed for students who usually feel threatened by science. In his courses, "Geology" and "Weather and Climate," he tries to "seduce kids" into becoming curious about their environment. But he is also interested in conveying attitudes towards learning, in undoing patterns that have often built up in response to the student's persistent experience of academic failure. He does not permit lateness, disrespect, or laziness in his classroom. "There are certain things that are just not allowed, without question. . . . No one is allowed to wear hats in my classroom and they can't leave to go to the washroom at the climax of my lecture!" he says with a wide grin.

The rich variations in abilities and origins among students make the Kennedy faculty and staff appear relatively homogenous. In comparison to the browns, blacks, and yellows represented among students, the faculty seem monolithic in their whiteness. There are the exceptions: the tall, attractive Black man who heads the music department; the gracious and kindly Black woman who is A.P. for foreign languages. Both are described by their colleagues as extraordinary professionals with high standards and good "human relations skills." I am surprised when Mastruzzi proudly proclaims that the minority representation on his faculty is twelve percent and that he has worked diligently over the years to increase those numbers. He compares that figure to other city high schools where the typical percentage of minority teachers is closer to one percent. After the principal points to the comparatively large proportion of minority faculty, I begin to notice more of them; a young Asian woman teaching computer programming; four Black counselors in the fourteen-member guidance department; seventeen foreign-born teachers in the foreign language department, many of Hispanic origins. However, a few teachers reluctantly admit that the minority representation among faculty should be higher. One says, "It would be nicer to have more role models for the Black kids. I think they can still get a distorted message about Blacks' abilities with so few of them on our staff." Another points to the negative effects of tokenism on the faculty members. "In the teachers' cafeteria they all sit together at one table. No one is unfriendly to them, nor they to us, but with so few they must feel they have to band together."

Most teachers that I spoke with, however, were adamant about their abilities and talents in relating to students from all backgrounds. Some of the statements were amazingly bold, "I don't think you will find one racist, or anyone with racist tendencies, in this whole faculty." Others were more measured, "I think people were attracted to this school partly because they felt comfortable working with all kinds of kids. The teachers who came to Kennedy did not feel threatened by Blacks or Browns." Most teachers responded to my inquiries with some surprise and claimed that race and ethnicity were not the critical dimensions. "The point is, are you a good teacher? If you are a good teacher, you can teach anyone."

In general, there is pride among the faculty. Many spoke to me about the unusual collection of able teachers at Kennedy by offering comparisons. "The level of teaching is much better than in the suburban schools. I am impressed with the laziness of the suburban teachers. They can look good without even trying. But we have to work hard." By far the most vivid contrasts were made with the Bronx High School of Science, the neighboring school of high status. Said one A.P., "Bronx Science rests on a reputation that it no longer deserves. Are we to call it a good school because it gets its kids into Harvard and M.I.T.? Look what they have to work with! No, a good school has to do with the quality of teaching and learning and it's much better here at Kennedy." Another A.P. was more balanced in his appraisal of the Kennedy faculty. "Every department has a couple of duds, lazy and selfish teachers who couldn't care less about the kids. Then there is a broad range of dutiful and competent teachers . . . and a few inspired teachers. They give with their full heart. They are amazing and can be like catalysts for the whole department."

An old-timer claims that the good teaching has cultural origins. "We Jews are natural pedagogues, and we work very, very hard," he says, only half joking. He points to the names of the faculty in his department, at least two-thirds of which have "a Jewish flavor": Greenberg, Silverstein, Weiss, Rosenberg, etc. A young woman of Italian origins counters, "Yes, it used to be Jewish, but now the Italians are taking over! Look at the chancellor, at our principal, at a lot of the department heads." Finally, someone offers an observation that a stranger might make. "Listen, you can't tell one from the other, a Mastruzzi from a Herzog—it is New York. We all have a style that only New Yorkers have."

Their likeness may have something to do with the blending of cultures and the powerful overlay of a "New York style," but it also may have to do with their similar social class origins, attitudes towards teaching as a profession, and their educational training. Although I was able to trace the story of only a handful of faculty, they all reported that their family backgrounds were modest. For many, their parents were illiterate or barely schooled but had an intense, uncompromised desire for their children to be educated. Teaching was seen as a respectable and honored profession, a reachable goal. Not able to afford the costs of elite, private schools, the parents sent their offspring to colleges that were part of the city university "at a time when these were the most competitive places in the country." Says a middle-aged English teacher, "Maybe I had a secret desire to go to Columbia and hang out with all those blond, blue-eyed, all-American kids, but I felt very proud of going to City College and all my family wept when they came to my graduation." When he looks at his colleagues in the English Department, many have similar histories. They are graduates of C.C.N.Y., N.Y.U., Fordham, Lehman, and Manhattan College. They grew up as working-class city dwellers and visit their parents, many of whom remain in the area, in rent-controlled apartments. "They're still proud of my accomplishments," says one teacher with a satisfied smile.

Even though a large proportion of the Kennedy teachers grew up in the Bronx and Brooklyn and may make Sunday excursions to visit their parents there, many of them are raising their families in the suburbs of Rockland and Westchester counties. Their commutes to and from school range anywhere from a half-hour to an hour and a half; and some see it as "a great escape" while others argue it's "the great mistake." Rockland county, with real estate prices somewhat less burdensome than Westchester, has become known as "Teacher County" because of the great influx of city teachers. One teacher exults about the tremendous advantages of the suburbs, "My kid can have a horse and feel some grass under her bare feet in the spring"; while another worries about the creeping changes that make it less idyllic, "We have the same problems in the suburbs, except they come ten years later and everyone is too shocked to do anything about it." A commuter, who hates the forty-minute drive each way, points sadly to an apartment building where he lived until four years ago, a ten-minute walk from the school. With the steep condominium prices, he can no longer afford to live in Riverdale. His nostalgia is echoed by a senior colleague who has lived in the same Riverdale apartment for almost thirty years. From his office window he can see his home, and he deeply enjoys the close connection between family and school. With his two children now in medical school, he believes that it is possible to get a superior education in New York City public schools. As he watches the caravan of cars heading out to the suburbs every afternoon, he is glad that he was never seduced into believing that green grass and horses were better than neighborhood roots.

With a large proportion of students and staff coming to Kennedy from far away, the school does not feel deeply embedded in the surrounding neighborhood. For the students who travel great distances to get there, Kennedy is seen as a very special and attractive place. And most teachers proclaim their pride in being associated with a school of high quality and standards. Some students will brag, "Kennedy is the best school in the city. Do you think I'd bust my butt to get here if I didn't think it was real good?" Others admit it is "among the top ten" in the city. But Kennedy's city-wide reputation is very different from the way it is perceived locally. A teacher who lives in a co-op close by and hears the local gossip about Kennedy says, "City-wide, Kennedy has a very positive reputation. In the neighborhood, it's negative. The Riverdale parents with money look down on Kennedy and the ones without money are afraid of it." In order to drive home her point of community fear and negativism she tells me the story of "The Fourth-Floor Incident," a tale I am told several times during my visit. Described as "the biggest sore spot at Kennedy," the story highlights the extreme case of community-school conflict.

Each weekday morning two thousand Black and Brown students ride from West Harlem to Riverdale on the Broadway subway. At 8:00, they pour out of the subway and walk the several blocks to school. Because of the school building's structure and the topography of the land, the street from the subway leads into the fourth-floor entrance of Kennedy. The community the students pass through is a blue-collar, largely Irish community known as Marblehead. Last year battles erupted between the Marblehead residents and the school when the locals claimed that the students were destroying their property and threatening their neighborhood. The residents demanded that the Kennedy students take another route to school; one that would not feel like an invasion of their privacy and property. The only other school entrance, on the building's first floor, would require the subway riders to hike almost a mile out of their way before arriving at Kennedy. Mastruzzi thought that the residents' request was unreasonable and reflected their racist fears of the "ghetto kids." He could understand their wish for the quiet solitude of the old neighborhood and their frustration with the strangers passing through. He could even sympathize with their worries about adolescent rowdiness. But he was shocked by the irrational threats and vehement attacks some of the residents hurled at the students.

Several weeks of intense negotiations between the school and the residents culminated in a series of compromises. The hostility was poisonous as each side took its case to higher borough and city officials. Finally, Mastruzzi worked out a settlement with top officials which would increase the possibility of an orderly procession of students through the neighborhood. He bargained, "You build me a wide sidewalk on one side of the street and I'll get the kids to walk on that side." The other side would remain free for resident pedestrians. When the city officials expressed skepticism about Mastruzzi's power over the adolescents' movement, he shot back, "You build the walk. I'll take care of the kids." A wider sidewalk was built and the students dutifully walked on one side.

Most of the residents were appeased, but a few "die-hards" continued to battle; telling the city officials that they wanted those kids off their streets. When the students continued to walk the Marblehead route, the few angry and resistant residents began to retaliate by letting their dogs litter the new sidewalk. Mastruzzi was furious. As he tells the tale to me his blood seems to boil, his face reddens, and it is the only time he admits to losing "his cool." Because they had reached an agreement, Mastruzzi decided to hold up his end of the bargain despite the outrageous behavior of the angered residents. Each morning a few members of his staff would be out on the sidewalk "scooping the shit" in order to make it passable for students. This lasted until June. When school opened this fall, Mastruzzi felt he could no longer ask the students to be dutiful when neighborhood adults were behaving abusively. Neither could he ask teachers to do the humiliating task of cleanup. Again students pour out of the subway and onto the streets and sidewalks; the battle is joined and feelings are raw. "Let's call it for what it is," says Mastruzzi finally. "If these were the White Riverdale kids walking through their streets, there would be no complaints."

Although many point to the Fourth-Floor Incident as a "sore spot," Kennedy people express a range of views about who the aggressors are in this battle. Some are even more vehement than Mastruzzi about the underlying motivations of racism. "These are the most bitter people I've ever seen," says one observer. "They are impossible to satisfy. They get into hate trips and it is so racial. Every time we reach out to them, we get slapped in the face." Yet there are others who do not believe that the residents' concerns are necessarily racially inspired or unreasonable. They can see how the daily influx of adolescent droves would feel like an invasion, and they claim that the handful of students who have damaged property and threatened neighbors have made it hard for all of the well-behaved and honorable students.

The morning that I arrive in time to see the hundreds of students walk from the subway to the fourth-floor entrance, the community looks closed down. Windows are barred, shades are drawn, and almost no one is out on the street except the students, who by their massive presence seem to own the territory. I spot one elderly lady, dressed in a faded, blue cloth coat and dark hat. She is leaving the corner grocery store, clutching her pocketbook close to her body. Four Black girls crowd behind her because their gaits have suddenly brought them close and they are trying to figure a way to pass. As they chatter casually, the old lady's body seems to crouch in fear, and she ducks into a nearby doorway. In the vestibule of a square, four-story brick building across from the school I see a small group of Black boys lighting up reefers. My companion says, in the residents' defense, "Now you know those boys don't live here. They've camped out there and they're getting high. Who knows what they'll do next. You can't blame the neighborhood for being up in arms."

Although the Marblehead-Kennedy exchanges are bitter and fester like an open sore, no one seems to fear the eruption of violence. The Fourth-Floor Incident remains complicated and unsolvable because it represents the broader problems of oppression and racism in society. Explains one teacher who feels sympathetic to both sides, "You see, these working-class Irish folks are barely making it. All they have is their worn-out piece of property. It scares them to death to see those Black kids getting an education and moving ahead while they stay still." Given the deep and intense feelings on both sides and the meanings attached to the symbols of territoriality and invasion, Mastruzzi's handling of the situation has been smart and judicious. He is described by many as a very political animal, and they point to his patient and calculating moves in the Marblehead affair as the best evidence of his political knowledge and intuition.

Mastruzzi believes that city high school principals must be political; that their connections to networks of power and decision making, and their understanding of the political process, are essential to a school's survival. More than any Bronx principal, he is known for his close association with political leaders. He is on a first name basis with the most minor council members and the most prominent state officials; with the fire chief and the police captain; with store owners in Kingsbridge; and businessmen in the high-rise apartments on the hill. He has developed a comfortable rapport with the local press. "How you are perceived is often as important as what you do, and many folks in the community never have direct contact with the school. The only way they can know us is through the press. So I go on television a lot."

His associations of "trust and mutual responsibility" with various constituencies have not magically appeared. Mastruzzi describes the "cultivation" of relationships as a slow and laborious process consuming a great deal of his time. He is also quick to assure me that his political activities are not inspired by personal gain or a need for flamboyant visibility, but by a very sober assessment of the community-school symbiosis. Particularly when school populations are not limited by neighborhood boundaries, the principal must convince the community of the cultural values and social benefits of a school in their midst. The principal, as the school's primary symbol and interpreter, must bear the responsibility of winning friends and building trust.

Mastruzzi has dedicated himself to the task on many levels. He walks the streets and meets and greets the locals. He lunches with businessmen in swanky private clubs, and he builds connections with politicians based on the promise of reciprocal benefit. All of this calculated groundwork pays off. When the Special Olympics were about to be held, Mastruzzi had to call in many of his chips. A call to the fire chief, and permission was granted for the elaborate fireworks display over the Harlem River. Another series of convincing conversations led to changing the street signs for the occasion—from Terrace to "Special Olympics" Avenue. And sports figures, well-placed politicians, and dignitaries appeared in force during the weekend of the great event.

Mastruzzi is aware of some muted rumblings about his public relations tactics and his not-so-subtle efforts at self-aggrandizement. But as I watch him in action, I become increasingly convinced of his honorable and generous motives. Certainly his style, energy, and enthusiasm are captivating, and he enjoys center stage, but his cheering is for Kennedy, not Mastruzzi. And his cheers sound engagingly authentic because he deeply believes he has something to cheer about. Perhaps worried that his political behavior and acumen will be interpreted as crass manipulation, he rephrases his extra-school affairs by saying, "I believe high school principals should be community leaders. That is our responsibility to the school and to the community."

SAVING SOULS

The attendance figures at John F. Kennedy High School reflect its attraction to students. In September 1982, the attendance figures reached to 84.5 percent, and the morning that I arrive in early October, the principal has just offered his effusive congratulations to the students over the public address system. "I got on the P.A. and told them how great they are. They should be rewarded for their sense of responsibility and commitment." The cumulative attendance records from last year were also above 80 percent and were seen as a strong indication of Kennedy's success. Mastruzzi watches the figures carefully. He admits that attendance rates are "a fetish" of his, but he regards it as the most tangible evidence of goodness. "It's very important. If the kids don't come, they can't be educated."

Each afternoon Mastruzzi receives the hand-computed attendance figures hot off the press from his record keepers. He writes the percentages on a pad that has a prominent place on his orderly desk, and then worries about each decimal. During the first few days of October the percentages have declined slightly and this causes a worried look on Mastruzzi's face. He points to the figures hovering close to 83 percent (Monday, 82.96 percent; Tuesday 83.05 percent, etc.) and begins by telling me that the percentages are probably ten points higher than city high schools with comparable ethnic and social class distributions. "Our attendance figures are more like the upper middle-class schools on Long Island." He ends by trying to account for the slight dip from September to October. "One of the problems is that these figures include lost kids on our rolls who never appeared in September. . . . If those kids were excluded from our count, the percentages would go up about two points."

Mastruzzi knows that there are ways to inflate attendance figures and that many schools report percentages that have been deftly doctored in order to give the illusion of success. There is always the temptation, but Mastruzzi believes that the "real figures" need to be faced. "What is the purpose of pretense or illusion?" he asks rhetorically. So he uses the hand-computed figures because the school's computer tends to falsely inflate the numbers. The machine counts full attendance when a teacher forgets to send down absence cards. The person, on the other hand, whose job it is to keep close track of the records, searches down the teacher to make sure that no attendance reports in fact means no absences.

In order to keep the attendance rates high, Kennedy offers students bold incentives. Most of the incentives refer to the negative repercussions of non-compliance. For example, if students have ten homeroom absences, they will automatically fail their subjects for that semester. If they miss twelve recitation classes, they will fail the subject. Both of these harsh warnings are followed by a softening clause which reads "unless there is approval of the assistant principal/supervisor to give a passing grade." The attendance rules are prominently displayed in the orientation folder that all Kennedy students receive each fall, and they reflect the school's serious intentions in this area. As one junior boy said to me, "About attendance, they simply don't play!" In the midst of all the negative warnings, there is one positive enticement. Each month the homeroom classes in each grade with the highest attendance scores receive a prize of MacDonald's hamburgers for lunch. Mastruzzi explains that this may appear to be a trivial gesture, but for many students it works as a powerful incentive.

In general, Mastruzzi believes that the biggest draw for Kennedy students is the good education the school offers. The negative and positive rewards would not make a dent unless there was something worth coming to school for. Beyond the general attractions, the principal points to the inspired work of the attendance office as the reason for the high attendance figures. The office is run by David Epstein, an energetic, empathetic figure with an unusual magnetism. "He is the kind of person that kids trust immediately," says an admiring colleague. "He is the opposite of your stereotype of a truant officer" explains another colleague. "He has none of the tough, hard, militaristic tendencies. He truly believes in the capacity and potential of all kids." During my conversation with Epstein, he exudes enthusiasm as he responds to my questions. He is relieved not to have to rehearse the rules and regulations of the official attendance policy. He is much more interested in using the occasion to think out loud about the philosophical stance that guides his behavior with students, particularly those who resist or refuse to come to school. Epstein feels greatly influenced by his own early antipathy for school ("I hated school. High school was the most unhappy period of my life"); and his parents' insistence that schooling was more important than anything else. Born and raised in Brooklyn, the son of Jewish immigrant parents, he remembers the burdens and inspirations of their great expectations and love. In his extended family there had been teachers whose work was considered honorable and worthy, and Epstein became excited about teaching as a way to recast and rework his wasted years in school. After graduating from City College in 1958, he entered teaching and spent his ten "most influential" years at a vocational high school that specialized in automotive skills. In this all-boys school that drew its population from working class Black, Hispanic, and Italian communities, Epstein began to develop his views about the ingredients of a good school. "It has nothing to do with the kids who go to it," he says forcefully, "It has to do with our *response* to the kids. The people I worked with were so into children that categories didn't matter." With 1,100 students and 87 faculty, Epstein's old school felt like a large and caring family. "When we saw a fight, we considered it a disruption to our house." When Epstein came to Kennedy to teach science, he was nervous about getting lost in its hugeness. He feared the anonymity and worried that it could be a great hiding place for students and teachers who resisted the essential human encounters of education. How could he recreate in this new environment the intimacy, visibility, and caring of his old school? Many of his fears were allayed by watching the ways in which teachers created feelings of family in their classrooms; the way they "saw each other face to face" and in that moment forgot the mammoth structure of which they were a part.

After teaching science for several years, David Epstein decided to take on the challenge of the attendance office; a job that still allows him to teach two periods of science each day. With an office that is often crowded with students in trouble, Epstein is in perpetual motion. He is helped by two para-professionals—an attractive Hispanic woman and a mature, benign-seeming white woman who do a range of supportive tasks and often talk to desperate students when Epstein is not immediately available. Epstein speaks about his approach as a dynamic mixture of toughness and sympathy. He admits that his toughness is rarely expressed in an adversarial mode. "I'm not confrontational," he says thoughtfully. "My strategy is to kill them with love. I do not view that as capitulation. . . . I want to make my office a place where kids can come and feel they will be listened to and trusted." The toughness is expressed in the persistent and uncompromising message that "there is no excuse not to come to school." Instead of searching for the reasons why students do not come to school, Epstein believes that faculty must find ways of getting them there. Teachers must "badger kids into coming. . . . They

95

must tell kids that if they are late, they are disturbing others. . . . They must insist upon the good citizen approach . . . if you mess up, you hurt all of us . . . attendance is an important self-discipline."

Throughout the day, teachers work closely with Epstein's office; corroborating student stories, calling Epstein when crises develop, and leaving notes on his desk requesting follow-up action. His partnership with teachers is essential. Without their responsible collaboration and support, Epstein could never identify the trouble spots or help a student become re-engaged in school life.

But Epstein looks to parents as his most important allies and reports that a great deal of his energy is consumed by establishing relationships with families. His message to families is double-edged. First, he wants to convey his respect for the hard work and passion of parenting. "Whoever they are, I want to say 'you are good, qualified parents and you have the most important job in the world.' " Second, Epstein wants to underscore the essential function of school as a window on the wider world, a place to expand life's options. "Many of these kids come from families where generations have never been schooled. In working with parents, I try to establish the value of education." Epstein is careful not to promise mobility, success, and profit to the parents of his charges because he knows in his heart that a responsible and mannerly school career may not culminate in those rewards. Besides, he seems to believe that schools should be devoted to reinforcing the more essential human qualities of kindness, generosity, and responsibility. If these altruistic dimensions get well established, students are more likely to become "good husbands, parents, and neighbors . . . and I regard that as at least as important as becoming a nuclear physicist."

In his conversations with parents, Epstein deliberately rearranges the traditional patterns of power and exchange. In most schools that serve poor and minority communities, parents have been systematically excluded from meaningful participation and made to feel powerless and "dehumanized." This imbalance discourages parent involvement, responsibility, and wisdom; all key ingredients to the successful education of their children. Because he believes that parental authority is essential for his work, Epstein strives to achieve balance between families and schools. "In some real sense, I am their servant . . . I establish with pride the fact that I'm working for them (the parents)."

To see Epstein in action is to witness his honor of parents, his integration of empathy and toughness, his belief in the capacities of each individual student, his awareness of the developmental cycles and crises of adolescence, and his boundless energy. Mostly one is aware of his sense of urgency, his impatience with human defeat. His favorite reference is to "The Marva Collins Story," a television movie that portrayed the fighting spirit of a Black teacher in Chicago who built a successful, alternative school for poor, Black children who had been considered hopeless public school failures. With relentless hard work and grit, Collins transformed her students from the depths of self-degradation to proud and competent achievers. Epstein offers a wide grin as he retells the story and rehearses the questions that formed the script's litany: "Who is the most important person in the world?" asks Marva Collins. "I am!" the children respond in chorus. "When is the most important time?" demands Collins. "Now!" chant the students.

The attendance office is located on the fourth floor of Kennedy at one end of the guidance suite. The principal claims that its location makes an important symbolic statement. Attendance is not to be seen as a disciplinary function; rather it should be linked with the programmatic and psycho-social issues of guidance. Along the corridors of the guidance suite, counselors work behind closed doors with students. The traffic in and out of the guidance offices is minimal compared to the congested scene at the attendance office. The morning of my visit, I arrive about an hour after the peak period of attendance business and see several students moving in and out of the small corner office and four "hard core" truants lined up outside the door. As they wait to see Epstein, they brag to each other about their accumulated absences last year. At first they boast about their truancy, but quickly the conversation shifts to defending their records. Each claims the others have been more delinquent. Only the subdued, motionless Black boy says nothing. Only his eyes reveal that he is listening to the banter of his peers. A Chinese girl, petite and tough-talking, brags, "I was only three months truant last year . . . but I passed anyway, didn't I?" Raphael, a Hispanic, admits to being absent only a month. "Compared to you guys, I'm a good kid," he laughs. Cindy, the most talkative, wears her blond hair in a shaggy cut and covers her face with layers of make-up. She wears tight jeans, a shiny red jacket, and chews her gum vigorously. At first she denies that her attendance record has been "all that bad," but then admits to five months of truancy last year. However, her terrible record allows her to brag about her close connections to Epstein. "I have him in the palm of my hand," she says almost defiantly as she makes a gesture of ownership. "Sure it's not the other way around?" asks Raphael teasingly. Cindy's last defense is poignant: "He talks to my mother more than I do . . . He's always on the case."

Inside the cramped office Epstein is seated behind one of the three desks in the room. He leans forward on his folded arms and looks intently into the eyes of the round, middle-aged Hispanic woman who is sitting across from him. Her hands are tightly clasped in her lap; her heavily accented voice is hesitant as she says about her seventeen year-old son, "I am suspicious . . . I don't know. He don't never talk about school. He don't never have any homework." Epstein seems to shut out the ringing telephones and office clamor as he listens only to the mother's voice. She continues, ". . . . and he says he wants to go to college, but he does nothing." Epstein's response is a mixture of sympathy, advice, and admonition. "Yes, they have great fantasies. He's going to college and he can't get through high school . . . but we'll have to be patient. This may take a long time. There is just so much pushing we can do. It has to come from within him."

He tells the mother about his plans for checking the attendance records, tracking down her son, and speaking with his various teachers. He needs more information before he can act. Just before departing, the mother's body slumps forward as she wipes away her tears with the arm of her sweater. It is the first time she has conveyed her desperation and sorrow. "I worry . . . I always worry," she says with a choked voice. Epstein's response is reassuring and firm. "Okay, I'll speak to him and follow up on this. Give me a call on Tuesday . . . but listen, don't take off more days from your work. It won't help anyone if you lose your job." At the door he shakes her hand gently and says, "We'll work together on this. . . . Try not to worry too much. Try to have a good weekend."

Before Epstein can return to his desk, Raphael is already seated in the empty chair just vacated by the mother. He is a handsome, muscular sixteen year-old whose voice reveals a trace of his Puerto Rican parentage. This is early October and Raphael has missed all but a few days of school. The note that he hands to Epstein claims he has been sick with a stomach virus for several weeks. With a look that is both skeptical and caring, Epstein asks whether the note is true. His eyes remain fixed on the boy who squirms under the scrutiny and finally admits that he was not sick during all of his days of absence. "Some or a few?" asks Epstein. "A few," Raphael says quietly. His whispered response seems to reveal a mixture of resignation and relief. Epstein shifts the conversation away from the note and begins to ask about Raphael's experience in school last year. Last year Raphael had been enrolled in the Mini-School (a small, alternative program within Kennedy for students who have trouble adapting to the demands and structure of the regular curriculum), but had been transferred out against his will at the beginning of this year. He had come to school for a few days in early September and had been overwhelmed by the rigors of regular school. "It's too much. . . . It's too hard . . . can't do it, man." After weeks out of school, he had returned with the hope of getting into the Work-Study Program at Kennedy. Every sentence he speaks suggests his ambivalence about returning. His plans are vague as Epstein tries to help him articulate his next moves. When they reach a dead end, Epstein offers his final challenge, "Raphael, listen, you have a problem, right? . . . . You are doing some good things in trying to solve it, but you still have a ways to go . . . I want to help you with this, but you've got to help yourself." Epstein waves the phony note. "And this is not the way to work this out." Before Raphael leaves, he points him towards the people he will have to contact to apply to the Work-Study Program and he makes an appointment with him for early the following week. "You'll have to come to this appointment for yourself first, but also for me . . . if you don't show, you'll be taking some other kid's time, so you have to come." Raphael tears out of the office, his face flushed and confused. He reappears ten minutes later and blurts out in frustration that the work-study people can not see him until the afternoon. The couple of hours delay seem to be enough to destroy his momentum. "I'm ready to give it up, man," he says with bitterness in his voice. Epstein, who is in the midst of another appointment, gives him the full responsibility. "You have to decide how important it is to you, Raphael." Just as the boy turns away in disgust, he says brightly, "See you next week."

At Epstein's desk a quiet, shy Black boy is trying to get permission to re-enter school after several weeks of absence. His mother has been in a serious car accident and since her hospitalization, he has not come to school. The boy, who is frail and awkward, looks strikingly vulnerable and Epstein's tone seems to noticeably soften. A call is made to the boy's aunt who is at work. "I'm going to dial the number," says Epstein, "but you say hello to your aunt, so she won't get scared. Tell her it's Mr. Epstein from the attendance office. Then I'll talk to her." The boy repeats Epstein's words verbatum and hands the phone across the desk to him. Epstein is gentle and respectful. "Hello, how are you? We wanted to call to confirm Robert's absences. He has been absent a lot and we've received no notes from home . . . He'll fail his subjects unless we hear from you confirming his absences." There is a long pause in which the aunt must be offering an explanation. Epstein follows with a few questions and then closes by saying, "Okay, we'll try to help him. He seems like a nice boy. Take care now and thanks for your time." Robert has been on the edge of his chair, his body erect and tense, during the telephone conversation. His eyes search Epstein's face. Epstein returns his full gaze and says with a stronger voice, "Let me tell you something important. What happened to your mom is very serious. No doubt about it. It was very scary, extremely frightening . . . but rather than be absent through all of the hard times, you must come to school. Come here and we'll talk about it. . . . Just think, if Mom comes out of the hospital and you've failed your subjects, she's going to be very sad and disappointed. . . . There are lots of people around here who you can get to know, who could care about you. But you have to be in school. If you must stay out, *you* have to call me. Not your Aunt Rose, *you*. It is *your* responsibility. If you want to visit your Mom in the hospital, you can come to school and I will give you a note to leave school a bit early." Robert seems to hang on each word and looks comforted, not chastised. He stands, offers a limp handshake, looks solemnly down at his shoes, and quietly walks away.

In each of these encounters, David Epstein gives his full energy and modulates his tone and style to match what he judges to be the individual's needs and demands. To the distressed mother, he is reassuring but not overly optimistic. To Raphael, he is probing and confrontational. To Robert, he is gentle and firm. To Cindy, he begins by being slightly flirtatious, then more seriously concerned, and finally skeptical and discerning. The traffic in the attendance office seems endless and Epstein confronts a parade of painful and complicated stories to which there are only imperfect solutions. His energy and stamina are amazing. His powers of persuasion are captivating. Mastruzzi says incredulously, "David literally salvages kids." However, Epstein is the first to admit the limitations of his person, his office, and the process. He worries openly about all the kids who are wasting their young lives out on the street and never make it to the school doors. He recognizes the number of students who come to school and fall between the cracks or get lost in the crowds. His interventions are rarely prophylactic. They usually occur after the crisis— when trouble has been brewing for some time, when he must help repair the damage already done. Watching Epstein's high energy and perpetual motion, I am reminded of the small Dutch child with his finger in the hole of the dike, holding back the dangerous water currents.

But Epstein does not work alone. He is not the only one with his finger in the dike. The attendance office is closely linked with the guidance department and with the Office of the Deans, the primary disciplinary body. The A.P. of guidance says that each office has its primary purpose, but that there is a great deal of overlap in the ways they function. "We do a lot of switching of roles . . . whatever it takes to get the job done." Clearly, the hardest job belongs to the five deans who receive the school's disciplinary problems and are responsible for issuing appropriate punishments. "They have the hardest roles in the school," he admits, "because they have to police the environment." Although Mastruzzi claims that the deans have a "guidance perspective," students speak about them with a combination of fear, respect, and bitterness. Says one who has had several run-ins with the deans' office, "They are brutal, evil people. They want to whip ass, that's all." Another boy claims that their effectiveness lies in their image of toughness. "They're not bad people. Someone's got to look scary so the other guys can look good." A third student is thankful for the deans' consistent and forceful punishments. "This place would go to ruin if it wasn't for the deans. They make it safe because people are afraid of them," she says.

The guidance department, on the other hand, tries to remove itself from disciplinary chores and focus in on academic programming, career and personal counselling of students. Gene DiStasio, its A.P., is a nurturing, generous man whose school-wide image of goodness gives the office its benign reputation. Just as many students refer to the tough ways of the deans, so do they point to Mr. DiStasio's "big heart." Says one sophomore enthusiastically, "He's the best grown-up I've ever met." Colleagues talk about his amazing dedication, his endless days at school, and his extraordinary rapport with students. "He is a rare human being who never turns anyone away—students or teachers," says a faculty member who has frequently sought his counsel. But even his bountiful kindness cannot possibly respond to the vast needs of Kennedy's huge student body. "I'm telling you that man gives all he has, but it's not nearly enough," observes a senior who feels the guidance area is terribly under-staffed. DiStasio has fourteen counselors on his staff and they each carry a caseload of 400 students. "You don't feel like a number when you go in there," claims the same senior. "You feel like a little, tiny, invisible dot. . . . This is the place you should be able to go and get personal attention . . . instead it's the place you don't feel like a person." Most people admit that the ratio of students to counselors would make it impossible for even the most gifted and caring clinicians to be effective. But many observers add that the counselling is uneven, and that there is not enough attention given to the leadership and administration of the area. Several students I spoke to described unsuccessful attempts to meet with their counselor, faulty information or guidance given during the course of conversations, and feelings of distance and distrust that accompany superficial relation-ships. A former counselor, now on the teaching faculty, spoke about the ways in which many of the counselors "hide behind the numbers." They are consumed by the paper work required to follow 400 students and, "They'd rather face the piles of paper than the real people."

The problem lies not just with the great numbers of students and the bureaucratic machinery that accompanies each case, but also with the numerous roles the counselors are asked to play. Clearly, the most imme-diate and time-consuming job involves designing the students' academic programs. At the opening of school each fall, hundreds of students arrive without a program in place, and the first weeks are spent meeting with parents and adolescents as schedules get developed. "There is a huge influx of off-the-street registration," says DiStasio. "That takes our atten-tion away from the in-house kids." Although the academic programming is mostly rudimentary, it offers new students the opportunity for contact with their counselor. "It is a time for mutual sizing up, even if it may not take advantage of the counselor's talents or skills." Yet often the pro-gramming displaces the counselling function as the counselors get locked into the clerical chores. For DiStasio, this is the major frustration of his work. "My biggest satisfaction comes from interacting with kids. But we can't be very effective in reaching out to kids when all of this paper work is hanging over our heads. The psychological stuff suffers." Like Epstein, Gene DiStasio worries about the students who get lost in the shuffle. His talent and temperament point towards the clinical counselling, towards saving souls and offering reassurance to weary and discouraged students. But the massive numbers and bureaucratic machinery at Kennedy require him to focus too much of his energy on clerical routines and brief ritual-ized encounters with students, therefore neglecting their more personal needs.

Paradoxically, it is in the offices where relationships with students should be most intimate and undefended that the numbers almost de-mand superficial treatment. Epstein and DiStasio, local folk heroes with enormous talent and tremendous energy, manage to find individual faces in the crowd and make intense and deep connections with troubled, dis-affected students. But they must recognize that for those few they are able to help, there are scores that will go unnoticed and unattended. It is in these caring corners of the school that one is most struck with the potential dangers of anonymity.

FINDING THE CORE: STREAMLINING THE CURRICULUM

Even though many classes are crowded with almost forty students, it is here where one witnesses the greatest intimacy and rapport among adults and students. In almost every classroom I visited, the desks and seats were entirely filled. The teachers' union requires that classes be no larger than thirty-five, but more than a month after the opening of school some courses were still oversubscribed and students were being reshuf-fled in and out of sections. Many teachers, frustrated by the crowds and chaos, made angry complaints to their A.P.'s, who passed on their con-cerns to Arnold Herzog, assistant principal for administration. A few threatened to begin formal grievance procedures because of the school's noncompliance with union regulations. But most teachers seemed to be unruffled by the "musical chairs" of the first several weeks and did not let the extra bodies distract them from their work.

Despite the large numbers, the teachers I observed had learned the names of their students and most made great efforts to involve the entire group in classroom discussions. Several times in my observational notes I wrote, "There is no back row in this class," a short way of reminding myself that I did not see the typical subgroup of uninvolved, unnoticed students who usually hide out in the back row. In some courses, particu-larly those inhabited by lively and ambitious Honors students, the teach-er rarely needed to call on students in order to get them to participate.

Rather, he or she could usually choose the respondent from a small collection of waving hands. In other courses, where students felt less confident, teachers tended to initiate contact with a wide range of students and were careful not to always return to the same few people. The teachers' determination to involve as many students as possible in the discourse and their ability to call on students by name seemed to be evidence of their intention to build smaller communities within a large universe. With each faculty member typically teaching five periods and supervising a homeroom, it was not usual for teachers to be in contact with 170 students every day. But in each course, most teachers seemed to focus on the thirty-five students in their midst and offer an unusually intense attention. The classrooms in which I observed seemed to be transformed from impersonal, institutional environments to highly personal places when students and teachers entered. Without material props or aesthetic surroundings, most teachers appeared to structure their own ethos by the power of personality and curricular substance. Said one to me, "When I'm teaching I live in the existential present. We inhabit that space and it becomes ours."

I am certain that I did not observe a typical or random group of Kennedy teachers. After making my interests known, the courses I visited were selected by the A.P.'s. They were all gracious in offering their time and responding to my requests, but I was aware of their wish to show me the best examples of good teaching. One candid and confident A.P. admitted that he was being "highly selective" because he did not want me to see the distortions of either extreme. "I don't think it's fair to show you our duds, but I also don't want you to only see our most special, gifted, and inspired teachers. . . . Let me try and find the good but regular teachers. We have lots of them."

Not only did classrooms become alive and personal when they were inhabited by teachers and students, but I also sensed a curricular clarity and pedagogical confidence that is unusual in most large public high schools. Each of the A.P.'s spoke to me about the structure and goals embedded in the curriculum and the ways in which the course offerings have been distilled down to the "basics." They all referred to the initial curriculum at Kennedy, which was packed with a wide range of courses that seemed to have minimal connection to one another and offered no intellectual coherence. In the first couple of years after Kennedy opened, the numbers and types of courses had mushroomed out of control as teachers tried to be responsive to consumer preference and the progressive rhetoric of the early seventies. Courses were taught as modules and rotated through several "cycles" each year. Everything was considered an elective and the choices were overwhelming. "There were no meat and potatoes courses, only the frills—no structure, only the embellishments," recalls one A.P. "Most of the electives were Mickey Mouse. Everything was confused and aimless," remembers another.

After a couple of years of "experimentation," Mastruzzi decided to return to the tradition of two semesters per year and pare down the course offerings to a manageable selection. Remembers one faculty member, "It was a return to sanity." Despite the fact that the number of course offerings had been dramatically reduced, students were still greatly attracted to the variety in the school's curriculum. In comparing Kennedy to other high schools, several students I spoke to referred to the wide selection of courses. Said one enthusiastically, "The best thing about this place is the choice . . . and its a choice between good things."

The high-powered Honors students tend to point to the special, selective programs in the major academic areas when they refer to curricular choice: the law program in social studies, the science honors program that includes a rigorous sequence of courses over a three-year period. Each year the thirty-five science Honors students are screened very carefully before they are admitted to the three-year program, and then they are required to take a toughly designed curriculum that includes advanced biology, advanced chemistry, statistics, research design, and an integrative seminar in science and society. The A.P. of the science department, who developed the curriculum and feels a special proprietary interest in the program, is extremely proud of the intensive experience offered to the chosen. He smiles when he says, "Every one in science Honors missed Bronx High School of Science by three points." But his face grows more serious when he recalls, "My kids went there and I really think our students are getting much more here at Kennedy." As additional evidence of the program's excellence, he points to some of the prestigious colleges and universities that have recently admitted the science Honors graduates: Cornell, Princeton, M.I.T., Cal. Tech., University of Michigan, and the bio-medical programs at C.C.N.Y. and Boston College.

But when most of the students at Kennedy refer to the attractive curricular options, they are not speaking of the academically elite experiences. They are usually pointing to the variety of course offerings in the nonacademic areas, particularly physical education. By far the most robust praise I heard from students was for "gym." They applauded the facilities, the teachers, and the imaginatively varied courses. Exclaimed a plump boy with a studious look, "You don't have to be a jock to like it. . . . It's geared for everyone." Said a more athletic type expansively, "It meets my every need." Principal Mastruzzi compares the full plate of offerings to the meagre menu of most other urban high schools and points to yoga, cycling, roller disco, jogging, slimnastics and winter sports as a few of the special goodies.

Although many students fasten on the physical education department as "the best part of Kennedy," there are some who point to the programs in music and fine arts. They begin by appreciating the variety of courses, and then move on to talk about the special commitment and creativity of the faculty. In music, for example, students can choose among several choral groups, ensembles, and bands. They can also study percussion, guitar, piano, and woodwinds. But the greatest enthusiasm focuses on the energetic A.P., who often takes his most advanced students on tours to distant places; or the voice teacher who loves to work with hundreds of students and produce momentous sound; or the head of the marching band who was proud to lead his group in Italian ballads for the Columbus Day parade. "They do a lot of extra stuff with us," says an admiring student.

The art department receives similar kinds of praise from students, who for the first time are introduced to pottery, photography, fashion, print making, calligraphy, book design, and cartoon animation. The lively and colorful murals that dominate the school's exterior, line the walls of the escalator, and decorate two of the three student cafeterias were all designed and executed by Kennedy art students. When I am introduced to one of the premiere mural designers, a Puerto Rican boy with lots of flair, he says dramatically, "This is my life!" as he points to one of his creations. Mastruzzi shows me the animal mural in one of the cafeterias and remarks that it has never been defaced by a student, "not a scratch. That speaks to the pride and appreciation kids feel." The A.P. of art, who explodes with creative ideas and tries to track down funding sources to support her many art projects, sees an essential integration between artistic expression and intellectual facility. She is eager to increase cross-disciplinary work at Kennedy and sees the murals as an aesthetic dimension of school culture. From the student perspective, then, the variety at Kennedy is ample; and variety is expressed through curricular choice and through the individual styles and commitments of faculty.

When the A.P. of English arrived in 1974, there were eighty-seven electives in English. By 1977, the department had revised its curriculum based on three central pedagogical themes (language, composition, and literature), and the electives had been reduced to ten (two sophomore year, three junior year, and five senior year). Currently, for each grade, required English is offered at three levels (Remedial, Average, and Honors), and only those students at the top level are allowed to choose electives. Occasionally, a strong recommendation from a teacher will allow an Average student to enroll in an English elective.

Not only are there few electives now offered to a select group of students, but also the electives must be carefully designed and attractive. "Teachers have to sell the courses . . . get kids hooked on the idea of the course before we will seriously consider adding it to our electives list," says the A.P. of English, who claims his background in advertising alerted him to the idea of "selling courses and gaining consumer response." When a faculty member in English wants to teach an elective he or she must recruit students from Honors English classes. The teacher visits classes, talks about the proposed course, and tries to "create a group of committed students." When pupils express an interest they are asked to submit a writing sample, and their teachers then offer evaluations of their work in the required courses. If the proposed elective survives the process of teacher recruitment and student scrutiny, it becomes part of the curriculum. In these courses, therefore, both teachers and students arrive with an unusual degree of commitment and interest. The electives "Advanced Journalism," "Heroic Literature," "Creative Man," and "College Writing" all were initiated through this marketing process and they enjoy a special kind of visibility and stature in the curriculum. They also tend to be closely linked with the personality and style of the instructor.

"Creative Man," a year-long course for seniors that focuses on "major writings and artistic movements in the history of mankind," has the vivid imprint of its designer. Students choose the course in order to study with Mr. Clifford, its forceful and erudite teacher; and because the academic image of the course imbues them with a special kind of intellectual status in the school. One student describes both benefits, "The way Mr. Clifford talks makes you feel smart. He just assumes you're bright . . . and when you're in the class, you feel like you're part of a special group. It's kind of like an identity." Principal Mastruzzi is fond of saying, "If you go in there and close your eyes, you would think you were in a sophomore English course in the best of colleges . . . sometimes it's so sophisticated that *I* don't even know what's going on."

Clifford, a large man whose ruddy face is covered by wire-rimmed glasses and a full moustache, holds a notebook in his left hand as he slowly paces the front of the room. Occasionally he pauses to lean against his desk. His voice is strong and his sentences are intricate. Until I grow used to the rhythm of his language I get lost in the tangle of complicated images that fill each paragraph. I look for direction from the single sentence written on the board—"Aim: How does Aristotle's *Poetics* guide the development of Greek tragedy?" The classroom

106

is crowded with close to forty students who are absolutely noiseless as they sit in rapt attention listening to the lecture. Some take occasional notes, others merely listen, a few ask questions. Clifford gives a straight, verbose lecture interspersed with a few questions that usually ask students to link the complicated historical symbols to their own experience. Towards the beginning of his lecture, Clifford quickly reads Aristotle's definition of tragedy as students follow the words on their own mimeographed copies. "Tragedy is an imitation of an action which is serious, completed in itself, and of a certain magnitude, in language embellished with every kind of artistic ornament which is to be found separately in different parts of the play, in a dramatic, not a narrative form; through pity and fear bringing about the purgation (catharsis) of these emotions." The students express relief when Clifford quips: "Isn't that interesting. It means nothing, right? . . . We can't make sense out of it until we break it into pieces and look at it more closely and carefully. . . . Aristotle laid down Robert's Rules of Greek Tragedy. He recognized that we can only approximate reality. We can try our damnedest to raise it to a level of perfection. . . . Tragedy comes closest to what imitation can be. Aristotle believed it represented the heights of what man can create." After some exchange with students about the objects of imitation, Clifford compares tragedy to comedy and prose. "Man can be represented in three ways. When you idealize man, you are talking about tragedy. When man is portrayed as he really is, that is prose. When man is seen as less than he is, that is comedy, buffoonery." Probably recognizing the abstraction of his language, Clifford refers to modern likenesses of Greek tragedy. "The closest we come to Greek tragedy is a Wagnerian opera. It affects all of our senses. We see, hear, experience everything . . . remember there were no KLH amplifiers to exaggerate the sensations. It was done through gesture, body language."

Clifford's discussion touches briefly on the importance of the plot in Greek tragedy and then moves on to consider character. He uses Oedipus as a vivid example of a tragic character, "Look at how Oedipus was portrayed. Oedipus has done a crime of such moral violence . . . one does not kill one's king. . . . He's killed his father, married his mother, broken every ritual taboo in the book. . . . Think of the repetitive theme of violence." A Hispanic boy raises his hand, "Why did the Greeks go for imperfection? Why were their characters so imperfect?" Clifford launches into a long and wordy response. He seems to savor the words he speaks. "They tried to portray man as a real human being . . . always reaching for perfection, but never realizing it. Oedipus may be better than the normal man, but he has the same appetites, the same fears . . . the tendency to anger first and repent in leisure later. . . . We see ourselves in Oedipus." The question of imperfection is followed by a series of student inquiries that focus on the quality and intensity of relationships in *Oedipus Rex*. The students' queries sound simple, almost pedestrian, against the elaborate language of Clifford. Yet they do not seem disturbed by the dissonance. Perhaps they do not hear it. Mostly they appear to appreciate the way he vigorously seizes their questions and launches into a poetic, embellished response. Despite the fact that Clifford's voice dominates and students are in the listening mode most of the time, the class seems to see him as responsive. A willowy girl with sandy straight hair and a studious gaze offers a paradoxical view. "He talks a lot . . . but he's the best listener."

Clifford's course is not typical in any sense. It gathers together the most capable students, appeals to those who want to be identified as intellectuals, and is an expression of the teacher's passionate interests. In addition, the pedagogical style contrasts sharply with most of the courses I visited where teachers actively enlisted student participation and discussion. At Kennedy, there seems to be a high premium put on "inductive teaching"; on drawing out student ideas, perspectives, and understandings. Teachers tend to direct and guide, but rarely take center stage in the way Clifford did. For less advanced students, inductive techniques are seen as essential strategies for gaining and maintaining the class's attention.

Except for two White boys, all of the thirty-five students in "Unified Biology" are Black and Brown. The course, designed for Remedial students, is full of "repeaters"; students who have taken the class at least once before. Although this is usually a sophomore-level course, the students' physical maturity is much beyond grade level. The boys appear tall, bulky, and bearded. Their long legs stretch out under the laboratory tables. Most of the girls look even older. It is not only their well-developed figures that give them an almost adult appearance; it is their weariness, their seeming loss of innocence, that is striking. The students settle into their chairs quickly with two seated at each lab table. Mr Romeo, the teacher, is dressed formally and impeccably in a blue suit, light-blue shirt, and conservative tie. He is a slender man with an erect posture. His shiny black hair, perfectly shaped goatee, and his stylized gestures make him appear almost imperious. When he calls on students, he often uses their last names and beckons to them with a long, extended arm and pointed finger. Romeo's tone seems to be an interesting mixture of arrogance and respectful regard for students.

After quietly telling a boy in the front row to remove his hat, Romeo walks around the silent room spot-checking homework assignments. His announcement of an examination the following Tuesday brings no clear response from the students' impassive faces. The lesson begins with a review of the material covered the day before. "Yesterday we discussed some artificial ways man has been able to propogate plants . . . who can describe the method we call grafting?" When six hands are raised, Romeo complains, "I remember teaching it to a *whole* class yesterday." In order to spark their memories, he offers several clues; asking specifically about "layering" and "cuttings." Without much success, he decides to draw on their experience, "Can you describe what a lawn looks like when it is first seeded?" The student's answer seems to be a partially memorized response, rather than an observation. "It doesn't have a green color to it because it hasn't reached the adult stage." Romeo provides a different, simpler answer. "It is patchy, isn't it?"

The confusion and obfuscation that accompanies the review of yesterday's lesson cause a frustrated and disheartened expression on Romeo's face and he finally decides to turn to the day's agenda. In precise script, he writes on the board, "Aim: How does natural vegetation and propagation occur?" and then carefully draws a sketch. "Will you look at the drawing, please. Describe what is occurring." A Black boy offers a tentative answer, "The roots go under further and pops up another stem." Romeo praises his efforts. "Very nice, an underground stem occurs. We call that underground stem a rhizome. . . . Why can we describe this as asexual reproduction?" A few hands are raised and the teacher waits for more. His gaze is stern as he calls on a Hispanic girl who was the last to raise her hand. " 'Cause only one parent is needed," she says softly. "Very good," responds Romeo crisply. Several times during the lesson, the teacher asks them to reflect on their experience. "Can someone describe what happens to onions when you've kept them around the house for a long time?" When only a pair of hands shoot up, Romeo's voice reveals a slight disgust. "I can't believe you *all* haven't seen that." A few other students are prodded into responding and they answer when he points at them. "Stems start to grow," offers the first respondent. "That's correct," admires the teacher. "That's very good." "Roots start to grow," adds the second voice. "Very good, can someone tell us what is happening?" "The onion is becoming a plant," says a third contributor with certainty. "Very good," responds the teacher again.

Most of the class proceeds in this way with the teacher asking short, factual questions, offering a series of clues when necessary, and giving reinforcing praise when the students' answers are mostly correct. The teacher insists upon raised hands, mildly admonishes the few students who call their answers out, and often waits for more people to show a willingness to contribute. The pace is painstakingly slow and the frustration palpable. There are moments of naiveté and misunderstanding. "Is that where onion paper comes from?" asks a boy after Romeo's explanation of the onion's "fleshy" leaves. "What does fleshy mean?" inquires another girl. There are also moments when the teacher's frustration turns into momentary cynicism. "Well what can I expect from city kids," he says when no one reacts to his question which asks students to refer to their gardening experience. But it is in the final minutes of class that students exhibit their first signs of anxiety. It is an anxiety that seems to derive from a fear that they will be singled out and called on and a growing recognition of how much they do not understand. "Who can quickly summarize for us the six methods of vegetative propogation?" inquires Mr. Romeo optimistically. The class is absolutely still and noiseless. "You mean no one can answer . . . now I see two hands . . . oh come on you were all here." Finally, a Black girl breaks the ice, "When you say summarize, what do you mean?" The teacher looks dejected and soon decides to break his big question into pieces. Teacher: "Vincent, would you tell us about rhizomes?" In a halting voice, Vincent reads the definition from his notebook. Teacher: "Miss Washington, describe a runner." Her answer is confused and partial but the teacher decides it is adequate. Teacher: "A bulb, Miss Soto." In answering the pointed questions, most students shuffle through their notes and use words that do not seem to belong to them. The teacher is determined to conclude on a more positive note. "Last question," he says with some drama. "Where did the first one [asexual plant] come from? It seems to be a problem." A Black boy answers clearly and immediately. "Sexual reproduction." "That's what I wanted to hear. This is only a secondary method. Aha!" exclaims Romeo as the first smile spreads over his face.

Described by many as being "the lowest of the low," the Remedial/ Repeater classes are by far the least attractive courses assigned to teachers. When we talk after class, there are tiny beads of sweat on Mr. Romeo's forehead that contrast with his otherwise smooth veneer. He has worked very hard. "It is like pulling teeth . . . very, very difficult," he says with a mixture of discouragement and pride. There seems to be some small pleasure in the meager accomplishments and a relief that he is able to survive the persistent setbacks. Although as I observe them I feel pained by the students frustration and limitations and the hopelessness that lines some of their faces, I am heartened by the perseverance of both the teacher and his class. No one seems to have totally given up. There are many examples of persistence from the students, even moments of dogged determination—and the teacher cares enough to prod, badger, and pursue them until something is understood. Never does the class disintegrate into the chaos that characterizes many high school classrooms filled with their least talented students. Instead, civility and order are emphasized. Even the teacher's slightly haughty style seems to be a demand for dignity and poise in his students.

"Unified Biology" and "Creative Man" represent the extremes in pedagogical style and curricular substance at Kennedy. They are also inhabited by students with strikingly different abilities and futures. Most of Kennedy's students fall somewhere within the broad range stretching between these extremes, and receive instruction that blends the slow, determined pace of Romeo and the elaborate, dramatic display of Clifford. Even though the differences between the Honors electives and Remedial courses seem great, they do not appear to be as vast as one might expect. In many big city schools, Remedial Repeaters are treated as discardable waste. They mark time in meaningless and empty courses or they are permitted to engage in subtle violence against themselves and others. In contrast, bright college-bound students exist in a different world, far away from the contaminating influences of the slow, disaffected students. At Kennedy, the differences are marked, but there are universal expectations of civility and humaneness that seem to shape teacher/student exchanges at all levels. Certainly, most faculty are quick to admit their preferences for the more rewarding experience of working with bright and gifted students and their discouragements, even despair, in teaching slow learners. But the despair is rarely expressed in disdain or defeat. Teaching may proceed at a snail's pace, but some teachers and students learn to recognize and appreciate the almost invisible progress.

BALANCING FORCES: INSIDE AND OUT

Although the coherence and simplicity of Kennedy's current curriculum was a response to explicit internal decisions by administrators and faculty, the academic structure is also partially defined by requirements imposed by the city and state of New York. Throughout my visit I was often struck by the tension between the particularistic goals, style, and decision making of Kennedy inhabitants; and the universal edicts of the state and city educational bureaucracies. These external bodies impose constraints on procedures and products that shape the everyday life of teachers and students at Kennedy. Some seem to regard the regulations imposed from outside as a source of security, a way to maintain decent educational standards across the city. But most people I spoke to viewed the bureaucratic layers encompassing Kennedy as potentially deadening to the creativity and productivity of their school. One A.P., who actively tries to diminish the intrusions of the city and state educational structures, refers to them ominously as "the central authority." He spends a fair amount of energy figuring out ways to circumvent policies and directives that, he believes, distort the educational experiences of teachers and students. Even though he finds the external intrusions "pernicious," he recognizes why they are necessary in a large, diverse city school system. He believes they were established to monitor the poor schools, the ineffective administrators, and the lazy teachers. But in trying to protect against inferior schooling, the "central authorities" have limited the freedom of the better schools and distorted the essential human encounters that shape education. "The independence of good schools is stifled because they are paying the price for poor schools that did not meet minimal standards . . . there is an increasing burden of clerical chores, an elaborate set of regulations . . . lots of bureaucratic machinery . . . the lock-step routine of the central authority inhibits our creativity. I must fight against it."

Others, who are critical of the external interventions but less vehement in their attacks, claim that some of the requirements are neutral and legitimate, while others distract energy away from the essential processes of teaching and learning. For example, they do not argue with the numbers or types of courses stipulated by the state and point to the fact that Kennedy's requirements are often more stringent. But they do chafe at some of the pedagogical directives, the prescriptions regarding how teachers should present material. "It is outrageous to require 'reasoning and critical thinking' and say nothing about the kind of institutional and interpersonal climate that would support that," complains one faculty member who tries to distinguish between "the spirit" and "the letter" of the law and only adheres to her "interpretation" of the former. Sitting around the table in one department workroom, several teachers told me increasingly funny stories about their noncompliance with regulations that strike them as "absurd." They told tales of "bending" the rules to adapt to their personalities, student abilities and needs, and the school environment and local context. One admitted to refusing to follow certain guidelines because they were morally repugnant and antithetical to her "view of professionalism." But a single voice offered a very different perspective. She saw the bureaucratic layers and huge system as a "wonderfully impersonal" structure that provided "the freedom that comes with anonymity . . . somehow I believe that the rules and restraints will never reach down to me. I am free to be myself because no one will ever notice."

The toughest critics of the state and city mandates spoke about Mastruzzi's critical stance in "softening" the external constraints. "A school can only develop into a viable culture if we all can negotiate our terrain without any interference . . . and Bob protects us as much as he can from that interference," said one teacher philosophically. Another pointed to Mastruzzi's political acumen and said, "He knows how to read and interpret the decisions . . . which ones to pay attention to and which ones to discard and that gives us a great deal of latitude here." A third observer spoke of Mastruzzi's self-confidence as a critical variable. "He is not afraid to say 'no' to them because he knows how good we are here. We have more freedom here than any other school I know of in the city."

Every assistant principal I spoke to began his or her description of the curriculum by reciting the city and state regulations and then told of the ways those are embellished by school requirements. For example, of the seven semesters of social studies required of Kennedy students, six are responses to state and city requirements. The state mandates one year of American studies; while the city requires three semesters of global history and one semester of economics. The school adds an additional semester of American history and permits students to choose electives beyond the seven term requirements (including courses in crime and justice, Black history, sociology, the American family, and American women). Likewise, the state guidelines for English require seven terms of English and one semester of speech. But Kennedy students must take a ninth term in order to meet school requirements.

However, it is not the numbers of state or city required courses that cause rancor among teachers and administrators. They seem to be perceived as relatively neutral guidelines shaped by a convincing intellectual rationale. In addition, the academic departments at Kennedy tend to be more demanding than the state or city in terms of the students' required fare. Rather, the complaints surrounding external regulation tend to be focused on the requirements of staff responsibilities, not the curricular structure. For instance, both teachers and supervisors speak negatively of the city system's regulations on faculty meetings and teacher supervision. On the first Monday of each month, every department is required to have a faculty meeting. The second Monday is reserved for full faculty meetings. Most teachers describe these occasions as "non-events," imposed rituals that rarely lead to substantive exchange. Some feel the perfunctory nature of the meetings is related to their rigid and dogmatic structure which does not permit a responsiveness to emerging issues or a spontaneity of exchange. Others believe that the boredom is a direct response to the compulsory requirement. "Somehow the edict from on high makes us all respond like resistant children who would rather go out and play," says a young woman half-jokingly. Still others fault their colleagues for "non-professionalism" and lack of commitment. Says one harsh critic, "most of them don't want to do any of the extras. They are unwilling to do anything that goes slightly beyond the literal duties listed in the teachers' union contract. Faculty meetings force them to tack forty extra minutes on to their day and they actively resent it. They're chomping at the bit to race to their car pool and head for the suburbs."

The Board of Education also has explicit regulations regarding the supervision of teachers. Based on years of experience and training, faculty are divided into three categories. Maximum salary teachers (M's) have had more than twelve years of experience and at least thirty credits toward their master's degree; tenured teachers (T's) have from three to twelve years experience; and probationary teachers (P's) have been teaching for less than three years and have not yet come up for tenure review. Most departments at Kennedy are dominated by more experienced teachers (M's and T's). The English department, for example, has only one probationary teacher out of thirty faculty members. Twenty-two are maximum salary teachers and seven are tenured. In social studies all of the thirty-one faculty are tenured, with twenty-nine on maximum salary. Although there are fairly elaborate regulations for the supervision and evaluation of new and inexperienced teachers, most of these do not apply to the A.P.'s duties at Kennedy. Instead, they are faced with experienced faculty who are safely protected by tenure. In many respects their job is tougher than it would be if the faculty were younger and less experienced. They do not have optimistic, energized teachers with unformed, malleable styles and approaches. Neither do they have the option of getting rid of incompetent or lazy faculty. Theirs is a challenge of revitalization, retraining, and re-energizing the commitment of experienced faculty.

Some A.P.'s take this challenge to heart by rigidly following the external guidelines. The Board of Education requires that they visit each maximum salary teacher once a year and observe tenured teachers twice annually. One A.P. I spoke to feels the guidelines trivialize an important supervisory function, so he doubles the number of teacher observations and adds several "mini-visits" during the year—short, spontaneous classroom visits that allow him to "keep in touch" with his faculty and diminish their apprehension regarding the more formal observations. This A.P., who laughingly refers to himself as a "grandfather type," has a benign, paternal approach to his supervisory work. "I try not to be too judgmental . . . I find it more effective to soothe problems among faculty." Other A.P.'s do not adhere as stringently to the letter of the law, and a few speak of the formal supervisory requirements as impediments to good faculty relations. One claims that informal encounters, over a cup of coffee or a bottle of beer after school, are always less threatening and more productive. "Teachers resent written reports. I get them done but I am often wasting my time. . . . With these very experienced teachers, there is a conservatism that comes with habit. My purpose should be to get teachers to think about throwing out, discarding materials, taking on a new form. I want to provide a climate for creativity . . . but the lock-step routines imposed by the central authorities exaggerate the conservative tendencies in teachers . . . the lesson plan becomes more important than the teacher."

A third A.P. neither regards the supervisory regulations as counterproductive, nor does he see them as benign. His cool approach matches his smooth temperament and his view of bureaucracy as a relatively neutral form. All regulations, he feels, must be "adapted" to the context and received with perspective and a measure of humor. He refuses to get bogged down in organizational details or spend his energy fighting external interventions. In his department of twenty-five, there is only one probationary teacher. The others express the broad range of talent and commitment, with most falling mid-range. "It is as you would expect," he says matter of factly, "most teachers are pedestrian, a few are losers, and only a handful are superstars. They are the ones who make the department go, do the extra work, and offer creative, energetic input. If you have three or four of those, you can build a decent, even good, department." To those teachers on the low end of the continuum, this assistant principal constantly prods and admonishes—"I am on their backs constantly. I drop in often, very often, and look to see if they are really teaching." To the broad middle range of teachers, he tries to offer supportive judgment. "Teachers are strange animals. They are very threatened by written evaluations. I usually tell teachers when I will observe them. I give them the opportunity to be at their best." To his superstars, he is "lavish in his praise." "I treasure the gems. In whatever way I can, I make their lives more pleasurable . . . I stroke their egos."

Even though the A.P.'s have different ways of coping with the requirements set by the Board of Education, they all claim to believe that teacher supervision is critically important to staff morale and pedagogical standards. They all refer in various ways to the irony that plagues their work: "The most secure and able teachers are the least threatened by supervision and of course they need the criticism the least." In addition, all of them point to the tension between standards set by the Board of Education and the regulations that are part of the teachers' union contract. The dual requirements often seem to be in opposition to one another. "We are squeezed from all sides," claims a beleaguered A.P. "The central authorities want to make sure that teachers work hard, and the union wants to guard them against hard work." These contrary forces are often expressed in the daily encounters with teachers. For example, one A.P., who believes that good supervision should include a careful review of written lesson plans, is not able to apply this standard to all his faculty because the union contract gives teachers the option not to comply with such a request. "I'm not going to play games with professionalism," he says with resignation in his voice. "But it is always the worst four of five teachers who deny me permission." Another mentions the opposite problem of not being able to adequately reward excellence in teaching due to union regulations of uniform treatment.

From both sides, therefore, the people most directly responsible for curricular and pedagogical standards experience constraints on their initiative and autonomy. In the same breath, they recognize the need for standards imposed by the central administration and the need for protection and security of teachers. Their job is to walk the tight rope between these often competing spheres and to find ways of interpreting both sets of requirements so that they can be made to appear compatible. Each of the A.P.'s I spoke to used some portion of their ingenuity and wit in balancing the external demands and standards; and a few complained that the "balancing act" consumed far too much energy—energy that should have been focused on educational processes within Kennedy.

As I observed the vitality and certainty of John F. Kennedy High

School, I was struck by circus metaphors that would either appear in my mind or in people's language. During my visit, I heard about the "tight-rope walk" of administrators who must engage in a "balancing act"; "the three-ring circus" that students must observe as they negotiate the huge and complex school environment; and Mastruzzi, the "master of ceremonies," whose dramatic flare shapes and defines life at "the Big Top." I was reminded of the energetic clowns who pranced amid the wheelchairs in the Special Olympics parade held at Kennedy last year, their painted faces showing the extremes of emotion; and the animal murals painted on the school's walls that show lions, tigers, elephants, and giraffes living peacefully together. I recalled the combination of spectacle and humor that seems to fuel the energy of the school. The circus metaphors did not convey to me a trivial, fantasy-like, staged event. Rather, they seemed to express attention to drama and performance as part of schooling, to the role of humor in maintaining perspective, to the dexterity and poise required in balancing forces inside and out. Mastruzzi is an elegant example of a ringmaster in his carefully chosen costume, his deft orchestration of events, his comfort with all of the beasts that inhabit the Big Top, and in his dramatic announcements of the attractions. He is smooth, articulate, and compelling. His stature and mastery depend upon the cooperation and participation of all the actors, and he watches their performance with pride, always cheering from the sidelines.

Certainly the symbolism of life at the Big Top can be taken too far, particularly if it begins to exaggerate the drama and performance and neglect the hard, grueling, rough-edged practice that goes on all the time— before, during, and after the staged events. It seems to me that people at Kennedy pay attention to both the performance and the practice and see each as essential to the survival of a big-city school. Mastruzzi's critics, for example, often point to his attention to public relations and claim that he focuses too much time on projecting the school's image. But Mastruzzi, in referring to his role as a "community leader," believes that he must balance school image and educational essence, and that each is dependent on the other. Unless he convinces the skeptical public of the school's goodness, they will subtly undermine the hard work of his teachers and students. Unless the students and faculty combine to produce high standards, all of his pronouncements will sound like empty gestures and not be believed by the wider public. His "fetish" with attendance figures reflects the same dual concern for image and essence. High attendance rates are critically important, says Mastruzzi, "Because unless kids come to school they won't learn." However, he is equally concerned about the *appearance* of high attendance scores. He believes they are a quick indicator of a school's goodness, a visible and measurable sign.

Likewise, many teachers seem to express a similar concern for smooth performance and rigorous practice. In every classroom I visited, there was a great deal of attention paid to form as well as substance. Teachers insisted on discipline, civility, and poise even when the atmosphere seemed relatively informal. Boys wearing hats were asked to remove them; students chewing gum were told to deposit it in the trash basket; and mannerly turn-taking was required. These disciplined forms were seen as an integral part of learning, not a reification of procedure. Said one teacher who claimed to be a recent convert to "traditional education": "I used to think that manners and discipline got in the way of real learning. I thought they somehow obscured the essential process. Since coming to Kennedy, I realize that structure is just as important as the substance. One is dependent on the other." Another teacher offered more pragmatic reasons for the emphasis on order and discipline when she referred to the need for consonance between family values and school norms. "Most of our kids come from working-class or immigrant families where parents want the educational basics. To them school is a place to be taken very seriously. They like the idea that we emphasize order. Then they know we're not cheating their kids."

The emphasis on form, therefore, is partly a reflection of the serious regard teachers have for their students; partly seen as an integral part of the educational substance; and partly viewed as an important visible indicator of the school's goodness. But form is also linked, I think, to an explicit ideological stance often voiced by Mastruzzi and his faculty, and occasionally echoed by students. The emphasis on discipline and manners is connected to a view of education for citizenship. Time and time again, I heard Mastruzzi refer to his belief that "all our students are winners" and that "winning" has more to do with being a good, caring, and generous person than with visible and lofty achievement. It is an inclusive, rather than an exclusive, educational vision—one that does not focus superior or prideful attention on the narrow band of top achievers, or create a school image based on their great successes. Rather, it is a vision that asks for "extra human effort" on the part of *all* students and asserts that they are all equally capable of becoming good citizens. Says Mastruzzi proudly, "There is an unbelievable emphasis on doing something for someone else." As an example, Mastruzzi points to a now-traditional holiday ritual. At Christmas time, Kennedy students collect hundreds of gifts for needy children. The students wrap each gift and deliver the presents themselves. Last year the presents were given to a home for mentally retarded children and this year they will probably arrive at an institution for the severely handicapped. The personal attention of gift wrapping and the presenting of gifts is central to the act of giving. It is not a distant, paternalistic gesture. It is an intimate act of charity. Each year the principal offers the same message of charity to the graduating seniors. He rehearses the words to me with great feeling, "I tell them, you need to leave this school with a sense of appreciation for other human beings. That is the primary lesson we teach at this school. I don't care if you are going to Columbia University pre-med, or if you have been tops in our Honors program. If you don't give a bit of yourself to someone else, you are a failure!"

PART TWO

SUBURBAN PORTRAITS

III

Highland Park High School

Hierarchies, Ambition, and Stress

SUBURBAN CHIC

Highland Park is one of a string of affluent suburban communities north of Chicago. To the outsider, it resembles its neighbors, Lake Forest, New Trier, and Evanston. To the insider, the distinctions among these towns are vivid and important to their individual identities. Insiders know about differences in the racial, economic, and ethnic ingredients of their neighborhoods and observe patterns of stability and change in the populations. Lake Forest, for example, is right next door to Highland Park, but its image is one of greater stability, civility, and affluence. It continues to be a largely Protestant town of old, established wealth and its residents look down upon the "nouveau riche" of Highland Park. Some Lake Forest people hope their town will remain protected from the rapid influx of "bourgeois Jews" they think have brought a new aggressiveness and pushiness to Highland Park that is not dignified. In Lake Forest, children are still said to have manners. They wave hello as they pass by on their bicycles, offering greetings of respect to their elders. Neighbors are said to speak in civilized tones to one another when they pass on the street, always keeping the appropriate distance, to insure privacy. These are the defensive self-perceptions of the more conservative sector of Lake Forest.

But many of their Highland Park neighbors see the Lake Forest civility as stodginess, and view their generational respectfulness as empty ritual. They prefer the more spirited tone of Highland Park and admit to a healthy assertiveness in their community. During my visit to Highland Park, the supermarket was the place where I witnessed heightened aggressiveness. Some residents joke that you "risk your life" when you go shopping in Highland Park. Perfectly coiffured and manicured ladies, in Adidas tennis outfits, race for positions at the check-out counter, pushing carts into each other and barking directions to the salesperson. Outside the store, the parking lot is a chaotic scene with lots of impatient honking and stealing of parking places. Occasionally shouting battles erupt as a silver Mercedes 450SEL outmaneuvers a burgundy Cadillac Seville.

The supermarket jungle contrasts sharply with the genteel face of Highland Park. A picturesque and immaculate town, it is an affluent version of a Norman Rockwell scene. Lining the main street are pristine dress shops stocked with designer clothes, colorful ice cream parlors, imposing jewelry windows with diamonds gleaming, and elegant bookstores. It seems almost like a theater set in its perfection and layout. Few people walk along the main street. The action is at the nearby shopping center which houses Lord & Taylor, Saks Fifth Avenue, and Marshall Field as well as some new restaurants, specialty stores, and movie houses. This is where affluent adolescents hang out on Saturdays spending their parent's money, and where housewives meet for a light lunch of quiche and salad followed by an afternoon of heavy shopping. This is modern, suburban chic, far from the ugly realities of Chicago's city scene; distant from poverty, decadence and other reminders of lower life.

The residential streets that wind away from the major arteries in town are quiet and tree-lined. Most houses are large and imposing with manicured lawns, two-car garages, and well-planned gardens. The houses do not all look the same. Some are traditional, ivy-covered brick houses; others are classic colonials; while others are strikingly modern with lots of glass and redwood. Even those that appear to be old structures seem to be of recent vintage. It is a town of recent design and construction, not one that seems rooted in history. In the early morning there are male joggers out, sometimes running in pairs, occasionally with the family dog tagging behind. I suspect that after their morning exercise, they will shower, dress, and drive into the smog-filled city for their sedentary work in a Chicago high-rise. Other than the morning joggers, there is little movement on the streets. People rarely walk, but move by car from place to place.

In the past few years, Highland Park has become known as a "settlers" community. Houses that sold for $80,000 a decade ago are now selling for $200,000; and these are ordinary homes, not extravagant structures. However, few houses are put on the market anymore. "Real-estate is sluggish." In the recent past, Highland Park was a more transitional community. Young, upwardly mobile, professional families would come to town, buy a house, and enroll their children in the good public schools. Once their children were off to college, the parents would leave Highland Park, often returning to a condominium in the city that required less upkeep, more options for entertainment, and a more adult-centered existence. Today's Highland Park families rarely follow this pattern of movement. Parents are far more likely to remain in their large suburban homes after their children are fully grown and out of the house—"two old people rattling around in twelve rooms." Their reluctance to move is partly related to increased fears about city dwelling and partly related to the fact that young families cannot afford to buy their $200,000 houses at inflationary mortgage rates. According to local observers, the stagnant market has made the town noticeably "older" and less vibrant.

The lack of new blood has had an enormous impact on the school population. Along with the declining birth rate that has marked the last two decades, the decreasing proportion of young families in town has led to the most significant shift in school population. School people, long used to the abundance of expansion and the extravagances of growth, have had to learn to accommodate budgetary constraints, school closings, and a stationary group of teachers. A town long used to transitions and mobility, moving trucks and farewells, now must anticipate forming enduring relationships and confront the pressures of continuity and stability.

At the end of town, right off the major thoroughfare and under the railroad viaduct, sits Highland Park High School. The viaduct has recently become famous. A few weeks before my visit, the *Chicago Tribune* published a series on the rapid rise of teenage suicide on the North Shore, and showed a picture of this viaduct with a graffiti message that read, "This town is no fun anymore."

The school is a large, sprawling brick structure surrounded by playing fields and parking lots full of teachers' and students' cars. It looks like many suburban high schools whose shape seems undefined and unplanned, the result of additions and expansions as the population has grown to 2,400 students. The original Sandwich building was constructed by bricklaying students in the early 1900s. Small and solidly built, it now houses the yearbook and newspaper staffs. In order to get to the old corner building, you have to wind down many corridors, past the swimming pools, student theater, ceramics area, graphic design department, and finally up several steps and back into time. It is the only place in town where one feels the weight of tradition, the old bricks laid by laborers' hands. The eastern wing of the high school was built in the early 1920s, and other sections sprung up in the decades that followed. The last construction on the building was completed in 1950, and included the gym and cafeterias. The three main buildings, labeled East, West, and Main, are three stories tall, joined together in a maze-like structure. Thankfully there are hall monitors, usually teachers, who are spaced throughout the building and can offer directions to the lost and weary traveler.

A LISTENING LEADERSHIP

The administrative activity takes place in the main building on the second floor. This is where Mr. Benson, the principal, and his support personnel are housed. The offices of his three vice-principals are scattered in other parts of the building, symbolically reflecting a decentralized, low-visibility leadership. As a matter of fact, Benson speaks proudly of the fact that the school runs with "very little administrative overlay."

Inside the central office is a comfortable waiting area with couches and chairs, and a friendly, accommodating receptionist who welcomes visitors. Mr. Benson's secretary, an efficient and warm person, sits behind high, decorated partitions close to the door of the principal's inner office. Everyone on the staff is unusually responsive and obliging. Collectively, they present a friendly face to the outside world. There is another entry door for insiders who seem to move in and out comfortably, telling the latest news, passing on messages, and making appointments.

These offices seem to be an extension of Mr. Benson's calm and affable demeanor. He is a tall, slender, mildly handsome man in his mid-fifties who greets people easily and has a gift for making others feel comfortable in his presence. In his elegantly appointed office, he rarely sits behind his large and imposing desk. He is more likely to join his visitors at the round table in the center of the room and offer them a cup or freshly brewed coffee. His style is cool; his manner is confident. He says of himself, "I am long on people skills."

Mr. Benson has been in the school system for twenty-five years. He arrived in 1956 after receiving his master's in history from the University of Iowa. The mid-fifties were a time of enormous expansion and growth in the "second ring" of suburbs north of Chicago, and Benson saw Highland Park as a town that offered opportunity and challenge. He joined the history department and soon took on the quasi-administrative role of advisor-chairman of the junior class. The principal at that time was a "very paternalistic" man who regarded his faculty like a family. Relationships among teachers were close, there was genuine collegial support and collaboration, and the future looked promising. But when a new school was built in nearby Deerfield four years later, Benson could not resist the challenge of becoming the dean, second in command under the principal. Deerfield was a small school of 300 students where everyone played multiple roles and there were "no hang-ups with titles." The staff was risk-taking and experimental; decisions were often openly negotiated. In 1963, when the principal of Deerfield left to get his doctorate, Benson became the principal. He describes his thirteen years at Deerfield with enthusiasm. The population expanded rapidly and the community "adopted their growing school," offering support and feelings of pride in its development. During the first ten years of his leadership, Benson recruited 30 to 40 teachers per year.

His work was made easier by the appointment of Mr. Petaccia as his vice-principal in charge of discipline. They have remained loyal and affectionate partners ever since, reflecting different, yet highly compatible temperaments. Benson is the smooth, urbane leader who establishes school policies, directs curricular decision making, deals with the superintendent, and makes public statements. His work appears to be so controlled and steady because Petaccia is "working in the trenches," dealing with the underside of school life. Benson readily admits that he could never do this job without Petaccia; that they work hand in glove; that Petaccia rarely receives the glory he deserves; and that the grinding, tough work his closest colleague does is ultimately distasteful to him.

Four years ago, when the superintendent asked Benson to take the principalship of Highland Park, he was reluctant to leave the school to which he had devoted so much energy and commitment. He remembered the people at Highland Park as more high powered, tense, and judgmental than his Deerfield colleagues; and he was well aware of the deep antagonisms and rivalries between the two towns. Route 2 divides them, a boundary Benson describes as "the deepest canyon next to the Grand Canyon." Benson would only agree to move to Highland Park if the superintendent also transferred Petaccia.

Together they moved across Route 2 to the rival town and faced a faculty that was divided by conflict and frightened by declining enrollments and diminishing jobs. After taking on his new post, the first thing Benson did was to visit and talk with every member of the faculty, classified staff, and custodial staff. He asked each person what they thought needed changing and refused to get involved in "old stories" and bitter battles from the past. "I would only consider events in the present." Benson was eager to cast a wide net, listen to the voices of all the participating community, and sought to be painstakingly fair. His leadership began subtly, listening for direction from the collective body, working behind the scenes to create alliances, and carefully but willingly delegating responsibility to others. Four years later, his style and approach is similar. Says one faculty member, "He is the best listener . . . I can just feel his support and confidence. He is always eager to learn."

Benson expects a great deal from his department chairpersons, most of whom he has appointed, others he has "inherited". He sees them as "the key persons for staff and program development. . . . I depend on them, I put pressure on them." Chairpersons are required to teach three courses each day, as compared to the five expected of regular teachers. Their administrative duties include intensive, weekly supervision of beginning teachers during their first two years. After teachers become tenured in their third year, chairpersons are required to visit their classes once each quarter and confer with them about career directions and goals every other year. Benson works with chairpersons, helping them develop more effective supervising skills and he personally evaluates their work. He complains that one chairperson is "a fine and good person, but does not like to deal with hard decisions" and hopes that another will soon "develop tougher skin." He feels sorry for another who has not had an opening in his department for several years and tries to work with him on strategies for rejuvenation and renewal of a stagnant faculty.

Over the years, the departments have emerged with distinctive reputations that are hard to undo or change. The reputations lag far behind the reality. For a long time, science, social studies, and fine arts have been perceived as first-rate departments; English has been seen as adequate but not great; and foreign languages and math have been the most criticized. Since the characterizations are no longer wholly accurate, it is difficult for the chairpersons of the departments perceived as weaker to continue to battle the negative images. Also, the lingering positive fallout enjoyed by the allegedly strong departments sometimes leads to a kind of complacency. Benson seeks to be even-handed and current in his criticisms and support, searching for the most relevant and precise evidence of success within and across departments.

Teachers enjoy a relatively privileged position at Highland Park High School. Every teacher I spoke to described the autonomy, support, and comfort they feel in the school. One English teacher compared their "freedom" to the constraints and prohibitions put on teachers in the neighboring district. "The kids here have a lot more freedom and so do the teachers. . . . In New Trier, they made them remove *The Merchant of Venice* from the library shelves. . . . Here, we can teach the most controversial material." When asked how curriculum gets developed in the school, Benson immediately points to the initiative and hard work of teachers. "For the most part, they are sophisticated about keeping up with the important trends in their fields. They go to conferences all over the country to collect new ideas and stay current." Teachers claim that much of the inspiration for their hard work comes from the demands and expectations of students. A very popular language teacher says: "At Highland Park teachers have to earn the respect of kids. You don't automatically get it because you are a teacher . . . but if you give kids respect, caring, and support, it will all come back to you." Many teachers spoke of their first year of harsh scrutiny by students, their determined attempts to gain acceptance and approval from them, and finally, their coming together in mutual admiration.

In seeking to encourage creativity and autonomy among teachers, Benson recognizes the need to allow for diversity and variation among them. He does not strive for uniformity, but seems to encourage idiosyncrasies to flourish. The drama teacher, a controversial school legend whose teaching and relationships are "most unorthodox," has a parade of followers who love her to death and a "line just as long ready to kill her." A young male teacher is adored by students, but causes eyebrows to be raised among some of his colleagues because of his highly emotional, charged, and seductive style. Benson does not agree with all of his pedagogical strategies, nor does he admire his immaturity, but he defends his individuality and sees one of his own primary roles as "protector" of these nonconformists.

Benson describes the administration's relationship to teachers as "non-adversarial." There are no teachers' unions and even negotiations around salaries are without conflict. He knows that such mutual accommodation is rare and considers it a great luxury to have strong support from his teachers. "I take advantage of that. I capitalize on that." For the first time last year, the teachers in neighboring Newtrier went on strike. Although the dispute was quickly resolved, Benson worries that the "trust factor will never be regained."

Not everyone agrees that the comfortable alliances between administration and faculty are good for the tone and spirit of the school. Dr. Kline, the head of the counselling department, observes that it can lead to a kind of dependence and caution among teachers. "The teachers in this school are treated by the administration like the students are treated by teachers. It is a very benign and benevolent relationship. They are taken care of, given high salaries, good benefits, and lots of rewards . . . why would they ever leave?" A teacher who has been at the school for over twenty years echoes Kline's sentiments. "We are all comfortable with one another and enjoy being here. But there is no new blood, criticism, or internal challenge."

Teachers and administrators appreciate the support they receive from the great majority of parents in the community. Parents are pleased by the consistent statistics. In 1956, 85 percent of the student body continued on to college. Two decades later, the figure was stable at 84 percent, with 75 percent completing college and 21 percent going on for advanced degrees. The list of colleges attended by last year's graduating class is full of prestigious schools, and the community is proud that its public high school can effectively compete with the elite private academies for the colleges of choice. In thanks for their fine work, parents generously support the school, and particularly Benson. "The P.T.O. thinks I'm God," he says with a smile. Last year the Parent Teacher Organization raised $30,000 to support an extravagant arts festival at the school. "They raised $14,000 from a single mailing," Benson exclaims incredulously.

The general feelings of good will between families and schools abruptly break down when an individual parent becomes frustrated because his child is not achieving in school. These parents become "caustic, critical, and demanding." They come to the school with a patronizing manner and demand an "immediate response" from Benson. But he always responds to them firmly: "I tell them I have more respect for their kids than to offer an instant response. They must wait for a considered response . . . and I will not deal with parents until they have the courtesy to deal with teachers first." In the end, Benson does "a lot of listening and diffuses the anger" of parents. He sits on the precarious boundary between school and community and recognizes the need to negotiate with parents, but he also works to protect students from their overly ambitious and competitive families, and guards teachers from their harsh assaults. The demands of diplomacy take their toll. He plans to retire in the next three years—"There is no disillusionment, only the recognition that it has been long enough."

UNDER PRESSURE

Parents in Highland Park express an early concern for educational excellence. They are anxious that their children get an accelerated head start in learning and that they never lose ground. Young mothers read baby and child care manuals on strategies for the intellectual stimulation of young children and struggle to get their youngsters into the best preschools. Most parents expect their children will read before formal schooling begins and are critical of kindergarten teachers who stress the social-psychological development of children.

Dr. Notman, a developmental psychologist who works for the school district, meets with the parents of prospective kindergarteners before the opening of school in early September. Each year, she gives the same message but it is rarely heard by the anxious parents. She asks them to "lay-off and don't push your kids. . . . The purpose of kindergarten is social learning. We want to help your children feel comfortable among peers and urge them to move beyond their egocentrism towards cooperative behavior." As Dr. Notman looks out at the tight, resistant faces of the young parents she makes one final plea. "Your children now belong partly to us so let us do our job." Even as she speaks these words, the experienced psychologist knows they will not be heard or heeded. The parents are horrified by a statement she makes to purposely jolt them into responding: "I wish schools would wait until boys are in the second grade before they would try to teach them to read. Most boys are not developmentally ready to attend to reading until they are seven or eight." The meeting usually ends without much discussion or public reaction from the parents. It feels like an empty ritual to Dr. Notman. Each year, she hammers away at the same message encouraging parental non-aggression and begging that they give their children space for autonomy and self-expression. Each year, the parents attend the meeting in full force and sit dutifully through her presentation. After the formal gathering, the veils from the parents' faces are dropped. Individually and with purpose, they approach Dr. Notman and ask the burning questions on their minds: "What books should I buy to get my Johnny reading early? . . . . Are there any extra-curricular activities that would enhance Susie's academic work?"

Local observers characterize the single-mindedness of parents in various ways. There are a few who feel no ambivalence about the origins of parental stress. Parents do it out of love and caring, they claim. Parents know what it takes to be a success in this world and they want to ensure their child's place on the high rungs of the hierarchical ladder. This is America, the land of opportunity; and they are quintessentially, enthusiastically American.

However, most observers express some ambivalence about the high-pressured world in which Highland Park children grow up. Mr. Cramer, a sensitive and expressive, youthful, middle-aged teacher, is outspoken on the subject. He has lived in Highland Park for seventeen years and has two pre-adolescent children who attend school there. They "love the community, enjoy being known by their neighbors, and intend to live in Highland Park forever." But at home, he and his wife consciously work against the prevailing pressures that their children experience from the school and community. They "downplay grades" and encourage their children to think more broadly about social responsibility and personal happiness. Most important, they try to model these contrary values in their own behaviors, avoiding flagrant materialism, volunteering for civic functions, and refusing to compete with neighbors and friends.

Cramer does not believe that the motives of most Highland Park parents are malignant, but neither are they pure. He believes that parents "live vicariously through their children," experiencing secondhand all of the successes and benefits of their achievements and status. When he sees parents at community meetings and asks "How are *you?*" they inevitably tell him about how their children are doing, "even if I don't even know their kids." Then parents tend to tell only the good news, the success stories. If Jason is at Harvard, Yale, or Princeton, he is heard about immediately. Rarely do parents speak about Jennifer who is studying drama at the University of Iowa, "even though she is a marvelous girl and Iowa is a great school." Cramer does not fault the parents for their pride in Jason, but he is suspicious of the disappearance of Jennifer from everyday parlance. "It is as if she is dead," he says with sadness and disbelief.

Cramer thinks this dramatic separation of parents from less successful children begins early in many of the town's families. He believes these children never really feel unconditionally loved and supported and that they therefore seek approval through external means, and further, that they rarely learn how to create enduring relationships in their own lives. Cramer traces "the problem" back to incomplete bonding between mother and child in "the first eighteen months" of life, the result of a mother too self-preoccupied to care fully for her child. He does not mention the father's place in child-rearing, neither does he look at the mother's own needs for nurturance and fulfillment. Indeed, Cramer's analysis does seem like a partial and incomplete story. Yet it is a largely untold story in this town, one representing an intriguing search for disturbances below the surface.

The competition among children begins early with the full support and encouragement of parents. By the time adolescents reach high school, the parental anxieties are fully internalized and further exaggerated by a healthy dose of peer pressure. Every teacher I spoke with at Highland Park complained of the intense competition among students and the extreme pressure from parents that their children achieve in school. Some teachers see a "flip side to this coin" that makes the school a "fantastic place to teach." The positive interest in academic achievement and the desire to be successful inevitably produce the negative fallout of competition among students.

Yet rarely do students reveal a burning intellectual curiosity that inspires their interest and commitment. More often their intensity is linked to winning the academic race, scoring points against competitors, and gaining a place on top of the pile. When teachers mention quiz questions or talk about a future test, a normally noisy classroom becomes immediately silent. The students' attention is riveted as they listen for any inadvertent clues or helpful hints. When graded papers are returned, the teacher may warn, "These papers are private matters, for you and your parents to see." Almost immediately, students begin to anxiously compare their grades—some suddenly low and discouraged, others exuberant with the good news of a high grade.

With such a premium placed on academic success, many students experience failure and deep feelings of inadequacy. The head of special education says, "Even an average kid is seen as slow in this school. . . . The overriding concern is academics, and if you don't fit in there, if you are not super-bright . . . you are lost." In a conversation with two bright and talkative senior girls, the theme of their remarks centered on the "pressure cooker" in which they live. Brenda, a bouncy and energetic member of the prestigious swim team described the "cutthroat competition" among her peers: "It is a very competive environment . . . but that is not always negative . . . it makes you work." With only slight embarrassment, she continued. "Inside you are always hoping someone else gets a worse grade." Mara, a quieter, more serious girl and a high achiever in all of the advance placement classes, echoed her friend. Even success does not bring relief, however. A kind of persistent and gnawing insecurity lingers on, a fear of losing one's precarious place.

It took Mara more than two years to feel comfortable at Highland Park, even though her family has lived in town for twenty years and her older sisters preceded her through school. During her freshman year, the large size of the school felt "confusing and overwhelming" after the more intimate environments of elementary and junior high school. She resisted trying out for school clubs and activities because the competition was so stiff and because she feared defeat. Afraid to move out towards people and initiate relationships, she "retreated into her studies," a safe place that brought rewards. By her sophomore year, the school did not appear so crowded and unfriendly. One day Mara dared to visit the offices of the school newspaper, a bustling and lively place where they were always looking for an extra pair of hands. Soon she was drawn into the fray. Her work on the newspaper forced her to be aggressive, push through crowds, and get the latest scoop. By her senior year, Mara had been voted a member of the student senate and was a major force on both the newspaper and the year book. "Now I am not so afraid of criticism," she says. But the struggles for inclusion were hard fought and her story is one of great success in this school. How much of Brenda's and Mara's experience is a part of the tumultuous journey of adolescence is hard to say. As I spoke to them, however, it did seem to me that these girls were, each in a different way, unusually resourceful, persistent, and energetic. I wondered about those groups of students who did not have those temperamental qualities, who never found the door of entry, and who continued to withdraw from the tough race.

School clubs do seem to provide some escape from the brutal academic competition, although students are still required to compete for the few choice places. Three hundred girls tried out for fifty-four places in the prestigious dance club; and one hundred and thirty students tried out for twenty-nine parts in the recent production of *Godspell*. Few are chosen. To those on the outside, the clubs are seen as exclusionary. Said one frustrated girl, who had been denied entry to the dance club for two years, "Clubs shouldn't exclude kids who don't have special training; they should be more open. I know it's hard to let everyone in, but clubs should be places for people to explore and take risks . . . even if you are a *klutz*." Others complain that club members are not always chosen on their talent or training, but because they have friends in the clubs who "play favorites."

For those on the inside of the clubs, however, membership and participation seem to provide challenge, pleasure, comraderie, and release from the daily grind of the school. After the close of school at 3:00, another life emerges. There is bustling activity throughout the building— swim club, cheerleading, ski club, student senate. Faculty advisors are assigned to each of these clubs, but students take the initiative in planning, organization, and leadership. It is here where many students seem to suddenly come alive, grow in stature, and reveal their competence.

The dance club practices in one of the large student cafeterias three afternoons a week. Girls dressed in practice outfits ranging from sweat pants and T-shirts to elegant, professional dance gear, are divided into three groups, each working on a different number. A few girls are well-trained dancers with lithe bodies and graceful moves. Others are pedestrian in manner and literal in their movements. Still others seem to be non-dancers, lost and clumsy. However, no one appears to be embarrassed or left out. A vivacious senior, who is a skilled dancer and president of the club, explains, "We think of this as a *club*, a place to teach and learn . . . not a performance group." The faculty advisor, who plays an appreciative but peripheral role, also speaks of the club as "a learning environment." Some of the ugly ducklings grow into beautiful swans. Each year she watches awkward freshman girls practice diligently under the tutelage of their upperclass peers and sees amazing transformations in confidence and skill.

One plump and graceful senior dancer exudes style and confidence as she teaches fifteen girls the steps she has choreographed to George Benson's "On Broadway." The music is rhythmic and pulsating; images of city lights, neon signs, and fast living on New York's Broadway seem far from Highland Park. Some of the girls are hopelessly stiff and confused by the steps; but others are filled with the spirit and rhythm, and for fleeting moments seem transformed into Broadway dancers. The student leader's manner is patient and firm. When girls lose their confidence, she inspires and supports them. When they become disruptive, she first cajoles, then mildly scolds them back into line. There is a wonderful spirit of working together towards a goal.

As we leave the practice sessions, the vice-principal in charge of student activities shakes his head and marvels at the self-confidence and certainty of the Highland Park students. "They are not embarrassed by anything. They'll practice their steps right in the middle of the hall, in front of anyone." When I ask where their self-assurance comes from, he points to the support and stroking they get at home. "The girls, particularly, are made to feel special by their parents. From day one, they are told that they're beautiful and talented . . . and they grow to believe it." This parental stroking does seem to breed confidence, but it also nourishes a kind of arrogance in these students. Their mannerisms and style reflect the fragile balance of boldness and vulnerability. School clubs seem to provide asylum for the chosen and encourage the development of confidence, as these adolescents turn from their parents to their peers for support.

KEEPING THE PEACE

From the outside, the student population at Highland Park High School appears to be homogenous. When I ask a group of students how outsiders would describe Highland Park, without hesitation, they exclaim in chorus, "We are seen as a 'JAP' school." Because of my obvious confusion, they explain further, "The school of Jewish American Princesses." The image describes a broader range of stereotypes associated with the school. From afar, it is seen as a haven for the privileged, the indulged, the overprotected, the ambitious, and the pushy—stereotypes often associated with successful Jewish populations. Connected to these fixed images are the perceived qualities of intelligence, success, academic achievement, and sophistication. Some students seem to wear these images proudly, even arrogantly. Their behaviors appear practiced as they parade around in casual, but expensive garb, brag about their winter weekend in the Bahamas, and remind friends of their brother who is a pre-med at Harvard. They are the walking caricatures for whom the stereotypes seem appropriate.

However, even a brief look inside the school reveals a diversity invisible from the outside. It is not a monolithic student population of bright and rich kids; it is a population composed of many groups where separations, divisions, and factionalism become more noticeable the longer one stays. Mr. Petaccia, the vice-principal in charge of discipline says wearily, "I work hard to keep the peace." Any student can quickly describe the factions and where they "hang out." "The 'Glass Hall' is where the 'scums' hang out. . . . They are the kids who party all the time . . . both rich and poor kids who are rebelling against their parents." The "Jock Hall" is by the cafeteria. This is where the "sports guys and popular girls hang out." The "Book Foyer" close to the library is where the "average-to-bright" kids gather, the ones who have "better attitudes and are active in organizations." The music and drama area is the place where students gather who are devoted to the arts and have become "disciples of the drama teacher." Put nicely, these are "interest areas" defined by common habits and traditions.

The administration and faculty are less delicate in their description of factionalism within the school. They point to the old divisions of race, class, and ethnicity. Mr. Petaccia knows the demographic figures by heart and is candid in his portrait of the tumult underneath the calm exterior. Standing over six feet, with broad shoulders, heavy girth, and a tough manner, Petaccia is a feared figure in school. A noisy, chaotic cafeteria will suddenly become calm and orderly when he enters the room. Rowdy, delinquent big shots become small, dutiful, and obedient in his presence. He will not tolerate belligerence or intimidation and stomps out trouble before it happens. That is Mr. Petaccia's public persona. Not far underneath this harsh exterior is a compassionate, caring man, "a teddy bear" as he is lovingly referred to by long-time intimates. Some students even sneak a view of this side of him which makes his sparing punishment seem all the more threatening. He is the favorite subject of a student cartoonist who exaggerates his rubbery features, his big ears, and his belly. In Highland Park, Mr. Petaccia is bigger than life.

In his mid-fifties, Petaccia is growing weary of the school battles and plans to retire in the next couple of years. Born and raised in a working-class Italian neighborhood on Chicago's South Side, Petaccia is still strongly identified with his origins and often feels like a fish out of water in the precious surroundings of Highland Park. He never ceases to be amazed by the arrogance and elitism of some students and is turned off by their overly protective and entitled parents who call his office "and talk to us the way they talk to Sears and Roebuck or Marshall Fields when they've received faulty merchandise." Yet he is quick to point out that these intrusive parents do not characterize the behavior of most parents.

Four years ago, Petaccia reluctantly came to Highland Park. He and Benson had been a successful team for several years at the neighboring Deerfield School where the disciplinarian's "life was a lark." A somewhat smaller and newer school, Deerfield had a largely white, Protestant population with "good disciplinary support from home . . . and not too many questions from parents." Occasionally, there would be "instances of minor vandalism," but "no real work to do." Coming to Highland Park was a shock—reminiscent of the struggles Petaccia had when he first began teaching in a Chicago public school in the early fifties, where disciplinary problems often reflected racial strife. He saw at Highland Park similar rigid divisions and the ever-present potential for disruption and violence.

The most recent statistics show that 65 percent of the student population is Jewish, 22 percent Italian, with a smattering of Blacks (33) and Latinos (45). The "serious flare-ups in discipline . . . the deep-seated hostilities," seem to erupt between the Jews and the Italians, who Petaccia says, "feel that Jews are the preferred group around here. They get the best teachers, the best counselors, while the Italians are advised to go into vocational work." A third identifiable group are the students from the nearby military base, called "the Fort Sheridan kids." Numbering 165, they are both White and Black, and often feel alienated from the rest of the school. Some have been in as many as seven or eight high schools before coming to Highland Park, and they are reluctant to form attachments and make commitments. There is also some racial strife within the Fort Sheridan group. They band together for protection against the outside world. But among themselves, they often fight bitterly. Rarely do they bring their battles to school. Petaccia explains, "The Fort Sheridan kids are suspended the least. . . . Their fathers are military men . . . and very scary. They wouldn't dare get out of line."

The upper middle-class Blacks, indigenous to Highland Park, see themselves as distinct from the Fort Sheridan Blacks and are described by some as "the most alone." The Latinos are also a lonely and peripheral minority. Most are Chicanos whose families live on the fringe of the community doing menial tasks for their more affluent neighbors. Some have a relatively comfortable and stable existence in the town because they have built reputable lawn services. But they are still regarded as part of the servant class whose existence is dependent upon the needs and generosity of the upper middle-class. Brown and Black faces are few, less than one hundred students altogether; and they do not appear as a cohesive group or a force to be reckoned with.

Dr. Kline, head of the counselling department, also describes the school as divided by factionalism and conflict. He is a sensitive, articulate, middle-aged man with a Ph.D. in consulting psychology from Northwestern. In the early 1960s, he came to Highland Park to teach social studies. His "love" was international history with a particular interest in North and West Africa. After several years of teaching, he became increasingly disenchanted by the "very presentist" orientation of students who were "rebellious, resentful, and disillusioned by the Vietnam War." He found it impossible to get them involved in serious intellectual inquiry, particularly in questions that probed the past. Kline's escape from student rebellion was to take a two-year sojourn at Northwestern for training in psychology. As a historian and psychologist, he has watched the changes in the school culture, adolescent preoccupations, and community norms over the last fifteen years. No longer moved by political events or ideological rebellion, today's students seem self-centered and withdrawn, detached from the real world. There is a strong focus on academic work and a great preoccupation with grades, but that is accompanied by a kind of intellectual boredom and complacency among students. Gone also is the school spirit, the sense of belonging, that students felt in the sixties. "Sports events no longer bring people together as they still do in some less affluent communities." Kline describes the deterioration of a sense of community within the school and says many students feel isolated and alone as they move through their day. Highland Park has become an "exclusionary community . . . the tone of the school dominated by a superficial sophistication . . . the primary preoccupations are in finding the right clothes, the right kind of car, the right friends." The troubles inside the school reflect a "depressive core in the community," worries Kline. Without goals or traditions to unite energies, hostility is directed inward and divisions intensify. "The Italians are offended by the loose affluence of the Jewish kids," and the students from the army base seem "rigid, uptight, and conservative." Differences are exaggerated.

The one thing that seems to unite the student factions is drugs—"the great leveler." Kline has seen a large increase in drug use over the past year after a decade of noticeable decline, and sees it as a poignant and sad effort at reaching out and making connections. Behind the haze of drugs, barriers do not seem as severe and life does not appear as boring. Drugs also are the focus of family battles that erupt at home and eventually reach the offices of Dr. Kline or one of his eleven staff members. Flagrant drug abuse is often an alarm signal to parents that their son or daughter is in trouble and needs help. Recently, a junior boy, who uses and deals drugs, sounded the alarm. He casually left large quantities of grass in the glove compartment of his father's car. When his father discovered it, he was afraid and outraged, and flushed it down the toilet. This precipitated a violent family crisis. Father and son arrived at school the following morning still screaming with rage. "Only when there are crises do some families begin to talk."

Clearly, Kline does not see a cross-section of students in his position as chief psychologist. His view is probably overly jaundiced, his prognosis overly pessimistic. Troubled students arrive at his door, but the troubles are deep and severe. Even with the help of several colleagues, it is not unusual for Kline to hospitalize five students in a week's time. Other less disturbed youngsters get referred to mental health clinics and private psychiatrists and psychotherapists around town with whom Kline works hard to sustain positive relationships. In fact, one could say that Highland Park is an unusually good place for troubled youngsters. Teachers, counselors, and administrators work collectively and seriously to save souls.

Benson is proud of the daily ritual that takes place during the seventh and eighth period of each day. The System for Coordinated Services (SCS) is a prophylactic measure designed to keep track of all students through the daily screening of attendance records. A small group of counselors, social workers, and teachers review the records each day and act on any case where the student has been absent without excuse for more than two days in a row. The first line of action is to notify the student's teachers, who are asked to call the parents. Since each student has several teachers, parents might receive as many as four or five calls from the school in a day. In response to these calls, defensive parents can become antagonistic and resistant. But most parents seem to appreciate the watchfulness and concern, and alliances between parents and teachers often begin with these initial contacts.

Petaccia claims that this stringent system has "reduced truancy a thousand-fold." Highland Park boasts an average attendance rate of 91 percent; 3 percent of the students are absent each day because of illness. Some of the truancy can be traced to parental initiatives. "They are professional people who do a lot of traveling . . . and without the slightest hesitation or any guilt, they will take their kids out of school for several days to go with them to the Caribbean, to Europe. . . ." Students are not suspended for truancy as they are in many schools. Petaccia explains matter of factly, "that is illegal . . . and every other father in this town is a lawyer, so we have been forced to become very legalistic." The one or two suspensions that Petaccia makes weekly are usually related to marijuana or alcohol possession. These suspensions are made sparingly, handled very carefully, and Petaccia "follows due process to the letter." "Philosophically," he does not believe in suspensions, but claims that they are an effective "deterrent to fringe groups and a warning to parents."

When the SCS groups uncover more serious student problems in their daily meetings, they are committed to making some immediate decisions on the case. No decision is allowed to be tabled; procrastination is prohibited. "This can be very frustrating," says one SCS teacher, "but it increases everyone's sense of urgency and responsibility." The most severe cases are referred to the steering committee, which includes Benson, Kline, Petaccia, the director of special education, and teacher representatives. They review the folders of students who have accumulated more than fifteen unauthorized absences and make various recommendations for special institutional supports. Parents may be called in for conferences, psychological tests may be administered, the special education screening committee may become activated, the curriculum may be altered, and students may be sent to the reading lab for individual help. The range of reinforcements and readjustments that the school makes in response to troubled students is indeed impressive. Nets are spread to catch those who fall. Kline says proudly, "It is this comprehensive network that distinguishes us from the other schools around here," where students' cries for help may not be heard.

But occasionally, a student can slip through the cracks despite all the collective efforts. On the second day of my visit to Highland Park, the school was stunned and saddened by the suicide of a young girl the night before. A student with a history of depression, she had been seeing a local psychiatrist for several years. For the last few months, however, she had discontinued her psychotherapy and seemed to be showing steady improvement. Since September, her life had been invigorated by her work on *Godspell*—a student production that consumed her energies and provided her with an instant group of friends. After *Godspell*, her spirits and enthusiasm declined noticeably. In her distress, she reached out to a teacher who had given her special tutorial support in the past, and the school machinery was set in motion. A meeting was scheduled for the following day to review her case. That night, after a visit to her psychiatrist, she killed herself.

The day after, the school buzzed with rumors as students passed on the gruesome news—their faces showing fear and intrigue. The special education teacher wondered out loud, "What did we miss? . . . Where did we go wrong?" as Benson responded tensely to the superintendent's fears of visibility and embarrassment. "I'll check it out . . . I'll get right on it." But I heard only one teacher speak of it openly and explicitly in class— the drama teacher who had produced *Godspell*. Her words brought tears and looks of terror in the eyes of her students.

> "We've lost a student today who was with us yesterday. We've got to decide where our priorities are. How important are your gold chains, your pretty clothes, your cars? . . . Where were we when she needed us? Foolish old woman that I am, I ask you this because I respect you. . . . While you can still feel, damn it, feel . . . reach out to each other. . . ."

TOWARD CONSERVATISM: ACADEMIC DIVISIONS

Not only are there divisions among ethnic and religious groups in Highland Park, but there are also clear distinctions made among academic levels and abilities. Almost all of the classes are homogeneously grouped with vast differences in demands, expectations, and status between the regular and the advanced placement courses. An advanced placement student expressed a common perception when she said "The A.P. courses are much, much harder. . . . I can't tell you how easy the regular courses are . . . the teachers spoon-feed those kids . . . there is absolutely no challenge." The distinctions among the "hard and easy courses" are vividly reflected in the weightings attached to each. Every course is "leveled"—a strategy designed to bring parity across the ability groupings and to ensure that the advanced students not be disadvantaged by the more difficult standards required of them. For the weighting of grade point averages, an "A" in an advanced placement course is worth 4.5; 4.25 in a medium-level course; and 4 in a remedial course.

The leveling of *all* courses reflects a new system-wide grading policy that has caused some squabbling within the Highland Park faculty. Some teachers applaud the explicit recognition of categories and view the new policy as a step in the right direction. Others feel strongly that it represents another move away from equality, justice, and integration and see it as a way to guard and coddle the elite at the expense of those who appear to be less able academically. The 1980 policy is a return to the leveling system used thirty years before at Highland Park. In reaction to the severe categories of the 1950s and early 1960s, the late 1960s and 1970s brought a much more open policy that de-emphasized homogeneity. Except for advanced courses in science and math, all classes were heterogeneously grouped.

Old-timers, who have endured all of these shifts in policy and practice, claim that the changes have reflected ideological shifts in the wider community. Ms. Silver, district-wide head of vocational education, has been at the school since the early 1950s. She left teaching for several years when her children were young, but was a close observer of school life when her offspring were attending Highland Park High in the mid-sixties. Ms. Silver takes a long view of the cultural changes and seems cool and unruffled by recent policies that plague some of her younger colleagues. She notices a correspondence between periods of experimentation, rebellion, and political involvement among students and the democratization of academic life. After a conservative period in the early sixties, when "athletics were important, student council was big . . . and a great emphasis was put on prom queens and cheerleading," students abruptly lost interest in the traditional high school activities. They moved into what many teachers refer to as "the hippie period," when they rebelled against conservative attitudes reflected in the curriculum and structure of the school. Football and cheerleading were no longer activities of status, it was hard to get students to run for student council, and student garb changed from neat to purposefully sloppy. Some teachers remember this period as a time when students were "threatening and menacing," when discipline seemed to break down. "You didn't dare tell kids to pick up the orange peel they just dropped on the floor . . . you feared the repercussions." During the tumultuous seventies, Ms. Silver recalls that students turned away from math and science and demanded more nontraditional courses. "There was an awful lot of pressure to do away with sex-bias courses. . . . Girls enrolled themselves in auto mechanics and boys in child development." A few daring boys chose to take home economics—long the exclusive preserve of "feminine" girls.

Now the pendulum has swung back and once again students are making the more conservative choices. For the first time in several years, a large group of girls showed up for cheerleading tryouts and the competition was stiff. Seniors brag about the great success of Homecoming Day this year. They worked hard on elaborate floats, costumes, and activities. "It was really special. . . . We had more spirit than any other year . . . even the teachers got a positive feeling from it . . . and for the first time, the Fort Sheridan kids got involved. . . . From the warehouse on the army base, they let us borrow a massive truck that used to carry missiles and we used it for our float." The new glimmer of school spirit is accompanied by a great preoccupation with grades, class standing, and "courses that count." Almost no boys appear in child development and interior design courses anymore, and girls are content to avoid learning the "masculine" skills of industrial arts and auto mechanics. There is a noticeable return to conservative attitudes and traditional roles.

"Family Living" is the one course in the school that continues to draw a cross section of students. One-third of the senior class chooses "Family Living." It attracts an equal number of boys and girls, and includes students from all ability groups. Part of the attraction is the teacher, Ms. Taylor, who is described by her colleagues as "vivacious, energetic, extremely competent, and demanding," and by some students as "the epitome of someone who cares. . . . She comes up with good ideas and makes you feel like a person, not a number." Another part of the course's popularity seems to be related to the students' perception of its relevance to their lives. They enter the course hoping that it will clarify some of their aching problems, answer their tough questions, and make them feel less alone. These are heavy expectations and unlikely to be met in the context of any single course. Ms. Taylor also notices a recent turn towards conservatism in the students' expectations of the class content. In the past, they would come anticipating support for their non-conformist behavior, wanting reinforcement in pulling away from the confining values and prohibitions of their parents. Now they seem to seek a kind of stability and reassurance from the course. "They talk more about building relationships than about sexuality . . . and recognize how unsatisfactory sex is without friendship," says Ms. Taylor.

The class straggles into the classroom after the bell. Students arrange themselves in an uneven circle on the periphery of the room. The circle is broken at the front of the room by the blackboard, teacher's desk, and a large overhead projector that Ms. Taylor sits next to during the discussions. A woman in her mid-thirties, Ms. Taylor is strikingly blond, slightly plump, and dressed in a white pant suit with high heels. She is confident in manner and smoothly articulate. She never talks down to the students but reveals in her attitudes and behavior a genuine respect for them, and a real concern for "what's on their minds." The course is highly structured with a clear outline, focus, and rationale. The difficult and messy material seems to demand the imposition of structure.

The day I visit the class, Ms. Taylor is concluding a unit on "love relationships" and is going over the outline and assignments for the next unit on "sexuality." "In our sexuality unit, we will be looking at issues of femininity and masculinity . . . are your parents comfortable talking about sexuality? . . . I have recognized some great differences in the background of students. . . . This will not be a local course in sex, we'll be looking more at your questions. . . . There's a whole lot we don't know. . . . The potential for you to do research on sexuality is vast." During her opening statement, most students respond to her obvious enthusiasm with looks of boredom, disinterest, and laziness. Bodies are slouched, eyes half closed, and there is a constant background of conversation.

The outline for the sexuality unit is distributed and Ms. Taylor goes through the list of research paper topics, giving some background information on each major area of inquiry. "Sex education is a controversial subject. . . . At what age should it be taught? . . . Who should teach it? . . . A group of parents in Southern Illinois protested against a private counselling service that was offering sex education to teenagers." Hearing this, a boy in the back of the room says vaguely, "You could sue them. . . . They said they'd get a lot of money." Ms. Taylor, not understanding the connection between her comments and his remark, tries to respectfully decipher what he means. The boy grows impatient with her questioning and withdraws from the conversation. There are other examples of miscommunication. Ms. Taylor uses the word "surrogate" and asks whether anyone knows what it means. No one responds, so she says, "It means substitute," and explains the increasing phenomenon of surrogate mothering. One student, who seems to understand, asks "Is it legal?" to which she responds, "It depends on the state." "I saw that on 'Dallas,'" offers another girl. The conversation is quickly diverted to a more animated discussion of "Dallas" plots—none of which show any connection to surrogate mothering. Ms. Taylor's attempts at explanation are constantly being interrupted by unrelated conversations among students. A redheaded girl exclaims to her neighbor, "You know what Roger just said about you, he said, 'look at Myra's tits,'" which causes laughter all around.

The class deteriorates further when Ms. Taylor begins to go over the details of the written assignment. "A research paper is other people's ideas about a topic you have chosen. . . . The narrower your topic, the better it is. . . . I don't want it any longer than three typewritten pages, double-spaced. . . . You've got to learn to cut out the garbage that doesn't say anything. . . . You need to learn research skills." For the first time students take out their notebooks and write down when the paper is due and "what they have to know." It is the first time that everyone pays attention. As Ms. Taylor goes over the details of footnoting, some students grow increasingly frustrated. There is a rising crescendo of noise that the teacher ignores as she says cooly, "Are there any questions?" "Yeah," answers an angry male voice, "why do we have to do this? . . . We've already had enough papers . . . I know enough to get by." In the midst of her halfhearted attempt to respond to his frustration, the bell sounds to end the period, and Ms. Taylor is besieged with another angry assault from a girl filing out of the classroom. Her voice is shrill and she seems to be losing control. "This is a dumb course. I can't stand it!" Still patient, Ms. Taylor says, "Well why do you say that? Is it because you don't want to do the work?" As the girl brushes furiously past her, she says plaintively, "Don't walk away. Communicate. Well, if not today, communicate tommorrow."

Throughout the entire class, Ms. Taylor has remained cool, patient, and respectful. Although there were a few students who seemed tuned in to her and occasionally asked relevant and substantive questions, most of them appeared lazy and disgruntled. I was amazed at the kind of abuse that Ms. Taylor was able to tolerate and absorb, and asked her about that after class. For the first time, she looks discouraged and frustrated, and begins by excusing the outburst of the girl who left the class yelling at her. "I think she is receiving enormous pressure from home to achieve academically. This is her senior year and her parents are insisting that she get good grades. . . . But she is not very capable intellectually and is struggling in all her courses. . . . She is afraid she won't get into college and is having to face her inadequacies for the first time." Ms. Taylor seems only slightly embarrassed that I have witnessed this exchange; she does not seem to have taken the student's fury personally. Her first response was to reach out to her, then try to search for the origins of her behavior.

However, Ms. Taylor does recognize the more general difficulties in this class and speaks of it as a "hard group to teach." She thinks her problems stem from the broad range of academic abilities and the large number of students with learning and emotional difficulties. Remembering the seating pattern, she is able to identify students at both extremes of the academic continuum and points to a large core of the class who have been labeled as having learning disabilities and behavior disorders. We recall together that the latter group had been responsible for the persistent disruptions throughout the class, and the former had mostly remained silent, occasionally trying to penetrate the chaos with a question or comment.

Most teachers in Highland Park do not have to face mixtures of students or struggle with finding a level of instruction that will not exclude any subgroup of the class. In Ms. Taylor's course, the intellectual content seemed to be defined by her images of the most capable students, but the exchanges and tone were primarily shaped by those who did not understand. In the end, frustration developed, and no one's needs seemed to be met. In her course, "Literary Persuasion," Ms. Wood does not confront this problem. Her course, reserved for the advanced placement students, is strikingly different in substance and mood from "Family Living." The room is traditionally arranged with rows of desks and chairs, and the teacher's desk sits center-front. Four of the twenty-five students are girls. The room is quiet during most of the class except for occasional whispering among neighbors, who seem to be making side comments related to the general discussion. The conversation between Ms. Wood and her students is rarely intense and animated, but they are on the same wavelength and there is an orderly process of raising hands, questioning, and commenting. The flow of the discussion is teacher-directed, but students often initiate lines of thinking or politely challenge Ms. Wood's interpretations. These are the students who expect to attend the prestigious Eastern schools. It is from groups like this that Highland Park's twenty-three National Merit scholars of last year came.

Ms. Wood is a short, curly-haired woman with a wry wit and an intense love of literature. She shows me "the original copy" of the book they are working with, tattered and worn from its many readings. With book in hand, she stands and leans casually against the front of her desk as she thoughtfully and carefully forms her first comments. The class seems to anticipate and enjoy her reflective, ruminative style. Before beginning the discussion, she remembers "the word for the day" written on the board, which is "phlegmatic . . . it is similar to sanguine . . . let's have a good sentence. . . . What does it mean when you refer to a human being as phlegmatic, Lydia?" "Slow to act," responds Lydia without hesitation. This is a ritual that begins each day and most seem prepared to offer the answer.

The discussion centers on Harriet Beecher Stowe's *Uncle Tom's Cabin*, a book the class has been reading and analyzing for the past two weeks. As they find the passages in the book, Ms. Wood begins, "This is a very didactic part of the book. She [Stowe] uses Sinclair really as a mouthpiece. . . . His major character flaw is his indolence. . . . Don't you think he also represents a general human flaw? . . . Where he brings in his own opinion is in the analysis. . . . A slave owner might have a great deal to lose, at least from his own perspective . . . remember we have said that we can't judge the characters by our own standards, we must see them in historical and cultural context." To bolster her analysis, Ms. Wood reads excerpts from the text. She almost seems to be having a conversation with herself when she exclaims in the midst of her reading, "interesting idea, an unorthodox notion."

The discussion fastens on the author's attitudes towards slavery as Wood asks students to contrast Stowe with Frederick Douglass, an autobiography they have recently read. The class is silent and tentative, so the teacher leaps in and says, "Stowe mitigates—aha! one of your vocabulary words from last week—the horror of slavery, but Douglass's book is too extreme . . . it makes people feel uncomfortable, and if you are writing a book of persuasion, you don't want to turn people off." These notions of the limits of truth and the uses of distortion are clearly themes of this course that Ms. Wood often returns to. "Next week you'll be reading Saul Alinsky's book, *Rules for Radicals* . . . a Machiavellian essay that takes the extreme position . . . distortion is all right if it is for honorable ends." Some students—all of the girls—are listening and taking notes, others are yawning and clearly bored by the esoteric distinctions.

Perhaps in response to the faraway looks in her students' eyes, Ms. Wood brings the discussion closer to home. She is trying to reveal the contemporary examples of enslavement all around them. "Having a slave in Highland Park is not the thing to do . . . it's also slightly illegal. But can't you picture how some of the folks here would deal with slaves . . . see them talk with people who work for them. . . . They are just as despicable as Beecher Stowe's characters!" Maybe they hear the urgency in her voice, but the students' faces show no change. I cannot see the face of the one Black boy in the class who sits in the front by the window, but I project pain onto him. How must he feel as this conversation swirls about him? And how does he experience the disinterest and distance of his peers?

The interest of all students becomes suddenly charged when Wood says, "I'll give you a clue . . . in fact, I'll *tell* you one of the questions on the next exam. . . . On the basis of your reading of *The Jungle, Grapes of Wrath, Frederick Douglass,* and *Uncle Tom's Cabin,* which would you rather be, a slave or an English laborer? . . . You have to carefully examine the question of freedom." Hands are immediately raised and responses come from all corners. As students struggle for "the right answer," they do not seem to totally believe Ms. Wood when she claims there is no correct response. She is looking for a reasoned argument, a thoughtful interpretation, and creative insight. They are trying to come up with what she wants to hear.

The students in "Literary Persuasion" have a sense of their special status in the school. They are part of the elite, the top group of academic achievers, and their lofty position protects them from the distractions of those less competent. In a school of such great size, students search for pockets of safety and connection. Academic excellence insures some degree of special treatment and separation from the masses, but the most protected spot in the school seems to be the drama department, where students receive heavy doses of nurturance and love from Ms. Newbury.

At fifty-one, she is just as theatrical and enthusiastic as she was when she won the best actress award at the University of Wisconsin thirty years ago. With gray-blond hair swept back from her face, a voice that projects across footlights and into the balcony, and a carriage that is both confident and elegant, Ms. Newbury is a seductive force among her students. They crowd around her like disciples; worship the ground she walks on. In turn, she offers bountiful affection and personal caring. Her graduates return year after year for her hugs and reinforcement, and the student theater is a home away from home for Newbury's special group.

The student theater is a large room with a stage, scattered chairs, pieces of discarded scenery, and rugs to lie on. Students spread out on the floor and sit on tables and chairs as they listen intently to Ms. Newbury's words. She weaves the web of intimacy.

> "My dears, this place offers an infusion—good word?—of comradeship. It is a built-in family . . . a built-in connection. . . . We will always have this tie. I look around for you because this is your place, your space . . . a magic place. . . . All our ghosts are here."

The delivery is perfect, her voice soothing and soft. No doubt it is a performance, but it is also experienced as genuine by students, who hear every word. Gone is the grubbing for grades and the cramming for tests. For this moment in time, the students seem far away from the rugged competition.

However, intimacy and good feeling is not all Newbury is after. She is also determined that her students will be introduced to the rigors and demands of acting and her standards are very high. She is fond of saying, "This is information that may be beyond you yet . . . you are so young . . . but you see I trust you enough to tell you this now and I know one day it will penetrate . . . and you will understand. . . ."

The class has just finished a screening of *Rebel Without A Cause,* a film classic starring James Dean and Natalie Wood. Students sprawled in front of the screen are still dazed by the powerful drama when Ms. Newbury begins her elegant critique of the film. Her comments are a mixture of lessons in technique, morality, and dramatic expression.

On morality: "I noticed you laughing at the Black maid. Why? Why? She is a paid housekeeper in that very wealthy home. . . . She was the *only* one there to love and care for James Dean. Do you find that funny? I find that touching and unbelievable."

On technique: "There are all kinds of remarkable things about this film. Watch James Dean and you'll have a mini-course in acting. He does things so

146

naturally that others of us would have to practice over and over. He's never, never melodramatic."

On emotional expression: "When Dean crumbles into tears and embraces the man, our first response to that is denial. We joke, experience disbelief. You say, 'I don't believe it. I'm numb. I refuse to feel this' . . . and then it hits you. . . . This, my dears, was a hard show to see. I wanted you to listen to Natalie Wood. Remember she said, "'I've been looking for someone to love me. Now I've found some one to love and it's easy.'" Listen to her words carefully. Learn it and learn it soon."

Newbury's words express themes that haunt the life of this school and this community, but often go unnoticed and unexpressed. She beseeches her students to become conscious of the hidden dogma, to work against the psychic malaise, bigotry, and isolation of their lives, and oppose the priorities and values of their families and culture.

Like most public schools, Highland Park reflects the community of which it is a part. Yet here the institutional boundaries between school and town appear even more penetrable than usual. Parents take an unusually active and initiating role in supporting and challenging the school. The reverberations of family crises, community conflicts, and economic cycles are felt within the walls of the school. Dr. Kline judges that most of the severely troubled children come from families of divorce, separation, or desertion. "It is not unusual in this town to have a mother living in a $200,000 house with four kids and a father living separately in a high-rise apartment in Chicago. With more affluence, there is more to lose. Because there are plentiful resources, people feel they should be able to handle the stress and are panicked when they can't. . . . I've seen some kids go from riches to rags in the midst of divorce. . . . There is enormous loss and anger."

Beyond the cases of extreme crisis, however, one senses that life within the school mirrors, and perhaps exaggerates, the culture and tone of the wider community. The divisions of race, ethnicity, and class, for example, are dramatically played out in the battles among Italians and Jews and the more subtle exclusion of Blacks and Latinos. Also, the general turn toward conservatism in American society is expressed in the building of more extreme hierarchies, a preoccupation with grades, and vigorous competition among students. Some observers claim that the healthy separations between community and school have noticeably eroded during the past several years. With barriers down, the school no longer serves as an asylum, a retreat from the real world for adolescents. Students do not perceive of school as a place where they can feel a part of a closely knit and accepting community. In fact, in school it is more likely that they will experience a heightened sense of exclusion and separation.

Parents, who were themselves students at Highland Park, worry that "the tone" of the school has dramatically changed. Students turn away from it, rather than towards it. Everyone notices the great increase in students who work after school; not so much because they need the money, but because they want to feel productive and useful, and because they want to feel connected to something larger than themselves. Benson comments nostalgically on changes in the centrality of the school experience, "School used to be the focus. Now it's the satellite in students' lives."

There are some indications that students are beginning to feel the need for a more invigorating school life; that they want to help create a place with which they can identify and feel proud. This year's homecoming was initiated by students and they were pleased with the crowds it attracted, the recognition it received, and the way it pulled people together. The enthusiasm for school clubs and after-school activities reflects the same wish by students for connection and involvement. As one put it, "I like the extra stuff, not the inner stuff of school." In the after-school drama, we see a kind of student comraderie, responsibility, and initiative that is not evident in most classes during the school day. The strong, aggressive girl who is directing more than a hundred of her peers in the annual, student-written production seems bored and unchallenged in her psychology class. In these courses, where students seem to be spirited and involved, there is often a larger network of relationships that sustains them beyond the commitments of a single course. The theater department is such a place of refuge.

Most students are not captured by these involvements, however. The clubs, activities, and networks only include those who are highly skilled, determined, or well-connected. For the outsiders, life at Highland Park can be disconnected and lonely. It is not the fault of teachers who work hard at challenging the status quo. They see the connections between the grueling competition, parental pressure, and student isolation, and they fight the aggressive rivalries by pointing their students toward the substance of the inquiry. Most teachers appear unusually responsive and respectful of students, actively encouraging relationships that will counter the depersonalization of the setting. When students show distress signals, teachers are quick to pick them up. Dr. Kline claims, "My work would not be possible without the active support of the teachers. If I have a student who needs help, I can count on getting the support and cooperation of his teachers. They respond confidently and professionally."

The top students, geared towards high-powered colleges, receive a similar kind of unusual care and recognition. Their special courses provide sources of identification and prestige. Not only are they driven by their deeply instilled momentum, but their trajectory is applauded by the wider community. They have high visibility and acclaim—in fact, their success shapes the primary public image of Highland Park. But for those students who are not dramatically achieving or in the midst of a visible crisis—the regular kids—Highland Park is a place they pass through unnoticed. The structure and tone of the school encourage their invisibility. Against the landscape of affluence and plenty, their neglect seems pointedly distressing.

IV

Brookline High School

Emerging Forms of Authority and Diversity

URBAN AND SUBURBAN IMAGES

The town of Brookline carves a triangular shape into neighboring Boston. It is bordered on three sides by Boston and on the west by Newton. Its proximity to the big city and the easy movement across town borders give Brookline a mixed image. Some consider it an urban community and even boast of its cosmopolitan spirit, lack of pretentiousness, and streetcars that can take inhabitants into the middle of Boston in fifteen minutes. These people enjoy the relative safety, affluence, and status of Brookline along with the bustling, heterogeneous, sophisticated character of city life. They can "have their cake and eat it too." In some ways, they feel more fortunate that their neighbors to the west who live a more suburban life, isolated from the mood and tone of the city. There are other Brookline citizens, however, who cling to its suburban, protected image and who underscore the differences in status and style between Brookline and Boston. They feel more identification with the habits and values of the people in Newton, Wellesley, and Lexington; and discourage their children from thinking of Boston as their neighboring playground. Depending upon whom you talk to, then, Brookline is variously described as an urban or a suburban community. For different reasons, the description is voiced with pride.

For people who see Brookline from afar, it has a homogeneous image of affluence and prestige. Outsiders tend to envisage large, stately homes, lush green lawns, well-tended hedges, and two-car garages. Inside the garages they imagine sturdy top-of-the-line Volvos, smooth BMWs, an occasional elegant Mercedes. Some even imagine the less sophisticated, opulent Cadillacs and Buicks parked in the garages of the more recently affluent who have not yet developed the taste that should accompany their class. A dominant part of the Brookline image is connected to Jewish stereotypes. The community is seen as largely Jewish, with characteristics often associated with successful Jews—a commitment to education; an aggressiveness about business matters; a heightened concern and protectiveness for their offspring; a sense of entitlement in relation to schools and other community institutions. A less vivid part of the stereotypic image portrays the town's people as enlightened and liberal, protective of civil liberties and resistant to the reactionary cultural and political trends. As with most stereotypes, this portrait of Brookline is largely inaccurate. It misses the mark partly because it exaggerates and caricatures the qualities of a group of people who express a broad range of styles and characteristics; and partly because the community is not nearly so uniform with regard to religion, ethnicity, and social class. The homogeneous image lags far behind the heterogeneous and diverse reality. Like most anachronistic labels, it often seems to obscure the great changes that are occurring in the community and seems to diminish the efforts of many who work hard at adapting to the social and cultural shifts.

In fact, as one seeks to capture internal rather than external perceptions of Brookline, the emphasis of people's remarks is on diversity. Students in the high school all speak of the many groups that form the school, of reaching out beyond racial and religious boundaries, of cliques that inhibit friendships with other kinds of kids. The teachers all speak of searching out pedagogical strategies and curricula that would be appropriate for a broader range of students. Beyond the walls of the school, a visitor is likely to see an old Chinese grandfather dressed in a simple gray cotton suit caring for his young grandchild at the park. Next to them on the park bench is a recent Russian immigrant mother, head tied with a peasant scarf, dressed in layers of sweaters who is bending over her child protectively. Her son looks all-American in his blue and white warm-up suit. Neither adult speaks any English. The offspring play with each other using the silent language of very small children, interspersed with Russian, Chinese and English.

An elderly woman in the supermarket, dramatically dressed in a silver fur jacket, black velvet slacks, plentiful face make-up, and a bouffant hairdo, complains that the town has changed for the worse. "It used to be a real community of like-minded people . . . and now I don't feel safe walking the streets in the late afternoon." Her comment is inspired by the actions of a Black teenage boy who has darted in front of her at the check-out counter. When he zoomed in front of her in line, making a high car-squeal and smiling, she had used her cart as a weapon. Growing increasingly outraged, she pushed her cart with great force into his thighs and backside. He responded with a wider grin, "Old lady, you're crazy!" The woman had sought my alliance when she spoke to me of the deteriorating neighborhood. Despite the image of privilege and stability, therefore, townspeople seem to be coping with diversity and change. One cannot help wondering whether the old image of outsiders and the nostalgia of old-timers combine to resist the new reality.

Brookline is a town of 55,000 people. The diversity of the town is reflected in the wide range of income among residents, from a median income level of $9,949 per family in the central village area, to $23,021 in South Brookline. Incomes in Brookline have not been rising as rapidly as those in some surrounding communities. Per capita income in Brookline rose 25.4 percent between 1969 and 1974, whereas income in the state as a whole rose 39.6 percent. Some Brookline residents, weary of their inaccurate image of affluence, point to places like Dover and Lincoln, where "real wealth" resides. In Dover, the landed gentry own large parcels of land and keep their horses in private stables. Their riding gear is impeccable; their horses are beautifully groomed. In Lincoln, zoning ordinances protect citizens from the threat of close neighbors. Creative, modern homes of redwood and glass look out over magnificent vistas. And 200-year-old houses, perfectly restored and cared for, nestle comfortably in the wooded landscape. A few years ago, no Black families lived in Lincoln. A single Black boy, adopted by a white family, suffered taunts and abuse from his schoolmates as he rode the bus to school. All the parents of the children involved were horrified. The episode did not match their liberal image of themselves. Many Brookline "liberals" compare these towns with theirs when trying to assert their identity as a hetereogeneous town of "real people."

As a matter of fact, rental units account for 72 percent of the housing market in Brookline. With an increasing trend toward condominium conversion, there is a very low housing vacancy rate (2 percent). Forty percent of the housing is under rent control and 7.5 percent is subsidized. There is a continued demand for assisted housing with about 400 low income family units at present. The economic base of Brookline is predominantly residential. Less than one percent of the land remains vacant. The industrial base of the town is divided into three business categories: wholesale and retail trade; finance, insurance, and real estate; and services.

But when Brookline residents refer to the "real world" quality of their town they are usually not commenting on the economic base, but on the population shifts which have become increasingly visible. A list of the ethnic and racial groups which form the town's citizenry reads like an idealized melting pot—Asians (including Chinese, Korean, Japanese, and Vietnamese), Blacks, Hispanics, Israelis, Russians, Irish, and East Indians. Although the population of the town has remained relatively stable over the last decade (with a 6.2 percent drop, from 58,689 to 55,062), the minority population has increased more than four times (from 695 to 3,110). The number of Blacks has increased from 487 to 1,060; those of Spanish origin from 656 to 1,162; and Asian and Pacific Islanders from 1,379 to 2,662. Many residents are proud of their town's willingness in reaching out to strangers and believe that the reputation for receptivity has encouraged the increasing numbers of minorities. Others worry that their town may not be able to absorb the influx of foreigners without losing its sense of identity, stability, and order; and an increasingly vocal minority resists the changes and fears the repercussions of diversity. This latter group feels besieged, intruded upon, and threatened by the growing number of minority faces.

Incorporated in 1705, Brookline is an old town with a rich history. Many of the fine, stately homes built in the eighteenth century have been restored and identified as historical sights. Some nineteenth-century sites are being rehabilitated, often with federal assistance. Townspeople are proud of the robust and sturdy architecture and seem to want to recapture as many of the old buildings as possible. The old parts of town, with majestic single-family dwellings, are in sharp contrast with the more ordinary apartment buildings and two-family homes that crowd next to one another in less affluent areas.

South Brookline, the section of greatest wealth, has many opulent homes hidden behind protective walls with long circular driveways leading up to the door. Houses are secluded and there is an emphasis on privacy. Mercedeses purr along the winding roads and joggers enjoy the

153

solitude of early morning runs when all seems still and untouched. After the first snow of winter, the land appears virginal. A path made by cross-country skis is barely visible across the smooth white landscape.

After the first snow comes a few miles away in Coolidge Corner, the town sends out its plows immediately to clear the streets for safe driving. Soon the pace of life resumes, people bustle among the shops and offices; and the snow becomes a dark city-brown. The action in this part of town moves at a different pace from the protected enclave of South Brookline. Moving in and out of the stores, one is likely to see the faces of elderly, widowed ladies, large Irish families, a group of Chinese adolescents, and a young Black boy being pulled by his big, galloping dog. Coolidge Corner is the major business district of Brookline with several drug stores, fruit markets, shoe salons, a movie theater, fast-food spots, and an amazing number of optometrists selling hundreds of styles of glasses. There are stores that appeal to sophisticated tastes—a very expensive women's wear shop that sells designer originals; a chic French restaurant that has a fine wine list and an irresistible pastry tray; and a lovely shop for home furnishings that has original ceramics, jazzy dishes, and subtle tapestries. There are shops that serve the ordinary needs of people—a well-equipped hardware store, a shoe store specializing in orthopedic models, a modestly priced clothing store for men and women, a delicatessen and a Woolworth's. There are excellent delicatessens, a Japanese gift shop, a large health food store, and a fancy cheese store where customers get expert advice on the subtle taste distinctions in Bries. There seems to be something for everyone. The center of Brookline's business district is lively and diverse.

As one moves away from Coolidge Corner, the town becomes residential. Collections of stores, usually serving the everyday needs of people, are found grouped throughout residential areas. There is a growing business enclave close to Brookline High School that serves the immediate neighborhood, but also has begun to attract people from the other parts of town. Most people come to this area to buy pastries, cakes, and bread from the Tour Eiffel Bakery, an establishment some Boston-area people describe as "the best bakery in town." Others come to poke around in the very large, well-stocked hardware store where you can find everything from roof shingles to car antifreeze or contact paper for kitchen shelves. The rest of the shops on this corner reflects the emerging mixture of styles and needs. A Chinese laundry is squeezed in between a twenty-four hour food market and a used furniture store. Beside the bakery is a shop that claims to have fancy antiques. Across the street, there is a laundry, a custom tailor, a shade store, and a delicatessen. A short distance down the street, but within easy view, is the Brookline Public Library—a stately brick building with a newly constructed wing that blends nicely with the older structure. A large statue of a man on horseback guards the library entrance. Just down the hill is the Pierce School, a modern building with bridges crossing the street below. It is one of the largest elementary schools in Brookline. Like all of the other elementary schools in town, it has a distinct identity and reputation.

Graduates of the Pierce School have to travel only five blocks more to get to the High School. Along the path from Pierce to the high school there are a few brick structures of several stories that used to be comfortable apartments and are now advertised as deluxe condominiums. The houses along the way are mostly large, wood frame buildings painted in pale New England shades. They are two-family dwellings with well-tended gardens and lawns and newly painted shingles. These houses appear somewhat crowded. Given their scale and elaborate detail, they seem to ask for more space than the few yards on either side for driveways and hedges. In a big, old, rambling house there is a nursery school with an elaborate wooden climbing toy in the front yard. The only sounds of life I hear when I arrive in this neighborhood midmorning are shrieks of laughter from young children coming down the long slide. A father arrives at the nursery school with his daughter in a backpack. She is dressed in a bright gold turtleneck and Oshkosh overalls, which seems to be the uniform for both boys and girls on the playground. Two blocks away and around the corner from this lively scene is Brookline High School.

When classes are in session, the mood is quiet around the school. On the morning of my first visit, it is early fall and feels like back-to-school weather. The air is crisp, the breezes fresh, and the trees are beginning to turn orange and yellow. A lonely boy carrying books walks casually towards the school, carelessly kicking the fallen leaves. On the long green field in front of the school, gym classes are being held. Athletic coaches dressed in light windbreakers and wearing whistles, stop the action occasionally and offer suggestions for improving playing skills. Young male bodies glide up and down the field playing an uneven game of soccer. Some are awkward, even afraid of the ball; others are reticent; still others appear more proficient and engaged in the game. On an adjoining field, there is a touch football game with boys and girls playing. Neither of these gym classes has attracted athletic types. The involvement of students ranges from disinterest and boredom to mild pleasure. The atmosphere is slightly lazy and the gym teachers do not push their charges to compete. None of the edge and vitality of competitive sports is evident. At the other end of the long green expanse is a playground for children that includes a handsomely designed jungle gym, swings, and benches. Bleachers and a basketball court separate the playing fields and the children's playground. While I am watching the gym classes work out, three- and four-year-olds from the nearby nursery school arrive at the playground. Fourteen children, with two teachers supervising their activity, attack the climbing toy and swings with energy and exuberance. Their obvious enthusiasm and high energy are in sharp contrast with the self-conscious and studied casualness of the adolescents at the other end of the field.

Three buildings form Brookline High School—a main building, a recently built athletic building, and an old brick structure that is in the process of being renovated for industrial arts classes. The renovations are well behind schedule; the money budgeted for the construction has already been depleted; and no one seems to know if the building will ever be occupied. The athletic facility houses the swimming pool, dance studies; well-equipped locker rooms, wrestling rooms, basketball courts, offices, and classrooms. Like many modern structures, it is difficult not to get lost in the maze of doorways, stairwells, and passages.

The entryway to this building is one of the favorite places to "hang out" for "jocks" and their entourages. Basketball players, tall and lean, stand in front of the gymnasium. They "shoot the bull" with each other and sometimes can be seen practicing their "moves" against invisible opponents. Many of the players are Black, impeccably dressed in their studied casual clothes, and often carrying expensive-looking duffle bags. The football players also gather outside the gym but they are harder to identify. They come in assorted sizes and shapes although some match the stereotypic image of brute and brawn. The jocks have a private language which is hard for a stranger to penetrate and decode. They gather in small circles and talk about "scores, moves, and fakes." There are often a number of girls hanging around the edges of these circles, rarely entering into the jock exchanges but choosing instead to gossip with one another. The girls tend to be special friends, often "steadies" of the athletes or cheerleaders. During my visits, I rarely saw young women athletes gathered outside the gym and often wondered whether they had favorite hangouts or a private language.

The main building, built in 1949, is a three-story brick structure. It is solidly built, with the classic academic symbols. Heavy, stately columns, three on either side of the door, support a wooden overhang upon which is printed "Brookline High School." A small circular driveway, no longer used, leads up to the central door. On the right side, as you face the building, are several steps leading up to bright blue doors which enter into the old gymnasium. On the left-hand side is the entrance that is used most often by students, teachers, and visitors.

One can also enter the building through a courtyard, a quadrangle surrounded by the building on all four sides. My footsteps echo as I walk across the courtyard cobblestones. As I face the back of the quad, there are two sets of steps, one on my left and one on my right. Groups of students are sitting or standing on them. On the steps to my right, five boys sit one next to the other in a straight row. Their conversation is minimal, and what they do say is delivered with their heads down, talking to the ground. Occasionally, a loud crack of laughter ricochets off the four inner walls of the building before silence settles back into the courtyard. On the left steps in front of me is a more fluid group of boys and girls. Individuals move in and out of the group as they enter and leave the building. They sit or stand, talking to one another in groups of two or three. Their mood appears serious, and their conversations focused. Like the front of the gym, the courtyard stairs are favorite hangouts for students. After a few days at the high school, I become familiar with who is in charge of what territory. On first glance, it already appears that the stance and style of the groups assembled in the courtyard are different from the jocks and their friends outside the gym.

Inside, the smell of years of chalk dust sifted down between the planks of old wood floors reminds me that I am in school. One teacher describes Brookline High as an "archetype." As I walk through the halls—with light brown and golden-colored bricks, institutional green and pale blue walls, low ceilings, and narrow walkways—it feels as if I am walking back in time. The bathrooms—free of graffiti and amazingly clean—feel almost antique. The low-hanging, dim lights have recently been replaced by more modern fluorescent ones that have less character but offer more light. But the heavy wooden doors on the stalls, the brass latches, the occasional marble decorative features, and the black and white tile floors, have survived the decades beautifully. Brookline High is comfortable and old feeling—free of the modern sleek lines, open spaces, and bright lights of many modern school structures. Over the generations, the building seems to have been used with care; not neglected or abused. An elderly woman, who cleans the building every afternoon, expresses affection for the old structure. We run into each other in a woman's faculty room which is full of tired and shabby furniture. With a strong Irish brogue she says: "This is a cozy corner. I come here for my cup of tea every afternoon. Don't you like the musty smell?"

Although the sights and smells of the school feel almost anachronistic, the people and action are strikingly contemporary. Like the town of Brookline, the tone of the school is reflected in the combined images of an urban and suburban school. It is not crowded by tall city buildings or surrounded by the clamor of traffic and commerce like most urban schools. The scale of the building in relation to the surrounding landscape gives it a gracious, almost stately quality. The doors to the building are never locked during school hours; there are no bars on the wide windows; no school guards stop you in the halls to inquire about your reasons for being there. Brookline High, therefore, has the relatively safe and secluded appearance of many suburban schools, but it does not have the sprawling, opulent appearance that often characterizes them. There are no large parking lots reserved for teachers' and students' cars. Everyone competes for parking along the nearby neighborhood streets, along one side of the green field in front of the school or in the precious few spaces around and behind the new gym. The streetcar that stops a few blocks away from the school connects Brookline with Boston and adds to the urban tone of the place.

When students begin to pour out of the school at the end of the day, one is convinced of the visible tension between urban and suburban images. Immediately one senses a mixture of students that is rare in any high school. Some look like stereotypes of suburban affluence and others have the style of more sophisticated, guarded city types. There is not the uniform dress that I have seen in many high schools, neither is there a Brookline "look" that is distinctive. A diminutive Chinese girl, dressed in black slacks and a purple windbreaker and carrying an orange backpack that seems half her size, heads to her ten-speed bicycle, unlocks it, and speeds away. Two studious-looking girls with long straight hair and pale skin walk away from school very slowly. They are deep in conversation. One carries a cello, the other a case which looks as if it is the size of an oboe. A group of stocky, wide-shouldered boys talk loudly as they walk towards a green pickup. They pile inside, crowding in the front, turn on the radio to a blaring rock and roll station, light up cigarettes, and squeal away from the curb. A tall, lean Black boy, smartly dressed and smooth in gait, has his arms wrapped around a much shorter, pretty Black girl. They walk away from school without seeming to notice the crowds of students swirling around them; alone together. Not only are the students diverse in color, style, and dress; one hears many languages spoken— Spanish, Chinese, Russian, and English in its myriad forms.

A RICH DIVERSITY: CONFRONTING REALITIES

No matter who you talk to about Brookline High School, the first thing mentioned is the diversity of the student body. Faculty, students, and administrators seem to want to correct the outdated, anachronistic images of the school that portray an elite suburban enclave. Bob McCarthy, the school's headmaster, says enthusiastically, "People used to say diversity was a weakness. Now we are saying diversity is a strength. This is an important shift in orientation for faculty, students, and the community." A prominent Black faculty member echoes McCarthy's optimism, "Brookline is a special place. I've never seen a better mixture of kids. You've got a little United Nations." A thoughtful, pretty sophomore who sits next to me in history class tells about the enlivening quality of diversity, "I went to a strict, Catholic elementary school where everyone was the same, very protected and very sterile. When I first came to this school I felt afraid of all the different types of kids. But now I feel *challenged* by all the different groups and much less afraid." Even those who assert the great advantages of a multi-ethnic school admit the tensions and conflicts among the groups. Says one new arrival to the school, "This is a very cliquish, very separatist place . . . I don't know where to break into the circle. . . . For every friend I make, there is an enemy."

There are 2,100 students in Brookline High School, with 20 administrators, 150 teachers, and 40 adults in other professional capacities (e.g., guidance counselors, social workers, career counselors, etc.). Thirty percent of the student body is minority, the largest proportion being Asian (including Chinese, Japanese, Korean, Indian, and Iranian in significant numbers). Twelve percent of the student body is Black. Half of those come from Boston's METCO Program* and half are indigenous to Brookline. Class divides this group. Most of the METCO students come from working-class backgrounds, and their Brookline peers tend to be offspring of professional, upper-middle-class parents. Says Bob McCarthy, "Historically they have been pressured into behaving as a group," despite their differences in background and experience. Another observer who is close to both groups claims that the divisions between METCO

---

*The METCO (Metropolitan Council for Educational Opportunity), now twelve years old, serves youngsters from the greater Boston area who travel to Brookline and other metropolitan communities for the educational opportunities not available in their own communities. Most of the METCO high school students have been in the Brookline schools since first or second grade. Brookline is the only METCO program where students can take public transportation rather than being bused to the school.

and Brookline Blacks are unfortunate but inevitable. "Brookline Blacks *naturally* take on the feelings, attitudes, and ways of the kids they've grown up with. I call it elitism. It never flares out in the open. There are no fights between them . . . but it bothers me. Maybe I am at fault. Maybe I want Black folks to be *too* close."

Forty percent of the students are Jewish, largely from upper middle-class families. The Jewish population in the school is declining as parents grow worried about the increasing diversity and what they perceive to be lowering standards. McCarthy claims that there has been a noticeable migration of Jewish families to the more distant and protected suburbs of Newton, Lincoln, and Concord. For the most part, the elementary schools in Brookline still enjoy a superior reputation and continue to attract the offspring of high-powered, academic-minded citizens. But the high school no longer has its old appeal as an elite school. Parents who have the resources and who are concerned about status and standards have begun to search out private schools for their adolescents, or move to more homogeneous towns.

The remaining thirty percent of the population reflects a mixture of white students from a variety of ethnic and social class backgrounds. The one visible and identifiable subgroup of students from this last category is Irish Catholic and working class. Known as the "Point" kids because they are from the High Point section of Brookline, they are long-time residents of the town. Most of their parents were students at Brookline High; many of their mothers work as secretaries in the school; and their fathers "keep the town running" as policemen, firemen, sanitation workers and mail-men. The Point kids are 10 percent of the student population and have a reputation as tough kids. "Historically they have battled with whatever group is lowest on the totem pole," says McCarthy. Their current com-petitors are the Black METCO students whom they claim receive more attention and resources than they do. They view the Black kids as advan-taged interlopers and often take out their feelings of deprivation and rage on this group. A teacher who has worked closely with the Point kids for a decade offers a different analysis of their hostility. "They feel this school really *belongs* to them. . . . They have always felt resentful of the upper middle-class Jewish kids whose image forms the public stereotype of the school. But the Irish kids feel the privileged Jewish kids are unavailable to receive their hostility—in some sense they are invulnerable—so they take out their anger on Black kids."

The diversity of the student population is additionally heightened by the presence of numerous language groups. One hundred and ninety students, about 10 percent of the population, speak English as a second language: they represent more than fifty-five languages, originated in twenty-five countries. Some of these students speak very little English and have great difficulty communicating with their teachers and peers. An increasing number of Russian Jews, recently immigrated from their homeland, speak no English and require special attention and expertise. A three-year, federally-funded bilingual program, called Project Welcome, seeks to reach out to the new arrivals, offering support and guidance.

Beyond the special programs for foreign students, the school curriculum seeks to be adaptive to their needs. "U.S. History for Foreign Students" is a good example of a social studies course offered for new arrivals with limited proficiency in English.

The teacher is a woman in her mid-thirties. Her wavy red hair hangs nearly to her waist. A hank of hair is gathered on top of her head in a coiled braid. Her pale skin is lightly freckled and her eyes sparkle light brown. The classroom is arranged so that all the chairs form a circle. Meredith, as she introduces herself to me and is called by the students, refreshes the students' memories concerning the day's lesson. "Today we'll hear from the Committee on Leadership." It seems that the class has divided into six committees. Each committee must report back to the entire class and all the students must reach a consensus before proceeding to the next committee report. The idea behind this course is shared by two teachers, both of whom are in the classroom. Although Meredith is teaching, Robert Hall, her co-teacher, is in the room observing the action.

Meredith asks Kay, a Korean girl, to sit front and center of the group to give the Committee on Leadership report. Meredith smiles at Kay, leaning down toward her, and coaxes her to begin reading. She speaks gently and with warmth and soon Kay begins to read from her report. Meredith writes Kay's points on the board. Kay comes to a word which she tries to read and just shakes her head. Smiling, she looks into her lap, shaking her head back and forth. Meredith moves quickly to her side and reads the words quietly to Kay. As she moves back to the blackboard she says, "It's alright Kay, you're doing just fine." Kay's smooth oval face is framed by black hair that falls in soft, sculpted waves to her shoulders. Her lips frame the words before she speaks them in a soft, tentative voice.

Another student walks into the room and stops to talk in Spanish to two other students sitting at the edge of the circle. Meredith moves toward him, motioning him to sit down. While this is going on, Kay is trying to read point number four. The other student settled, Meredith walks over to Kay and apologizes. "Kay, I'm sorry, I missed that. What was number four?"

All points on the board, Meredith says, "I think I understand Kay's points. Let me repeat them." She checks with Kay when she is unsure. The committee has developed seven recommendations. Meredith says to the class, "What questions do you have?" Silence in the room. "Does everyone agree that we need a leader?"

One boy questions why only the representatives of the six committees get to choose the leader. Meredith is listening intently to him. She leans gently over

Kay. "Kay, do you think you can explain your committee's reason?" Kay just shakes her head, her faint smile looking more fixed. Meredith turns back to the student. "Norris, why don't you develop your reasons for another way of selecting a leader?" The room is silent. She asks, "Does everyone understand the issue? No? Let me draw a diagram." Most of the students face the board and appear to listen.

There are four Venezuelan students in the room. I am able to locate them by their orientation to one another in the room. One of the two girls asks a question. "Can one of the representatives be a leader too?" Kay says, "No." "Why not?" questions Sophia. "Just tell me why not." Kay begins to respond, but stumbles on a word. She seems to shrivel in her chair. She shakes her head back and forth. Meredith moves close to her. "Kay, just take a deep breath, it's hard I know."

One of the Ethiopian students offers yet another alternative. Meredith works hard to keep the choices in front of the students by writing them into her diagram. She watches the students' faces carefully and moves quickly around the room, touching students gently.

Lugo points to the diagram saying, "I don't understand very much. Will you explain?" The request "Will you explain?" is one that Meredith uses a lot to encourage students to amplify their responses. The students seem to have picked up the question and use it in their questions to her and to each other. Meredith speaks clearly, slowly, and patiently. She leans forward urging words out of the students.

"We need some more opinions from some other people. Lenora, what do you think? Would you please give me your reasons? This is not just a vote, I'm looking for your opinions."

A second Ethiopian student, a tall, thin young man, speaks very softly. Meredith is by his side in a moment. She asks him to speak louder for all to hear. "I can't," he murmurs. Meredith urges, "Speak to Sophia across the room." Meredith leans down, "I know you speak quietly, you always do." She smiles fully on him, "Okay you speak to me and I'll shout it out for you."

There is no talking among the students. They shift in their chairs so that there is an occasional creak. One of the Venezuelan girls exchanges flirtatious glances with Lugo on the other side of the room. Lenora is dressed in pink—pink sweat pants, pink socks, pink sneakers, and a pink shirt under a pastel blue sweater. Her makeup is dramatic and she is singing to herself, keeping time with her head. Meredith barely touches her shoulder, "Lenora?" Lenora stops her rhythmic motion.

As class breaks, the Venezuelan students speak in Spanish to one another and the Chinese, Korean and Ethiopian students likewise seek each other out for a few moments of easy conversation. For Meredith, it has been an energetic session. She has moved among the students, watching them carefully, helping them to frame their words, assisting them in whatever ways she could. In a later conversation, she turns the same full, warm smile on me and says, "I can't help it. I get a kick out of the students. I like them."

When people speak of ethnic and racial separations at the high school, they are usually not referring to the national groups represented in "U.S. History for Foreign students." Rather, they are speaking about the visible categories of the more entrenched groups—the Blacks, the Asians, the Jews, and the Irish. Luke Simon, a social worker who is revered as "The Saint" by students and faculty alike, has been intimately and unflinchingly involved in the "interracial stuff" since he came to the school fourteen years ago. He has carefully watched "how this community receives strangers" and his observations recognize the great progress and the profound resistance to mixing among the groups. When he first came to Brookline, he remembers the Irish kids casting aspersions on "those fucking Jews." The Irish resented the abilities and agressiveness of the Jewish students and responded with "territoriality and physical prowess." Fourteen years later, Simon feels that the school is much more of a melting pot. "The old Jewish liberal spirit still exists. . . . There is good will for people and strong commitment to the philosophy and goals of public education." As minority groups grow in size and visibility, the school has had to find ways of adapting to their presence. Simon underscores the emerging tensions: "As the number of Black kids has gotten larger, this has become more *their* place. . . . This puts a new kind of stress on the institution which has not been wholly played out. There continues to be a small core of resistance . . . status games . . . and old-timers still resist surrendering their town to newcomers." Given the severe territoriality of a decade ago, Luke Simon finds these reverberations promising. "I'm very optimistic . . . I don't feel as much tension as I used to. . . . There are always lots of kids who want to take risks to reach out and know other kinds of kids, to cross the barriers."

Simon is wary of stereotypes, categories, and myths about groups. He knows the danger of static, dogmatic perceptions and recognizes the great variations within groups. When I ask him to characterize the ethnic and social groups in the school, he flinches at first and then risks the misunderstandings and inaccuracies of speaking in global terms. He is not the kind of liberal who says everyone is the same. He is a tough realist who recognizes the humanity in all people but perceives the striking cultural differences in style and values. Perhaps he believes that facing the differences and admitting the separations are the first steps toward tolerance and acceptance. I am impressed by the insight, pragmatism, and daring of his characterizations:

> "Irish kids screw themselves. . . . They have directed their energy into a negative tradition, shut down their horizons. . . . Are they going to always have these attitudes? We should try to challenge the way they feel . . . help them to see the beauty in other people . . . I think this is their last chance, and ours, to help them.
>
> "I feel out of touch with the Chinese kids. We don't see many of them

in our roles as social workers. They just don't get in trouble. . . . They seem to invisibly move through the building. . . . They must have a rich private life. Their publication, *The Inner Voice*, speaks about their mode of expression.

"The Black kids are spiritually and physically together. They are as one—not just in a hostile way but in a supportive way. They don't want to be messed over. If anyone is the target still, it is the Black kids. For people who grow up needing an enemy, they are the great, visible target . . . but that is being gnawed at from every possible angle."

The differences seem extreme, but they grow less pronounced with each year. School seems to be a good setting to work out hostilities, to straddle barriers, and to test the assumptions of stereotypes. Says Simon poignantly, "Sometimes Brookline High School has to deal with the waves of tension coming out of the city. At times I've thought of this building as a sanctuary . . . away from the more painful street stuff."

The racial and ethnic cleavages are exaggerated by the long-established "leveling"system. Although almost everyone claims that students are not tracked, there are four definable levels of instruction: Basic, Standard, Honors, and Advanced Placement. (Some departments, like social studies, have three levels: Standard, Honors, and Advanced Placement.) Students are assigned to these levels through an elaborate combination of self-representation and choice, parental preference, testing, former grades and standing in elementary school, and counselor evaluations. The guidance department describes the placement process as judicious, careful, and flexible. A student who is not faring well in an Honors class, for instance, can move to a Standard level class without embarrassment or humiliation. The shift is made with the consultation of teacher, parents, and student; and the effort is coordinated by the guidance counselor. Many students I spoke with talked about the ease of entering and exiting from one level to another and the coordination of judgments that makes that possible.

One parent, who is a school psychologist working in a neighboring suburb, marvelled at the responsiveness of Brookline's guidance department, "There is communication and availability. . . . When I had anxieties I could get response. . . . They are always there." When her daughter, a sophomore, felt pressured by the demands of her Advanced Placement courses, a collective decision was made to move her to Honors sections, where she is now thriving. The counselor, housemaster (the administrative head of one of four subdivisions in the school), relevant teachers, and parents met with the student to consider the options and a decision was made that seemed to respect all voices and satisfy most needs.

Another mother, who works as a secretary in a local business, tells a less positive story about negotiating with the guidance office regarding level placement. In the beginning of the year, her daughter, a "bright but manipulative" senior, was having some difficulty mastering the material in her Advanced Placement mathematics course. She complained to the counselor that the work was too hard and received permission to move to an Honors level class. A form was sent home for parent comment and signature, but this mother felt the decision had already been made. "I felt powerless to change the course of things. The counselor never asked me about it *before* the plans were set in motion. My daughter followed their plan. Parents should have more power in these decisions." The experience of exclusion hit this mother very hard. She felt that parents have a knowledgeable and different view of their child of which the school should take advantage. Decisions should be based on collective evaluations, and parents should have a prominent voice. "I know my child is an operator. She needed to be pressed into working harder, not given the easy retreat to another level." She spoke of the lingering feeling of subtle discrimination against working-class parents. "Maybe if I were a lawyer instead of a secretary they would value my opinion more highly . . . maybe they don't know I'm a college graduate."

These mothers of achieving daughters both viewed the leveling system as flexible and responsive to individual needs, but had different perceptions of the decision-making process. To one, the process was careful and systematic; to the other, it was careless and impulsive. Although many people who defend the leveling system point to the movement it permits, most teachers, parents, and students recognize its static, separating effects. The Advanced Placement classes are filled with ambitious, articulate students from privileged backgrounds. They are safe from the contaminations of the more mediocre students and can expect to receive a superior, even creative, education. The minority and working-class students are disproportionately represented in the Basic and Standard levels. For instance, there are one hundred METCO students and the large majority of them are in Basic level classes. Seventy METCO students received D's or E's on their grade reports during the third quarter of last year. These are not students who have recently transferred from Boston's public schools. They have been in the Brookline system since kindergarten, and their failure cannot be blamed on the negative, oppressive environment of an inferior school system. Headmaster McCarthy claims that these striking differences in achievement patterns have remained unspoken about for too long. "Now they *must* be confronted. We must face the realities." He underscores the point more dramatically: "There are two schools here. I have two children in this school and they have no idea of the range of problems I deal with up here. Theirs is the suburban school, smooth and peaceful . . . and then there is the other school rumbling underneath all the time . . . the challenge is to bring these two schools together."

A more ardent critic of the leveling system describes it as "insidious and discriminatory." An upper-level administrator, she is the only one I spoke to who claimed that students are "tracked." "The initial assignment is critical and it occurs in elementary school. . . . It completely determines what the student will come away with. . . . Some students come into school, get lost in a non-academic life . . . do nothing, learn nothing . . . just hang around for four years. If you go into A.P. classes, you're not going to find Black students . . . and no female students in A.P. science classes . . . maybe some of that has changed recently." Despite the school's liberal rhetoric, there are only a few faculty who recognize the contradictions between "a just and democratic community" and the leveling structure. In her view, the accepted stratification is related to preserving the image of excellence and elitism in the midst of major shifts in the student population. "As I speak to students, alumni, and teachers about Brookline High School, I hear a recurring theme—B.H.S. is constantly compared with Harvard. The references are almost interchangeable." These images are important to parents and students of high status and comforting to some teachers whose self-image is linked to old visions of an exclusive education.

One distinguished old-timer echoes these sentiments. He has been at Brookline High for more than two decades and enjoys teaching Advanced Placement courses in the dry and laconic style of a college professor. Many students, bored by his delivery, are pleased with his assumption of their excellence. He brags that his A.P. students can enter any elite college and excell. "One of my friends who teaches at Amherst said, 'Hey, you guys at Brookline are putting us out of work.'" Nostalgic, weary, and a bit timid speaking about his negative responses, he describes the inevitable tensions between diversity and excellence: "Maybe I am not supposed to say this, but definitely standards are lower than ten years ago. . . . They try so hard to include everyone, to keep everyone involved in the school, and that's good—industrial arts, cooking classes, et cetera—they have courses in *everything*, but the quality . . . well I would not vouch for that." He wonders out loud about the limits of inclusion, "I don't know whether you've heard about these problems from others but there are now a whole bunch of kids from Southeast Asia who are fifteen, sixteen, and seventeen years old and they've *never* been to school. They are illiterate; can't read in their own language. And there are increasing numbers of Russian students. Some are very talented. Others are impossible. They get here and don't know what to do with all the freedom." The veteran's voice trails off. His emotion seems to combine a deep longing for the old days and genuine puzzlement about how to face today and tomorrow with integrity and fairness. With some apology, he admits that teaching is no longer a joy. There are too many persistent struggles and unanswered questions.

Just as there are some teachers who can only feel inspired by the brightest students, there are others who intentionally choose to teach the Basic level courses. One English teacher has an excellent reputation among her colleagues precisely because she is capable of teaching well at all levels. Says one admirer, "We all knew that she was extraordinary in working with the articulate, bright kids. Their facile minds could play with ideas. But then she managed to do a bang-up job with a bunch of Basic students and we said, 'Now we *know* she is a fine teacher.'" An energetic and committed science teacher chooses to teach Basic biology. "I love it!" he exclaims. "It doesn't mean they get watered-down biology. What I teach they get in Standard and Honors. But it means that I have to work harder." A Black scientist, he is determined to attract young Black students into the sciences—"It is my personal crusade."

At Brookline, there does not appear to be the negative stigma attached to teaching low-achieving students that one finds in most tracked schools. Occasionally one hears derogatory comments about the Basic students, but mostly these remarks are couched carefully and designed not to offend. Sometimes they grow out of feelings of frustration teachers are feeling in "making a dent" or "communicating." Yet one also hears faculty complaints about the more privileged, high-achieving students who are occasionally accused of being overly competitive, indulged, and uncreative; fearful of losing their lofty position.

Group differences and boundaries are most clearly visible in the cafeteria. Students and faculty point toward the cafeteria when I ask about the "culture" of the school. It is here where the "natural" inclinations of students are allowed to flourish. One is struck by students' "groupiness"—the variations within groups, students' understandings of why separations exists, and the ways in which some of them try to cross group boundaries.

167

During the first lunch period, I sit down with Marion, a senior who has recently run for school-wide office, and three of her companions. Marion is sitting with three other seniors, a blond girl and two dark, curly-haired boys. In the course of the conversation I learn that these four students are enrolled in Honors and Advanced Placement courses. I ask the students about school pride. Peter Rosenberg leans across the table and says, "It's not cool to have school spirit. For about ten years there's been no spirit, but it's making a small comeback now, right Marion?" Peter is a thin, nervous person. He pulls apart a brownie he is eating and rolls the small pieces into balls in the palms of his hands. His hands are always moving. He is either tearing his brownie apart and rolling it, or twisting his fingers. He leans in close to talk to me, but nervously checks his companions for validation. He tends to defer to Marion when she is inclined to answer. Having just run for school office, Marion has a lot to say about school pride and spirit. She states emphatically that "B.H.S. is just like college." She explains, "The courses are just as hard, the teachers are just as smart as at college." The blond girl to Marion's left has long hair that sweeps the table top when she leans toward me. She also talks with intensity. "Yes, it is just like college. I know that because last year in chemistry I had a student teacher and he said that we used the same book they had in college." Marion says, "This is a great place to see and get to know all kinds of people—Russians, Chinese, Blacks, Jews." The two girls look at Peter and Jason. The blond girls says, "Truthfully Peter, if I'd gone to private school I probably would never get to know Jews and here I am friends with a Jewish person." Peter says, "My brother goes to prep school and he really misses out. You know, everyone is white." Marion says, "My brother goes to prep school but he's better off there. He just can't control himself. He'd have trouble here." I ask why he'd have trouble here and she answers, "He's not as tolerant as I am about people." I say that it does seem to me that there are lots of different people and I tell them my observations about the student groups who occupy different steps in the quadrangle. All four students lean toward me. Peter twists his hands and moves his face, stretching it from ear to ear as he tells me about student cliques. "Of course there are cliques. There are cliques everywhere." He lowers his voice. "Behind you are the jocks. Over there," he points his head briefly, spinning back to face me, "are the preppies—White preppies, Black preppies and Chinese preppies." The pace of the conversation is frantic. All of the students are trying to talk at once. The subject of cliques is of interest. They explain that ethnic groups more or less hang out together, but there is lots of mixing. I have noted that every fourth table seems to have a heterogeneous grouping of students. Jason says, "If you think the students are separatists, you should see the teachers, they're even worse." (Later in the day when I mention that observation to two teachers they both agree emphatically. They are surprised that the students have noticed.) With the lunch half-hour almost over, the tone of the conversation is hyper, not simply animated. These students are active in Brookline High School student activities, they recognize and appreciate the standard of academic work expected of them, and they want to put the best face of B.H.S. in front of me—the stranger. Yet their curiosity about the ways students and teachers stratify into groups—according to them, "exclusive groups that are almost impossible for a new person to break into"—leads them to expose what they see as a possible weakness of B.H.S. Peter grabs my wrist. "All of the groups are exclusive. Of course there are always some exceptional people who can break into any group, but that's rare. Mostly people just like to stick to a group."

In the second lunch half-hour, I ask two Black girls if I can join them. Both smile shyly up at me and move their books to make space. One of the girls explains that she's late for class and must leave. She speaks with a lilting, rhythmic accent which I'm told later is Haitian. The young woman I face has a pensive, pretty face. Bahai tells me that she is from Africa, from Ethiopia, where her parents still live. She moved to the U.S. over two years ago to live with her older brother and sister. She was first enrolled at Brighton High School which she hated. She explains, "The students at Brighton come to class with their tape recorders. They wear headphones while the teacher talks and they make noise all of the time. Brookline is much better, it is serious. The students here are very serious and that's good." Bahai explains that she came to America to get a good education. "That's why Brookline is the best place to be," she says with certainty. When I ask if it was easy to meet people at Brookline she says, "Yes, it is most easy to meet white students. The Blacks know we are different. They know we're African and think we're racist." I say, "That must be hard for you sometimes." She replies, "Yes, it is hard for all of us who are not American Blacks. It makes us feel hurt." Later when I talk to an indigenous Black senior girl I ask her about the foreign Black students. She explains that foreign students tend to stick together and not mix much with anyone. When asked how welcoming Brookline High School students are to foreign students she says, "I guess it's hard to incorporate new people into your group, especially if you've known these friends all your life. You don't make the effort. Not that we shouldn't, but we just don't."

For an hour and a half, the two rooms of the cafeteria are full. Teachers walk singly throughout the rooms during the whole lunch period. They are unobtrusive and generally ignored by the students. Occasionally a teacher will stop and chat with a table of students and then move on. The students settle among the rectangular, round, and square tables systematically. Most students tell me, "I always sit at this table." The underclass students move like flocks of swallows. They arrive in large groups, chattering and squawking, and settle en masse around three rectangular tables. The juniors and seniors tend to move more slowly and in smaller groups—in pairs or even singly. In the first room, Black students occupy six rectangular tables against the folding partition. In the next room, Asian students occupy three rectangular tables set end-to-end. In both rooms are tables with Black and Asian students, but the territory seems to be bounded for others.

NEW LEADERSHIP: CHANGE IN PHILOSOPHY AND STYLE

Dr. Robert McCarthy introduces himself informally. "Hi, I'm Bob McCarthy." His dress matches his casual greeting. He wears a loosely fitting, light blue sweater; slightly rumpled dark trousers; and walks with a weary gait. His gray-black hair is tousled and he runs his fingers through it often as he furrows his brow to think. McCarthy's tired look is deceptive. When he begins to talk about things that are important to him, energy and enthusiasm show in his intense eyes. He thinks out loud as he says, "I don't know if this is what you came for . . . what you want to hear . . . why don't you just let me go on . . . stop me if I go too far off the track." But nothing is rambling about his comments. They are organized, perceptive, and contemplative. He is surprisingly open and self-critical, and doesn't have the guarded reticence of many school administrators.

McCarthy has been at Brookline High since September 1980. He came from a principalship in Hanover, New Hampshire, where he enjoyed a challenging but easy life heading a school of 650 students. "I liked it there very much. My kids were in good schools . . . we lived five minutes away from the Dartmouth campus." Occasionally during his decade of tenure at Hanover High he would be tempted to sniff out other jobs, but he had no intention of really leaving. He was comfortable. The challenge of Brookline was seductive. "This is the *only* school in the country I would have left Hanover for," he says enthusiastically. The attraction of Brookline lay in the combination of the critical and interesting problems facing the school and the resources available to respond to those problems. He saw it as an "urban" school shaken by major crises, but he also saw a community committed to its salvation. Several months earlier he had been called to apply for the South Boston principalship, "But I wasn't that crazy." The complacency and homogeneity of the more affluent suburban schools did not interest him; neither did the chaos and deterioration of South Boston. Brookline lay somewhere in the middle of these two extremes. It had big city problems, but a cushion of money and positive sentiment that could challenge the difficulties if used wisely and bravely.

Brookline High, long known for its fine academic standards, had deteriorated in the decade before McCarthy arrived. Built in 1854, the school had enjoyed a reputation of stability. Since 1854, there have been only nineteen principals. Most of them had long tenures; only one stayed for a year, until he was elevated to the superintendency. The school's reputation as a solid, abundant institution still lingers today, even though the image is long outdated. Although McCarthy points to the troublesome seventies and the "authoritarian" leadership of his predecessor, Joseph Lombardi, he does not view himself as the sole guiding force that got the school back on track. "You know, from what I'm telling you, you might be thinking that everything was rotten until I came. Then things suddenly got better. . . . But I know you are too perceptive to believe that," he says to me.

Lombardi had been a teacher in Brookline for a long time before he became principal. He had enjoyed the school's fine reputation and supported its high academic standards. But as the population of the school began to shift and the cultural norms of the community were transformed, he proceeded as if nothing had changed. He ignored the new diversity of the student population, claiming "everyone is the same and must be treated the same." The teachers and administration seemed blind to the eruptions of violence, episodes of racism, and human indecency. Says McCarthy, "If you were walking through the courtyard and some kid pulled a knife, you tried to avoid seeing it." During the first two months after McCarthy's arrival, there were sixteen serious fights. "My head was in a different place . . . I wasn't used to this . . . I felt scared."

More shocking than the fights were the complacent responses of faculty to the violence. "They seemed to see it as part of their job to break up fights . . . they didn't seem to be angry." In talking with the faculty, McCarthy discovered that they too were frightened and angry, but had not felt that it was legitimate to express their rage. In some ways, they were ignoring the profound troubles surrounding them by pretending that fights did not disturb them. McCarthy challenged their pretence of complacency. "I would not accept breaking up fights as part of my job. I would show those kids how angry I was." Soon the "crackdown" began. Students were not allowed to congregate in ominous groups or bully fellow students who wanted to pass through blocked doorways. When there were incidents of violence parents were brought in immediately, and teachers expressed their outrage to the student and his parents. The new expressions of anger seemed to have an effect. Many students were shocked by the expression of feelings and the seriousness and intensity of their teachers, who had seemed not to care so much before. Parents may have been embarrassed by the public outrage, but seemed comforted by the attempts to bring a new order and safety to the school. Since the opening of school a month ago, there have been no fights this year. The norms appear to be shifting, and memories of last year seem to have transcended the summer sojourn.

The violence among students had often been associated with episodes of racism. A fight would break out between a Black kid and an Irish Catholic kid and ripple throughout the school as other groups chose sides. In the late seventies the violence against Black students had become so severe that their parents took action. Says McCarthy sympathetically, "It was not easy for these Brookline parents to confront the School Committee. They were risking their relationships to neighbors and friends . . . their place in the community." The parents formed a group called "Concerned Black Citizens" and began to meet regularly to talk about the racist tone of the school and the violent assaults against their youngsters. They met denial from Lombardi, who refused to admit there was trouble, and reticence from the School Committee, which took a protective attitude towards the principal. As the violence became more flagrant and visible, as the parent group grew in numbers and sophistication, the School Committee could no longer ignore the charges. During one School Committee meeting when Lombardi was under attack from the Concerned Black Citizens' group, the committee "just let him hang there . . . swinging in the breeze." Soon after, Lombardi left.

Everyone talks about the sharp contrasts between Lombardi and McCarthy. Lombardi was "authoritarian, dominating, theatrical," and McCarthy is "low-key, soft-spoken, thoughtful." Lombardi was "visible, definitive, and uncompromising." McCarthy is "invisible, contemplative, and ambiguous." No one had any difficulty understanding and interpreting Lombardi's actions. Many claim to have difficulty comprehending the motivations and intent behind McCarthy's behaviors. Some faculty allude to differences in style related to their ethnic origins. Lombardi had the flair and drama of Italians, and McCarthy the restraint and seriousness of his middle-class Irish upbringing.

Even though some express a nostalgic wish for the clear-cut messages of the old regime, I spoke to no one who wanted to have Lombardi back. Most agree that the school grew to be too complex and tangled for the straight-forward, dominating leadership of Lombardi. The problems of the seventies required a more flexible, subtle, and questioning style which did not fear change. Even though everyone seems to have recognized the need for a change in leadership, there is a lingering affection for their old leader. In one voice, people praise McCarthy and speak caringly about Lombardi. Their affection for Lombardi springs from their long association with him, from his genuine commitment to the school, from his outspoken protection of his faculty, and even from his human vulnerabilities. Paradoxically, one senses that his aggressive and charismatic style made him more open and approachable than the more sophisticated stance of his successor. "Lombardi let it all hang out," says one veteran teacher. Claims another, "With Lombardi, it was what you see is what you get." When he finally got in trouble, many teachers recognized his weaknesses and limitations, but identified with his fate.

The connections to Lombardi and his shadowy presence remain and make it difficult for some teachers to fully respond to McCarthy. One administrator who is strongly approving of McCarthy explained it this way, "By the end of his reign here, Joseph had successfully alienated almost everyone. He had been a man who was loved and feared, but his departure was weird. No one understood it. One day he was just gone and there was no way to say good bye. . . . We never really severed the relationship and his presence is still deeply felt. . . . No one says 'I wish Joseph were here,' but it was difficult making the transition."

Just as some faculty experienced more comfort and protection with Lombardi's "autocratic" style, many told me of the liberation and autonomy that McCarthy's leadership permits. Raved one teacher with an excellent reputation, "I love him. He is just wonderful . . . the best thing that has ever happened to this school!" Said another, in slightly more restrained tones, "Bob followed a witty, energetic, articulate, but very authoritarian headmaster who gave orders and told everyone what to do . . . but McCarthy is low-key, sensitive, and secure and won't take that position. . . . Lots of people have trouble with that but I think he is wonderful. . . . Let me tell you something he did the other day. One of the guidance counselors, who was well-loved by everyone, died of cancer. McCarthy got on the P.A. and talked about the sadness, the separation, the loss, and the anger we feel at being abandoned by her . . . and the kids really got it; the teachers got it." Tears come to the storyteller's eyes as she recounts the incident. "I think it is because he is a runner," she says smilingly. "We runners have great inner strength and lots of patience."

Those who express boundless admiration for McCarthy's personal qualities also tend to speak positively about his views on leadership and power. McCarthy is outspoken on the subject. "I have always found that the more power you give people, the more responsibility they take." He is eager to dismantle the top-down, hierarchical arrangement of roles and relationships in the school; and is trying to create a school structure that will increase the sense of community (a word he often uses) and participation among students, faculty, administrators, and staff (that is, custodians, cooks, and secretaries).

Soon after his arrival, McCarthy established a "Fairness Committee" to deal with disciplinary problems. Students and faculty sit on this committee and their recommendations for action, made to the administration, are binding. There are no empty gestures; this is real power and decision making. McCarthy hopes that over the years the Fairness Committee will increase its scope and become like the judicial arm of the school—not merely responding to incidents of crises, but also creating policy.

This year a new and important experiment is being initiated. The "Town Meeting" will become the major decision-making body of the school. With 80 representatives from all parts of the school community, the Town Meeting will establish the beginnings of a democratic structure that gives participating members an equal voice. McCarthy speaks about the new innovation with enthusiasm—recognizing the vulnerabilities of an open system and the inevitable problems of initiation and growth. Five years from now he hopes that his role will be reduced in scope and resemble the executive branch of government. "They can take *all* the power for all I care."

McCarthy's strong allies among the faculty share his vision, recognize the risks involved, and offer their good will and support. Others share much of his philosophical orientation, but feel his methods are unfocused and unrealistic. One supporter spoke about the hazards of transitional periods, "No one knows who is in or where the power is . . . McCarthy's signals are sometimes mixed. . . . He seems to want it, then he doesn't want it . . . so everyone spends so much energy trying to figure him out." This observer told about McCarthy's ambivalence towards power (despite his rhetoric to the contrary). Last year when they were searching for a department chairperson, he claims McCarthy designed an elaborate and cumbersome process for the review of candidates. After many rounds of interviewing, the search committee proposed three names for his consideration. McCarthy did not like any of the names and chose the candidate that he had favored all along. "He was unwilling to relinquish power."

Many faculty seem to recognize that McCarthy's "mixed messages" are an inevitable part of the acclimation process. "McCarthy is working out a style in relation to the school. Half the time I'm invigorated by his approach, and half the time it drives me crazy." However, they also recognize their wish for a visible, lofty leader. "He wants to come across as a normal person, but some people have trouble with a normal person as head master." No matter what people's inclination is towards McCarthy, everyone seems to agree that this period has ushered in a great deal of uncertainty and shifting ground. There is a self-consciousness about actions and responses; a searching to find out where one stands in relation to others; a "staking out of territories and protecting of flanks"; and the optimism and fears that always go hand and hand with change. Everyone is trying to figure out the puzzle as pieces get rearranged and patterns get reset. At the center of the puzzle is McCarthy, a man with a well-articulated vision, but some say, a measure of ambivalence.

THE TOWN MEETING: SHARED POWER

The Town Meeting structure is designed to approximate Lawrence Kohlberg's notion of a "just community." Convinced that moral development and growth can only thrive in a context that supports shared power and responsibility, last year some Brookline teachers and administrators wrote a grant proposal that recommended the Town Meeting as a way of altering hierarchical relationships in the school. The Town Meeting, comprised of students, faculty, and staff, would have the authority to govern Brookline High School within legal constraints set by Massachusetts and in concert with the headmaster and School Committee. This was not to be a vacuous form of student government or an empty gesture that camouflaged old patterns; it was to be a real attempt to change deeply rooted patterns of power and decision making. The proposal was funded and, the day before I arrived in early October, the project director was chosen to lead "the experiment."

Steve Stone, a recent graduate of the Harvard Graduate School of Education and a disciple of Lawrence Kohlberg, arrived with a realistic blend of skepticism, commitment, and hope. Despite the fact that many teachers shared McCarthy's enthusiasm for the process and supported his commitment to the goals of democracy and equality, many were reticent to become overly optimistic, while others were suspicious of motivations and purpose. Some teachers' complaints were focused on the choice of Steve Stone. "He looks like a typical Harvard type . . . his language and style are wholly academic," said one. "An insider should have been chosen for this position. You have to know the school intimately in order to do this job," said another. However, the dominant concerns of skeptical and resistant teachers seemed to be related to their views of the Town Meeting form as an administrative and decision-making structure. The most adamant faculty complained that the Town Meeting was a way for McCarthy to avoid the demands and liabilities of leadership. "He is afraid of power, afraid to be the bad guy," said one teacher, who admitted her penchant for conservatism, order, and certainty. Other, less critical voices, worried that the Town Meeting was based on a wrong-headed view of school culture, values, and norms. In their view, schools do not work best as democracies. Not only is shared decision making wildly inefficient, but it leads to ambiguities of power that make everyone unsure and uncomfortable. Clarity of roles and defined authority structures, they argued, are liberating, not oppressive; they support, rather than undermine, communication. In addition, these teachers believed that adolescents may not be ready for wielding power and making informed decisions. "My greatest worry," said one sympathetic but wary teacher, "is that Town Meeting will degenerate into the student government I knew in high school; be a popularity contest; stand for all the wrong values. . . . It would be one thing if this had been an oppressive environment for students, but the kids have always had a voice, always felt cared for, always had their piece of the power. Why are we making all these changes in a system that has worked well?"

The elections for Town Meeting are held in early October. During the week before, the elections posters and leaflets begin to appear, plastered carelessly in the hallways. Most are written on colored construction paper without much attention to precision or aesthetics. The great majority of the candidates do not appear to have made election posters or canvassed their peers for votes. A few posters have the practiced script of careful sign-makers, but these tend to be advertising freshman candidates for office. One enthusiastic and very earnest freshman boy has slick publicity material that appears to have been professionally produced. Perhaps he has not yet learned that it is not "cool" to try so hard, to appear to want it so much. Some of his classmates seem to be embarrassed by his vigorous attempts to get elected. The upper classmen seem half-amused and slightly scornful of his too obvious enthusiasm.

The election speeches are given in each of the four houses: Akers House, Roberts House, Lincoln House, and Packard House. With 500 students in each house, they serve as major subdivisions of the larger school. All students and faculty attached to each house gather in large meeting rooms (the cafeteria, the student-faculty lounge, the old gym, and the auditorium) to hear the speeches of the candidates. There is a mood of anticipation and excitement as five hundred students crowd into the gathering places one Tuesday morning at 10:00. I am struck by the crush of bodies and the volume of noise that fills the room—and with a sense of order and control. At no time do I fear violence, or even chaos. More important, the teachers in charge do not seem worried about outbreaks of disorder. Their attitudes are calm, affable, and restrained as they urge students to get seated anywhere they can find space—on chairs, on tables, on windowsills, and on the floor. Once everyone is settled, members of Roberts House listen to their housemaster, Selma Hill, make the introductions: "Welcome to the first annual Town Meeting campaign session . . . we have well-qualified, eager, articulate members . . . a crowded field. Each candidate will tell you why you should vote for them. Voting will take place tomorrow in my office. You will be able to vote for two candidates in each grade, eight total . . . there will also be at-large representatives if there are groups who feel that they are not being fairly represented."

The Lincoln House election meeting, held in the cafeteria, follows the same general pattern, but the atmosphere is a bit more informal.

The housemaster at the microphone has the easy good looks of someone who fits in. He has reddish-blond hair, thinning at the top, a wide and frequent grin and dancing eyes. He banters with the students who cheer and boo him excitedly. The candidates assembled, his tone changes slightly as he begins by saying, "The people here in front of me are running for Town Meeting. They will be allowed to speak for one and a half to two minutes. I ask you to please be attentive and polite and to listen carefully to what they say. This is an important decision you're making. You'll be able to elect two people from each class in Lincoln House." He jokes, "Now let's see, that's four times eight or ?" There's no answer from the audience. He points to his temple and shakes his head. The students laugh uproariously as he says over their noise, "That's what we like, an informed electorate." He waits for quiet. "If you are Chinese or Black or Irish or Russian or any other ethnic group and you don't think that your group is repre- sented by any of these candidates, please speak to your housemaster. We all want representation." With a few more introductory comments, delivered in a respect- ful and an accepting way, he introduces the first speaker, "Ms. Marion Best." Marion has shoulder-length brown hair, parted in the middle. Her slightly freck- led face is serious as she asks, "Is there school spirit and school pride among us?" The crowd murmurs a hushed "No." She moves ahead with her recommenda- tions for increasing both spirit and pride. She says, "We should use the house system as a melting pot, where the students of all ages and backgrounds could get to know one another." To illustrate how much she cares about "B.H.S." she says, "I cared enough to postpone getting my braces removed until after this speech and this election. I'll end up wearing them three more weeks than I had to." The applause seems genuine, the calls from the crowd supportive.

The next senior speaker is a blond ponytailed girl. Her face is somber as she approaches the microphone. Joyce Hart is wearing a lime green turtleneck with a rag sweater and a single strand of pearls. She gives her political experience, but no platform.

The third senior to speak stands up, squares his shoulders and ambles for- ward. Brad has dark hair, parted in the middle, an athletic build, and a popular following of girls who yell, "Yea, Brad!" He doesn't have a prepared speech. (He tells me the next day when I am watching the soccer team practice that he thought seniors would speak last, so he was going to write the speech as the first three classes spoke.) "Hey," he begins. He waits, looking at the crowd. They laugh and the second-row girls yell. "Listen, I'm not going to stand up here and give a speech, I just want you all to know that I'm here to represent you." He rambles on with apparent ease and ends by saying, "I just want you all to know that any of us would do a good job, except for Mark Stein." The students laugh and the teacher moves to the mike to introduce the last senior speaker: Mark Stein.

177

Mark has a head of brown curls and the same muscular, athletic build as Brad. He moves to the mike with a serious face. He nods toward Brad and says with deadpan delivery, "That's a real tough act to follow, Brad." The students love it and whoop and laugh. Without cracking a smile, Mark waits for the noise to subside and gives a short, clear speech with obvious poise and confidence. Finished, he smiles and heads directly to Brad. Placing his hand on Brad's head, he ruffles his hair and moves on to his own seat. At soccer practice the following day, I learn that both are friends, teammates, and competitors on the field. Brad is from a middle-class Irish family and Mark from an upper middle-class Jewish family. They tend to see Brookline High School differently. When I tell them that I've noticed that certain groups of students seem to congregate on particular sets of steps in the quadrangle, both nod. I say, "I'm told that the group on the left steps are SWS [School Within a School, an alternative school within B.H.S.]." Brad says, "Hey, they're the freaks. Did you talk to any of them? Spaced out on drugs, fried." Mark interjects, "SWS is a program that attracts lots of real individuals. You know, some kids just can't stand the pressure of being in the classroom and need lots of individual attention, so they're in SWS. Some kids maybe did some drugs once and need to go a little slower." Brad snickers. Mark continues seriously. "Some of them are just so brilliant, so up there that our classes move too slow for them." Brad says, "Freaks, all up on the fourth floor, weird." I say, "I was also told that the students on the right steps are called the Point kids, whatever that means." Brad looks a little uneasy. He digs his running shoes into the dirt. "They're just a gang. They wear leather jackets and hassle small freshmen with glasses." I ask why they are called Point kids. Brad replies, "They all come from a neighborhood called High Point. Their families are the townies, you know, the policemen and firemen. Really, by the time you get to be a senior, they're just kind of a joke." "But not for freshmen," I say. "Right," says Brad, "They scare freshmen." He waits a moment then says, "Some of them are really good kids. They just have to live in that neighborhood so what are they supposed to do? They've got to join the gang, I mean, they've got to live there, don't they?" Mark lets Brad's question hang in the air. He says, "Mostly, they're Irish Catholic working-class guys looking to be tough." He watches Brad's face out of the corner of his eye. Brad's face remains unchanged as he scuffs his running shoes in the dirt. "Some of their mothers are like secretaries around here." The day before when I was talking to a group of girls about the same student groups, one of the girls told me that she had been warned that there would be a lot of fights at B.H.S. She said, "I'm a junior now, and I've never seen one or heard of any serious fights. Certainly no gang fights." The others agreed immediately.

The four seniors finished, the juniors begin. Anthony Doxiadis is introduced. He is a heavy, dark-haired young man with a shadowy mustache on his upper lip. "I'm going to be different than the other candidates. I represent the right-wing. I'm conservative. Not like the left-wing candidates who are running. I support Two and a Half* and that makes me different." The crowd moans, but Anthony persists, "I think we need some conservatives on Town Meeting." He

---

*The reference here is to Proposition 2½, a recently passed state law that reduces the amount of tax revenues. It has had a significant impact on the monies available for schools and other public services in the Commonwealth. It's impact on B.H.S. will be discussed later in this chapter.

makes a mental jump: "I don't want people running after me, telling me what to do all the time. I'll tell you what to do, if I'm elected." He steps away from the microphone, the first speaker to get little applause.

Myrna Rosen scurries up to the microphone. Her wavy brown hair bushes out around her shoulders. She straightens her pink turtleneck and Fair Isle sweater and firmly grasps her speech and charges into the text. She speaks rapidly without looking up. "I would not be a passive candidate. . . ." Each sentence trips over the next in rapid succession. She finishes, takes a deep breath, receives her applause and returns to her seat.

Roger Duke is introduced. A tall, slim young man with a short Afro walks to the microphone. His handsome black face slowly spreads into a contagious smile. "Hello, I'm Roger Duke." The students return his laugh. The audience seems to ease into Roger's sincere delivery. "I'm a person who wants your ideas for this Town Meeting. And I want to help this committee work." With one hand in his brown corduroy pants, the other is free to gesticulate. He thanks the students for listening and gets enthusiastic applause.

The fourth candidate's introduction is the first to be greeted by audible hoots. A low "Hey, Jean" rolls forward from the back of the cafeteria. A short, sturdy Jean Goodwin seems to ignore the hoots, which die down almost as quickly as they began. Her square shoulders seem broad in the navy blazer she is wearing. In a stern voice she informs the students that she has experience, dependability, and good judgement. She levels her dark glasses on the bridge of her nose as she looks out over the audience. The gesture seems staged, almost as if her speech told her to pause and survey the audience. Jean finishes her speech and receives some applause.

The housemaster who is acting as the emcee perhaps feels the boredom in the cafeteria. He tells us, "A bulletin from election central reports that teachers will not be able to vote for students." His announcement is greeted by huge applause and whoops. He raises his hand to calm the students. "But I must tell you, that means no students can vote for teachers." He claps and they boo him with high spirits. He introduces the first sophomore.

Betsy James reads her speech so quickly she simply can't be understood. Her racing, quiet voice blurs each word into a stream of words and no one from the middle of the cafeteria to the back can hear her. The noise of the crowd increases substantially. Students turn to talk with one another, laughing, poking, and teasing.

Matthew Miles follows Betsy. A straight, slim, blond-haired young man, he says, "I come before you an honest politician." The audience laughs hard and interrupts his speech with applause. Seeming unruffled, Matthew continues his speech with seriousness, clear enunciation, and a loud, clear voice. The students have become more attentive now that they can hear the speaker again.

The next two speakers, Donald Turner and Joan Spielberg, have written speeches that they read with clear, loud voices.

The last sophomore to speak is Jennifer Howell. As she walks to the microphone a supportive male voice in the back yells "Yea, Jennifer." Without acknowledging her fan, Jennifer pats her long blond hair, which is pulled back. Her pretty smile flashes as the light reflects from her braces. When she finishes her speech she grimaces and hunches back to her seat.

Sammy is the first freshman speaker. A large, overweight boy, Sammy lumbers to the microphone. He wears a yarmulke and clothes that seem to belong to a fifty year-old rather than a fifteen year-old. The gray pants are held tight at his waist with a belt, and he scuffs his shiny black leather shoes against each other as he speaks. "I'm Sammy and I'm not going to say very much." A voice in the back of the room yells, "Good!" Sammy scuffs harder. "I'm a good leader. Those who know me know that." The students laugh. Sammy grins back at them.

The second freshman has his own cheering squad. Students have pinned campaign cards on their clothes and all of them clap long and loud when their candidate, Zachary, is introduced. An impish face framed with bright orange curls faces the students. His supporters cheer his silence and his speech with equal zeal. He says, "Not many critical issues have been raised today." His fans respond, "Right." For a couple of minutes, campaign fever infects the audience.

The next speaker is a young Black man. Martin is a round, somber-faced boy who says of himself, "I am a man of very few words." Like Zachary, Martin also has a cheering squad sitting near the front. He directs his speech to them and they respond enthusiastically.

The audience is growing more restless. Pairs of Chinese boys at the next table are playing some game on a piece of paper they keep passing between them. The freshmen boys behind me are jostling each other and whispering loudly. A teacher in a gray suit joins their table. A young man, he looks directly at the boys, straightens his tie and settles into his chair ostensibly to hear the rest of the speeches.

A small-boned, blond-haired girl whose name is Betsy begins, "Flash, thirty-two teachers, two secretaries, thirty-two students announce. . . . " She catches their flagging attention and the room becomes silent as Betsy reads her mock news flash. She finishes and looks up and introduces herself by name again. She completes her speech with clarity and poise. The students seem almost surprised that they were caught up in Betsy's fantasy news flash. They applaud her speech with enthusiasm.

The last speaker is a short Black girl. Under five feet, she needs the microphone lowered. As the housemaster-emcee attempts to lower the microphone, some male voices yell out, "Where is she? Where'd she go?" With the microphone adjusted, Nicole presents her platform step-by-clear-step. A clear speaker and the last speaker, Nicole receives a lot of applause.

On the following Friday, during homeroom period, McCarthy announces the winners of the student election over the public address system. With a voice that sounds reverent and deliberate, he expresses the seriousness of the new community enterprise, "I have the privilege of announcing the winners of the Town Meeting election. Thanks to everyone who participated in the process. . . ." In the homeroom where I am hearing the announcement, students show little interest in the news. Most of their conversations continue uninterrupted, despite the protestations of the teacher, who urges them to listen carefully. A few students listen for the names of their friends and show visible disappointment when McCarthy does not mention them. Out in the hall after homeroom period, there is some buzzing about winners and losers. The victors receive congratulations from friends, "Way to go, man"; while the losers quietly accept bemused condolences. However, the victories and defeats do not seem very charged. Perhaps the prize is not highly valued.

The moderate enthusiasm among the students seems vigorous compared to the lack of interest among the teachers. Departments were to select faculty representatives to Town Meeting. For reasons of reticence, skepticism, and overwork, the teachers declined to become involved in election proceedings. To most, the Town Meeting was a high-risk venture that many teachers feared would demand time and energy away from their already over-committed schedules. In most departments, teachers were asked to volunteer for seats on the Town Meetings Committee; and by the time of the first scheduled meeting, the faculty representation was below the designated numbers. Those teachers who volunteered their services tended to be vocal supporters of the new system, "the few who always get involved and do all the work," or people who greatly admire McCarthy.

The first Town Meeting showed all the signs of a beginning experiment. There was the rhetoric and optimism of the leader followed by restraint and reserve on the part of the members. There was a disorganization and lack of direction as people wondered who was in control and who had the power. There was confusion about roles, agendas, and purpose as everyone struggled with the self-definition of this newly formed group. Teachers appeared more tentative and tense than students, probably fearing they had more to lose. Steve Stone, the project head, expressed ambivalence in his every move. He needed to grab the reins in order to move the group forward, but he did not want to give off signs of unequal power and authoritarianism. To one observing the awkward process, there were feelings of empathy for the pain and fears connected with change and admiration for those willing to endure it.

Dr. McCarthy stands before the first Town Meeting assembled in the faculty dining room. "This is an important day, if not an historic day. Brookline High School opened in 1854. In the 1930s we initiated the house system which was the first of its kind in the country. Brookline High School has introduced many firsts. I will predict that the concept of a Town Meeting for a large high school is another one of those firsts. I understand that you have some questions. Will the Town Meeting run the school? Who's in charge now that we have changed our system of governance? First, don't worry that no one around here can make a decision. We're going to see power shared in this school, though. The reason why it's important that decision making be shared is because we're not an army here.

And we're not at war. If our lives depended on immediate decisions, we'd have a different decision-making system. Very logically, the process of decision making in a school should be established where all aspects of the school are subject to review. People must accept that this is a school where agreed upon regulations will be supreme, not idiosyncrasies of individual men or women. Better decisions are made when a lot of people are involved. That's my basic conviction and what my experience has been."

Students are listening indifferently. They seem more interested in checking out who else was elected to Town Meeting. Recognizing each other across the room, they exchange smiles, small waves. The teachers and staff seem more intent on McCarthy's comments.

He says, "I promise you that a priority for me is to provide release time to all the staff involved in this process of Town Meetings. Students, if you desire that credit be awarded, we may work that out as independent study. You'll have a budget—money. Money is now available to repair vandalism in this school."

Looking around the room I count seven Black students and two Black staff. There are no Asian students, but one female Asian staff. It's difficult to evaluate whether or not Town Meeting is representative of the B.H.S. student population.

McCarthy: "You have the authority to review and to make recommendations to the School Committee, to the Massachusetts Department of Education, if necessary. In this room we will disagree, argue with each other, but if we can go to the outside boards as a united front, we stand a better chance of being heard." He has a list of issues which he thinks Town Meeting will have to address. "We have an AWOL (Absent Without Leave) policy at Brookline High School which some believe is applied differently by different teachers; you will have to deal with that. Dope policy—in my opinion anyone under the influence of either alcohol or drugs should be reported to the Police. Guardian Angles want to come and recruit here. Some of us question that. Is it appropriate? What do you think? Litter and vandalism—what can be done? Methods of discipline are open to your scrutiny. Student-faculty lounge—perhaps there should be pinball, maybe supervision [murmured agreement in the room is loud], maybe we should put furniture in there."

In his final comments McCarthy tells the Town Meeting, "We want to show that a large metropolitan high school can be run democratically." He introduces Steve Stone who he says is working full-time on Town Meeting under a federal grant.

Steve Stone introduces himself. He is standing in the center of a circle of Town Meeting participants. The students are getting a little more uneasy, but they remain polite—looking at Stone as he speaks, refraining from talking among themselves. He says, "I'm sorry that I will be doing so much speaking during this first meeting. This will not happen as we get ourselves organized. I have worked for the past several years with schools experimenting with democracy. I've worked with smaller schools, but I bring a faith and a confidence that this will work out. One of my jobs here is to work with this group to help in any way I can. I will take on a coordinating role to help the committees as they're established. People all over the world are looking to see how these democratic structures work in large, metropolitan high schools.

"I am most interested in issues of school climate. I would like to be taping all of these meetings because, number one, we will be doing some future training and tapes are invaluable for that. Number two, we'll have a permanent record and, number three, we'll be able to help other schools who are interested in setting up a democratic structure. So, I would propose we do tape our meetings." A student asks, "Could we stop the tape if we wanted to speak off the record?" Stone: "Well, that's an issue. We could discuss that."

A short, student-dominated debate of ten exchanges ensues. Stone terminates the debate saying, "We could have two votes—first, a general policy. Will people be in favor of taping?" He asks for a show of hands. A unanimous approval of a general taping policy.

"The second vote I would like to put off," he continues. "If there are matters that should be kept private, we'll discuss that as a special issue as it arises."

He looks at his watch. "I promised I would get all of you out of here by 2:15 and we still have several agenda items." Students and staff look at their agendas. "I need volunteers from this group. First, Dr. McCarthy wants five students to represent Town Meeting to the School Committee." A faculty member interjects that according to state law the school needs two seniors, two juniors, and one sophomore to sit in on the School Committee. Stone asks that students who are interested in volunteering raise their hands. At least one-third of the group raises their hands. A discussion on how to resolve the large number of volunteers with the five places takes place. Finally, Stone is able to say: "I think we have three different approaches and I suggest we vote. We can have a lottery by class. A ballot election, or we can use rotating numbers." The discussion is still confused and it's 2:15. Stone simply asks that all interested students and staff sign up after the Town Meeting with one of the students.

He is rushing a little. "Second, I would like to see volunteers to be on an agenda committee for the next few Town Meetings. I would especially like people with experience working with Town Meetings to help out on this. We could meet in the faculty lounge after the meeting.

"Thirdly, we're going to have a half-time assistant who will be the Town Manager. We need people to serve on a screening committee. Students and staff are needed to do screening as soon as possible. We'd like to interview next Monday and make a hiring decision later in the week. Would volunteers for the screening committee stay here after the meeting?" A short round of questions from staff, on whether they can have release time, ends this meeting.

Everyone rushes off. Steve Stone must be reminded of similar beginning attempts to change entrenched patterns and structures in other schools in which he has worked. His comments to me a few days later express both patience and weariness. He knows it will be an uphill battle to build trust, confidence, and a sense of community. He knows, also, that pessimism and optimism are both appropriate emotions. The odds of failing are at least equal to the possibilities of success.

A SENSE OF COMMUNITY

Brookline's student population is divided into four houses: Akers House, Packard house, Lincoln House, and Roberts House. Many faculty explain, "They were designed to be like the houses of Harvard and Yale." (The reference to elite connections is not lost on this observer, who often hears students and faculty define their institution in these high status terms.) They resemble the houses of Harvard only in a structural, bureaucratic sense. Houses create smaller communities with which a student can be identified and affiliated. But at Brookline they are not intellectual frameworks, neither are they communities that inspire loyalty and commitment. Although some students I talked to said that they had vague feelings of affiliation with the houses to which they belonged, they did not speak of the houses as places of connection and solace. Faculty, administrators, and students seem to agree that the houses as they are presently organized serve little more than an organizational function, and many express a wish that they could have more force in the life of the school.

Five hundred students are randomly assigned to each house, except for siblings, who are always assigned to the same house. This makes it possible for parents to build relationships with a single house even if they have more than one child in the school, and it makes it more likely that houses will feel familiar and comfortable with younger siblings if their older brother or sister is already ensconced there. The houses are administered by a housemaster (a full-time position) with the assistance of a houseteacher (a part-time position). With the recent budget cuts of Proposition 2½, the houseteacher is now required to teach three courses along with his administrative duties. Before this year, houseteachers taught two courses and had more time to administer. The division of roles and responsibilities between housemaster and houseteacher appears to be negotiated by the incumbents, not rigorously stipulated in advance. Housemasters certainly have the ultimate authority and accountability within the house, but houseteachers play prominent roles as disciplinarians, advisors, counselors, interpreters of school policy, advocates for students in relation to other faculty, and negotiators with parents. There is often an overlapping function of the teacher and master role as they work in concert, collaborating with and supporting one another. From the students' point of view, it is better to have two, rather than one, authority figure connected with the house. "If you don't like one, you can approach the other." Usually, one adult seems to be more available or responsive than another to particular students and this allows for some choice.

Everyone agrees that since McCarthy's arrival, the housemasters have been permitted more power and autonomy, but it continues to be an administrative, not an instructional, role. One housemaster describes his increased authority. "With Lombardi, the housemasters were like lieutenants. The metaphors were very male, very military. . . . But McCarthy has opened the door for housemasters. Lincoln House students are *my* students. I can make all the decisions about them." And to watch him in action, one sees a person with a wide range or responsibilities and tasks. The job does not seem glamorous. His office is functional, cluttered with papers and books, empty of aesthetic expression, and open for people seeking attention and help. Mr. Barclay is in perpetual motion, always trying to figure out what is in need of the most attention and what might be delegated to someone else. Within the first few minutes of our conversation, Barclay is responding to a telephone call from an irate parent who is calling long-distance from Canada and wants to have a conference with Barclay as soon as he returns to town. Next, he speaks briefly with a boy we pass in the hall about some housing Barclay has located for him. "That kid has a lot of strength. He is a reformed alcoholic; his mother is dead; and his father's a gigolo. In order to survive he needs to move *away* from his father." In consultation with his counselor and social worker, Barclay has been trying to organize alternative living arrangements. His contact with the boy is a brief but very caring exchange. His arm is wrapped gently around the boy's shoulder and he seems, for a moment, like the great protector. Next, my conversation with Barclay is interrupted by a student helper in the house who says that there are two Hispanic boys who need to be enrolled in school and they only speak Spanish. Barclay gets on the phone trying to track down a Spanish-speaking student who can serve as translator. The duties are far ranging, the pace is hectic, the relationships with students seem almost parental. There is no time to get wrapped up in status-maintaining behavior. In order to do his job, Barclay provides an easy access, an affable style, and a clear respect for students.

Even though the role often seems overwhelming, there are limits that are defined by the structure of the house system. Although counselors and homerooms are affiliated with houses and faculty have house assignments, teachers identify with the departments of which they are a part and see them as the primary educational settings. Says one housemaster self-critically, "Houses really have no identity. . . . They are a superficial overlay. . . . Departments and houses find themselves often clashing over their educational role. . . . Housemasters are very often seen as separate from the educational function and I see this as a flaw." Inevitably the housemaster must be responsible for the overall functioning of the house, attendance, conferences with teachers and parents, and working with the counselors in the house. This demands that housemasters must sometimes assume a distant, supervisory role and become less passionately involved in the fate of individuals. A female housemaster talks about shaping the role to fit her temperamental style and philosophical inclinations. "My role is more the heavy . . . counselors are more likely to function as advocates . . . but since I can't function as a heavy, I try to function as a role model. . . . I try to make the kids feel responsible for their own actions in a way that is educative . . . to help them grow. . . . Additionally, I think it is important for people to see that a woman can function in an administrative position and still have womanly qualities. Before I was appointed to this position, there were only male housemasters . . . disciplinarians who had a cut-and-dry approach to the function. . . . I consciously tried to broaden the job to match my temperament and to enhance the school . . . I wanted kids to see this as a warmer place." The tone of the houses is largely influenced by the personality and orientation of the housemaster. Through his or her own style, the atmosphere and norms get shaped and the relationships to students become established. One housemaster describes the tone she tries to develop. "I see kids as emerging adults. The more dignity and respect you give them, the more it will come back to you." Although many recognize the housemaster role as critical and of high status, it often feels cut off from the real business of schooling. Taken seriously, the challenges and responsibilities of the role are overwhelming and endless. They require a kind of dedication and toughness that sometimes feels unrewarded. Always confronting problems, always negotiating compromises, always orchestrating human resources, there is little opportunity for self-renewal. Says one housemaster who is not eager for additional responsibilities, but is eager for a "substantive challenge": "I would like to teach . . . develop a course. That would enrich my life."

In contrast to the houses, which are experienced as partial communities, the School Within a School emerges as a real community that embraces the lives of its inhabitants. The School Within a School, or "SWS" as everyone calls it, is an alternative, "democratic" community of one hundred students and five teachers. Tucked in a fourth-floor corner of the school, SWS has a dramatic identity and strong reputation as a "different place." The nature of the difference is a source of some discussion, mixed interpretations, and much stereotyping. Twelve years ago, when SWS was organized, it seemed a natural outgrowth of a more general cultural trend towards progressive, collective forms of education. Brookline, like many other enlightened high schools, saw SWS as a response to students' needs for choice and an effort to recognize diverse philosophical and pedagogical stances on education. Immediately it was seen by most outsiders as a place for the "far-out," nonconformist kids—a refuge for the crazies and outcasts. "You could tell the SWS kids because they all dressed like hippies, had long, straight, dirty hair, and smoked a lot of dope." These kids were feared and disdained by their peers as their reputation became bigger than life.

SWS survived the criticisms and assaults of the wider community during its early years and no longer appears to be a major threat to nonbelievers. With a twelve-year history and a very stable faculty, SWS is firmly entrenched. The stereotypes linger but they do not stand up against the tests of reality. Even though SWS students claim that as freshmen they "were afraid to come up to the fourth floor" because the SWS kids had such bad reputations, an outsider can hardly distinguish SWS students from others unless they are gathered in SWS hangouts. Even though they are commonly referred to as "the freaks," conversations with SWS students reveal a great deal of variation in style, goals, and modes of expression. A young woman who is a senior is neat and preppy-looking. After feeling lost and faceless during her freshman year at Brookline, she applied to SWS because she hated the competitive atmosphere of "the downstairs school" (the name used by SWS-ers to refer to the rest of the school). It has been good for her. She reports that competition among students is reduced, there is less concern about grades, and no one is invisible. She plans to apply to a string of elite colleges—Yale, Brown, Swarthmore, Wesleyan—and thinks she now has the self-confidence to thrive in a more highly structured setting.

Even though the stereotypes of SWS are overdrawn and no longer seem to apply, its identity as a vital community, with a unique ethos and encompassing power, still prevails. Insiders enjoy and often exaggerate its singular qualities. Says one ebullient student, "In SWS people care about learning. There is a real sense of community." In the weekly SWS Town Meeting I attended, students' and faculty's comments often underscored the contrasts between their school and "the downstairs school." The collective body was trying to decide whether to attend the election forum for Town Meeting representatives that would be organized around house structures. There was some curiosity about the big-school process, a slight sense of superiority about their extensive experience as a democratic community, and a wish to maintain their distance and autonomy.

FIRST VOICE: "I don't think we should go. We are not the downstairs school. We're the upstairs school."

SECOND VOICE: "Yes, we are a community here, but we're also part of Brookline High School."

THIRD VOICE: "Maybe someone could go and report back what they say . . . in the world outside of Room 401."

The ambivalence about how much to become involved in the life of the larger community and how to maintain the boundaries is related to a persistent theme, constantly being faced and negotiated by SWS. The director of SWS refers to it as a "natural process" of identity formation. It is difficult to establish feelings of cohesion and commitment within SWS without some turning away from the outside world. In trying to nurture the "we"-feeling of SWS there is the inevitable rejection of the downstairs school. For some this rejection sounds exaggerated and defensive; the boundaries are overdrawn. Says one girl who is opposed to following the school-wide rules of detention and suspension, "If you are up here (SWS), you're more responsible than the rest of the school by definition." But for other students, there is a searching for a balance between separation from and integration into the larger school structure. SWS is a strong anchor and a comfortable home that makes the entry into the downstairs school less threatening.

Part of the sense of community in SWS comes from its small scale, but part comes from the fact that it is primarily an educational enterprise and its members are a much more homogeneous group than the diversity reflected in the school at large. Additionally, the SWS students must apply and be selected for membership. At the end of their freshman year, students can apply to join SWS. They are interviewed by SWS faculty who make a judgment about whether they are likely to become responsible members of the community and thrive in a less structured and open environment. Some applicants seem too immature to tolerate the increased choice or confused about what they want; others are really hoping for a school that will demand nothing from them. These students are turned away in favor of those who appear to have more maturity, energy, and direction.

SWS tends to attract a relatively homogeneous group of students. It is a mostly upper middle-class White community with only two Blacks and one Asian. The director explains undefensively, "It is hard enough being different in this school without also separating yourself off in

SWS—with all its negative images." She claims the Black students, in particular, feel that coming to SWS is "like selling out . . . like joining the White forces." After spending some time in SWS meetings, classes, and hangouts, I can also imagine that minority parents would not feel inclined to encourage their adolescents to join what they might perceive to be a loose and permissive atmosphere. The relatively unstructured environment of SWS would be unappealing or threatening to parents who emphasize order and structured authority within their families.

One SWS teacher feels slightly defensive about the homogeneity and says that his concern is more with the social class separations than with the racial sameness. He thinks the community would be more interesting and vital if it were more diverse. Instead there is a tendency for subcultural, within-group phenomena to be exaggerated. He points to the large proportion of SWS students who come from homes with separated and divorced parents and the assumption of abundance by students. Parents, often guilty about their split families, tend to indulge their offspring with material gifts. With large numbers of students living similar lives, there is less opportunity for witnessing other lifestyles and a tendency to assume that what they know is normal and good.

When pushed to characterize the SWS students, the director at first demurs from making facile generalizations and then says tentatively, "They are individualistic risk-takers, nonconformists." Some clearly suffer from emotional and social problems and look to faculty and peers for heavy doses of psychological support. Their pain may be expressed in severe learning disabilities. Many are gifted intellectually, are extremely articulate, and unusually creative. The hundred students display a range of skills, competencies, and intellectual styles, but most agree that SWS has more than its share of "bright kids."

The faculty of SWS also have a school-wide reputation as competent, caring, and highly committed teachers. One downstairs teacher says, "If I had to choose one spot in this school for my son, where I would know he would get excellent academic attention, I would choose SWS." The director describes its image as "paradoxical." On the one hand, SWS is resented for "siphoning off" the leaders and skimming the cream of the crop from the downstairs school. This image portrays SWS as an elite academy for the privileged. While on the other hand, there is relief that SWS is an asylum for the wild, uncontrollable types and the rest of the school can be saved from their negative influences. In this picture, SWS is a place for misfits. To some extent students and faculty must labor under this conflicting imagery and feel the mixed messages sent by outsiders. But mostly they seem to go about the hard work of sustaining a community committed to democratic ideals and developing an academic curriculum that is responsive to student needs.

SWS students take about half of their courses within the small community and half in the downstairs school. The five SWS faculty members teach courses in math, social studies, English, psychology, and counseling. The two women faculty, who teach English, share a single job. All of the faculty have been at SWS for more than three years and there is a strong tone of continuity and stability. They share a sense of history, rare in alternative schools, that offers a good perspective on pressing, immediate concerns. They also seem realistic about the limits and liabilities of the democratic structure and try to train students to take more responsible roles. Says one faculty member, who notices some progress in student leadership skills, "We have learned to work very hard behind the scenes before meetings, setting the agenda, and coaching the kids." Twelve years after its creation, SWS is a sturdy community less threatened by negative perceptions and assaults, but still confronted with the persistent struggles of making a difficult process work and still a distance from its idealized goals. Ironically, its survival has a lot to do with the tone and culture of the downstairs school. The director recognizes that fact. "Brookline High, as a whole, is unusual in its individualistic approach to students." Without that bedrock of agreement in fundamental philosophy between the downstairs and upstairs schools, it is unlikely that SWS would have survived and ultimately thrived.

CLOSE STRANGERS

Communities are also defined by those who are excluded from them. At Brookline High the group of students that most people identify as "separate," "alienated," "victimized," or "different," are "the METCO kids." The one hundred students in the METCO (Metropolitan Council for Educational Opportunity) program are not a monolithic group, but people often refer to them as if they were all alike and as if they all cause trouble and "make waves." I met several METCO students who are thriving at Brookline, feel comfortable in the setting, and appreciate its abundance; others who hate the place. Said one bitter sophomore girl, "There's too much trouble here. It's like a soap opera and I don't like being part of a soap opera." A middle range of METCO students cope with episodes of exclusion and prejudice, but also enjoy moments of accomplishment and friendship at Brookline. Yet most people agree that more than any other identifiable group, the METCO students do not take full advantage of the environment, neither are they treated with the same level of respect by their peers and teachers.

At nine in the morning when I arrive for my appointment with Grace Taylor, the METCO coordinator, she is streaking down the hall responding to an emergency. She sees me and yells "You can come if you want to—I'm dealing with a very hot situation." Sitting in Taylor's office is Irene, a ninth-grade METCO student. Irene is jet black—almost the color of her black knickers. She is carefully dressed in white sneakers and socks, a new-looking, tan down jacket. Her hair is pressed neatly and closely cropped. There is a hardness to her face that makes her appear much older than her fourteen years. As I meet her, I think to myself that she would be an attractive person if she only felt good about herself. My next thought is how hard it must be for a young Black adolescent girl—with her color and her hair—to have a positive self-image in a society that still devalues those qualities.

Taylor, a slender, attractive woman with reddish brown hair and light brown skin is beautifully dressed in a soft-gray pant suit. Her outfit is decorated with gold chains and her wrist jangles with charms and bangles. She gives off every sign of confidence in who she is. Taylor sits behind a desk piled with papers and introduces me to Irene, who is sitting in the chair closest to her. The small, cramped office is decorated with proud Black images—posters of jazz musicians, scientists, judges, and sportsmen. There are sayings on the wall that are designed to encourage pride in Blackness and inspire hard work and discipline.

Taylor's face shows a mixture of weariness, pain, and anger as she confronts Irene. The METCO coordinator has heard rumors of a fight that is planned for after school and Irene has been targeted as the provocateur. The fight would be among METCO girls, off campus at the streetcar stop. Irene admits to the planned rumble and slowly divulges her part in it. In response to Taylor's tough and persistent questions, Irene confesses that she tends "to talk a lot" about other people and "get into their business." Her talking "gets her in trouble." When Taylor asks how she might change her behavior, Irene looks down at the floor as she whispers, "Well, maybe I'd stop being bad if they would beat me up. . . . If they beat me up maybe I'll stop." "Look at me, Irene. Lift your head up and *look* at me," demands Taylor. "Is that the only solution you can come up with . . . to get beat up?" After much prodding Irene thinks of a less violent alternative, "Well I could just stay away from them." "Well, that is a start," says Taylor with slight relief.

In the course of the intense exchange, Taylor makes several points that reflect her tough realism, her sensitivity to Irene's pain, and her absolute intolerance of violence and fighting. "It is all right not to like each other. . . . There are lots of people I don't like . . . but it is unacceptable to get into fights in school. . . . Here are the cold, hard facts. There will be no fight this afternoon. If there is a fight, you will be back in Hyde Park High tomorrow. I will not tolerate this!" Irene's shock and sudden grimace indicate that she believes the threat; that she does not want to be sent back to the big city high school where the dangers are even greater.

Before she sends the girl off to class, Taylor gets the names of the students involved in the anticipated fight. "Who are they? . . . Whose side are they on? . . . Are they friend or foe?" Irene reveals her allies and enemies; Taylor writes the list down and promises to talk to each one individually and to all of them together if it becomes necessary. The harsh words seem to have an impact on Irene. She is clearly concerned about the repercussions of fighting and worried about how she can retreat without losing her honor. Her face shows some relief and perhaps gratitude. Taylor's intervention may save her from self-destruction, and she now knows that she has been noticed and attended to. She is not invisible.

Before she has a chance to take a break, Taylor begins to track down the other accomplices. She calls the houses with which each is affiliated and leaves an urgent message: "Tell her she must come to my office at the beginning of homeroom period. It is *very* important." These conversations take place within the twenty-minute homeroom slot, before Taylor has to go off and teach her social studies course.

Grace Taylor has been at Brookline High School for ten years. For the first three years she was a full-time teacher in the social studies department and then became the full-time coordinator for the METCO program during the next seven years. With Proposition 2½ (a newly passed state law that reduces tax revenues), the METCO funding has been drastically reduced and Taylor now teaches three classes and coordinates the METCO program only part-time. All of her METCO business must be reduced to the two morning hours between 8:00 and 10:00. The casualties of lost time are great. "I am overwhelmed, overworked, and can't give my kids the attention they need," she complains. In the past, Taylor saw herself as "the protector" of METCO students, in touch with every sphere of their lives. She knew their families, would meet them at the trolley in the morning, have breakfast with them in the school cafeteria, and be available to hear their problems and put out brush fires. Her full-time status gave her the chance to know them intimately and recognize subtle signs of trouble. Gene Brown, a handsome senior boy, always came to school dressed in snazzy clothes. When he would occasionally arrive in jeans, sweatshirt, and sneakers, Taylor recognized that this was the signal that he was prepared to fight. "You see, he didn't want to get his fancy clothes all messed up." Spotting his casual dress, Taylor would collar him and make him cool off in her office. The fight would be avoided, and Gene did not have to lose face with his peers. "Taylor docked me. She made me sit in her office," he would complain. Explains his protector, "You see, he was *asking* for someone to stop him because he couldn't stop himself."

With her time severely reduced, Taylor is no longer able to know every METCO student or recognize their cries for help. She complains that she does not even know many of the names of the thirty-six METCO freshmen who arrived in September and there has been no way to develop the all-important trust and sense of connection with them. Instead of reaching out to her and seeking her support, they are more likely to respond to her approaches with "who are you? What right do you have to tell us what to do?"

The coordinator feels very strongly that METCO students need a vigilant advocate in Brookline High School. She offers examples of the "benign racism" and subtle hostility that they receive from a few of the "pseudo-liberal faculty." One morning during first period, Taylor looked in the cafeteria and discovered a bunch of METCO students eating break-fast. When she asked why they were not in class, they explained casually, "Oh, you know, we told our teacher that we couldn't concentrate be-cause we didn't have breakfast . . . and she said go get some." Taylor is floored—by the teacher's gullibility, or her eagerness to get rid of these students. She does not view it as a sympathetic act. "Those kids *all* have breakfast at home. Their *families* see to that. If not, they can get it *before* school." Another example: At the *end* of last year, a teacher approached a group of METCO students in his class and said that they should not have been disruptive in class because that confirms the stereotypes that White kids have of Black people. Taylor fumes, "Why didn't that teacher come down hard on those kids at the moment of misbehavior? Why did he wait until the end of the semester? Why did he speak to them as a group rather than individually? Some of them were well-behaved and man-nerly students, a few were being terribly disruptive." Taylor judges that the physical education department is most culpable of this subtle racism.

"The gym is a place where lots of the Black guys hang out and some of the coaches will come and say, 'Taylor, you want to know what *your* kids said' . . . and I say to them, as long as you say *your* and not *our*, the problem's going to be there. . . . If teachers always send kids to me when they have trouble with them, then they are relinquishing some of their power and handing it over to me."

The passion and outrage with which Taylor tells these stories probably reflects her deep commitment to these students and her role as their protector and advocate. She does not pretend to be dispassionate or objective and is willing to risk the anger and hostility of some of her colleagues in order to do her job. "Sometimes they see me coming and say, 'Oh no, here comes Taylor' . . . I don't mind them feeling that way about me as long as it helps my kids."

Even those faculty members who are as vigilant as Grace Taylor about assaulting racism in the school do not necessarily share her views of the oppressive environment. Without the encumbrances of the protector role, they see a less discriminatory community than she does. Says another Black faculty member who is very supportive of Taylor's efforts and admires her courage and aggressiveness, "Brookline High School is not perfect, but it is better than any other school I've seen. White administrators and teachers will not be intimidated by Black kids and that is rare. These are good, strong teachers and you will be jammed if you don't do your work. Black kids have to make the grade."

Despite the differences in perception, both agree that the presence of Blacks on the faculty is critically important to the tone of the school and essential to their sense of support. There is a "strong cadre" of about ten Black faculty (two houseteachers, two teachers in English, one librarian who is new, two in math, two in social studies, and one about to be hired in physics) who refer to themselves as "The Summit." They wanted to avoid the separatist image of listing themselves as the "Black Faculty" when they were announcing their meetings in the school bulletins. Besides offering counsel and alliance to one another and serving as important images for Black students, they have worked hard to plan programs designed especially for the Black students. Last year they sponsored a weekend retreat for twenty-five selected students in New Hampshire. They worked with them on "some leadership skills and some fun stuff. . . . Then brought them back and turned them loose on the school, saying 'spread the good word.'" With Proposition 2½, everyone feels too overwhelmed with work to harness the energy for another retreat. There are tentative plans in the works for a meeting with seniors to do some practice sessions for the S.A.T. exam, or maybe a get-together with fresh-men to talk about "how one survives for four years in this place."

Black faculty seem balanced between their special affiliations with Black youngsters and their general commitments to the school commun-ity as a whole. A houseteacher talks about the precariousness of the balance. "You know, some of the Black girls that I've been working with on this dance coming up feel that they own me and get angry when other kids come around. They want to claim me as theirs . . . but I am a house-teacher for *all* the kids. Negotiating this thing is sometimes tricky. . . . It *is* possible to feel a special commitment to minority kids at the same time as I feel a commitment to the well-being of all kids."

McCarthy recognizes the balancing act. He describes the Black faculty as intensely committed and "thoroughly professional." When "enough trust had built" after McCarthy's arrival last year, the Black teachers met with him to talk about the ways they had been misused as faculty members and their needs for administrative support. Because they were Black they were often expected to counsel all Black students, put out brush fires that erupted among Black students, rescue Black students from trouble spots, and be authorities on the Black psyche and Black culture. All of these expectations were loaded on top of their regular teaching chores and committee assignments. Their special status also meant that other teachers were not forced to learn how to deal with Black students, or even consider them their responsibility. McCarthy claims that slowly perceptions have begun to shift. When a Black kid gets in trouble, the appropriate housemaster is now called, not a Black teacher. If he or she is having emotional problems, the counselling office offers supportive services. Yet the burdensome expectations still persist to some extent. Observes one young white female teacher, "Brookline High School has the art of tokenism down to a fine point. . . . The few Blacks are expected to sit on all the committees just so the school can say there is equal representation."

Minority faculty are also important in the lives of majority students. I am told a story about Mr. Hall, a thoughtful and caring Black social studies teacher with an excellent reputation among his colleagues. Last year one of the girls from the Point searched out Mr. Hall and said, "I have a friend who may be pregnant and if she is, her parents will kill her." Mr. Hall guessed that the young woman was talking about herself and gave her lots of his own time and directed her to counselors and a social worker. At the end of the year she walked up to him with her girl friend and gave him a gift. The teacher who related the story was there and marveled, "It was really something to see this Irish Catholic girl from the Point hugging Bob Hall and giving him a poem she had written on a parchment scroll." She shakes her head. "See, it's those kids who need minority role models, not just the minority kids. . . . Don't you think it's amazing that the girl from a neighborhood that is basically racist would choose a Black teacher to confide in? It is testimony to Bob's understanding and empathetic personality."

ACADEMIC LIFE: A BROAD CURRICULUM

In recent years, some concern has been expressed about the quality of education at the high school level in Brookline. Most parents feel fairly confident that their children are receiving a fine education at the elementary school level. The eight elementary schools are small in scale and have distinct identities and affiliations with neighborhoods in Brookline. Inevitably, there is more sense of connection and accountability between teachers and parent groups in these schools. Brookline High, on the other hand, is the "great melting pot," receiving students from all over the town. Some people link the melting pot image with dilution of excellence, with a lack of purity. This concern for the reduced standards created by mixtures is heightened by the recent growth in minority populations and general population shifts. Observers who support the high school claim that the elementary schools are parochial enclaves, while the secondary school is a cosmopolitan community. These protagonists see what others call dilution as enrichment.

However, these perceptions are relative; derived from contrasting the status of elementary and secondary education within Brookline. If one simply looks at Brookline High without benefit of contrast or comparison, one is struck by its persistent and unchallenged academic image. The high school population is unusually stable. Ninety percent of the students stay for four years, with only a two percent rate of transfers and dropouts. An eleven-year longitudinal survey (1970-1980) done by the guidance department, indicates that an average of 78 percent of the graduates have gone on to higher education—66 percent to four-year colleges and 12 percent to two-year educational institutions. The guidance office also identifies the 19 percent who were accepted at "colleges considered prestigious." It is this latter group that shapes much of the image of Brookline High, not the 22 percent who do not go on to post-high school education, deciding instead to work or enter the armed services. Even though the high school's reputation seems fixed on the academic image, the curriculum and pedagogy embrace the whole population of students.

The course catalogue for the high school reveals the broad spectrum of students and the faculty attempts to respond to diverse needs. There are 300 courses in the formal curriculum (and more than 500 courses listed in the catalogue). These include academic offerings at the "Basic, Standard, Honors, and Advanced Placement (A.P.) levels"; offerings in the arts—fine, performing, physical, visual, and industrial; in home economics; and occupational education. To an outsider leafing through the catalogue, the choices seem endless and the possibilities overwhelming. For example, in the catalogue, twenty-three pages are devoted to Career Education with eleven different courses of study (including Business/Accounting and Administration, Early Childhood Education, Food Service Careers, Medical Careers, Technical/Industrial, and several others). Career Education became part of the high school curriculum in 1966 and efforts are made to provide optional part-time work experiences outside of school for those who are interested.

With twenty-one pages in the catalogue, the foreign language department offers Chinese, English as a Second Language, French, German, Italian, Russian, Spanish, and Latin. The English department and Individualized Study Program each have seventeen descriptive pages in the catalogue. The English department offers an array of writing courses from composition to journalism; literature courses including American, British, and Minority literature; and supplementary courses in public speaking, and grammar and usage. The Individualized Study Program provides alternative ways for students to learn both inside and outside of school. There are volunteer experiences and apprenticeships, college courses throughout Greater Boston, independent study with individual teachers, and so on.

The social studies department, with fourteen pages in the course catalogue, offers diverse courses in history, social sciences, and civics. Among the history courses are "American History for Foreign Students," "Black Studies," "Afro-American History," and "American Constitutional History." The social sciences include "World Culture," "Women in Society," and "American Studies." Civics courses include "Law and the Individual," "Law and Society," and "Introduction to Criminal Justice." The other academic areas of science and math reveal more classical selections, but the same broad array of courses.

It is in the performing and visual arts that one is struck by the most eclectic range of courses. It is rare that public schools, even schools for the privileged, are able to provide these rich aesthetic possibilities. Visual arts include drawing, painting, sculpture, printmaking, ceramics, jewelry making, cartooning, photography, and filmmaking, among others. The performing arts department provides experiences in music (with fifteen courses), dance (with six courses), and drama (with five courses).

Faculty express mixed feelings about the great proliferation of courses since the mid-1960s. Some view it as a worthy attempt to respond to the increasingly diverse needs and goals of students. Others are critical because they see it as a retreat from academic excellence. In their view, the broad range of courses reflects a diminished standard, a subtle discrimination against those students who are judged inadequate to make the academic grade. Still others see the thick catalogue as evidence of the school's unclear goals, an unwillingness to decide what is most important in the curriculum. This latter group of teachers see unanticipated advantages in the recent budget cuts. "We'll finally have to decide what is most important," says one critic.

Perhaps in response to reduced resources, but certainly inspired by new school leadership, a group of faculty developed a statement of philosophy for Brookline High School. Beyond these more organic reasons, the faculty were responding to the dictates of the 1980 Ten-Year Evaluation which required the development of a statement of educational philosophy. Working over the summer, four faculty members engaged in deep discussion and prepared increasingly coherent drafts. By this ambitious effort, they attempted to create a document that would "guide, confirm, and incite thought about the ways in which knowledge is held and acquired." It is through this document, not the course catalogue, that one begins to gain a sense of the ways in which this institution seeks to confront a changing and diverse society. Largely the inspiration and language of a faculty member who is described by his colleagues as "deep," "literate," and "philosophical," the words are often labored and cloudy. The document certainly does not express a collective view, a common voice. However, I was very impressed by how much faculty-student relationships and educational exchanges imperfectly fit the lofty, philosophical language. It is clearly a statement of goals, but many teachers seem to take those ideals seriously in their work with students. After several laborious drafts—each becoming clearer and less encumbered by opaque prose—this fall, the faculty voted unanimously to approve this five-point "Statement of Philosophy."

1. *Education Presumes a Climate of Care*

The schoolhouse must be a kind of home which offers its inhabitants a sense of belonging, of individuality strengthened by expectation, of security born of respect. As in the home, the student should feel known but revered; the teacher, exposed but esteemed. Reason should prevail, and where reason falls short, tolerance abide. Regard for excellence need not preclude acceptance of human foible; neither should devotion and understanding be devoid of rigor. Care is by nature compensatory, seeking to provide that which would otherwise be lacking.

II. *Thoughtfulness Is the Social As Well As the Intellectual Aim of Education*

The habit of reflection is the ideal trait of the educated mind, taking for its concern what others may be satisfied to take for granted. Education should foster this habit, should teach us patience in the understanding and construction of ideas. But it should also teach us to consider feelings, to anticipate the probable effect of our actions and words on others, and to temper these when they augur injury. Education is thus forethought rather than afterthought, abiding thought rather than sporadic thought.

III. *No Style of Learning or Teaching Is Privileged*

Learning and teaching are two sides of the same coin. Both rely on a sense of timing, a state of readiness, a heightened sensibility which enables one to see or say or think something not seen or said or thought before. Readiness is achieved in different ways, depending on what there is to be learned. Sometimes it requires painful and protracted effort—thinking, reading, watching, writing, talking, doing. Other times it is attained effortlessly, almost inadvertently. Either way, timing is critical. Knowing how to learn or how to teach is essentially knowing when to press and when to wait. Styles of learning and teaching are characterized by their mix of pressure and patience. Thorough education will expose teachers and students to a range of styles so that they come to know their own.

IV. *Learning Is a Mixture of Pleasure and of Pain*

The love of learning is an acquired taste, an addiction for the tart rather than the sweet. To learn is to change, and to change can be both exhilarating and wrenching. As creatures of habit, we must approach learning with trepidation, not expecting those who learn to experience a smooth trajectory of triumphs, nor those who teach to effect unrelieved excitement about their subject. While it is true that what is most easily learned is usually hardest taught, it is also true that love of learning cannot be taught; it can only be exemplified. As is so often averred, teaching requires patience. Let it also be said that what teaching requires, learning must learn.

V. *Education Examines Not the Individual but the Species*

The value of learning lies not so much in its immediate utility as in its generality. Schools are instituted and maintained to serve their communities as havens of learning, not as microcosms of the market place. Here students are apprenticed to life in its ideal form, life that is devoted to inquiry, touched by beauty, informed by justice, guided by reason, girded by simplicity, graced by elegance. At the very least, graduates should exhibit competency in the exercise of certain skills—computation, composition—but the aim is to make them literate about the full array of human achievement, so that they will know what it means to do anything well.

In December, the school newspaper, *The Sagamore*, summarized the "Statement of Philosophy" and compared it to the one developed a decade earlier as part of the school's 1970 evaluation. "The old philosophy stressed individual growth. The new philosophy stresses the idea of the school as a community conducive to all types of learning; where respect for differences encourages caring; and where students can learn from students as well as teachers; where all styles of teaching and learning are valued; and where reason, patience, and tolerance improve the school as well as our understanding of ourselves and others."

The apparent shift of emphasis from individual to community, from competition to caring, from sameness to diversity, fits with the current rhetoric and ideals faculty move towards in practice. The rhetoric and goals seem to express clarity and general consensus. As one would expect, in practice people reveal their ambivalence, their wishes to hang on to old values, and their difficulties in facing the transition. It appears that in practice the community is now precariously balanced between old and new educational and philosophical ideals, poised somewhere between the extremes of separation and integration, individuality and community.

It is only when one contrasts educational practice with philosophical ideals that one feels some sense of discouragement. Mostly, one is impressed with the level of academic engagement in this high school and only occasionally disgruntled by imperfections and breaks in the generally good standards. There is visible evidence of educational commitment. When you walk through the halls of the school during class periods and peer through open doors, students tend to be attentive and busy. A typing class is energetically engaged in pounding the keys, working against a stopwatch. In a physics laboratory, small groups of students work collectively on an experiment while the teacher circulates around the room offering encouragement and clarification. It is very quiet and all eyes face forward in a U.S. history course where the teacher is lecturing with little affect or drama. A quick, passing gaze finds things going on in the classrooms, minimal chaos, and directed attention. Most teachers seem to feel confident enough about order and quiet in their classrooms that they leave their doors to the hall open, or offer no surprise when an intrusive observer stares through the glass of a closed door. Classroom boundaries are not severe. The educational settings seem open and highly penetrable.

Another indication of educational engagement is audible rather than visual. I am surprised not to hear the harsh sounds of bells that indicate the beginning and end of class periods. The day's rhythms appear to be internalized by both faculty and students, who do not rely on the external alarms. Despite the absence of bells, all the classes I visited started easily on time and without much fanfare. The only times when bells are used is to mark the homeroom period, a largely procedural event. It seems to me that a school that was not serious about education could not proceed without bells. They would be a needed enforcer of student and teacher behavior. Instead, Brookline students show surprise when I inquire about the lack of bells. Says one to me in mock alarm "This isn't a prison, you know! We're not Pavlov's dogs!"

Beyond these immediate signs of educational engagement, there is a great deal of evidence of the seriousness attached to schooling as one enters classrooms. The seriousness of purpose is not limited to courses for bright, academic students. In a reading class for students with major learning disabilities, the room is noiseless as the students work individually at their seats. The teacher insists upon quiet and helps them focus on their assignments. When their attention wanders, she directs them back to the task; when they become discouraged and begin to turn off, she supports them and re-engages them in their work. When one begins to be disruptive and distracts his classmates from their reading, the teacher will not tolerate it and reprimands him severely. With only a few minutes left to go in the class period, Christopher resists getting another assignment from the teacher: "But it's only four minutes left." Says the teacher firmly, "I know, but you have to do something in those four minutes. Hurry up or you'll only have three minutes left!" When Randy approaches the teacher for approval because he has gotten a perfect score on an exercise, the teacher pushes him to do more challenging work. "Randy, if you got one hundred, it was too easy. Did you feel it was too easy?" This teacher is dedicated, skilled, and committed to teaching students who might be considered unteachable and unreachable in many other schools. The atmosphere is serious, the rules clear, the caring certain, and the methods eclectic. "I will do anything that works," she says with force.

The same seriousness is attached to non-academic courses. In an advanced dance class, the teacher has a friendly but no-nonsense approach. In a studio well equipped with bars, mirrors, and a shiny wood floor, Ms. Shelley directs students in the ritualized exercises. With soothing, melodic music, the twenty-five female students go through their practiced movements with silent attention, some showing an intense involvement in their faces, others with glazed eyes and automatic responses. The teacher's attention is even and focused. She walks around the floor, adjusting movements, occasionally demonstrating, and softly counting the beat. When she presents a new stretching exercise, an anxious student asks, "Will you talk this through when we do it?" Ms. Shelley responds supportively, "Yes, I'll talk it through." When small groups are practicing a short jazz sequence that is part of a larger piece choreographed by Ms. Shelley, the range of skills is revealed. The more able dancers capture the syncopation and difficult, arched-back movement by watching and trying it a few times. The less confident dancers break down half-way across the floor and show some embarrassment at their awkwardness. Ms. Shelley continues to prod and direct, and then offers restrained approval. "This is looking so much stronger." These are the best dancers in the school. In order to enter the advanced class you must audition. One would expect a level of skill and attention here, and one would imagine that a teacher might feel more committed to these potential protégés. However, when I observe Ms. Shelley with her class of beginning ballet students, there is the same expectation that students will work hard.

Ms. Shelley is realistic in her assessment of her students' abilities. She knows that for the most part she is not training future dancers, but she is committed to teaching the discipline of dance and to offering dance as an important avenue to self-awareness. She sees connections between mind and body: "I've heard so many times from the counselors that dance has had an incredible impact on the girls' self-images. . . . They begin to have a different feeling about their bodies." In giving herself fully to this enterprise, Shelley recognizes her psychological limits. She knows she cannot give indefinitely without the aesthetic highs that all artists need to remain involved in their work. Her teaching is sustained by her own artistic commitments outside of school. She explains, "I find teaching a pleasure because I also perform. . . . I have rehearsals late afternoon and evenings . . . and that feeds *me*. I need that. It also helps me stay vital in teaching the kids." In order to be a dedicated teacher, Shelley searches for a balance between giving out and taking in and finds renewal beyond the boundaries of school.

Even in courses that tend to attract noncollege-bound students, there is attention to pedagogy and curriculum, and a commitment to good form. In a food service course, the teacher shows an industrious style, clear goals, and high standards. The students will have futures different from their achieving academic peers, but they are given respect and taken seriously as part of the school community.

The nine students in the food service course are making Italian feather bread. All nine are girls who range from freshmen to seniors. They are working in the large, sun-filled, warm, good-smelling kitchen. There is very little discussion among students, who, with the exception of one girl, are working in pairs. I am told that they saw a demonstration of the process in class yesterday, so today they are excited about making their own loaves of bread. They work quietly, familiar with their kitchen work stations. The stations, like the room, are spacious and well-equipped. I wander among the students, talking with them first about their task and, as they choose, other topics.

The only girl working without a partner tells me that her partner isn't in school today. She says, "It would go faster if she was here but working alone is okay." She is about 5'6", a heavyset, large-boned young woman who tells me she washes, sets, and styles her short hair each morning around six. She has carefully applied blue eye shadow, blue eyeliner, and thick mascara. Her lips and finger-nails are glossy and red. The loaf of bread she makes will be served to her father and her boyfriend at dinner. She cooks for them four nights a week because her mother is a cocktail waitress. Her mother has been either a cocktail waitress or bartender all her life. She tells me, "My mother's hours are crazy because of her work. She can never go to bed before 4:30 A.M. In the summer, I used to try and stay up with her sometimes because she looked so lonely sitting in front of the TV all by herself. But my dad and I need to go to bed by one A.M. We've changed a little for her though."

She's taking this course along with sewing, a foreign cooking course, English, and typing. "I need English to graduate this year. The other things I'll use. I already do. My boyfriend and me are getting married next October. I want to be able to cook and sew good. I think it's important that a family have good food, you know, good nutrition. They should all eat their dinner together. That's the way I'll be." She tells me how busy she is getting her hope chest organized. "I want everything in order by October [1982] so we can move into our own place. We're looking for a house now in Mansfield, Mass. My brother lives out there and we go out, me and my boyfriend, every weekend. My sister-in-law does a lot of cooking. She even jars jelly and does yeast bread. It's that kind of place—real country. My boyfriend does construction so he's looking for work there." She explains that she's from a large Greek family so they're already planning the wedding.

I join another pair who work smoothly, moving in and out of each other's movements. Both are about 5'7". The young Black woman is wearing navy slacks and a red, V-neck terry shirt with "B.H.S." in white letters over her left breast. Her navy slacks are dusted white with flour. Her partner, also a junior, is White with shoulder-length brown hair, curled limply around her pale face. The Black girl looks directly at me, her shoulders squared, and asks, "What are you doing here?" Her tone is directly curious, straightforward. I smile involuntarily and explain. She interrupts me to ask if I'm working on "that racial study." I tell her I don't know about "that racial study." She says, "B.U. has a project here to improve the racial and social climate at B.H.S." She grimaces. I ask what that face means. She says, "You been hanging out here?" I respond positively. "Well what do you think about our cliques?" Without waiting for an answer, she says, pointing her head at her partner, "We don't belong to cliques. There's no one we want to impress around here." I look at the other girl who looks down at her bread dough, keeping her eyes averted. Sensing my gaze she looks up, smiling shyly. "We don't want to be in a clique with all the same people. We have lots of different friends, that's better." "Yah," says the Black girl, nodding her head. "If you belong to a clique, you do what they do. Wear the clothes they do. Talk like them. Who needs it?"

The teacher is moving among work stations. She is a woman in her fifties, with gray hair, plainly and neatly dressed. Throughout the class, she has tended to work with a pair of freshmen who look especially confused. She never approaches the work stations when I'm there. She is teaching constantly. When answering questions which she thinks might help all the girls, she raises her voice. This signal suffices. All the girls turn to look at her and to listen.

Twenty minutes into class, three girls walk in and approach the teacher. She looks at the clock, then in a loud voice says, "This time I'm going to be nice to you and give you dough from the other girls who started on time. That way you can make your own loaf. Girls, I want all of you to weigh your dough. Keep one pound to make your own loaves and give me the rest for these girls."

None of the girls complain, but quietly commence weighing. The teacher collects the dough and gives it to the three newcomers. They are different in appearance from the rest of the students. Their style of dress is preppy. One girl is wearing turquoise pants, a striped shirt with collar turned up, a yellow sweater, Nike running shoes, and a yellow ribbon at the end of her long, elaborately woven blond braid. I watch her throughout the rest of the period and am amazed that she never moves faster than a desultory pace, never touches the bread dough, and never gets her hands wet in the cleanup effort. Instead, she manages to eat three pieces of buttered bread prepared by the last class. She seems to have an easy rapport with the teacher. They exchange frequent smiles and small talk.

The rest of the class continues to work efficiently, watching their time carefully. There is a serious air about the room as pairs murmur quietly, coaching each other. Out of the twelve girls present, five are Black, two Asian and five White. They are fourteen to eighteen years old. Later, the teacher tells me that most have taken several home economics classes, but a couple have taken the class because they "need easy credits for graduation."

As the class nears the end, the out-of-class conversation increases. The teacher announces loudly, "No one can leave until your station is cleaned-up and checked-out." The cleanup process is purposeful and rushed. At the end of the period, the students are speeding out the door. I stay behind in the now quiet kitchen to help the teacher clean up and to talk. She tells me, "The primary stress in home economics is preparation of food for yourself. In food service it's different. They learn about institutional cooking and cleanup as an integral part of their work. There are different stresses related to the job demands. Since last spring, when they opened the student-run restaurant, we've had to divide Food Service I in half. In the first half they are in classes and in the second half they work in the cafeteria. Some stay in the cafeteria for Food Service II, III, and IV, but now students can work in the school restaurant, too. In the restaurant, students cook and serve the food, order supplies, and keep the books with a little supervision from Mr. Kearny, a food services teacher. The restaurant is opened to the general public Tuesdays and Thursdays. Breakfast and lunch are served."

She says, "Up here [second floor] I order, buy, and keep inventory on all the food needed for classes. There's a lot of work involved in teaching cooking and now because of Two and a Half, the School Committee has got it into its head that we should be teaching more students per class. Can you imagine trying to teach more than twelve kids each class? You've seen this place in action. It would be impossible." She shakes her head. "They've never been in my class. They don't care about quality of teaching at all—just numbers. Churn those students out. Who cares if they learn."

Even though academic images shape Brookline's image, the school seeks to be responsive to the range of people in its student population. Certainly there are lost souls who slip through unnoticed and unchallenged. Certainly not all teaching is at a high level. One hears the typical student complaints about teachers who are uninspired, tedious, and boring. Yet the general standards for teaching and learning seem to be high, and the standards remain high across the range of academic abilities and choices.

Even more impressive are those "star" teachers who challenge students to even greater heights, who test their limits: the biology teacher who chooses to teach the Basic level courses in order to seduce students into science who would normally not dare to take such a "scary and hard" subject; the Constitutional history teacher who has developed an innovative curriculum using primary sources and original documents, and has created a pedagogical style that uses role playing and simulation activities; the English teacher who has developed a course called "The Art of the Essay" where students write and critically respond to each others' pieces. Risk-taking, passion, discipline, and honesty are encouraged by the teacher, who reveals all of those qualities in her own approach to the work.

In a Standard level American literature class, the students are in the midst of reading and discussing *Death of a Salesman*. The desks and chairs are arranged in a circle and the teacher's style is supportive, thoughtful, and responsive to student needs and direction. Many students in this class have been judged to have learning disabilities and their behaviors show that they have difficulties in focusing their attention. At the beginning of class, Ms. Dickerson's comments about their written assignments reveal a beautiful balance of empathy and intellectual challenge. She returns their papers and warns, "Now folks, don't panic. Some of you got low grades . . . but consider this a little grade, the equivalent of a quiz. . . . This is like the core of a paper, beginning ideas . . . if you have a low grade, it is a sign that there has been a misunderstanding." She clarifies the assignment due the next day. "You will need to develop a thesis statement. . . . A thesis statement means it must be a debatable idea or opinion, not a factual statement. . . . Pitfalls for a debatable statement—it can be too huge and expansive [she offers an example]; it can be so obvious that only a ninny would debate it. . . . Virginia Woolf says a writer is one that sticks his neck out . . . a firm stand with some intellectual risk. . . . Then backs it up with evidence." The atmosphere is comfortable and unthreatening even though Dickerson is urging them to be both disciplined and free, careful and courageous in their writing.

When they turn to the discussion of *Death of a Salesman*, many of the students' comments sound confused and inarticulate, but the teacher pushes for clarity. The discussion centers on Willie Loman's decision to commit suicide. The teacher encourages students to talk to one another rather than direct all their comments to her. To one girl who is having difficulty penetrating the barrage of comments, Dickerson says quietly, "Assert yourself . . . get in there . . . you have something to say." When the conversation begins to feel scattered and directionless, the teacher breaks in. "We have a whole lot of separate ideas on the floor. Let us take a few minutes of silence to sort these out. . . . If you can't remember anyone's ideas except your own, you haven't been listening. . . . I have heard at least fifteen explanations for Willie's suicide. . . . See if you can reconstruct it." The class grows quiet as students begin to write their ideas down. Dickerson walks around the room, encouraging students who seem stuck or discouraged and restating her question for greater clarity. Then she offers a clue to the whole class: "See if you can remember Cynthia's question . . . it was a turning point in the discussion. She didn't give an answer, only a question." After several minutes of silent contemplation the teacher says, "Let's combine our reasoning." Students immediately begin to offer reasons for Willie's suicide: "He wanted to quit a world where nothing was going right for him." "He felt he had failed terribly and was a disgrace to those who loved him." "He wanted to have people pay homage to him at the funeral." "He had only half achieved his dream."

The contributions are energetic and fast-paced. When the exchanges become heated and confused, Dickerson intervenes with a tentative and thoughtful voice. "Let me ask you a very hard question. . . . What happens when a dream you've lived by turns out to be a lie? How do you feel about that? . . . Or are you too young?" The responses are charged and unrestrained. One girl speaks with passion: "People shouldn't circle their lives around one idea." Another disagrees, "But it is not just one idea, it is their whole reason for being." A third comments, "There is always a danger in being too committed, too closed. . . . You should have one or two goals. You should choose . . . you don't have to die with one ideal." The discussion becomes argumentative but not hostile. The teacher does not direct them towards a tidy conclusion. They are struggling with unanswerable questions, profound dilemmas, and she wants to encourage them in the struggle. She wants them to recognize Willie's pain. Class is over abruptly and there is no closure.

I am struck by all that has gone on—by the open criticism, hot debate, level of trust, and spirit of inquiry. I am baffled when Dickerson says apologetically to me after class, "It is not merely false modesty . . .

but I don't think that went well. . . . *I* was unsure of where I was going in the discussion, uncertain about what I wanted them to get out of it . . . *they* were wonderful. They tolerated my ambivalence." One of the qualities of a "star" teacher seems to be tough self-criticism; never accepting oneself as a star.

A COMMITTED AND SERIOUS FACULTY

The perceptions of the faculty at Brookline High School range from good to extraordinary. The most critical voice I heard said that there are three categories of teachers: a small group of "stars," a large group of "slightly above average" teachers, and a few "duds." To one who has visited numerous schools, Brookline seems to be rich with talented and committed teachers. A department chairperson describes her peers as "gifted and highly professional . . . I always think of them as people who could do whatever they chose to do." A houseteacher is even more enthusiastic about his colleagues. A relatively recent arrival to the faculty, he exclaims, "If I had my choice of all the high schools, I would send my kids here! I think this is the best school I've ever been in. They have the discipline . . . and tough academics . . . you can't slip through. If you can't make it here, you can't make it anywhere. Faculty will always be sensitive to students' needs."

Teachers do not only seem to be admiring of one another, they also express satisfaction with the tone of professionalism, resourcefulness, and good will that the school culture seems to generate. "Almost everyone loves coming to work," says a ten-year veteran of the school. Through their appreciative smiles, however, there are persistent complaints. "Brookline teachers tend to complain. In fact, they *enjoy* complaining. This should *not* be misread as dissatisfaction with the school . . . perhaps their standards are too high and they are struggling to meet those unrealistic goals."

Throughout my sojourn at Brookline, I was struck by the competence and dedication of the faculty. Occasionally I heard teachers talking about ideas, pedagogy, and styles of learning. More often, I saw teachers conferring together about how to help a difficult student; how to support and comfort a girl whose mother had suddenly died; and how to ease the racial tensions that had erupted at a recent football game. They seemed to be joining together as student advocates—pooling information, perspectives, and skills. Although I heard many conversations about students, I heard very few careless, derogatory statements about them. The backstage behavior in faculty rooms is not fueled by the abuse of students—common casualties of loose teacher-conversation in many schools.

In class sessions, most teaching seemed to be at a high level. I was impressed by the careful preparation before classes I observed, the respect teachers showed for student opinion, and the focus on curricular matters rather than discipline. Although I heard rumors about fracases and mischievous behavior among students, discipline did not seem to be a problem in the classrooms I visited. Teachers appeared not to be threatened by the possibility of disruption, and students did not seem to want to provoke disorder or create chaos merely for the purposes of undermining the teachers. When I asked a fifteen-year veteran teacher about disciplinary battles in the classroom, she looked slightly puzzled. "That has not been a problem for me. Nor does it seem to be a problem in this school. Teachers offer kids respect and it comes back to us full circle."

One does not sense the tensions and sharp divisions of power that often accompany teacher-pupil relationships in secondary schools. The tone of the school is more relaxed, with teachers admonishing students who get out of line or encouraging them "to focus" their attention, yet teachers seem to be free of the policing function. Both in and out of class, teachers and students seem to mix well, relationships appear comfortable, and there is minimal adult dominance. During a fire drill, for example, with crowds of people streaming out of the school, I was impressed with the general calm of everyone, the minor supervisory role teachers took, and some of the informal, friendly conversation between students and teachers as we gathered outside the school.

Another teacher offers a different view of why disciplinary problems are minimal: "Brookline is unusual in its individualistic approach to students. . . . Teachers know students well and are concerned about the whole person. They work towards communicating at many levels." Violence often accompanies anonymity. Faces lost in a crowd are more likely to act irresponsibly and be moved towards anarchy. Brookline teachers seem to see individual faces and students respond to the focused attention.

Many students spoke of appreciating the unstrained, nonthreatening setting. When a teacher asked her class to tell me what was special about Brookline High School, there were many recent arrivals from other high schools who testified about "feeling safe for the very first time." Said a pretty blond-haired girl from New Jersey, "This is the first school I have been to where you can walk in the hall without being supervised." Echoed another girl from Connecticut, "In my school, there was graffiti all over the bathrooms and kids used to torch lockers." After several statements about the threats of violence in other schools and the feelings of asylum in this one, a thoughtful boy summed up the tone of his peers' remarks: "This is a sort of a *free* school. . . . Teachers are not abusive."

The feelings of circular respect and good will must sustain teachers in their work. Yet one also has a sense that teachers are supported in their individuality as well; that there is little pressure to conform to prescribed patterns or styles from administrators or colleagues. A social worker is admired for his unorthodox methods and his unending, limitless commitment to the lives of students. Two history teachers, with greatly contrasting pedagogies and philosophies, are both perceived as extraordinary. Their differences are valued. Claims one observer, "There is lots of variety in the faculty. Kids can plug in where they want to. . . . There is an adult for every student."

A few faculty that I spoke to did not share this view. They spoke of the difficulties of innovation and change in a faculty overly committed to conservative academics and traditions. One member of the biology department has designed a course entitled "Body/Mind Research." Proclaimed as "great and fantastic" by many students, the course has slowly gained a mixed reputation among faculty as "esoteric," "different," "controversial," and "fascinating." Inspired by student responses to the course, a few faculty and administrators have enrolled in a summer-session course and become converts and enthusiasts. Julie Wilson has been teaching at Brookline High for almost a decade. For several years she taught conventional biology courses and experimented "for free" with other forms of scientific exploration using "paradigms and frameworks" that caused suspicion among many of her departmental colleagues. Three years ago she introduced her new course for the first time. Ten students dared to take it; all from the School Within A School. "They were considered on the fringe of life here," explains Wilson, "and that is the way I was perceived as well." Much of her energy was spent fighting the traditions and conservatism of her department. Her style, pedagogy, and the course content were thought to be too unconventional and people suspected her missionary zeal. Whenever the department's budget required trimming, Wilson's course would be immediately threatened. She blames some of her colleagues for lack of courage, not malice of intent.

The course has not only survived; it has thrived and grown. This year one hundred students applied and there was space for only fifty in two class sessions. Wilson could choose whom she wanted and she selected very carefully. Juniors and seniors only; students who had parental support and interest; and students who were school leaders. "Now I have the college-prep, all-American kids . . . they are great and I love them," she exults. The large numbers and "chosen ones" have increased the visibility and status of the course in Brookline High. Clearly, Wilson is the inspiration and drive behind the course. To her it is more than a course. It represents the potential for a different world view, a transformed image of self; a chance for increasing human capacity and potential among students.

"Body/Mind Research" meets in the bowels of the new gym, in a huge padded room usually used for wrestling. "You can tell when it's wrestling season," Wilson smiles, "it begins to stink in here." When students walk in the room, they take off their shoes. The temptation in this large space is to whirl around and do cartwheels, and upon entering students begin to move in space—tussling with each other, slowly turning in absent-minded motion, or charging across the room at high speed. They seem freer, unencumbered, and glad to be there. Wilson, an attractive woman with dark curly hair, alive eyes, and a dramatic style, directs all of us to sit in a circle on the floor. (She is not willing for me to merely observe, but wants me to "experience the process." Perhaps she is also concerned that an observer might distract others from being involved.) "In the beginning of the year, there are spaces in the circle. By the spring, the circle is closed. . . . The feeling is wonderful. . . . In the fall I have to drive them and be the task master. Later on I can let go and let it happen."

The class is active and physical, with students and teacher exploring physiological questions through direct experience. We all do a series of experiments on muscle strength. With a chosen partner, Wilson demonstrates the exercise, but leaves questions unanswered. Her demonstrations are lively, and theatrical, compelling the class's attention. Students then choose partners and try out the experiments themselves. Data are gathered from each pair of students and compared with the "results" of more conventional, carefully controlled experiments found in the scientific literature. Wilson explains to the students her motivation for leading this journey of discovery. It is an explanation that points to different ways of knowing, the nature of evidence, and the problems of bias. "Some of you have been worried about the unscientific nature of what we are doing here. It makes you feel uncomfortable. . . . How can we grow increasingly critical and systematic while we still remain sensitive and open?" She warns them that even scientists who claim to be doing the most careful experiments are guided by unconscious assumptions of what they expect to find. It is important to become increasingly self-critical about those hidden assumptions and to recognize that more of our senses can be involved in exploring scientific terrain. Wilson's explanations are not defensive but reflect the open-mindedness she is exhorting in her students.

Even though Wilson recounts the subtle exclusion, skepticism, and misunderstandings inflicted upon her by some reticent colleagues, the tale of her course and its great success also point to the eclecticism and diversity that this institution is able to tolerate and absorb. Many remain unconvinced, but they seem willing to "let her do her thing" without interference.

Strong alliances among teachers may support this openness for diversity. Faculty seem to create friendships and gather support within their departments. There are some generalized stereotypes about the character of departments that seem at least half-true. The biology and math departments, for example, are described as more conservative than the English and social studies departments. Wilson's philosophies and pedagogy may not have made waves in another department with more sympathetic colleagues. A member of the social studies department claims that social studies teachers have earned a good academic reputation among their colleagues, but that they are considered "a little left of center" in their ideological stance. They no longer wear the 1960s' garb, but underneath their more conventional, "grown-up" clothing is the spirit of those who wear "jeans and sweatshirts."

Faculty in the English department also seem to be admired for their commitment and skill. Many are described as gifted, even "poetic" teachers. Yet they are also resented by members of other departments because they are given a lighter teaching load. Historically, it was expected that English teachers would spend a great deal of their time individually counselling students. Writing and reading, the essential skills of academic work, were the province of English teachers; and they would be responsible for instilling those in students. In order to support that special responsibility, English teachers were required to teach four courses, rather than the normal load of five. That policy is still in effect today. In this period of diminished resources, however, many faculty resent what they consider to be the privileged position of the English department. Admits one English teacher, "I understand why others are indignant. After all, faculty in other departments now do as much individual work as we do. The historical distinction no longer makes sense."

These generalized characterizations of the departments do not appear to be firmly entrenched or markedly divisive. Departments are less expressions of territoriality and image than they are environments of support and exchange. Some teachers speak of departments as if they were extended families, with the positive qualities of loyalty and connection and the strains of competition and closeness. One teacher complains that her productivity and happiness at work are diminished by her complicated, adversarial relationship with her department chairperson. In the same breath, she appreciates the enduring friendship and nurturance she gets from a few close colleagues in the department. These friendships sustain her through tough personal and professional times, and allow for the kind of criticism that is only possible when there is high trust.

One chairperson I spoke to describes her department as "very close." It is not that everyone feels trust and intimacy, but that they share common goals and care for each other's well-being. "If you are out sick, you can expect a call from someone in the department who is concerned about you." There are two or three people whom she perceives as being "on the fringe" and hopes to "bring them into the fold." Still, she does not believe that they feel excluded and ultimately respects their decision to remain aloof.

A woman in her mid-thirties, Janine Jones, was recently appointed as chairperson. She succeeded an older man who had a benign, fatherly image within their department. He expressed his caring by being protective and taking younger colleagues under his wing. When Jones entered the job, she was determined to see administration as a "task to be done," rather than play a superior, maternal role; and she wanted to increase the sense of responsibility and leadership from within the ranks. Since September she has seen subtle, but very moving changes. Some of the younger faculty, who had been fathered by the former chairperson, have "been able to grow up" since his leave-taking. They have begun to assume leadership roles in departmental committees and act more responsibly in relation to colleagues. One departmental member had anticipated how the change in leadership would effect her behavior. She admitted to Jones, "I wanted you to be chairperson but I was worried when you got it because I knew that I would have to work hard." Departmental chairs have a prominent place of clout and status at Brookline. Their style and temperament seem to have an imprint on faculty life. Because the high school's image still rests securely on an academic reputation and because teachers primarily view themselves as thinkers and pedagogues, the traditional departmental arrangements of academic life appear to have force here.

DIMINISHED RESOURCES AND MORE DEMANDS

This year faculty enthusiasm has been dampened by Proposition 2½, a recently passed Massachusetts law that has substantially cut tax revenues in the Commonwealth. The budget cuts have devastated many of the state's public services. Hospital staffs have been depleted, firemen have been laid off, and policemen with long years of experience are suddenly without jobs. Public parks suffer from lack of upkeep; municipal pools have been closed because there is no money to pay the salaries of lifeguards; and publicly funded child-care centers have had to drastically reduce staff and supplies. However, public attention has been primarily focused on the ravage done to schools.

In the Boston school system more than a thousand teachers were laid off in September, many with more than a decade of teaching experience. The "extras" of art, music, gym, and field trips have all been eliminated as teachers and students face a bleak future without abundance and resources. Increasingly, those parents who can afford alternatives have decided to take their children out of public schools. The waiting lists for private schools have grown impossibly long. Many families, once committed to the conveniences and style of city life, have decided to move to the relatively affluent suburbs. Parochial schools are being oversubscribed by desperate applicants. As one public official said recently, "Boston's public schools are becoming the prisons of the poor." Without alternatives and clout, the poor are left to inhabit a rapidly deteriorating system.

In comparison to the gloomy picture of Boston, Brookline schools appear relatively untouched. They still seem to enjoy the resources and privileges that have been denied Boston. Last year, Brookline's superintendent was a visible and powerful spokesman for the opposition to Proposition 2½, and parents and community people rallied to save their schools from the destructive cuts. When it was rumored that the proposed cuts for 2½ would lead to a double-session kindergarten, the community was up in arms, ready for battle. Says one slightly cynical observer, "Parents were outraged. They were convinced that their kids' lives would be unalterably damaged!" The parents of high school students tended to be less threatened about the repercussions of Proposition 2½ than the vocal and protective elementary school parents. There is always a tendency for the parents of secondary students to be less involved with the schools than they were a few years earlier. But some citizens claimed that in this case, high school parents showed extreme irresponsibility towards the schools and their children, and did not fully recognize the potential damage of diminished resources. An angry parent of a high school student, who felt she was fighting the battle "all alone," claimed, "No one said anything in opposition to a proposal that the first year of language at the high school be eliminated . . . if the faculty had not gotten enraged, that proposal would have gone through . . . why don't parents scream when the number of guidance counselors are cut? There are now two hundred-fifty students to every counselor. It is impossible!"

Despite the comparative view that Brookline has suffered little in relation to its big-city neighbor, school people in Brookline feel a sense of loss and discouragement. From the superintendent who was used to winning and wielding power effortlessly, to the individual teacher who feels less supported and rewarded, the sense of loss in this town is palpable. Because the superintendent's fight against Proposition 2½ had been so dramatic and visible, its passage was a personal defeat for him—a defeat with high political and professional costs. Said a budding administrator who has always admired the superintendent's inspired leadership and deft style, "I had always thought he was invulnerable and suddenly I recognized he was mortal and could lose."

Beyond the personal defeats, faculty in particular speak of the harmful repercussions of Proposition 2½. Many paragraphs begin "Well, before Two and a Half, we could . . . " and end, "Now we are not able to . . ." An invisible line seems to divide the time of abundance from the period of retrenchment. Some faculty speak of being "discouraged and frustrated"; others more dramatically talk about the assaults of a "conservative reign of terror." However, most seem to be seeking a resourceful and responsible approach to the losses. A housemaster captures the mood eloquently, "My sense is that morale is down . . . the spirit is being tested. Before Two and a Half, faculty would go to unbelievable lengths on behalf of kids. Now their efforts have to be more realistic, more circumscribed." The chairperson of a department is slightly more buoyant in her perception of faculty responses to the budget cuts. "Last year, there was a lot of fear and anguish. Everyone worried about losing their job. Over the summer, people seemed to rally and return feeling renewed . . . faculty are now doing a much more difficult and consuming job but they have somehow discovered the inner resources." As a department chair, she has had to meet the harsh realities, protect her department, and stimulate her colleagues' morale. A relatively new appointee, she is eager to be seen as competent and finds her energy and ambitions can sometimes become liabilities. "Everyone says you're doing a great job and I say I'm in a double bind. I want to do a good job because I am ambitious and want this to lead to other good jobs. . . . But if I prove I can be a super-woman, under impossible conditions, that is not right either. The structure is still all wrong."

To conform to the requirements of the law, Brookline had to decrease its budget by 18.5 percent this year and will have to cut back 15 percent in 1982–83. Part of the anxiety among faculty stems not so much from present conditions, but from anticipations about a more difficult future. This year, the high school managed to keep most if its faculty despite the large budgetary cuts. Administrators and teachers agreed that monies should be taken from other corners. Middle-level, system-wide administrators were let go rather than deplete the core teaching faculty. For example, the curriculum coordinator for social studies, who is responsible for orchestrating efforts across grades and among schools, was fired. Now there is no longer anyone who can serve as a resource for teachers and department chairs. Some of the recently hired guidance counselors had to leave and the custodial staff was substantially cut. Explains one teacher, picking up trash as she walks through the quadrangle, "For the first time in my fourteen years here this building is not being kept absolutely clean. Some of the custodians have been fired and their buddies are resisting with a work slow-down, in defiance."

Mostly, the high school has tried to cut the nonhuman resources. Money for books, paper, and other supplies is very low. The chairperson of social studies has only $1,000 this year to buy all of the books for her department's use. In parts of the school building the roof if leaking badly, but it was decided that a repair should be neglected for at least another year. The brass sign on one housemaster's door still bears the name of his predecessor. "No money for new signs," he explains with a smile.

Some of the attempts to save money seem fairly trivial until people begin to point to the subtle and unexpected repercussions. Several teachers told me about the impact of budget cuts on the food service. The lunches have become almost inedible, and faculty no longer have a separate food service for their exclusive use. They still gather in the faculty dining room but they have to wait on student lines to get their food. Rather than endure the crowds, the hassles, and the bad meals, most faculty have begun to bring their lunches from home and to gather in their department offices. On a given day, the faculty cafeteria is likely to be almost empty while teachers gather with their brown bags at their desks, or around conference tables. "No one really leaves work. They talk shop talk or they don't talk at all," complains one teacher, who misses the comraderie and humor of the old cafeteria days. A more compelling complaint made by many more teachers focuses on the unanticipated divisions among faculty that have arisen. Brookline is a large school and the lunch room was one of the few places where teachers could gather informally and meet across disciplinary and departmental boundaries. Now they are forced to retreat to more circumscribed patterns that diminish their sense of community.

Clearly, the impact of Proposition 2½ is central to the concerns of adults at Brookline High School. McCarthy speaks proudly of their efforts "to hold the line" on those things most critical to the process of education, and he admires the resourcefulness and resilience of his teachers. Yet he worries out loud about how much they can endure and does not want to test the limits of their good will and energy.

Beyond the press of Proposition 2½, faculty and administrators are facing another major intrusion. This is the year of the Ten-Year Evaluation of the New England Association for Secondary Schools (NEASS), and a great deal of energy is being channeled into this self-evaluative effort. In response to these later demands on their energy and time, teachers speak with a collective voice. They feel harassed, resentful, and frustrated by a process that seems largely superficial and predetermined. Evaluation committee meetings are held every Tuesday and Thursday afternoons from 2:30 to 4:30 and most faculty members are assigned to two committees.

The only time I heard angry and accusing exchanges among teachers was in connection with committee assignments for the evaluation. A chairperson of one of the larger committees was trying to track down a reticent faculty member whom she had never met by sending notes and leaving telephone messages with his chairperson. He was enraged by her pursuit and felt she had gone over his head to his superior in order to get him in trouble. The accusations exploded on both sides. As I listened to the heated exchange I sensed that they were both overwhelmed by the demands of their work and furious at the intrusions. Quite by accident, they became each other's targets. Once their anger was released, they became the reasonable and dedicated people I had met before.

The committee meeting I observed reflected none of the hostility but all of the boredom and weariness that often accompany unwanted chores. The School and Community Relations Committee is trying to decide how to portray their school—the level and depth with which they should try to respond to the prescribed questionnaires provided by NEASS. The struggle of defining their task and setting their goals combines the tough issues of work-load, methods for gathering the needed information, and ethical considerations. The questions stipulated on the evaluation forms seem inappropriate and superficial to the committee

members. Says one, "This assumes that each area of the school is monolithic. . . . If you begin to even touch on the complexities it makes our
task even more difficult." The chair of the committee, a housemaster
known to be politically wise and knowledgeable about community
forces, tries to shift the discouraging tone. "I think we have to grapple
with attempting to describe the complexity of the school. It helps to respond in the most honest way possible." Eleven faculty, weary from a
long school day, rally in response to her urgings. They try to figure out
how to design responses that will conform to the prescribed forms as well
as how to gather information that might be useful for them to know.
Their spirits are slightly enlivened by the thought that this exercise could
be ultimately beneficial to their knowledge of the community and their
interactions with parents. An enthusiastic participant feels that the form
does not reflect the concerns of Brookline's diverse population. "One
question that is not on the form concerns that growing population of kids
who are deciding not to go on to college. Don't we want to ask their
parents if they think the curriculum is adequate for persons who do *not*
plan to go to college?" Another worries about the tone of the questions, a
tone she feels encourages bias and negativism: "In sympathy with the
striking Philadelphia teachers, I'm feeling a little paranoid and threatened by these questions that ask for subjective judgments. . . . Can't we
include some clear, objective questions like how many times they have
come to parent-teacher conferences and how they decide when to let
their kids drop a course? . . . Some parents let their kids drop a major that
they haven't attended for five weeks!"

Although some good suggestions emerge from time to time, the discussion seems labored and inefficient. The mandatory instrument for
gathering data gets in the way of progress, inhibits their exchanges, and
depletes their initiating energies. By the time the chairperson begins to
assign tasks to people at the end of the meeting, everyone is worn down.
"Will you do an announcement about the Back-to-School Night, Rose?"
the chair asks one of her more resilient members. "Do I have to?" pleads
a childish voice. Then Rose says with a smile, "Gee whiz, I suddenly felt
like a kid being given an assignment by the teacher." Rose's plaintive
voice and her immediate recognition of "quick regression" captures part
of the experience of this process. For teachers who mostly enjoy autonomy
and confident feelings of adulthood, this task seems almost infantilizing.
It is the way most try not to treat students and its infliction on them feels
doubly unwarranted. Despite their complaints, one has a sense that these
teachers will produce a more than adequate evaluation report. They are
too wise and too realistic to pretend this hurdle is trivial.

One should not overemphasize the recent experiences of deprivation and loss. Brookline High is a brave and resilient school which is facing important changes. Unlike many schools, it does not seek to ignore the world around it, but tries to confront the hypocrisies, endure the uncertainties, and rally against the assaults. In responding to the persistent challenges, there are imperfections. It is a school that seems divided. It is a school where class, race, and ethnicity are vivid markers of status. It is a school where bright, academic, and efficient students continue to form the public image and get more than their fair share of admiring attention. However, these imperfections are not being ignored by faculty, students, or administrators. The struggle is palpable. It is a school searching for a clearer moral code and standards of behavior. It is a school testing the limits of diversity. It is a school experimenting with new and unconventional arrangements of power and responsibility. It is a school in visible transition.

One senses that the risk taking, the unusual openness to change, and the responsiveness to community are possible only because of a long history of security. The contemporary bravery follows generations of stability and certainty. That self-confidence is a bedrock for responding to the uncertainties and threats that will shape the future. It will require the patience and endurance of a long-distance runner, but also some of the quick, intuitive responses of a sprinter.

PART THREE

ELITE PORTRAITS

V

St. Paul's School

Certainty, Privilege, and the Imprint of History

THE AESTHETICS AND COMFORTS OF ABUNDANCE

It is a magnificent spring day. The sky is clear blue, the air crisp, and the sun golden in the sky. The landscape is lush green and the azaleas are exploding with blossoms of magenta, lavender, and deep orange. In short, it is the perfect day to visit St. Paul's School, which seems to stretch on for miles before me—aristocratic, manicured, perfect. I arrive midafternoon, the time for athletics, and see playing fields full of hockey and baseball players—lithe, graceful, and practiced bodies moving across the grass.

Everyone is helpful and welcoming. A man in a blue truck—probably one of the custodial crew—finds me lost on the road and tells me to follow him to my destination, the School House. Everyone waves greetings. A young man on a small tractor mower offers a wide, enthusiastic grin, and a tall, distinguished, slightly graying man gives a stiff and formal wave. I park behind the School House, next to a car with windows open and a young child inside. Having just arrived from the city, I wonder immediately how anyone could feel safe about leaving a precious child in the car. Fearing that I will frighten her, I smile and speak softly to the little girl. She babbles back, unafraid. The child's mother returns after

221

a couple of minutes. A plainly attractive woman of about thirty-five, she is one of five females on the teaching faculty. She greets me warmly, introduces me to her daughter, and drives off quickly to play tennis. I am struck by how safe, secure, and beautiful it feels at St. Paul's. It is a place where windows and doors are left open, people exchange friendly greetings, and babies wait in cars unattended.

The land belonging to St. Paul's seems to stretch on forever. There are 1,700 acres of woods and open land surrounding over 300 acres of lakes and ponds, and over 80 buildings. A shimmering lake carves out a graceful shape in the central campus landscape. On an early evening walk from the School House to dinner in the dining room, you can cross the lake by way of a quaint stone bridge. The evening light makes the lake a mirror; the lily pads that dot the water gently sway back and forth; and all feels serene and still. The traditional and graceful architecture of New England characterizes the campus buildings—sturdy brick structures with ivy growing up the walls and white, flatfaced houses with black and green shutters.

Among these quietly majestic old buildings are three sleek modern buildings that house the programs in dance, theater, and the plastic arts. A parent of a student at St. Paul's, who was interested in supporting the development of the arts program, gave three million dollars for these new buildings. Elegantly designed and highly functional, the buildings were conceived to be adaptive to the artistic mediums that they house. The theater in the drama building is layered, movable, and sparse, allowing for myriad rearrangements of space. The stage can be dramatically transformed from one performance to the next.

Mr. Sloan, the director of dance, worked closely with the architects and builders in the design of the dance building, and it shows the wisdom and inspiration of the artist's experience. The major dance space in the building is used for both classes and performances. Bleachers and balconies surround two sides of the dance floor, with mirrors and dance bars lining the other walls. Sunlight sweeps in the high windows and casts tree shadows on the dance floor. The internal lighting is soft and effective. The most extraordinary detail can only be fully appreciated by dancers. Mr. Sloan takes me into his office and proudly shows me the miniature model of the dance floor. It is a five-layered construction that took several months to build, and it moves and ripples when it is jumped on. "It is the best in the business" says Mr. Sloan. "The American Ballet Theater has the same floor."

The arts buildings symbolize one of the major missions of St. Paul's

School. In his ten-year leadership of the school, the Rector says that the building of the arts program is one of the developments of which he feels most proud. Along with the superb physical facilities, new faculty positions have been added in the arts; students can receive academic credit for course work; and there are numerous opportunities for students to give concerts, performances, and exhibitions. In his 1979 Annual Report, William Oates, the rector, stressed the connections between art and culture, art and intellect, and art and personal growth:

"Work in the arts provides an opportunity for participants to learn about themselves. And this opportunity is particularly valuable for students at St. Paul's School because it allows, and in some ways demands, consideration of fundamental issues through observation, and testing, and experimentation. From fourteen years old through eighteen this chance is eagerly sought and required. This is the period of questioning and exploring, of self-doubt and braggadocio, the period of developing self-confidence and of maturing personality. In the arts are found cultural contradictions and conflicts, insight, informed speculation, tradition and discipline, and a general pattern for testing achievement and apparent success. The arts afford the use of uncommitted space for thoughtful and considered growth through consolidation of experimentation. And increasing knowledge of the self promotes and supports its realization."

In stark contrast to the angular lines of the art buildings, the chapel of St. Paul and St. Peter stands as a symbol of classic beauty. The hundred year-old brick structure was the first building on the St. Paul's campus and its stained glass windows, ornate wood carving, and regal dimensions mark the history and roots of this school. It is in these modern and traditional edifices that St. Paul's reveals its connections to past and present, its commitment to sacred traditions and contemporary change.

A BINDING TOGETHER

Chapel is the most precious moment in the day. It binds the community together. The 500 students from the third through sixth forms, and 80 faculty of St. Paul's come together at 8:00 four mornings a week. There is time for peace and reflection, for beautiful music and poetic words.

Streams of sunlight filter through the magnificent stained glass windows, shining down on all inside. They seem like the enlightened people, the chosen ones. There is the connection between mind and soul, body and spirit, the sacred and the secular. The baroque organ with pure and clear sounds is "one of the best in New England." It fills the space with rich, reverberating sounds. The organ playing is impeccable.

Chapel services are an expression of unity, fellowship, and a commitment to Christian traditions at St. Paul's. As a church school, it has had a long-time association with the Episcopal church, and the rituals and structure of the Episcopal ceremony still form the basis of morning chapel services. However, the denominational ties are no longer deeply engrained. The school catalogue stresses the relationship between spiritual commitment and community life:

> "Chapel services, studies in religion, and our common life in Christian fellowship are expressions of the unity and fundamental faith of St. Paul's School. . . . The school supports the beliefs of each faith, encouraging students to recognize the strength and loyalty of the commitments of their families. The school recognizes that all its members should discover the meaning of the Christian tradition in their own lives through free inquiry, and the experience of community life in that tradition."

The beautiful and old architectural lines of the chapel are in contrast to the ruffled and contemporary people sitting in the long, carved pews. Dressed in typical adolescent garb—rustic chic—the students' faces are still and attentive. Some slump over in weariness, some eyes are half-closed, but most seem to be captured by the ritual. When their fellow students make music, they receive full attention and generous applause. The day I visit, the service is an all-musical program of Bach. The first piece is played well by a trio of flute, harpsichord, and violin. It is a slow movement that requires sustained and disciplined tones. Occasionally the violin is clumsy in technique and flat in tone, but that is the only evidence of this being an amateur performance. The second piece, which is the first movement of Bach's Third Brandenberg Concerto, begins energetically, but quickly degenerates. The students, led by a faculty conductor, barely struggle through the difficult string variations, but no one winces at the grating sounds. There is strong applause for the ambitious attempt. I am struck by the extraordinary difficulty of the music and the willingness of the students to do less than well in public. I am also impressed by the sustained elegance with which this musical disaster is carried off. This seems the ultimate in certainty and style. There is no embarrassment, a full acceptance of the efforts made, and the expectation of applause.

The faculty sit in the upper pews, also in assigned seats. Chapel is a compulsory community event for faculty as well as students. Along with the formal evening meals, chapel is considered one of the important rituals that symbolizes community and fellowship, emphasizes discipline and ceremony, and reflects a sense of continuity between past and present. Looking down the row of faculty, the dominance of whiteness and maleness becomes immediately apparent. Most are wearing tweedy jackets and ties, and the unusual ones stick out—the blond and pregnant history teacher; the beared, tall, Jewish, head of the English department; the casually dressed dance teacher with a head full of irreverent ringlets. It is not that there is no diversity within the faculty, it is that their sameness is exaggerated in this setting as they sit lined up in the back pews of chapel.

It is also in chapel that one experiences the impressive orchestration of the school. All seems to flow so smoothly and evenly, almost effortlessly. Behind this smooth scene is the hard, disciplined work of many. "Chapel Notes" for the week tell what music will be played, what hymns sung, and what lessons will be read. A faculty member is assigned to regulate the acoustics system just in front of her chapel pew to insure the right volume for each microphone. Notes are delivered to the rector well in advance of the "Morning Reports." The rector arrives the day I am there and opens an elegant note from the senior class. The script is like calligraphy, the image above the writing shows a bird in flight, and the message inside combines poetry and allusions to scripture and prayer. The senior class has decided that this sunny day will be their senior-cut day and they are off to the beach in rented buses. Their absence is no surprise to anyone. Their actions are certainly not devious or even assertive. This is part of the anticipated ritual. The person sitting next to me whispers, "Of course the rector was informed about this well in advance." It is beautifully orchestrated—the anticipated "surprise" event, the ceremonial note to the rector, the announcement to the assembled people, and the restrained approval of everyone.

The supreme orchestration of events and people at St. Paul's reflects, I think, the abundance and privilege of the school. In order to be able to anticipate and coordinate life in this way, one must be able to foresee a future that is relatively certain. Years of experience rooted in tradition seem to guide the present. Some things seem to fall into place without conscious effort. It has always been that way. History has cast a form on things. In his concluding remarks on graduation day, the rector underscores the mark of tradition and history, "This ceremony has become traditional, and, therefore, mandatory." In schools where things inevitably fall apart, where patterns of the past are not clearly defined, and where futures are neither certain nor promised, one doesn't sense this feeling of an orchestrated and smooth existence.

"Morning Reports" follow chapel. All gather outside on the chapel steps as the rector announces the day's happenings. He begins by formally welcoming me into their midst. "We have the pleasure of a visit from Professor Sara Lawrence Ligthfoot, and I would like to introduce her to those who have not yet met her." Applause and smiles follow with some picture taking. Then an announcement that startles me: "Robert Brown has been off bounds for smoking marijuana and will return on Friday." This is said with the same tone and demeanor as the welcoming words of the rector. This is the first time at St. Paul's that I have heard words of public discipline or sensed the exclusion of a community member—off bounds. It is also the first time in a very long time that I have heard "pot" referred to as "marijuana," its real name. It seems a throwback to the old days and sounds more forbidding and dangerous in its three-syllable incarnation.

Four times a week, faculty and students gather at the close of day for a formal, family-style meal in the dining room. This is the second major community ritual that echoes the traditions and ceremony of St. Paul's and encourages fellowship among students and faculty. On Wednesday evenings and weekends, eating is done cafeteria-style and dress codes are relaxed.

Ms. Susan Thompson, a vivacious, middle-aged woman, has been on the St. Paul's faculty since the school became coeducational a decade ago. She leaves her office at the School House in the early evening with just enough time to freshen up and change into a slightly fancier dress. The door of her apartment on the second floor of a girls' dormitory is wide open. For me, it stands as another sign of the feelings of trust and safety at St. Paul's and as a first sign of the obscuring of public and private boundaries between faculty and students. Anyone, at any time, can walk in and talk, make requests, and seek counsel. There are two other faculty members who live in the dormitory. A young, single woman lives on the third floor, and a married woman with a husband and child has the most sumptuous accommodations on the first floor. Each is primarily responsible for supervising the dormitory on alternate evenings. Ms. Thompson speaks of all three faculty as "strong" dormitory counselors and feels pleased at the disciplined and comfortable rapport that has developed among those who live there. Among students, this dormitory has the reputation of being overly strict and inhibiting.

In late spring, when students make room selections for the following year, most do not list this dormitory as their first choice because they want to escape the rigorous supervision. More than a few girls, however, seem to seek out the peace and security of this more disciplined setting.

Ms. Thompson's apartment has four rooms—a large living room, a study, bedroom, and tiny kitchen. It is simply, barely decorated with modest furniture. One bright, colorful canvas dominates the living room, a picture of brown people in a bustling market place. It seems strangely out of place contrasted with the severe, colorless environment that surrounds it. Home does not seem to be important to Ms. Thompson. She describes herself as a "workaholic," not much interested in homemaking. Life is not centered here, but in the school as community. Within a few minutes we are off to dinner. The campus is alive with students converging from all directions, walking briskly up the hill to the dining hall.

Students and faculty congregate in small groups in the outside hall of the great dining room, waiting for doors to open for dinner. Boys must wear jackets and girls the "comparable" attire. After the cut-off jeans, bare feet, and T-shirts of the daytime dress, the students look transformed in their formal attire. Ironically, the third-form boys appear even younger in their jackets and ties while the sixth-form girls look like mature, fully formed women in their spring dresses. The great dining room with high ceilings and stained glass windows is only used for formal evening meals. On the wooden paneling that lines the walls from floor to ceiling, names of the students in each of the school's graduating classes are carefully, aesthetically carved. A boy at my table can turn around and see his uncle's name carved in the wall behind him. It is misspelled.

Each faculty member sits with eight students at a long rectangular table with straight, high-backed chairs. Seats are assigned and rotated every three weeks, and students are chosen to create a mix of grade levels and interests. Grace is said by a man with a booming voice as everyone stands behind their chairs with bowed heads. Dinner conversation is somewhat formal and subdued. My presence may have been inhibiting, but I hear many students and some faculty complain of the forced quality of these occasions. The adults ask most of the questions, with polite responses from students. A willowy, blond girl in the fifth-form has come from upstate New York to study in the excellent dance program. A lively, bright-eyed, Black boy from Chicago is practicing for the Latin play to be given on the weekend of graduation. He tells us about an invention which he is trying to patent and seems to be knowledgeable about the legal steps that will be required to protect his idea. A sixth-form girl from New England is the most socially sophisticated and smooth. She speaks of her plans to go to the University of Colorado next year.

Dinner is swiftly consumed despite the ceremonial conversation. When the students are finished, each says dutifully, "Miss Thompson, may I be excused?" and she grants them permission. The permission granting seems almost archaic. As they seek permission to be excused, they appear suddenly childlike. Many times during my visit to St. Paul's, I am struck by the swiftly changing adolescent images. At any moment, the smooth exterior of the mature, worldly, adult-like image fades and exposes the awkward vulnerability of a child.

227

THE EDGES OF REALITY AND UNREALITY

The incredible beauty, seclusion, and abundance of St. Paul's makes it seem far away from the reality most people know. It is hard to conceive of anyone growing used to this magnificence. It is easy to imagine that people might quickly forget the ugly facts of life beyond this serene place. Occasionally, rumblings are heard underneath the smooth facade of St. Paul's.

Last year, just two days before graduation, several sixth-form boys decided to steal away into the woods and drink beer. Knowing well that alcohol consumption was against the school rules, these boys—some of them school leaders—decided to tempt fate in the final hour. Slightly high from their beer party and elated with the anticipation of their graduation celebrations, they sang loud songs and walked back along the public highway towards school. When they saw a car coming their way, the rowdy group stuck out their thumbs to hitch a ride. As luck would have it, these normally good boys were picked up by a faculty member who smelled liquor on their breath and felt compelled to report them. Disciplinary measures were harsh. None of them was permitted to attend graduation even though many of their families were already enroute to the ceremony. The boys were sent home immediately.

Although this sounds like a typical adolescent prank with grave repercussions, the underside of this near-perfect place reveals more serious problems of alcoholism, plagiarism, cohabitation, and drug abuse. One suspects that these cases are few and that the surprise at their mention reflects their relative infrequency. Mostly, St. Paul's seems to proceed without severe crises. The tempestuous period of adolescence is subdued in this setting, or at least it appears that the tempests are channeled into productive energy.

Although "real-life" often feels distant from life at St. Paul's, the truths told here sometimes seem unflinchingly real. Many times I was surprised by how students and faculty confronted worldly issues that usually remain unspoken or camouflaged, particularly in the context of school life.

A Pulitzer Prize-winning journalist from the *Boston Globe* is a visiting speaker in a sixth-form class on advertising and the media. The speaker is intense, witty, and probing. This semester, he is a visiting professor at Yale and his style with the St. Paul's students bears the same dry humor and sophistication that he must use with university students and colleagues. There is no talking down, no attempt to simplify. He begins his monologue on political advertising with a high-level, penetrating discussion about the packaging of political candidates. His sentences are laced with difficult concepts and words. He speaks of metaphors, symbolism, conceptions of human nature, and the creation of images in political advertising. Uncertain about whether he is reaching his audience, from time to time he encourages questions. The students need little encouragement. Student: "Newspapers are historically known for having commitments to certain political candidates. . . . Is it true with television networks? Do they show favoritism?" Speaker: "CBS is a little to the left. ABC is to the right. NBC is asleep. . . . Mostly the networks research the prevailing attitudes of the audience and they match those fundamental biases."

Inspired by this line of thought, the speaker wants to make a more general point about ideological influences in the media. "In the media, being 'objective' does not mean being without bias or prejudice. It is a bias towards the mainstream. It means being white, middle-class, Christian, and capitalist." Even though these characteristics would seem to describe most of the students sitting in the classroom, the listeners seem unthreatened by the harsh criticisms. They listen intently, but their faces show no change of expression, no signs of emotion. The speaker's provocative words are heard, but not visibly challenged. The teacher, who has remained silent since introducing the speaker, fears the bold cynicism of the message and tries to offer balance to the discussion by referring to the democratic nature of the political process, the opportunity for people's voices to be heard through the ballot box. The teacher's comments are measured and reticent compared to the biting criticisms of the speaker, who continues to assert his pessimistic perspective. "Everyone gets to vote, so that seems to validate the democratic process. Consent implies democracy, which implies consent. . . . If the citizenry cannot make informed choices, should they be making uninformed ideological choices?" The dialogue between the teacher and the speaker grows increasingly intense and obscure. A student lost in the barrage of words interrupts with what he thinks is a straightforward question about Anderson's chances for success in the presidential race. However, the speaker responds with complicated notions, refusing to submit to facile generalizations or easy answers. "Consider the effects of not advertising. If you are not advertising, journalists will not take you seriously—the case of Anderson—because they think if Anderson doesn't advertise he will not be able to bring out votes. So journalists think he is not serious and generally disregard him."

In this discussion, I am struck by the pursuit of truth, the recognition of competing truths, and the spirit of inquiry and debate. The adults are not afraid to disagree publicly, nor do they alter the nature of their discourse in order to present a simpler, prettier picture of the world to their students. The speaker underscores the ugly undersides of the political process and attacks any remaining illusions of a fair race. The reality presented by the speaker seems very faraway from the serenity and perfections of St. Paul's. Ironically, the accounts of real-life events are far more truthful and probing than the stories normally told to students in other high school settings where ideals and illusions are more carefully guarded. The students at St. Paul's seem to greet the uncovering of truths with a certain detachment. When the class is abruptly over, the students rise quickly and pour out of the room. The teacher offers a few last words, "Wrestle with the issue of democracy. . . .", but the students have moved on, seemingly undisturbed by the disturbing message they have just heard.

THE INQUIRING SPIRIT

The rector's address at the Anniversary Chapel Service on graduation day points to the "developmentalist perspective" that pervades the culture of St. Paul's. It is a stark and clear essay on facing the ambiguities and uncertainties of life beyond the relatively safe and nurturant environment of St. Paul's. "Can we learn to reconcile ourselves to imperfect choices. . . . We send our sixth-form friends on to a complex world, but we do so with confidence." In negotiating the myriad commitments and pursuits of St. Paul's, the rector is confident that the graduating class has "tested and explored options," met difficult and competing challenges, struggled against temptation, and emerged from the four-year odyssey ready to face the world. The challenges confronting St. Paul's students, however, are cradled in an environment nurtured by certainty, abundance, and respect. These qualities are deeply rooted in history. "St. Paul's is the center of love and care for many generations," says the rector after warning the graduates of the possibility of growing rigid and threatened as one faces life's imperfections. The certainty of love and care allow one to take risks and ask probing questions. "The inquiring spirit turns the words of the psalm into a question."

There is a connection, it seems, between feeling safe and protected and daring to move beyond safety. There is an invincible quality about these young people that probably reflects their privileged station, but also grows out of the maturity and confidence that come with positive and productive intellectual, social, and psychological experiences. Never once at St. Paul's did I hear a teacher diminish or undermine a student in any way. Never once did I see students act disrespectfully of one another. With no fear of abuse, there is plenty of room for open inquiry, for testing limits, and for trying very hard.

In an advanced dance class, the teacher is a benign but rigorous task master. A dancer with the American Ballet Theater for over a decade, Mr. Sloan has "retired" to teaching. He approaches it with the same seriousness and dedication that must have sustained his successful dance career. Nine students dressed in traditional ballet garb go through their practiced motions at the bar. Without much talk, the dance teacher demonstrates the next step and then walks around the floor offering individual support and criticism. Suddenly, he claps and says "No." Music and motion stop. One dancer is singled out, "Maria, get your arms down . . . in the same rhythm, open your arms and plié." Maria, a tall, angular Hispanic girl, tries the step again without embarrassment, as everyone turns silently towards her. An hour later, when the dancers are doing complicated, fast-moving combinations across the floor, the teacher singles out Michelle, a pretty, petite Black girl, whose steps have been tentative and constricted. "That's a good start, but take a chance, a risk. . . . Go for it, Michelle," he bellows. It is a tough challenge as he makes her do it over and over again. She is awkward, unbalanced, and almost falls several times, but the dance master won't let her stop. As Michelle struggles to master this complicated step in front of her classmates some watch attentively, without laughter or judgment. Others practice on their own around the edges of the floor waiting for their turn. Everyone, including Mr. Sloan, exerts great energy and tries very hard. Imperfections are identified and worked on without embarrassment.

There is a rising crescendo in the mood and tone of the class as the steps get tougher, the music gets more rigorous, and the instructor and students more charged. The exhilaration and vigor of the final moments contrasts with the serious and subdued attentiveness of the early bar work. As dancers execute the swift steps across the floor, the wide range of skill and talent is revealed. Kara is a precise and elegant dancer whose hopes of becoming a professional dancer seem realistic and promising. Even when she is tackling the most difficult step, she is smooth and graceful. Yet she doesn't escape criticism. Mr. Sloan insists on the subtle, almost invisible points. There is always room for improvement. A very tall and lean young man, who looks awkward and primitive in comparison, tries just as hard, but never produces a step that even vaguely resembles the one demonstrated by the teacher. No one laughs or grimaces as he breaks down half-way across the floor. The challenge remains: "You'll do it like that for awhile and you'll build up to doing it better. . . . It's a very difficult step."

Another example: Thirty sixth-form students sit in scattered chairs, vaguely forming a semicircle, facing Dr. Carter Woods, in their first period class on human personality. Sitting, Woods tilts his chair back with arms clasped behind his head and begins to speak thoughtfully and tentatively. As a prelude, he says, "We're all good friends in here. We know each other well." Then, without notes and looking up at the ceiling, the teacher begins to ruminate out loud. "Freud had a little help from his friends, but they started out on a really good tack. . . . They all came out of biology. . . . Free association was an amazing thing . . . totally existential, totally client-centered, a total departure from tradition. Carl Rogers wasn't even imagined in those times." The contemplative monologue soon turns into a conversation as students move in and out of the discussion. The words are often sophisticated and the thinking convoluted as Woods and his students explore together the murky waters of psychodynamic theory. The teacher encourages them to think out loud, and search for meanings by modeling that approach himself. "I am not sure what it means to get in touch with one's senses. I thought

I'd work that out with you. Let me struggle with it for a moment." Then, in even more searching tones, Woods says, "I find myself wanting to know how I can best instruct myself in finding out what Frederick Perls means." Not everyone is with him on this exploration. Some are visibly confused, some attentively listening, others daydreaming, a few are not quite awake for the first period in the morning. Six or seven students are completely involved and challenged by the probing questions. Occasionally, a down-to-earth, concrete question is asked of Woods as some students seem to want to establish boundaries and limits to the wandering conversation. Woods resists getting pinned down. "*I don't know, I'm asking you.*" When Woods approaches the board to review material covered before, most students respond to the certainty by copying the categories and lists from the board. The pedagogical message is clear: In order to understand, you must inquire and struggle to find meaning. To explore the full range of ideas, one must take risks and tolerate ambiguities. But this must be done in a nonjudgmental and accepting environment. When one of the students begins to slightly ridicule the "simplistic thinking" of the early psychologists, Woods responds immediately to her cynicism and encourages her to appreciate the slow evolution of ideas. "Science changes very slowly. We have the advantage of history. It is hard to move away from former, earlier authority." When the class is about to end, Woods says exuberantly, "The struggle—I'm happy in it."

Although the styles and substance of these two classes are very different, the themes of "love and caring" are prominent in both. The encouragement of risk-taking and moving beyond the safety zones are also stressed by both teachers. The success of the latter seems to be dependent on establishing the former.

Although it is likely that the nurturant and challenging experiences of students at St. Paul's help to build a community of trust and kinship, the careful selection of applicants is supportive of that goal as well. Choosing one out of every thirteen students who apply, the admissions committee makes a conscious effort to select young people who will thrive in the St. Paul's setting. When I ask one of the two psychologists at the school what kind of students are most successful at St. Paul's, he lists a number of characteristics: those with ego strength, a commitment to relationships and community; those who are outgoing, intelligent, and academically able. The applicants who are unlikely to survive the selection process tend to be those who are inward and withdrawn, who seem to be able to do without other human beings—the "young savants" who feel awkward socially. There are a few admitted who may at first "appear to be unresponsive" to people, but "manage to respond in more indirect ways." St. Paul's feels it can tolerate these more reticent souls if there is promise that they will make a unique contribution to the life of the community. There is some sense that diversity of backgrounds, styles, and temperaments is an integral part of a rich community experience. Learn-

232

ing to relate to those different from oneself is an important preparation for facing a diverse society and a critical part of articulating one's self-definition.

The best way to describe "the ethos of the St. Paul's community is that it is Eriksonian in emphasis." That is, there is a stress put on trust, industry, and autonomy. The rector, who admits to being profoundly influenced by Erikson, speaks of an evolutionary change in the school under his decade of leadership; "The school has moved towards a more developmentalist approach." From an administrative point of view, the "new approach" was visibly initiated by hiring two school psychologists who have become an integral and critical part of community life. One trained in counseling and consulting psychology, the other originally trained as a researcher in psycho-biology, these two men have carved out unusual, nontraditional roles at St. Paul's. Along with teaching half-time, they participate in all community responsibilities, including attending chapel and dining room meals, coaching sports, and living in student dormitories. Beyond these regular daily duties, they offer counsel, advice, and support to individual students and faculty. Carter Woods's office door is always open. "I had to work very hard to keep my door open. At first, everyone thought of the psychologist's work as secretive, mystical, something that happens behind closed doors." Now when students come to see him about personal dilemmas and stress there is little separation made between the intellectual and psychic spheres of life, but an attempt to see students as "whole."

The developmentalist view offers a "different view of human nature"—a view that can anticipate universal patterns of behavior and attitude formation. The psychologists seek to convey the progression of these patterns to students and faculty alike so that neither group will be surprised or upset by characteristic human dilemmas that tend to emerge as prominent at different stages of development. As one student said with enormous relief, this new knowledge of human development "helps me forecast my life," offers new interpretations, and some solace when things feel as if they are falling apart. For faculty, the developmentalist view changes their perception of students as "good or bad." Now when they have lost all patience with the antics of the thirteen year-olds, they can be gently reminded that these are anticipative and appropriate behaviors for third-form students, and that these characteristics are transitional and transforming. By fifth form, these students will appear as changed human beings and "we know some of the reasons why."

Not only do the psychologists offer individual counsel and guide the interpretations of behavior, they also give direct consultation to faculty

233

who are struggling with problem students or having difficulties negotiating with one another. For a few years now, Derek James has sat in on the faculty meetings of the history department, where there are a couple of "volatile members." After their not infrequent fights and disagreements, James helps them discover the origins of their struggle and supports them through a temporary resolution. Carter Woods offers the same sort of listening and counselling role for the religion department, a department often fractionated by polarized views of the appropriate curriculum for adolescents facing contemporary realities. And every Monday at lunch time, the rector, vice-rectors, chaplains, and psychologists meet with the trainer, who runs the school infirmary, to share information on any students who seem to be having academic difficulties or physical and mental health problems. They go around the circle offering their pieces of information on individual students, encouraging other perspectives and interpretations, gauging the seriousness of the problem presented, and finally assigning one of the group to follow-up action. It is an attempt at gathering and synthesis of information, orchestration of efforts, and careful attention to detail. Says the rector, "We don't want anyone to fall through the cracks." The Monday lunch is also another indication of St. Paul's efforts to work with "the whole child." It is here that "experts" of the body, mind, and soul gather to piece together their perspectives and offer their images of health.

The academic courses taught by the psychologists provide an opportunity for students to learn important material on culture and human behavior, as well as confront and express their own feelings and attitudes on questions of personality development, sexuality, and human relationships. The psychology courses are filled with sixth-form students who, having already met the academic requirements for college entrance can now take the more freewheeling courses that might be considered less than serious by college admissions officers. Envious third- and fourth-form students, and some unconvinced faculty, continue to refer to the psychology curriculum as "breeze" courses. It is likely that the readings and written assignments are not as demanding in these courses as in others, but the intensity and seriousness of the issues raised must surprise and baffle some unsuspecting sixth-form students.

Dr. James, a thin, bearded man with a gentle and inquisitive style, teaches the seminar on human sexuality. Twenty students sit around a large, rectangular oak table, many of them draped casually on chairs, some sitting on the edge of their seats with intense animation. Several students wander in late and the atmosphere is easy. No one opens a book or takes notes. James begins by presenting statistics on a study reported in the *New York Times* that surveyed attitudes towards homosexuality. "What would you do if your best friend said that he/she was a homosexual?" James merely recites the study's findings. He does not elicit responses from his students because he judges it to be "an invasion of their privacy," and in opposition to "the cultural norms" well established in this classroom. Almost without direction or provocation from the teacher, the discussion heats up to an animated pitch. Sometimes James makes brief comments or tentative suggestions, but mostly students direct their comments to one another, offer opposing opinions, and disagree vehemently. The girls, sounding womanly and worldly-wise, dominate the conversion. One very straight, handsome young man seems to have accepted the role of "traditionalist," or worse, male chauvinist and welcomes the abuse that is hurled towards him. The discussion of homosexuality is short-lived. It quickly turns into a discussion of differences in the ways men and women express feelings of rage, sadness, joy, and love. James willingly follows the shifts of direction and mood and says, "The culture comes down so hard on males being tough and hard . . . they are not supposed to be tender . . . if you're not hard and strong, you're not male." A rush of responses follow as the conversation grows increasingly autobiographical. One girl challenges, "But I've seen *both* my parents cry." The "traditionalist" stirs a response by claiming that only the weak cry, "My mother rarely cries and my father *never* cries." Another boy speaks up for the first time, with some embarrassment, "My father comes home, walks down into the basement, and hurls pyrex glasses—(he's a chemist)—against the wall . . . comes upstairs, takes a deep breath, and eats. . . . He takes his anger out on objects rather than people. . . . It is sort of bizarre." Family stories are revealed as most students try to make distinctions between themselves and their parents. They recognize the profound influence of parental values and behaviors, but they also stress their conscious intentions to find their own style of expression. Affect and intellect, information and expression, are fused in the student conversation. The atmosphere remains nonjudgmental. Trust is high and the discussion flows from being charged and forceful to moments of humorous release. When the bell rings to mark the end of class, I am startled. For the past fifty minutes, this has not felt like school and I am shocked by the intrusions of school sounds. The students seemed undisturbed by the abrupt transition. Immediately, they are out of the room and on to the next class without apparent confusion. To them, this is part of school.

Although St. Paul's explicitly recognizes the dimensions of the whole child and the inextricable interdependence of the psyche, the soul, and the intellect, it views its mission and purpose as clearly educational. "St. Paul's does not try to be a therapeutic community," warns Carter Woods, who is constantly having to delineate the boundaries between educational and therapeutic efforts. These boundary lines are not always so easily drawn. "St. Paul's goes to every length, uses every resource to provide educational resources for a student. . . . We spend thousands of dollars a year on an individual student, trying to help him or her over an academic hurdle . . . we would rather spend it on a student than on a building." But when problems seem to originate in families, beyond the boundaries of school, and when the response of the student is to be disruptive in a way that "infringes upon the good of the community," or the space of other individuals; then the student is asked to leave. Woods has recently returned from the West Coast, where he accompanied a troubled boy home on the airplane. After months of trying to "incorporate this boy into community life," St. Paul's felt it had no more resources or energy to offer. The boy's problems were too profound to be addressed by the faculty, and his acting out was beginning to negatively affect the lives of other students. At the other end of the flight across country, Woods had to face the sensitive task of communicating the bad news to the parents, their harsh defensiveness, and then their sense of defeat and guilt at their son's return.

On many occasions, families are included in the school's attempts to help a student who is having major problems. The parents of a girl who had serious trouble with alcohol were asked to come to St. Paul's to meet with the psychologists and members of the faculty. Attempts were made to explore the history of alcoholic problems within the family, and long-distance calls were made to a psychiatrist in the Midwest who had treated members of the family for mental distress. As parents, siblings, and outside professionals rallied together to pool information, offer support, and express their feelings, Woods orchestrated the combined effort, carefully negotiating the terrain of family and school responsibilities.

In seeking the counsel and support of parents, St. Paul's has begun to take a different view of family-school relationships. Traditionally, families were systematically and purposefully excluded from participating in school affairs. Told when they delivered their child to the campus in September that they should return at the close of school in June, parents were expected to be invisible and silent, uninvolved in their child's acculturation to St. Paul's. Never did anyone suspect that parents and teachers would disagree on the basic values and cultural perspectives that should be imbued in their young charges. Trust and partnership were assumed because there seemed to be harmony of values between home and school, an unspoken consensus. Besides, many of the fathers had themselves been students at St. Paul's and were confident and knowledgeable about what happened behind the closed gates. As the world beyond St. Paul's has become increasingly complex, as family structures grow more diverse and uncertain, and as St. Paul's adopts the developmentalist perspective, it has seemed increasingly important to welcome families as a vital resource and as an important source of information. Woods speaks of families as a critical "connection to the culture," and recognizes their profound and primary role in the lives of students. Some families are not comfortable with this change in the school's view of them. The father of a troubled boy, who had been asked to come up to St. Paul's, felt awkward and inappropriate as they sat talking together in Wood's living room. Expressing his initial wariness, he said, "I'm feeling uncomfortable here. When I was here as a student, families were made to feel unwelcome."

UNIMPEACHABLE POWER

At St. Paul's, the rector wields great power. Everyone describes Bill Oates as powerful—a power that is defined both by the traditions and expectations of his role and the character of his person. He is energetic, uncompromising, and focused in his goals. Yet he does not wield power carelessly. It is a restrained authority, always held in check and used sparingly. Although faculty emphasize his great powers, they also talk about his political intelligence, his keen understanding of decision-making patterns, and his thoughtful and balanced consultation of the people involved. For example, there are fifteen faculty and three students on the admissions committee who work for months reading and making judgments on over a thousand folders. After reaching carefully negotiated decisions, they make recommendations to the rector. The final decision about who gets admitted rests with the rector, "but he is wise enough to recognize when an overturned decision would greatly violate a difficult and consuming selection process or offend an important constituency." In every entering class, there are inevitably the rector's choices; students whose families are important donors to the school or who have connections to external sources of power that the Rector wants to tap into.

Faculty rarely argue with the rector, or even dare to disagree strongly. No one risks being late to meetings with him. People who normally seem strong and sturdy in their roles appear strangely submissive and accommodating in his presence. One teacher, who challenged the rector with an opposing view in a small planning meeting, told of his restrained but scathing response, her sense of bravery and risk-taking in even raising the issue in his presence, and the buzz around the faculty room when the word leaked out that she had acted irreverently.

Even though his dominance is without question, his style is not dominating. Rather, he appears supremely civilized and benign in manner. He takes on the demeanor of the rectors who were his predecessors. The weight of the role, already well established and deeply forged by history, seems to shape perceptions of him just as much as his own actions. As a matter of fact, many students describe him as friendly and approachable. He knows every student's name and can speak knowledgeably about their special and unique styles, personal struggles, and important triumphs. Every Saturday night, he and his wife host an open house with punch and their famous chocolate chip cookies. Most students stop by at some point during the evening. Says one, "It's fun to go and shake his hand and chat with him. I have a friend who goes to Exeter and she says they never see their headmaster. He just disappears and never comes out." Some faculty say that with reference to student life, Bill Oates is the best rector of a preparatory school in the country.

They speak differently about the life of the faculty, who seem to be the least powerful, most disenfranchised group at St. Paul's. Faculty receive no contracts or terms of appointment. In December, they receive a letter from the rector stipulating the next year's salary. (The one I saw was a Xeroxed form letter with name and details written in hand). Occasionally there is a mild word of encouragement or support, but mostly letters are short and only explicit about the salary. Faculty do not view these letters as perfunctory. Even those faculty who feel confident about their work and contributions to St. Paul's silently worry about their fate on that December day when letters arrive in the mailbox. One young faculty member spoke of seeing an elder of the faculty, "a 'lifer' as the kids call them," who had been at St. Paul's for over forty years, anxiously awaiting his letter, trembling when he opened the envelope. "It was then that I began to think something was wrong with the system."

Although the notion of a system that works without contractual arrangements seems archaic in this day and age, all faculty do not see this as a problem. As a matter of fact, there seems to be a fairly clear line of demarcation between the old and the new faculty. The old, themselves raised in preparatory institutions, many from very privileged backgrounds, steeped in the traditions and habits of St. Paul's, see little problem in the established patterns of the faculty role. At times, they view the new faculty's demands as irreverent, whining, and threatening to the comfortable stability of the place. New faculty, who tend to come from less affluent backgrounds (without independent incomes), many of whom were not raised in exclusive schools, are more likely to view their role as a professional one and want some legalistic and contractual safeguards. Says one new faculty, "On almost every vote there is a divided faculty. It makes it impossible to make any progress on most of these issues."

Even though there is a divided view of faculty privilege within the current system, most seem to agree that beyond the walls of St. Paul's the faculty have options open for them that are indeed extraordinary. One of the first things the rector mentions in my conversation with him is his attempts to provide support and encouragement for faculty growth and development. He has gone out and raised funds for the generous provisions of faculty leaves, travel, and study. The faculty have a full paid year of leave, travel grants for the summer that will be raised to $3,500 next year, and study and tuition grants for further graduate study. Recently, the rector arranged for the endowment of the "Dickie Fellowship Program"—a program of visiting scholars and experts in the various fields of study offered at St. Paul's. Every year, each department is able to invite to the campus for two days a nationally renowned person in their field who will offer counsel, support, and advice to the faculty. These visits offer renewal and an opportunity for reflection and self-criticism.

All of these life-giving benefits seem critical to the survival of faculty members who must give seven days a week, twenty-four hours a day to their work at St. Paul's. It is a special kind of work that demands an extraordinary level of commitment and participation. All faculty must live on campus; all must attend chapel and evening meals with students. Beyond their classroom teaching, they are required to coach sports every afternoon, counsel and advise students on a daily basis, and serve as dormitory residents with disciplinary and overseeing chores. This is a total institution that blends the realms of work and play, private and public roles, and parenting and teaching. The rector chooses faculty whom he judges will embrace the totality, not resist it. Some faculty are superb in the classroom, but are let go because they do not give totally to the community. A faculty member must be ready to offer his full and complete commitment. "It is a life with a different kind of rhythm," says the rector—a rhythm different from those that shape the work-life of most other adults. The full-time commitments of faculty are balanced by "22 days off at Christmas, 22 days for spring break, and 13 weeks of summer vacation." Despite the generous periods of time off, the demands on faculty are extreme and one wonders why faculty do not break down under the pressure or rise up in revolt. Surely some people thrive on this lifestyle. The totality of commitment feels comfortable; the inclusive quality embraces them as well. Others must find ways "to get others to nurture them . . . so they don't go dead in the process . . . unless we give to ourselves or find others who will give to us, then the demands of this life are too extreme." Returning to graduate study provides this nurturance for some. As one faculty member put it when he began to take courses at Harvard, "Finally I had to do something for myself." Outside study may offer intellectual stimulation, adult interaction, and a great escape from the boundaries of St. Paul's. However, most speak of their sojourns at the university as nurturance, as a time to give to themselves in a way they have had to give to others. It is what the students call "a feed," a filling up on goodies that helps sustain them through a work life that often feels selfless and other-directed.

Faculty life, therefore, is precariously balanced between giving out and taking in, with pressures that impinge from above and below. They must be willing to fulfill the multiple roles of teacher, counselor, parent, and even confidante to students, all requiring adult-like responsibilities. Yet they must be willing to leave their fate in the hands of a benign, but authoritarian rector, assuming a childlike role in relation to the supreme parent. There could be tension, then, between the demands of the mature authority they must exude in relation to the students, and the docility required to submit to an even greater authority. For some, there may be comfort in the ultimate submissiveness of their position—a comfort that allows them to respond fully to student needs and demands. For others, I would imagine, there is a basic contradiction between how they are treated and the roles they are being asked to assume in relation to students—a contradiction that forces some to leave, some to find external sources of stimulation and support, and some to become stagnant and dissatisfied, no longer in touch with their needs.

BETWEEN TWO WORLDS: A MINORITY PERSPECTIVE

The majority of students at St. Paul's come from families of affluence and privilege. They exude the casual certainty and demeanor of entitlement that reflects their upper middle-class status. Many already have the savoir-faire and cosmopolitan style of people much beyond their years. Their Calvin Klein T-shirts, Gloria Vanderbilt jeans, L.L. Bean jackets, and Nikon cameras dangling from their necks show restrained opulence. Their sophistication is accompanied by an open friendliness. Every student I spoke to willingly and spontaneously responded to my questions. Some approached me with generous words of welcome and eagerly told of their experiences at St. Paul's. Their stories of life at the school were uniformly positive. They praised the rector, their teachers, the academic program, and the school's rituals and ceremonies. Mostly, they echoed the rector's words of "love and caring." There were the typical and expectable complaints about dress codes and dormitory rules, but surprising praise for the food. For most students, St. Paul's is an inspiring and demanding place where they feel challenged and rewarded.

A decade ago, St. Paul's became coeducational and now girls make up 40 percent of the student body. The theme of the graduation symposium this year focused on the first decade of coeducation at St. Paul's. Several fifth- and sixth-form students (including a boy from Central America and a Black girl from New York) and a female faculty member with the longest tenure at the school, gave short presentations about their experiences with and perceptions of coeducation. The presenters were carefully selected by department heads and the rector. Speeches were written, critiqued by faculty, and rewritten several times. One student, exasperated by the close scrutiny, complained of the "censoring" of her ideas when she tried to speak her mind. But the public stories that emerged conveyed the success and richness of coeducation at St. Paul's. Said one student enthusiastically:

> "As males and females living together, day to day, we see each other both at our strongest and at our most vulnerable moments. We encounter each other in the classroom—and at breakfast. Superficiality *cannot* survive fried eggs in the morning. Casual, regular interaction compels a better knowledge of ourselves. In my personal experience here at St. Paul's, I have seen a great change in my own ways of thinking. One that I had not been consciously aware of, but a change that I had taken for granted. In my first year, I tended to think of people in distinct male or female roles. Now I realize, by encountering people in a coeducational setting, that I must free them to be individuals, free them to develop the full spectrum of human responses and potential."

The audience of parents and alumni greeted the messages with polite, but restrained response. Even with the rector's encouragement of candor, the audience did not speak of what was on their minds: the issue of sexual norms and practices among the boys and girls.

To a visitor, the girls at St. Paul's seem fully integrated into the setting. They are serious athletes, sensitive artists, bright and inquiring students, aggressive journalists, and student leaders. In ten years, the comfortable assimilation of girls into the historically all-male environment appears to have been accomplished. There are other signs of the incorporating arms of St. Paul's. Admissions committees stress their concern for diversity among the student body. In a small history seminar that I visited, students came from all over the country and the world: Germany;

Japan; New York City; Capetown, South Africa; Denver; Maine; and San Francisco.

Less impressive is the minority presence at St. Paul's. Black and Brown faces are few and far between. A Black student says that they are now 4 percent of the student body; a more knowledgeable source claims a 7 percent Afro-American presence. I was eager to learn about the history and experience of Blacks at St. Paul's and turned to Lester Brown, one of two Black faculty and the new assistant dean of admissions. Brown's perspective reveals an intriguing blend of historical recollections and contemporary views.

A student at St. Paul's from 1969–73, Brown graduated with an engineering degree from the University of Pennsylvania and has returned to his alma mater for his first job. Lester Brown was born and raised in West Philadelphia and calls himself a "Philadelphia boy." He went to school not in the familiar Black territory of West Philly, but in Kensington, a working-class, Irish Catholic neighborhood where he experienced open hostility and some violence towards Blacks. It was a fiery, dangerous time. He rode the elevated street cars and buses on his hour and a half trek to school. His walk from the streetcar to the school sometimes had to be protected by police and national guardsmen. Because Kensington was a magnet school with special resources and a more academic climate, Brown decided to become "a sacrificial lamb." He soon discovered that the white kids inside were friendly and good, while the white kids outside were hateful. "It was not a matter of race, but of how you behaved that counted." He and two other buddies of his from West Philadelphia were discovered and "adopted" by a generous Jewish woman—a volunteer in the school who offered them "cultural enrichment," friendship, guidance, and support. Brown called her "my fairy Godmother." Everything she touched magically turned into something good. It would happen invisibly. "We didn't know how things happened. Suddenly, everything would come together." So it was with Brown's coming to St. Paul's. When he was about to go on to high school, this woman asked him about his plans. He had thought of going to Central High School, a Philadelphia school with a good reputation, but she said, "You know, Lester, there are other options you should consider." Without much effort, he and his two friends found themselves spread apart in fancy private schools, faraway from family.

Brown remembers the transition to St. Paul's as immediate and easy. His experience with "good whites" in the Kensington School made him not prejudge or stereotype his white peers at St. Paul's. When Brown arrived in 1969, a strong, cohesive group of Black students provided solace, support, and a source of identity for individual Blacks. (Brown remembers there being forty-five Blacks in the school as compared to twenty-three eleven years later.) A strong group consciousness permitted individuals to move forcefully out into the sea of whiteness and not feel overwhelmed or confused. Brown remembers the leader of the group, a strong articulate, political figure, who gained respect and some measure of fear from faculty and students. He was not considered radical, but he was disciplined and outspoken, and everyone knew he was serious.

Blacks were a clear presence on the campus in the early seventies. "Believe it or not, we even had a Third World room—a space we could make our own, decorate the way we wanted to, a place to gather." The energy and vitality of this cohesive Black group infected the campus spirit. Aretha Franklin's and Ray Charles's sounds could be heard across the manicured lawns; poetry readings portrayed Black voices; and parties were dominated by a Black spirit. "We were so sure of ourselves, we invited the *whites* in!" The irony of their success as a strong and dynamic force on the campus is that it led to their own demise and failure. Soon there was little differentiation between Whites and Blacks. The boundaries that had helped them establish their identity and made them strong enough to reach out eroded, fading into blurred distinctions.

Now the Afro-American Coalition has become the Third World Cultural Group. The "Coalition" label was seen by faculty and students as an overly political symbol, and the "Afro-American" image was deemed as too exclusive. In its recent incarnation, the Third World Cultural Group is an integrated club, generously sprinkled with whites. With no clear identity or purpose, many say it should be disbanded. "It's not doing anything for anybody." Others say it should be expanded to include a more generalized service role. There are more than fifty people signed up for the the Third World Cultural Group—"It looks good on their college applications." However, rarely are there more than ten or twelve who show up at meetings. This year, a white girl seems to be a favorite choice in the slate of nominations for president—a far cry from the spirit and ideology of the early seventies.

All recognize that the transitions within St. Paul's are a reflection of changes beyond the walls of the school. With fewer cities bursting into flames, with a lessening in the threat of violence and force, and with a softening in the rhetoric of Black consciousness, the thrust of affirmative action has diminished. Additionally, many Blacks feel more reticent about becoming "sacrificial lambs." In the last several years, the Black applicant pool at St. Paul's has yielded fewer and fewer qualified students. Increasingly, prospective students have been turned off and intimidated by approaches and images that have worked well with their more privileged and white counterparts. Since his return, one of Brown's major roles has been the recruitment of minority students. His active and sustained efforts have produced a significantly larger applicant pool that will bring fifteen third-form Black students to the school next fall—a major ripple in the still waters of St. Paul's.

Even those who have worried about the invisible and weakened status of Blacks at St. Paul's do not seem to be suggesting retrenchment or a return to isolation and separatism. But many Black students do speak of the need for a swelling of numbers and an encouragement (or at least validation) of togetherness. Group consciousness now seems to symbolize weakness rather than strength. The third- and fourth-form boys, who play junior varsity basketball together, have found a way to withstand these negative perceptions of their groupiness. They justify their togetherness by claiming that they have athletics, not necessarily race, in common. According to Brown, the Black girls have no such vehicle for group awareness, and so they suffer more from isolation at the school.

Class also divides the group. Most Black students come from working-class, urban backgrounds in New York, Chicago, and Boston. When they come to St. Paul's, they are overwhelmed by the abundance and plenty that surrounds them. At first, nothing is taken for granted. "They appreciate the green grass and woods; they appreciate the gym floor; they appreciate the room accommodations." It takes them almost a year to make the major cultural shift, cross the class/ethnic boundaries, and begin to feel comfortable. At the same time, they are required to make a difficult academic leap. Courses at St. Paul's demand a kind of thinking they may have never experienced in their prior schooling. "They've never had to think before." They are expected to be questioning and articulate, and their academic skills are not as practiced or sophisticated as their peers'. The dual demands of cultural assimilation and academic competence bear down on them with great force. It is amazing that they hang in, survive the onslaughts, and return the next year ready to face the challenges.

But where does this lead? Most likely, a prestigious college career will follow. Next fall, Cheryl will go to Amherst. Others have gone to Harvard, Yale, Princeton, and Williams. Stephen, the only Black boy in the sixth form, will not go immediately on to college. He'll travel to Spain with no clear plans, no job lined up, and no facility in Spanish. His career plans seem to be distantly related to his travels. He hopes one day to enter the foreign service, and he wants "to get Spanish under his belt." He seems apologetic about his vagueness, adrift and alone in the school.

244

Stephen and Cheryl will be sad when school ends and they will have to return to New York and Chicago for the summer. "We have no friends at home," they say. Away from their family and friends for four years, they are strangers at home, feel distant and awkward in their old neighborhoods, and will miss returning to the now-safe environment of St. Paul's. Their profound connection to the school, and their sense of disconnection and alienation from home, seem to be related to what Lester Brown describes as the "breeding of arrogance." He fears that successful accommodation by Blacks to St. Paul's means that they are likely to leave as "different people" with well-socialized feelings of entitlement and superiority borrowed from peers, from faculty, and from a culture that inevitably separates them from their own people and, perhaps, from themselves. The naturally smiling and open face of Lester Brown grimaces at the thought. He, too, feels implicated and guilty about his participation in this process of cultural and personal transformation.

VI

Milton Academy

Breaking New Ground: Humanism and Achievement

CITY BACKDROP

From Boston you travel along the Southeast Expressway, a three-lane highway crowded with fast cars and roaring trucks. You pass the great hulking oil drums with splashes of Corita-painted designs and the modern architecture of the University of Massachusetts Harbor Campus. I. M. Pei's Kennedy Library stands sleek and poised over the water, drawing a clean line in the sky. From the swiftly moving traffic you can spot the gaudy billboards, fast-food joints, and crowded shopping centers just off the expressway. After fifteen or twenty minutes of driving, the East Milton exit approaches quickly and the landscape abruptly shifts. During the late afternoon rush hour, it takes an hour to travel that same stretch of highway. The traffic is bumper-to-bumper. In the heat of summer, car radiators and human tempers rise to match the soaring temperature. In the winter, the slick, icy roads cause traffic to move at a slow, cautious pace and accidents are frequent.

The lush green landscape of Milton comes as a welcome surprise after negotiating the tortuous traffic. If you turn towards town, you find a small suburban village—a collection of drug stores, a twenty-four hour

246

grocery store, dry-cleaning and laundry establishments, dress shops, and luncheonettes. The tone is quiet, motley, and unpretentious, reflecting mixtures of this town's affluence and middle-income styles and tastes. Traveling further in that direction, towards a section that some of the wealthier residents call "the other side of the tracks," there are modest suburban dwellings on small plots.

But if you turn in the opposite direction when leaving the expressway, you soon approach the more affluent sections of Milton. Stately homes built of solid brick with sturdy white columns or New England wood-frame, century-old structures sit on larger parcels of land surrounded by well-tended lawns and elegant gardens. A few turns later, Center Street becomes the central artery of Milton Academy, and you are advised to go twenty miles per hour. It is difficult to recognize the boundaries of the campus because it blends so easily into the residential landscape. For several days I thought the imposing brick mansions, close to the school and along Center Street, were extravagant private homes and discovered later that they were the girls' dormitories for Milton Academy. Some faculty view the town street running through the center of Milton's campus as important symbolically. "It reflects our close connections to the wider community, to intercourse with life beyond our borders," says one.

Eclectic architecture combines to form a handsome campus. The modern angular buildings face restrained old brick structures. It is not an opulent, overly-precious scene. The buildings are sturdy, the grass is green, and the campus has lovely scenic spots. Yet there is a well-used, slightly frayed feeling to many of the older buildings, and the new ones are not extravagantly built. The Yankee restraint of upper-class New Englanders is evident in many of the structures.

On the day I arrive in early April, the sun is golden, the air is clear but still brisk, and the budding crocuses promise spring. Students have shed their coats and are pushing the season in their warm-weather regalia. Many girls look light and feminine in spring frocks and flowered skirts. A girl with straight, blond, waist-length hair smiles broadly as she twirls barefoot on the grass. "I'm celebrating spring!" she explains to me. The boys wear corduroys and khaki pants with open-necked, longsleeve shirts. (The dress code that does not permit boys and girls to wear blue jeans causes some complaints from students.) It is midmorning break and several students are gathered in small groups on the square lawn in front of the library. Some are completely sprawled out, trying to soak up the sun's rays. Others are engaged in casual conversation while they sip coffee, and a few are leaning against a nearby wall reading school books.

Three boys and a girl are tossing a frisbee to one another. It is the day following spring vacation and many students find it hard to make the transition back to school. "It is always awful returning after the holidays and facing the grind . . . simply distasteful!" complains a plump sophomore who is carrying a pile of books into the library.

I follow him into the Cox Library, a modern building with comfortable spaces for sitting, reading, and studying. It is a well-equipped and functional facility with 40,000 volumes, 121 periodicals, microfilm, and non-print materials. It is also an aesthetic place with original art work, comfortable furniture, and lovely patterns of light and shadow coming through tall windows. As you enter the library, two prominent pieces of art mark the extremes of human emotion. A metal sculpture called "The Tense Man"—tall, thin, and brittle—exudes tension and anxiety. On the wall close by hangs a modern quilted tapestry called "Planted by Living Waters." Done in soft, warm colors, it is a hanging that symbolizes calm and peace.

In an alcove to the right of the library entrance there are restful easy chairs, arranged around a low table. Four students are sitting in the chairs, feet propped on the table, quietly reading the *New York Times,* the *Boston Globe,* and the *Wall Street Journal.* There is a display rack next to the wall that has shelves for journals and recently published books. The titles offer a glimpse of the intellectual climate of Milton. The faculty journals include the latest editions of *Modern Language Journal, Harvard Educational Review, Journal of Interdisciplinary History, Foreign Affairs,* and *Daedalus.* A young male teacher is leaning against the wall reading an excerpt from *American Quarterly.* Under a pink-orange, handwritten sign indicating "Our New Titles," is an intriguing array of books including: Richard Rodriguez's *Hunger of Memory,* Janet Malcolm's *Psychoanalysis: The Impossible Profession,* Archibald Cox's *Freedom of Expression,* Marjorie Shostak's *Nisa: The Life and Words of a Kung Woman,* and Guy De Mallac's *Boris Pasternak: His Life and Art.* The study of family, culture, history, and community; the concern for exploring the psychodynamic roots of human learning and behavior, are themes central to these volumes. They are also themes that shape the philosophy and values of life at Milton.

Milton Academy has 50 buildings on its 125-acre campus. There is a Lower School for 185 children in the first six grades, and an Upper School for students from seventh through twelfth grades. Seven hundred students (420 boys and 280 girls) attend the Upper School. (A Middle School, for 110 seventh and eighth graders, is a subsection of the Upper School. It has a few core faculty but shares most of its teachers with the

Upper School. In the past several years, the Middle School has gradually gained elements of an individual identity.) Not only does Milton have a lower and upper school, it is also divided among boarders and day students. Students from ninth through twelfth grades can be admitted as boarders. Many of the boarders hail from distant places around the country and the world. The larger proportion of day students arrive each morning from nearby Boston and suburban towns and depart after school, some coming by car, others by bus and subway. During the school day, the lives of boarders and day students are integrated with assemblies, classes, and activities in common. However, at the close of the day, their experiences are sharply contrasted. Milton encourages the mixture of these groups through day-boarder exchanges that allow day students to spend a week at a time in the dormitories and boarders to stay with families of day students during the week. The tuition for boarders at Milton is $7,900, and $5,500 for day students.

During my visit to Milton, I was exclusively interested in the Upper School, with a particular focus on the experiences of students and faculty in grades nine through twelve. Although the Lower and Upper schools are in proximity on the campus and both are under a central administration, they are relatively separate institutions. There is an intraschool program allowing the older students to tutor the younger children, and sometimes dance or theater groups from the Upper School give performances for the Lower School; but the adolescents seem a world apart from the younger children, and the two faculties rarely come together for school-wide functions. The collective faculty gatherings are largely ceremonial or social rather than substantive. I am sure that Upper School students feel the ripple effects of the younger children's presence, but in conversation they almost never mention them and occasionally complain about "their getting under foot." It is possible, therefore, to describe life in the Upper School as a relatively distinct environment and to view it as roughly comparable to other private secondary schools.

The Milton catalogue pictures the city backdrop. Its cover, in tones of blue and brown, shows Milton's campus with Boston's skyline in the distance. Compared to most secondary school catalogues, Milton's appears slender in size. I am relieved by the straightforward, jargonfree style of writing and by the friendly, low-key tone. There seem to be no brash claims or seductive allures, only a convincing pride about the rich offerings. Sprinkled generously throughout the pages are candid pictures of administrators, teachers, and students in action; a counselor listening caringly to a student, a girl pitching a baseball, hands molding clay on a potter's wheel, a small choir singing in the chapel, a teacher explaining a physics problem in a science laboratory, and pretty girls all dressed up in long white graduation dresses. The pictures project an image of a lively environment with myriad attractions and the intense and active involvement of participants.

The catalogue text, though restrained, also portrays a world full of interesting, healthy, and inspiring people and activities. Buckminster Fuller (Class of 1913) is shown demonstrating an experiment to a rapt audience of faculty and students, and it is mentioned that over the years Milton has had such distinguished visitors as Franklin D. Roosevelt, T.S. Eliot (also a Milton graduate), Dr. Jean Mayer, Julian Bond, and Ralph Nader. A section entitled "The Student World" refers to the student government, sports, glee club, orchestra, jazz groups, theater productions, public speaking competitions, art festivals, newspaper, and much more. A few days on campus reveal that these attractions are not merely advertising gimmicks. Students often refer to the rich array of extracurricular activities, "too little time to fit in all the wonderful possibilities"; faculty are actively involved in directing and organizing clubs, festivals, exhibits, and sports teams, as well as teaching classes.

Beyond the sheer quantity of student activities, faculty and students are proud of their quality. The speech team, for example, is a highly disciplined group who have won numerous statewide and regional competitions. Tanya, a senior who exudes style and grace, tells me that she is interested in pursuing a career in the theater. She joined the speech team in order to improve her "performance under pressure and her spontaneity." She has found it "exciting and energy-draining." She feels both compelled by and apprehensive of the brutal competition. "I am learning to lose without feeling that I am a loser," she says. Tanya is also involved in tennis, photography, the octet singing group, the House Committee, and a drama production. She has to monitor her energies carefully and make sure her studies are not neglected. Yet she recognizes the ways in which the extracurricular activities give her "courage to face her studies . . . they bolster my self-esteem."

The Milton Measure, the school's newspaper, is also seen as an activity of high quality. It demands time, energy, and discipline from its committed student staff and a wise guiding hand from its faculty advisor. Some people claim it is the best high school newspaper in the country. A reading of the *Measure* reveals fine reporting, writing, analysis, and the diligent pursuit of evidence.

The curriculum and academic requirements are clearly displayed in the catalogue. The opening paragraph stresses discipline, creativity, and self-discovery.

> The academic program combines demanding training with innovative approaches. It attempts to foster a creative spirit and independence of judgment. The program prepares students for college; it also helps them to discover and enjoy their own capacities.

There are nine major academic departments listed: English, Language Skills, Classics, Modern Languages, Mathematics, Science, History and Social Studies, Religion, and the Arts. Each department offers an array of courses that follow a careful sequencing for grade levels. English, with a prominent place in the curriculum, is the first to appear in the catalogue. There is an elaborate explanation of the purposes and values that shape the English curriculum.

> After more than a decade of self-examination and experimentation, the English Department at Milton has achieved a dynamic balance of educational theories and practice. While one class may spend a month in a close analysis of *King Lear*, another class will be preparing oral interpretations of writers as various as Tennessee Williams, Chaucer, and Anne Sexton. The point is this: there is a continuous interplay between the traditional and the innovative, the ancient and the modern, the basic skills and the imaginative encounter.

With seventeen course offerings, English has the greatest number and variety of classes. There are the introductory courses in reading, writing, and speaking; the analysis of novels, plays, poems, legends, myths, and fables; and the writing of critical and imaginative essays. Intermediate courses focus on English literature from Chaucer to the early seventeenth century. There are more advanced courses—"Literature and the Human Condition," "Introduction to Western Philosophy," "Introduction to Shakespeare," "Man and His Fictions," "Major Writers in America," "Modern Comparative Literature," and "Creative Writing." The chairperson of English, proud of the high caliber of teaching in his twenty-person department and the tradition of excellence and creativity among his faculty, says that they give a careful, substantive review to the curriculum every four years. A couple of years ago, there was a serious proposal for a major overhaul of the entire English curriculum, a proposal that would have dramatically changed the pattern and substance of learning and required the faculty to develop new course offerings. The discussions among faculty were "sharp, vigorous, and passionate," remembers the chairperson, and caused some "momentary divisiveness" among the members. "With six Ph.Ds, former headmasters, and other charismatic people in this department, you have a lot of firepower." The proposal lost by one vote, but the "process was important and enlightening to faculty development," he recalls.

Although other departments are not as large, and perhaps not as vociferous, one has a sense that curricular decisions are carefully considered and critically reviewed, and that curricular innovation is seen as an opportunity for faculty development and exchange. The selection of courses in the catalogue reflect faculty care and restraint. One does not see the smorgasbord of courses that is typical of many secondary schools; rather, one finds the kernels that symbolize what faculty regard as primary to the students' intellectual growth. For example, the science department's display of courses only fills two pages in the catalogue with such courses as Life Science, Physical Science, Earth Science, General Biology, Geology, Physics, Chemistry, and Astronomy. The relatively short list of course descriptions is accompanied by a thoughtful explanation of the goals and values that shape the curriculum, a rationale for the sequencing of courses, and the possibilities of enriching the course offerings with independent study research projects and off-campus opportunities.

It is in the arts that one sees more diversity and depth of courses than one normally finds in a secondary school of this size. "The Arts Program is a fellowship of the arts which recognizes the universal impulse to create," states the catalogue. Within this program there are a range of courses in creative writing, drama, dance, music, oral interpretation, and the visual arts; and many of the faculty are serious artists who combine pedagogy with the practice of their craft. Students can witness their teachers at work, developing their ideas, skills, and craft, and the curriculum is infused with a lively spirit.

A painter on the faculty speaks about the integration of her two worlds of work: "I have two full-time careers as a working artist and teacher. At first I thought teaching was *ordinary* work, designed for making money to support my art. Now I see that my natural calling is teaching. It is an important vehicle of expression . . . and I now believe that my worlds enrich one another." In an effort to achieve balance between practice and pedagogy, last year she built a small personal studio in a room connected to the much larger studio for students. She shows me the space and some of her work in progress and beams. "Students can see me in the process of creating and recreating. We can share a process together and they can see how hard this work really is!"

During my visit to Milton, I visited several classes in three departments: history and social science, English, and the arts. I knew it would not be possible to cover the entire landscape, so I chose these departments strategically. My choices reflected a combination of my own peculiar interests and the areas that many faculty identified as "strong, special, or unique" at Milton.

Beyond the academic departments, the catalogue reserves pages and photographs for describing the physical education and sports program. Milton has a well-deserved reputation as a school with a fully developed and enthusiastic athletic program. The director of admissions cites athletics as one of the key attractions of Milton and many students talk about its importance to their lives at school.

The playing fields seem to stretch on for miles beyond the school's buildings and every afternoon you can see boys, dressed in T-shirts and shorts, kicking soccer balls across the grass or lugging baseball gear towards the practice field. Their female counterparts, many with strong, muscular bodies, head off in the opposite direction towards the girls' fields. Dressed in similar jock attire, they carry field hockey sticks or tennis rackets and have the same enthusiastic gait. At 3:00, there is a shift of tempo in the school day as students and many faculty move from focusing on cerebral issues to disciplining their bodies.

In physical education, the girls' and boys' programs are clearly divided by separate classes and facilities. Classes for boys and girls are taught by trained physical education teachers but most of the boys' team coaching is done by male faculty members. Girls' teams are coached by women physical education teachers. There is a rich array of both interscholastic and extramural sports. The interscholastic sports for boys include football, soccer, cross-country, hockey, basketball, wrestling, squash, sailing, Alpine and Nordic skiing, baseball, tennis, track, and lacrosse. The intramural sports list is not as extensive but includes the less expected offerings of frisbee, cycling, weight training, and outdoor education. As with most activities at Milton, there are ardent enthusiasts and recalcitrants. Some students see sports as their only salvation and tolerate the accompanying academic program, and there are others who can barely cope with the demands of the physical education courses. Because of its strong reputation as an avid sports school, I asked the principal for boys about the students' involvement in athletics. "For many of the kids, it is their life blood . . . but there are also a lot of kids who feel uncomfortable in athletics, who feel there is an overemphasis on sports here." He summed up his observation, "I would say 25 percent of the boys are ardent jocks, 25 percent are anti-athletic, and 50 percent represent the broad range in between."

TRYING TO FIND A BALANCE

Although the catalogue's description of Milton's structure seems straight-forward and clear, the institutional arrangements appear baffling in reality. In its organization and composition, Milton defies easy categorizing. It combines suburban and urban elements, a lower and upper School, boarders and day students, and boys and girls. The Milton catalogue begins by referring to the complex mixtures:

> What is worth noting about Milton is its diversity. Visitors to the School often ask: Is it coeducational or single-sex? Is it a boarding school or a day school? Is it a big or a small school? Is it a country or a city school? In fact, Milton is all of them. As one of its teachers remarked, 'Milton is not an either/or school but a both/and school.'

Although the public relations material emphasizes the attraction and richness of combining diverse elements, administrators, teachers, and students are more likely to refer to the difficulties of embracing the diversity and the challenge of balancing constituencies. The most potent division within the community seems to mark separations between boys and girls. Everyone I talk with mentions the awkward boundaries between boys and girls; the imprint of history on contemporary structures and relationships between sexes; and the feelings of imbalance and inequality that result. In order to begin to understand the powerful and complicated sentiments surrounding boy/girl interactions, one needs to look back in time.

Before I have been at Milton for half a day, Carol Gregory tells me the long saga of the boys' and girls' schools at Milton as a way of helping me interpret present attitudes and behaviors. She knows I will be baffled by the anachronistic expressions of sex divisions and confused by structures and arrangements that seem to invite conflict unless I am told the historical origins. A veteran of twenty-three years, Ms. Gregory combines a fierce loyalty to Milton with perceptive criticism. A wonderful storyteller, her images are vivid, with attention given to composition and detail. She is careful to remind me that the story she tells is shaped by her prejudices and reflects her perspective, not universal truth. Despite her warnings of bias, I am impressed by the balanced presentation, her attention to opposing views, and her recognition of competing truths.

In 1798, Milton Academy was chartered by the Great and General Court of Massachusetts to provide education for the families living in the small colonial village of Milton and on the farms scattered through the forested Blue Hills Valley. It catered to the wealthy families of the South

254

Shore who worried that their children would not be able to accommodate successfully to public schooling. Its original clientele, therefore, came from backgrounds of privilege, and the school was explicitly oriented towards an individualistic, humanistic approach that would support the mind *and* spirit of young people. Explains Gregory, "The theme was tender loving care, fostering the individual. In its generic character, Milton has not been Exeter or Andover. It has always been interested in academic excellence, but not with the ferocity of the elite, male schools."

By the turn of the century, the small minority of girl students felt "bullied" and mistreated by their male peers and it was decided that they should have separate institutional arrangements. In 1901, an annex was built for the twenty girls in residence. It was designed as a boarding house with the girls living "family style" with nurturant and caring house parents. Students sat around big oval tables at meals, grace was said, candles were lit, and manners were emphasized. The girls played with the children of the house, sought comfort and protection from the family's dog, and experienced an atmosphere of intimacy and warmth. According to Gregory, the "great success [of this family approach] set the tone for the way girls would be treated at Milton." Many of the early family rituals still survive today in the girls' dormitories at Milton.

Just before the First World War, Ware Hall was built for housing the girls' school. It was a solid, substantial brick structure and its construction symbolized the deep roots of girls' education at Milton. The boys' and girls' schools developed separately, each entrenched in its own structure, values, and norms; each building with its own administrative and organizational structures. The schools, separated by a narrow street, became increasingly distinct entities. Over time, their boundaries were reinforced and exaggerated by strongly divergent philosophical orientations. Not always clearly articulated, the ideological inclinations were often expressed in "silly rivalries" between the faculty and students of the two schools. Sometimes the differences were reflected in extreme avoidance behavior. "Someone who taught Latin at the girls' school for twenty years had not met someone who taught Latin at the boys' school," says Gregory incredulously. "The schools were separate to a degree that was mind boggling!"

The internal separations became sources of the school's identity to the external world. The boys' school, thought to be in the same sphere as Andover, Exeter, and Groton, often suffered from negative comparisons. Considered by the inhabitants of other elite schools as "not quite top drawer," the boys' school struggled with gaining status among peers. Milton boys were thought to be pampered and privileged, not tough and cerebral. The fact that in the early days "Milton shipped all of its male graduates across the river to Harvard" was not seen as evidence of the graduates' serious intellect, but as a mark of their wealthy connections.

At the same time as the boys' school struggled with issues of identity and status in contrast to well-established male academies, Milton's girls' school enjoyed a relatively comfortable existence, with few competitors. At that time, there were few places in the country that provided boarding for girls, and Milton soon gained a national reputation in this area. The girls' school did not have to use valuable energy shoring up its public image, or rationalizing its mission to other competitor schools. The focus was inward and the energy could be directed towards strengthening educational processes.

The girls' school also enjoyed an unusual stability of leadership. In eighty years, it had only three headmistresses and there was a rare continuity of perspectives and goals among them. Everyone speaks of the arrival and tenure of Miss Pierce, the third headmistress, who was the dominant shaping force in girls' education at Milton. In 1950, Miss Pierce became headmistress at twenty-eight years old and remained a powerful and uncompromising leader until she retired thirty-two years later. She is remembered by many as an "idealistic, beautiful and elegant" woman with a "capacity to arouse great loyalty"; an ambitious leader with a rare clarity of vision. She is also remembered as a great pedagogical mentor who knew how to build a strong and committed faculty. A veteran teacher, known to be one of the school's best pedagogues, says simply, "All I know about teaching, I learned from her." As with most potent figures, memories of Miss Pierce's reign are not all laudatory or approving. No one denies her great power and influence, nor her charisma, but there is disagreement about whether her potency was positively channelled. Just as one hears tales of her elegance and goodness, so do people speak of her demanding style, her dominating ways, and her occasional blind spots. A portrait of Miss Pierce hangs in a prominent place in a sedate room in Ware Hall. When I first see it, I am surprised by her diminutive size, by her small and delicate features. The stories have made her seem bigger than life to me. The teacher who introduces me to the portrait complains, "Actually, she is much more beautiful than that picture portrays." A few days later, a faculty member points to the same portrait and warns, "It masks many of her powerful qualities." Both perceptions admit her prettiness, but one regards it as the surface of a deeper beauty while the other sees it as evidence of underlying toughness.

Even though there are sharply divided views on Miss Pierce's goodness, everyone seems to agree on her power and on the articulation of her vision. She had a deep sense of the values that should guide education for girls and she found effective ways of articulating and institutionalizing her vision. Carol Gregory, one of her admiring prodigies, describes the way Miss Pierce transformed the school into a "more and more utopian society. . . . She minimized competition, hierarchies, and distinctions of status among the girls. . . . She introduced art and culture. . . . Everything was informed by moral purpose." Prizes were not given for academics or sports, class standings were not publicized, and there were no valedictory speeches given during graduation ceremonies. The faculty sought to create an environment that supported trust, warmth, and a sense of community. Most people agree that over the years, the stability of leadership, Miss Pierce's charismatic style, and her unambivalent purposes combined to create a strong and successful school; somewhat sturdier and more confident than the boys' school.

At the same time as the girls' school became increasingly "utopian" in its vision, the boys' school grew in the opposite direction. Concerned about its status among the elite academies, the boys' school focused on improving its academic image. There was an emphasis on tough competition, high achievement, valued prizes, and a preoccupation with grades. The boys were to be inspired by aggressive competition and visible hierarchies. Differences in the diverging philosophies of the two schools were reinforced by their physical proximity. The contrasts were stark and clear to all observers.

When Jerome Pieh arrived in 1973, he had to confront an extremely difficult and complicated set of circumstances. He was appointed headmaster of Milton Academy and his leadership was supposed to encompass the Lower School, the boys', and the girls' schools. Milton's board of trustees had recognized the powerful and divisive differences between the boys' and girls' schools and may have worried that the extreme separations and competition between them would eventually undermine their collective purposes. Some observers feel that the decision to merge the schools was less a response to the educational liabilities of the institutional divisions that existed and more a wish to present a unified front to potential big donors. Pieh quickly undertook a major capital campaign and the trustees reasoned that he would be more successful if he could speak with one voice, present a coherent and unified philosophical stance, and not have to choose sides or loyalties.

The deep historical divisions were resistant to the more facile administrative restructuring. Not only were habits and loyalties deeply engrained, but Miss Pierce was still a powerful presence who would always represent the separateness of the girls' school. "She was a force with whom Pieh had to reckon . . . and it was not easy," remembers one teacher, who is known for his understatement. With Pieh in charge of the unified operation, a man was chosen to match the role of Miss Pierce in the boys' school. Nathaniel King, a former French teacher with a strong reputation, became the principal for boys, but "no one could match the dominance and charisma of Miss Pierce."

With the retirement of Miss Pierce a few years later, the potential for finding a balance of power emerged, and the administrative structure was again altered to support the process of institutional integration. Directly under Pieh, the headmaster, sits Nathaniel King, who is known as assistant headmaster of the Upper School. In explaining King's new role, a faculty member says he is like the dean of faculty, in charge of the academic side of life at Milton. Then there are two principals, for girls and boys. The same interpreter claims "they should really be called deans because they do not have schools." The department heads are responsible to King, who is most closely related to the academic side of life; and "the pastoral side" is under the direction of the principals, who supervise the head advisors for girls and boys.

The long history of deep boundaries and the recent explicit attempts at integration of the two schools has led to current structures and practices that are difficult for a stranger to discern or comprehend. One finds vestiges of the old and awkward attempts at inventing the new. For example, although most classes are coeducational, homerooms and assemblies are single-sex. Three mornings a week, the day begins with assemblies. The girls all gather in a large room in Ware Hall, announcements are made, information is exchanged, and occasionally, small programs are organized or guest speakers visit. The Principal for girls is in charge of organizing these morning rituals. At the same time, across the street, the boys are having their assembly. Because of their large number, they can not all crowd into one room, so they are also divided by class rank.

Clearly, the most vivid difference in boys' and girls' experiences at Milton is centered on boarding life. At one end of the campus are the boys' dormitories, undistinguished, solidly built brick buildings that house 45–50 boys. At the other end of the campus are the girls' dormitories, more dignified dwellings with circular driveways and careful landscaping. Before being told they were girls' houses, I drove by them several times and thought they were the stately, large homes of wealthy Milton residents. As you get closer to them, they do not have the carefully manicured quality of a fine home, but their scale and dimensions are very similar to the domestic surroundings of the very privileged. The marked differences between the girls' and boys' dormitories lie less in the physical structures of the buildings than in the quality of life inside. Life in the girls' houses echoes the civilized, nurturant beginnings of the first boarding school at the turn of the century. At meal times, the thirty-six girls, houseparents and their family, and other faculty dormitory counselors gather around a large table; grace is said by the faculty person on duty and plates are served by an appointed hostess. The girls can rise from the table only after the faculty member in charge stands and declares the conclusion of the meal. At bedtime, the goodnight rituals are highly personalized and maternal. The faculty member on duty that evening visits each girl in her room and says goodnight. Sometimes, the nightly exchange is brief and uncomplicated; at other times, it becomes the opportunity for a girl to talk over troubling concerns or seek adult attention. One housemother, who is known for her warmth, caring, and sense of humor, says that she must put aside one and a half to two hours of her evening for the goodnight rituals. "A couple of girls will always take fifteen minutes of my time. . . . There is no way to avoid it. . . . Sometimes, I just dread going in there."

In the boys' dormitories, there are no planned personal encounters at bedtime. Rather than the ritualized goodnight from the houseparent, there is a bed check. Bodies are counted to make sure no one is missing. Rather than sitting family style around a large table, boys travel down to the main dining room, pick up their food cafeteria style, wolf it down quickly, and move on to their evening activities. There is little civility or grace in this rushed, institutional process. There are rarely interesting conversations held over dinner and adult-student interaction is minimal. The principal for boys views the cafeteria scene as symbolic of the inequalities between girls and boys at Milton. He believes that the boys should have the same opportunities for intimacy and adult attention, be forced to practice their manners and learn the habits of conversation and civilized exchange. "It is possible," he claims, "to be a boy at Milton and never sit down at a meal with an adult for four years."

The differences in faculty-student exchange in the boys' and girls' dormitories creates noticeable variations in the environmental tone. A housemaster of one of the boys' dormitories speaks about the problems of defining and sustaining a "livable community" in the dormitory. He worries about the acts of vandalism done to the property, tries to get students to act responsibly, and seeks to instill pride in his charges. He is often annoyed by the childishness of the adolescents and links that to their backgrounds of privilege and indulgence. "I try to hold them to reasonable standards of behavior and responsibility, but that takes enormous vigilance," he says wearily.

Having lived in both the boys' and girls' dormitories, Tom Gray has a rare comparative view. Six years ago, when he first came to teach at Milton, he lived with his wife and newborn baby in one of the boys' houses. Gray remembers, "It was a very tough environment. I felt like a proctor, a policeman." He had the additional onerous responsibility of being a dining room monitor and quickly gained "a reputation as 'the school Fascist.'" When a job opened for his wife to become housemother at one of the girls' houses, they happily moved into their new roles. He no longer finds it necessary to be "tough and authoritarian" in relation to students. A new, more subtle, challenge emerges for adults in the girls' houses. "The atmosphere is nonconfrontational and you have to find the delicate balance between kindness and control," says Gray thoughtfully. He much prefers the subtleties of the new role and welcomes the humane climate. "It is much nicer here. The girls treat us like people and there is a sense of mutual respect."

It would be an overstatement to claim the harshness of the boys' boarding experience and the warmth of the girls'. Worried that I might exaggerate the differences between the boys' and girls' environments, one observer pointed to the recent structural and cosmetic improvements in the boys dormitories and reminded me that although the rituals of bed and board are not as ingrained in the boys' houses, the relationships between the houseparents and the boys are generally "very caring and generous. . . . You should not be deceived by the elegant exterior of the girls' houses," he warned.

The responses of the inhabitants also reflected a more mixed picture. Although most girls I talked to claimed their advantaged position and spoke about the niceties and comforts of their living conditions, some reported unhappy experiences with an unkind and domineering housemother, or wished for greater autonomy and freedom from the community requirements. A few girls reported that it was unrealistic to expect to experience "feelings of closeness" among thirty-five girls in a dormitory. The expectation, they felt, was a source of dishonesty ("It is impossible to like, or even relate to everyone!") and made them feel as if they were "suffocating."

Many girls complained about the school requirement that they change rooms and roommates three times a year, a requirement not expected of boy boarders. Three times each year, they must pack up their possessions, hope for a congenial match, worry about the room lottery, and create a new environment. A housemother reported that the moves cause great anxiety and disruption in the girls' lives. "They complain bitterly, but somehow manage to accommodate quickly to the new setting." On the eve before the April move, several girls told me of their worries. "First, and most important, you hope to get a roommate with a good stereo and a big record collection!" exclaimed an energetic and smiling junior. "Then you hope she doesn't snore." In more serious tones, a senior who had been living alone in a small room called "the cheesebox" told about the problems of developing and severing relationships throughout one's school career. "I finally have decided it is more comfortable to live alone than to continually have to make and to lose close friends." When I asked a female faculty member why girls are asked to endure these rearrangements, she replied cynically, "It has always been that way . . . Miss Pierce felt it was a good thing to do." Others defended the system by saying that Miss Pierce saw it as a way of breaking down cliques and building a sense of community and group loyalty. But the school's counselors reported that many girl boarders arrive at their doors during these transition periods and that their experiences are traumatic. "For some girls, their family lives are chaotic and fragmented and the roommate becomes their only source of stability and support. When the roommate leaves, the girl feels abandoned and devastated. A Black girl from Washington, D. C., who has silently and stoically tolerated the numerous shifts, summed it up forcefully: "This is not about building community, it is about destroying friendships."

At the same time as girls expressed a range of experiences, boys did not seem to feel that they were the disadvantaged group. As a matter of fact, many boldly claimed their relative advantage. After all, they receive less adult supervision and this gives them more freedom and autonomy. They do not have to be restricted by the rituals and decorum that inhibit the girls' movements. Perceptions of the boys' deprivation seem to rest mostly with adults who worry that "the quality of life is not as good as it should be." Such disparities prompt the principal for boys to say: "I see myself as an advocate for boys in this school. . . . Historically, advocacy for girls has been much more successful than for boys."

Numerically, the boys dominate at Milton. There are 420 boys and 280 girls in the Upper School student body, and the asymmetry gives the environment a distinctly male tone. There are obvious differences of scale and the more subtle signs of inequality. One concerned faculty member observes, "Boys seem to appreciate the opportunity to be with girls, but they do not yet see them as equal. . . . They know the eighties' rhetoric but they have the fifties' feelings toward girls." An administrator worries about the subtle harassment of girls. "When a girl comes into the boys' assembly to make an announcement, the boys will hoot and holler when she leaves. . . . She often goes out red with embarrassment." Another example: "When a group of boys and girls are having a conversation, sometimes the boys will engage in sexual innuendoes in an attempt to see how much the girls will tolerate before walking away. . . . In part, this is typical adolescent behavior . . . but this school does not send clear messages that this is wrong, that the culture is intolerant of these interactions."

Many faculty and administrators express concern about the more abstruse repercussions of the greater proportion of boys than girls and the lingering effects of the historical separations between them. Students, on the other hand, express a range of views on the quality of boy/girl relationships at Milton. Some seem to feel that the boundaries between sexes are eroding, but that some separation permits a welcome privacy rarely found in coeducational schools. Others speak about the "unnatural" and "false" relationships that exist between boys and girls. Said one frustrated senior girl, "The social side of life at Milton is very strange. There is lots of tension. The times when boys and girls can be together are always earmarked 'social' and it creates an atmosphere that is awkward and uncomfortable." A popular student council leader remarked on the recent shifts in attitudes among many of her girl friends—from supporting integration of the sexes to defending the need for some separation in order to hang on to historically female traditions. "Last year, there seemed to be a strong feeling that you *had* to be for coeducation. . . . Now lots of girls are standing up and saying 'we like the girls' traditions . . . we don't want them diluted by mixing with the boys.'"

The range of student views was revealed in a senior American literature class where the teacher asked the students to "tell me about differences between boys and girls" at Milton. In a class where the girls' voices dominated the student exchanges, where the girls seemed more confident and more aggressive than their male peers, it was interesting to listen to the boys' perspectives:

> FIRST BOY: "There are definite separations between boys and girls. . . . It makes it hard to communicate."
>
> SECOND BOY: "Boys have more friends, but girls have better and closer friends."
>
> THIRD BOY: "I would say the opposite, girls are *encouraged* to be friendly to one another while boys are cliquish. They only associate with small, closed groups."
>
> FOURTH BOY: "Yes, girls seem more open to someone new . . . They take strangers under their wings. . . . Boys need to work themselves into things."

Although there was no clear consensus of views, the boys saw differences in patterns of intimacy and friendship and felt that girls knew better how to create and sustain relationships with one another. Some viewed the differences as stereotypically male and female ("Society imposes those expectations"), and others believed that Milton helped to reinforce the stereotypes. Only one student in the fifteen-member class claimed that Milton supported genuine friendships between boys and girls. As she spoke, she anticipated rebuttal: "I know that a lot of people don't agree with me, but in this school a lot of boys and girls are just friends—real, trusting friends!"

The institutional transformations toward increased balance between boys and girls are difficult, complicated, and replete with passionate feelings. The Coed Committee has been charged with the responsibility of pondering the tough questions of institutional balance and integration. With Carol Gregory as its deft and competent chairperson, the committee includes thirteen faculty and staff who represent different constituencies and perspectives on the coed question: the director of admissions, head of counselling, chairperson of the arts program, head of the Middle School, and director of financial aid. In the meeting that I attended, the Coed Committee was presenting its tentative proposals to the chief administrators of Milton—including the headmaster, the assistant headmaster for the Upper School, the principals for boys and girls. As Gregory recited the proposals that had been formulated by the committee, she offered the members' collective reasoning and careful justifications. Her voice was cautious, combining tentative and decisive strains; hoping not to be misinterpreted. The meeting, held in the room where Miss Pierce's portrait hangs, seemed to symbolize the lingering divisions. Without seeming to notice their moves, all the men sat on one side of the room, with the women on the other. Carol Gregory sat centrally, under the picture of her mentor.

The conversation was careful on all sides as the committee and its guests struggled with the questions of territory, balance, tradition, and change. The exchange of views moved from highly traditionalist arguments for stasis to proposals for reorganization unencumbered by historical imperatives. Everyone seemed to recognize the complex puzzle that they were trying to piece together—the inevitable links between structural rearrangements, philosophical values, and curricular decisions; the need to consider the contrasting perspectives of students, faculty, staff and alumni. Although strong feelings were expressed, the tone was always respectful and minimally defensive. Holding down his rage, one committee member said to another, "How can I say politely that you have just incurred my anger?" When the meeting was over, I approached Carol Gregory and commented on the intensity of the discussion. "This must be the most vital issue that Milton is now facing," I said with the naiveté of a stranger. With a knowing smile, Gregory did not deny the compelling nature of the subject, but warned: "Well, I think you'll find that people are generally intense here. That is part of the tone of the place . . . very deeply felt, trying *very* hard. . . . It's very New England, don't you think?"

Beyond the territoral questions concerning boys and girls, the Coed Committee is also responsible for considering issues of balance between boarding and day students at Milton. Although the latter does not seem to inspire the same kind of deep emotion as the former, there are opposing perspectives and a concern for discovering the optimal ratios between boarders and day students. The concern focuses primarily on the search for ingredients that will support a healthy, invigorated educational climate. The concern is also one of image—how Milton wants to be perceived by the outside world.

Currently, there are about 250 boarders out of a student body of 700. Each of the four boys' dormitories comprise some 45–50 students. Two girls' dormitories each house 30–35 students. The catalogue minimizes the distinctions between day students and boarders and underscores the school's attempts at integrating the diverse experiences:

> Little distinguishes the day student from the boarder during the school day. They lunch together, take midmorning coffee together . . . have sports together and join activities and classes together. Day students share all the School's programs and facilities not only during the week but also, if they choose, on weekends, too.

Yet students tend to describe two relatively separate communities that reflect sharp differences in daily experience. In general, neither group seems to feel happier or more privileged, but they do voice different complaints. Some day students, for example, complain of the travel time from home to school which prevents them from joining in after school activities, or they speak about the persistent tensions between the pull of family and the attractions of school. Says one energetic senior girl, "Occasionally, I want to stay overnight at school in order to get deeply into the activities and my parents insist that I come home. . . . They don't want to lose me. . . . It's almost a jealousy."

The boarders, on the other hand, tend to complain about feeling isolated from "real life." Even though there is relatively direct public transportation into Boston, many insist that campus restrictions combine with heavy doses of homework to discourage their making the trip. Said one boy incredulously, "The kids from Amherst get into Boston more than we do because they have private buses that take them in . . . and they're almost one hundred miles away!" Only one student I spoke to admitted her timidity of the big city and her fear of urban dangers as the reason for remaining campus bound. I did have a sense, however, that many of the elaborate excuses for not venturing into Boston masked apprehensions of moving beyond the familiar and comfortable terrain of Milton.

The complaints of boarders do seem to have a harder edge than those voiced by their day school peers. A perceptive day student senses the bitterness of boarders and explains, "Day students are more enthusiastic and less cynical because they can always get away from school. In one dorm, I know a group of girls who sit around and cut other people down . . . everything gets magnified in the group. . . . I don't think that they are cynical towards the school, they just take out their aggression on the nearest thing . . . and when you live at school, it's school. The day school girls complain endlessly about their mothers!"

Whatever the student perceptions of the experiences of boarding and day life at Milton, everyone seems to agree that there are vivid separations between the two groups. These are not antagonisms. It is just that different daily experiences shape contrasting group patterns. One day student who wanted to describe the degree of separateness between the groups said, "There is a wall that all the day students sit on. . . . The other day, a border was passing by the wall and some of us said to him, 'Come on up and sit with us.' Do you know his response? He was shocked and said to us 'Have you ever seen a boarder sitting on this wall?' . . . He climbed up on the wall as if he was entering foreign territory."

Although the complaints of boarders and day students refer to differences in their relationship to Milton, they are also an expression of adolescent turbulence. Many remarks point to the struggles for autonomy and individuation. Both boarders and day students, for example, refer to the tensions and attractions of family, missing the warmth and intimacy or feeling inhibited by parental power. The psychological counselors at Milton [called "personal counselors"], who have watched generations of students struggle with these vacillating feelings, recognize the special vulnerabilities of adolescents. The more experienced of the two counselors observes that these conflicts are more difficult to resolve within the context of boarding school. "Sending kids to boarding school circumvents the *natural* process of breaking away from family . . . students come to boarding school with unfinished family issues. They do not have the opportunity to do the daily work of separating and integrating with family. . . . Day students, on the other hand, can work with families and gain *real* independence . . . an independence that evolves naturally through hard and difficult work." The premature independence of boarding students can lead to a kind of pseudo-maturity. They can more easily become "protected, defended, and isolated."

In more measured tones, her colleague admitted that boarding school may be the healthiest environment for some students whose families are unusually tension-filled, but said that he had also noticed differences in adolescent resolution of autonomy struggles between boarders and day students. He remembered poignantly his own experience of going to boarding school at fourteen. It was as if time stopped there. After he left for school, his parents never knew him deeply or intimately again, were not in touch with the developmental changes he was experiencing as a young man, and forever after perceived the fourteen year-old image in their grown son. His mirror response was to easily regress to fourteen year-old habits when he visited his parents as a young adult. Smiling at his autobiographical memories, he was quick to point out that these patterns are not inevitable or universal, but more likely for adolescents who do not experience daily life with their families.

The struggles for individuation during adolescence are further complicated by the communal experience of boarding school. During adolescence, young people are confronted with a great many decisions about lifestyle. Should they experiment with drinking, drugs, sex? Both counselors agreed that a fourteen year-old needs some guidance and supervision in coping with the myriad seductions of adolescence and that houseparents are unlikely to be able to provide adequate individual attention. "Real parents know the kid well enough to be able to detect subtle changes . . . but dorm parents are likely to miss the changes. . . . Problems can begin early and be sustained throughout the school career."

The psychologists' skepticism about boarding school life does not seem to be shared by most faculty and staff. Admittedly, the counselors tend to see students in trouble and miss the broad range of responses. Given their training, they are more likely to focus on pathology and their perceptions are more likely to be skewed towards intrapsychic explanations. But most faculty and staff do worry about balancing the experiences of day students and boarders and easing some of the separations. Many believe that the combination of boarders and day students produces a unique dynamic that shapes the culture of the school. Each group offers the other a critical perspective that is missing in schools that are distinctly boarding or day environments.

Franklin Jones, director of admissions, is the most persuasive proponent of this point of view. He is responsible for creating images and attracting good applicants (for "selling the place"); and his rhetoric about the boarder/day student dynamic sounds surprisingly convincing. He claims, for example, that day students are welcome to attend the supervised weekend activities at Milton and they can experience the diversity of an international student body. A number of the boarders are students from abroad—either children of Americans living abroad or foreigners whose parents want them to be educated in the United States. Both of these attractions are not available at day schools that are open five days a week and serve a localized clientele. But these are easy arguments to make to an already oversubscribed day student applicant pool.

It is much more difficult to convince people of the unique attractions of Milton's boarding life. Parents of prospective boarders, for example, worry that Milton will not provide the exclusive, protective environment enjoyed by other elite boarding schools, "that their kids will be running around with all that local riffraff." Or they are concerned that when the day students leave on Friday, the school will feel lifeless and abandoned and their children will be isolated and unstimulated. Franklin Jones tries to counter parental fears by focusing on the enriching qualities of the day student presence. He believes that day students bring two critical ingredients with them: connections to home and the real world, and avenues to familial nurturance and worldliness. Here, Jones does not merely seem to be rehearsing glib public relations rhetoric; rather, he seems to be describing a phenomenon he observes and believes in. "Day students bring a sense of home with them. Many of their parents have a very strong presence here and work hard at creating a vital community. More importantly, day students bring the world in. . . . What happens on the front page of the *Boston Globe* has repercussions at Milton. . . . You can look out of a classroom window and see the Boston skyline . . . this provides a very important context for education here." This "plug in with the real world" offers Milton students a chance to face fears about their future and apprehensions about adulthood. "They become attuned to the pulse of the world. . . . They see their parents' great stresses and sacrifices and they have deep worries. Our connection to the real world says to kids, 'What you are perceiving is real, but you've got to learn how to face it, confront it, deal with it,'" Jones concludes with unbridled enthusiasm. The mutual benefits of the boarder/day student exchange produces a community that is "fresh, vital, and current."

The ratio of boarders to day students shapes faculty and staff responsibilities. Unlike most boarding schools, where faculty live in campus housing, or day schools, where faculty leave at the end of the school day,

Milton's faculty have mixed living experiences. Of the 120 faculty in the Upper School, 30 have direct dormitory responsibilities, 60 live on the campus but have no dormitory duties, and 30 live off campus. The range of campus supervisory responsibilities is reflected in variations of faculty perquisites. Although faculty salaries are equalized (based on chronological age and years of experience), those who live in dormitories receive free housing, utilities, and food benefits in exchange for their caretaking duties. Those who live on campus without dormitory duties are given free housing, but have to pay for their utilities. Those who live off campus must fend for themselves.

Knowing of the burdensome responsibilities of houseparenting and the relatively low salaries of teachers that would make good off-campus housing difficult to find, I am immediately struck by the apparent inequities. The middle group of faculty, living in comfortable campus dwellings but free of major responsibilities, would seem to have the most appealing arrangement. Few faculty talk to me about the relative privileges. But those who wax eloquent about the glories and comforts of a Milton teacher's existence all come from this middle group. One who will be leaving next year says enthusiastically, "I can't complain. It is the best deal I've ever had, very seductive, and hard to leave." Another, who is living in recently constructed faculty housing, speaks about the advantages of being both close and private: "I feel a sense of security living on a campus . . . but it allows me to be separate from school and yet have something to bring to the school."

The handful of faculty who complain to me about their colleagues' lack of commitment, or connection to the "pulse of the school," are all teachers who live in the dormitory. A housemaster of a boys' dormitory sees Milton as "fighting to be seen as a boarding school," and the faculty as ambivalent about how much attention to give to the quality of life in the dormitories. He credits the new principal for boys with offering creative and insightful leadership in this area, but fears that three-quarters of the faculty are "out of touch." Having worked at a boarding school for several years before coming to his present position, he feels frustrated by the imbalances and the sense of a divided community at Milton. Another faculty member, residing in a girls' dormitory, is more vociferous about the negative effects of the non-boarding faculty: "They are *totally* out of touch with our kids. They have no way of understanding their problems." Although he recognizes their relative freedom from the parental demands of teaching, he also believes that his colleagues are missing something special by not knowing the students intimately. "I have always lived in the dorm. It is an important part of my work . . . I would probably not enjoy civilian life . . . I must get something from this." Finally, he ends by saying that dormitory life provides a retreat from real life that is very comforting and, with only a touch of humor, he observes, "I think that boarding schools tend to attract insecure people who have the need for power and safety . . . the need to withdraw from the outside world." An off-campus dweller echoes this comment, "I need that connection to the real world. I would suffocate if I lived here . . . but living in town also means I am never really integrated into Milton's life."

There does seem to be an imperfect but workable match between faculty temperament and institutional needs. However, members of the administration have begun to worry about the apparent inequities in faculty responsibility and privilege. Although the administration is concerned about the faculty bitterness that might result from the imbalances, they seem primarily focused on ways of keeping more faculty in touch with the boarders' lives at Milton. In the hiring of new faculty, the administration has recently decided to require that new recruits spend at least three years in the dormitory before pursuing other living arrangements.

The complex, varied views of institutional balance and integration are immediately apparent to a stranger. It is not that it feels like a divided school full of antagonisms and bitterness. On the contrary, one is struck by the open, direct, and friendly tone of the place. I have made hundreds of visits to schools of all varieties and I have never been more generously welcomed, more enthusiastically received. But it is not only the openness that is impressive, it is the lack of defensiveness that is most striking. Faculty, students, and administrators do not seem afraid of exposing their vulnerabilities, voicing their self-criticisms, or focusing on their weakness. Most institutions try very hard to present a united front to the outside world even if they are fractionated within. Yet Milton seems unwilling to cover up the raw scars, the jagged edges, or the persistent confusions; and this is immediately apparent to the visitor. One administrator remarks undefensively, "There is a little bit of an identity crisis here . . . I am often frustrated by the confusion. . . . It is hard to be half-and-half and still be whole." The director of admissions seems inspired by the "yeasty" tone of the school, as he proclaims enthusiastically, "Milton is a questioning joint, a self-critical culture . . . not a stale school."

The students also recognize the legitimacy of criticism and tend to respond to my queries first with complaints, later with enthusiastic judgments. A junior boy says matter of factly, "We're taught to complain. . . . I mean, we're encouraged to ask tough questions." For an observer, therefore, it is often difficult to interpret the apparent negativism voiced

269

by so many. Are people really dissatisfied and unhappy? Do they tend to focus on imperfections in order to move towards greater wholeness? Or are they expressing what Carol Gregory describes as the New England tendency to "try very hard"? Probably, their persistent complaints are a reflection of all these tendencies. My sense is that the "yeasty" culture derives less from negativism than it does from a healthy climate of questioning. The climate of self-criticism has its origins in a deep self-confidence, rather than in weakness or petulance. The institutional imperfections are not cause for defensiveness or retreat, but rather seem to inspire more scrutiny, diagnosis, and lots of talk.

A HEALING AUTHORITY

The tone of self-criticism is modeled and encouraged by Jerome Pieh, the headmaster. With a listening and gentle approach, he invites vigorous exchange, does not deflect harsh disagreements, and seems inspired by healthy debate. It is not that he seems to like confrontation, but that he deeply believes that institutional invigoration and change will only come with the difficult work of challenge and debate. He is aware of the differences in people's tolerance for uncertainty, and he recognizes the threats of institutional chaos and disintegration that often accompany a questioning climate. But he seems willing to risk the impending chaos in an attempt to encourage the self-criticism that he believes is the bedrock of a healthy educational climate. Pieh refuses to rely on the habits of tradition and yet he recognizes the need for roots and continuity to a rich past. He looks forward to the imperatives of the future, yet he resists the facile, trendy remedies. His is an uncomfortable posture, poised on boundaries and never comfortably settled. The last paragraph of his opening letter in the Milton catalogue reads:

> Milton Academy introduced to you in these words is a constantly evolving school, neither shackled by its own past nor impatient to overturn its special traditions. Its focus on the individual student, its commitment to rigorous standards, its rich store of experiences make it a challenging but friendly school. Welcome!

This paragraph sits below a casual, smiling, quietly handsome photograph of Pieh. He is grinning, his hair is slightly tousled, and his eyes seem to express an edge of melancholy. The image is of one who appears wholly approachable, thoughtful, and empathetic. The picture is not of a distant, aloof, authoritarian headmaster.

When Pieh arrived at Milton in 1973, he had to call on all of his human relations skills. Asked to do the difficult and subtle job of bringing together a divided school, Pieh had to search for the balances between tradition and change and work towards institutional integration. The resistances of habit and history and the complex arrangements of structures and roles combined to form a culture that was hard to discern or penetrate. Says one sympathetic old-timer, "He thought the arrangements were wild and strange."

In some ways, Pieh was entering foreign territory. A product of public schooling, he did not have autobiographical private school experiences as sources of guidance and direction. More important, he probably did not have the subtle imprint of privilege and entitlement that often accompany the career of a private school person. Before coming to Milton, he had been the principal of a public high school on the North Shore of Boston; and although many of his practiced administrative skills must have been transferable to the new environment, there also must have been some surprises in moving from a public to a private setting.

Despite the environmental shifts, Pieh brought along his philosophical inclinations intact. He had a sturdy, unwavering sense of education as a complex, human enterprise requiring the enlivening of head, heart, and spirit. A disciple of Ted Sizer, former dean of the Harvard Graduate School of Education and at that point the headmaster of Andover, Pieh followed the "humanistic" approach to education—an orientation that is concerned with the substance of education, but also with process and context. "His first concern was 'the welfare of the community,' " says one observer who watched the transition of leadership very carefully. "He met the difficult circumstances very cleverly."

Wisely, he initiated his leadership without aggressive fanfare—observing, listening, and trying to discern the forces at work. During the summer before the fall of 1973, he gathered together ten key faculty and staff for a four-day conference. During this "briefing," one participant recalls that Pieh "set up the scene for himself so he would know what he was getting himself into." Early on, he revealed "his extraordinary capacity for listening, summarizing, and synthesizing." Although several faculty can point to tactical mistakes made by Pieh during the first months of his tenure, most were sympathetic with his goals and admiring of his initial strategies.

Jerry Pieh's focus was on welding together a divided faculty. He approached this process from several angles. First, he provided informal social occasions throughout the year that would help people cross factional lines without feeling threatened. The wine and cheese parties began to break down some barriers of social intercourse and help faculty see each other out of their rigid professional roles. Second, he began the slow process of combining formerly distinct departments under a single chairperson and housing the group in a single physical space. Third, he organized an all-school meeting once a year; an opening ritualistic occasion that would bring together faculty and staff from the Lower and Upper Schools around a substantive concern.

At these annual opening meetings, Pieh presents an inspirational message introducing the theme that will shape faculty concern for the year. Often outside speakers are invited to address the substantive theme and workshops are organized for small group discussions. The meeting takes place the week before students arrive, when there is a mood of reunion, anticipation, and excitement as teachers return from their summer sojourns. This year the theme centered on pedagogy, the craft of teaching—and I was asked to come and deliver the opening lecture. The scattered notes in my journal after my introduction to Milton reflect the optimism and promise of this ceremonial occasion and my idealization of the community spirit.

On this glorious fall day, Pieh has awakened and run several miles in the early morning air. In his early forties, tall and lean, he seems to combine the elements of mind, body, and spirit—believing the expression of one enlivens the others. I imagine that he must run in order to think. There is a balance and composure to his presence, a gentle and benign leadership. Everything is understated and said with a slight hesitation as if he is still thinking about it. There do not appear to be the sharp distinctions of power between headmaster and faculty that are often found in other secondary schools, but a comfortable and easy exchange between them.

The faculty and staff assemble in the handsome library of the administration building. Their dress is casual and uninspired—the uniform I had expected. Many women wear simple wrap skirts with flowery blouses and minimal jewelry. Men are in pullover alligator shirts of pastel colors, penny loafers, and loosefitting cotton pants. There are even vestiges of the madras era. A few faculty stand out in bright colors, inventive jewelry, or sophisticated, tailored jackets. One young man has long, shoulder length hair held in place by a purple scarf. His blousy shirt with generous sleeves is a matching purple and he sits cross-legged on a table in the back of the room as he listens to me speak. But mostly, the faculty garb is simple and matches my image of Eastern privilege. Their faces are friendly and seem to welcome the return to work and the beginnings of the year with energy.

People are gathered in small groups close to the coffeepot and elegant bakery treats, many engaged in charged exchanges, others offering minimal greetings

272

to one another. Pieh rings a large brass bell as he tries to assemble people for the meeting. Conversations linger and the bell is rung again. Slowly, the faculty make their way to chairs arranged in a horseshoe shape facing the podium.

The beginning of the meeting is devoted to welcoming new faculty, congratulating newly married members, and announcing the arrival of babies. "Tom and Joan got married this summer . . . Christine has a new son . . . any other news of this kind?" Only first names are used. The tone is personal and seems to reflect a sense of close community among them. The boundaries between personal and professional spheres are not clearly drawn. One of the new faculty babies, who is three months old, is nursed by his mother. When he makes cheerful baby noises, everyone smiles in response.

The faculty moves quickly from informality to focused work. There is a short coffee break after the initial greetings and they return to their seats ready to listen intently. Their applause at the end of my speech is warm and generous and many express thanks for inspiration, new thoughts, troubling ideas, and the chance for introspection. Some see themselves as risk-takers. A bearded man with a permanently furrowed brow approaches me and exclaims, "I think of my work as play . . . a great adventure." A young, modestly pretty woman comes forward with some intense but unshaped thoughts about "trying to be *there* for students," and "building a community at Milton that will support them." After our brief acquaintance, I am left with an impression of a group of teachers who are rarely complacent, who continue to ask probing and difficult questions of themselves and others. I am impressed by the easy expression of feelings and turmoil and by the headmaster's deft hand that seems to accept and calm.

My journal entry, idealized and naive, picks up half-truths; many of which are overturned in my week-long visit later in the year. But some impressions are firmly underscored through more systematic inquiry— Pieh's concern for mending fences and building a whole community, his tentative listening style, the questioning and critical voice of faculty, and the blurring of personal and professional spheres.

Most faculty seem to appreciate the now traditional opening ceremonies and the opportunity to focus on some aspect of the educational life of Milton. A small minority find Pieh's attempts a bit naive and then are surprised when some interesting intellectual or philosophical exchanges flow from ideas inspired by him. A few faculty are turned off by his "folksy" style. "It is too 'family-ish' for me," complains an older faculty member who is slightly embarrassed by what he views as an "unsophisticated" approach.

A fourth strategy Pieh used to bring faculty together at first appeared to be a trivial effort, but turned out to be "a very important turning point in faculty relations." Three years ago, Pieh had a faculty room constructed in the basement of Ware Hall. At midmorning each day, faculty gather there for coffee and conversation, or to pick up their mail and messages.

It has become a very important meeting place, an opportunity for building casual connections, and a spot for resolving points of tension. In my visits to the faculty room, I heard conversations about a recent trip the varsity baseball team took to a sports camp in Florida, a discussion about a controversial lecture given during the girls' assembly, a hurried planning session for the anticipated arts festival, and helpful hints from one parent to another on authority struggles with their children. During that half-hour in the morning, the faculty room is buzzing and busy. At other times of the day, it can serve as a space for small group meetings or quiet retreat. One can imagine that this ecological change has altered faculty patterns of interaction, whittling away at the territorial boundaries.

(Similar environmental changes were made to bring together a once divided student body. Formerly, girls and boys had dined separately and now everyone ate the midday meal under one roof. The student lounges were combined into one, and girls' and boys' mailboxes were brought together as part of a unified activities center.)

Finally, Jerry Pieh has sought to bring the faculty into a cohesive whole by scheduling full faculty meetings every three weeks. With 120 members, the meetings are large, unwieldy, often inefficient occasions that Pieh describes as "the biggest frustration" he faces as a headmaster. He quickly adds that, "the tone of the meetings has gotten pretty constructive, accepting, and unthreatening . . . but it has been a long time in coming." Another observer sees little progress and labels the meetings "a horror show." A faculty member who is fascinated by the evolution of group process finds the meetings "like spontaneous theater, with people trying on masks and roles, forging images for public display." As with most faculty meetings anywhere, there are the persistent complaints of inefficiency and boredom, and the wish that "Jerry would just go ahead and decide what to do."

The faculty meeting that I observe takes place from 2:00–3:00 one Wednesday afternoon. People begin to drift into the library of the administration building a quarter before the hour, help themselves to coffee and a delicious assortment of cookies, and exchange brief greetings. The early arrivals occupy the comfortable sofas and chairs lining the back wall, and the others begin to fill in the rows of chairs facing the podium. Sun is streaming in the tall windows and offering brilliant light and penetrating heat. With almost full attendance, the meeting begins promptly with the announcement of a former colleague's death and a moment of silence in his memory. Pieh initiates the discussion for the day: "The business of the meeting today is the calendar. As you know, we have agonized over the calendar in former years . . . much of the discussion has occurred in departmental meetings . . . but we need your counsel and advice." The faculty refer to two recommendations for changes in the school calendar drawn up by the

Academic Policy Committee; the first having to do with the scheduling of semesters, and the second with the timing of final examinations.

Most of the discussion time is devoted to the latter, with faculty offering comments and critiques that refer to procedural issues, pedagogical concerns, motivational questions, and philosophical ruminations. As with most large group discussions, the conversation tends to be diffuse and unfocused; the same few people usually dominate the exchange; and many grow frustrated by the redundancies. Pieh navigates the meeting with a gentle style and tries to offer summaries and intepretations of what has been said. Several times, he refuses to bring premature closure to a decision despite the prodding of some impatient faculty. At other moments, he decides to cut off a conversation that seems to have reached a dead end. When faculty comments begin to sound like rehearsals of old, worn battles, Pieh says, "Many of you may be beginning to recollect old discussions, echoes of former conversations." I think this reminder is designed to move people beyond repetition of often discussed issues, but one faculty member views it as an opportunity for seeing new possibilities: "Just because we decide to change our minds and return to an old pattern doesn't mean that we're losing ground. Flexibility should not be seen as schizophrenic . . . who knows, we might find new insights!"

He is immediately and hotly contested by a colleague who is less interested in the process of discovery and more interested in the effects of exam scheduling on pedagogical practices. "Having a June exam seduced us into teaching for the mastery of exams. . . . It is not an issue of flexibility. We've run that experiment already." This comment is reinforced by a woman who is admired for her educational leadership. She says forcefully, "An April exam is a completely different animal from a June exam. April exams can become part of an educational process, a learning experience. A June exam is merely an evaluative procedure. We are sending that message to children and I *lament* that message." A more tentative voice provides support for this argument. "In my class last spring I saw an increase in student involvement after the April exam and it was very rewarding. The students were released from anxiety and they really blossomed."

With those related comments the exchange breaks down, with faculty offering suggestions and criticisms that sound disjointed. A frustrated voice complains that his earlier motion has been lost in the "irrelevant" conversation and pushes for procedural correctness. Pieh counters: "In a parliamentary sense, there is always the possibility of tabling the motion if that makes sense to our discussion." A woman leaps in with a strong concern that seems to be related to the conversation held a half-hour ago: "It is an extremely bad and difficult thing for those who are parents to begin school, or even faculty meetings, before Labor Day. It is totally disruptive. I feel *very* strongly about this!" A young teacher, who has now spoken five times, offers another contribution. There are some muffled groans when she rises once again. "My point is a point that some people here are not going to like," she says almost defiantly. "I don't think that exams are so seriously on the minds of our students that we would destroy their peace and happiness if we had exams after vacation." The possibility of another revision in the calendar and exam schedules (with all the accompanying rationales and justifications), finally strikes one man as outrageously absurd. He says, exasperated, "We've now succeeded in creating two semesters with two midterm exams which we're now calling finals. It is zany!" Laughter fills the room as many seem relieved by the break in the ponderous tone. The decorative clock on the library wall reads 3:00, and a few people quickly filter out. The motion on the floor is tested by a hurried vote and there is general confusion about how to interpret the results. Without reaching a clear resolution, and with frustration lingering in the air, Pieh adjourns the meeting.

In the days following the faculty meeting, I hear a variety of reactions. The views are markedly divergent. The most enthusiastic response comes from one of the active participants, who exclaims, "Wasn't that a great meeting! The faculty is finally finding its voice. . . . We have had no way to express our indignation quickly and we're beginning to learn the legitimacy of dispute." In stark contrast, a quiet young woman worries that "Jerry is trying to give faculty all the decision-making authority . . . trying to create a faculty run school . . . and we're ruining the whole thing." A third comment points to the issues of group process: "The same people always dominate faculty meetings, and Jerry just refuses to bring closure to the discussion. He can't say 'no'!" Pieh's reflections on the meeting are almost philosophical. "It was pretty good, wasn't it? There was a fairly constructive tone and people were talking to one another." He recounts the progress of this once fractionated group and views the more civilized, tolerant tones of the most recent meeting as evidence of positive change.

The mixed reactions to the faculty meeting echo more general responses to Jerry Pieh's leadership at Milton. Many admire his honesty, decency, and listening qualities. Others speak of his political acumen: "He knows *everything* that is going on. He is very political, very astute." But almost everyone, even his staunchest supporters, claims that he has trouble saying "no" to people. Says one close and trusted associate, "He simply has trouble putting his foot down and being clear about what is possible or acceptable." Another friendly ally, a great admirer of Pieh who shares his philosophical stance, observes: "The major criticism of Jerry is his reluctance to make decisions. The faculty would be happier if he took a more decisive role." More critical voices seem to be in the minority. They are suspicious of his nonauthoritarian style, claiming it is ineffectual and causes needless frustration and confusion. A harsh critic believes that Pieh's "humanitarian front" is subtly dishonest and masks enormous power and control.

Pieh would probably not be surprised by these differing reactions. He is keenly aware that some faculty are still suspicious of his motives and that others do not share his views of collective authority. Others, he notices, are temperamentally ill-suited for the more cumbersome quality of shared decision making. A few may even wish for a "Big Daddy" figure who will tell them what to do and protect their interests. Pieh seems to recognize and appreciate the mixture of concerns and needs expressed by his faculty, but he steadfastly resists the paternalistic role and refuses to capitulate to some of their wishes for the more traditional arrangements of power.

As a matter of fact, when I ask Pieh to describe the strengths and weaknesses of Milton he points to the philosophical stance of collective authority and to the force of individual expression. He recognizes the potential power and vulnerability of this orientation, saying they are "the flip side of the same coin." He seems to be thinking out loud as he illuminates the core values that shape Milton's culture:

> "This school makes an enormous commitment to the individual person. Faculty and students have a substantial amount of independence. This is a dynamic, complicated, and highly personal place . . . without a core of institutional expectations ordering all of this process. . . . My style is one of trusting and assuming the best. I am interested in creating a context that will support a diversity of talents, a sense of individual responsibility towards the community, and an integrity among all of us. But there is no formalistic structure, no rigid arrangement of power and control . . . and this great strength also makes us vulnerable—particularly to the lawyer-types who create a style of confrontation which we have trouble with. . . . We are like a house of cards that could come tumbling down. But we are pretty glued together, I think."

THE INDIVIDUAL SIGNATURE

Although there seems to be a variety of views on Pieh's philosophy and style of leadership, there is a consensus among the faculty about the value of responding to the individual needs of students; the wisdom of supporting a diversity of talents. Everyone regards this individualistic approach as a critical ingredient of educational life at Milton. A faculty member calls it "the signature" of the school. Milton, in its original charter, sought to offer students tender loving care; and the empathetic, nurturing stance still thrives today. The headmaster believes that adults and students should be treated as individuals with diverse needs, talents, and

277

vulnerabilities. He wants to create a context in which students will thrive intellectually, emotionally, and physically; feel safe enough to take risks; and regard each other with trust and concern. "We have the opportunity to create an ethos that reflects care. . . . One day I would like to go to Tavistock in England [a clinical training program in psychodynamic theory and practice] and sensitize myself to it . . . get my antennae in shape," he says wistfully.

One of the ways that faculty seek to convey the humanistic ethos of Milton is to offer contrasts with other elite—primarily male—private schools. A history teacher who spent several years on the faculty at Exeter describes the academic excellence and inspired teaching at his former school, but says, "It was a cold nest, just like a boot camp . . . if you didn't shape up, they'd throw you out." Milton, on the other hand is a "humane place" that supports students through troubled times. Echoing similar sentiments, a faculty member who taught for almost a decade at Andover, recalls the high-powered intellectual exchanges ("the fantastic horsepower") in his Andover seminars, but is more inspired by the diversity at Milton. "We really care for the kids here and know them very well . . . at Andover there was always the concern for grooming kids for the tough, male, real world and less interest in knowing them. . . . There, it was possible to see a student in ninth grade and never see him again until graduation. Here, we meet the kids throughout their careers." Also the varsity baseball coach, he enjoys the chance of seeing the dimensions of students revealed in different contexts, and believes in the balanced development of mind and body. "I love baseball, always played baseball," he says with glee. "Coaching also allows me to express myself differently. It is tangible, different from teaching." Student and teacher can see each other's multiple sides, experience playful intellectual exchanges and grueling physical exercise, and get to know one another very well. It is this integration and holism that continues to inspire this teacher. "It keeps me alive," he says as he races to the window to see if the rain clouds have blown over for the afternoon scrimmage.

The visitor to Milton immediately notices the humanistic orientation in the faculty's regard of students. There is a genuine concern for the nurturance and growth of each student and a sense of disappointment and guilt when one falls by the wayside. In a weekly meeting of the head advisors for girls, the principal for girls announces that Angela Watson, a Black girl in the junior class, has withdrawn from school. Around the table, faculty express sadness and frustration. With her long history of trouble adjusting to the intellectual and social climate of Milton, the school has finally decided it can no longer offer the resources and support Angela seems to need. Although weary of all the struggles, the principal does not seem fully convinced of the wisdom of this final action. Her tentativeness is countered by a colleague who says strongly, "It is right and fair that she has been asked to leave." "I know that in my head," responds the principal sadly, "but in my *heart* I feel differently." With the tough decision made, the advisors worry out loud about how they might support Angela's friends during this time of loss: "They might be terribly demoralized." One advisor expresses a concern that everyone seems to feel: "Her friends might interpret this racially . . . something against Black kids."

Everyone knows Angela's story—her history, her background, her troubles, even the elusive bright moments in her career at Milton. But the faculty do not only know students in trouble; they seem to know all the students. The clearest sign of this individualized attention was revealed after almost every class I visited. I would approach the teacher with gratitude for allowing me to visit and with questions about the substance, process, and purpose of the discussion I had witnessed. At some point in the after-class exchange, the teacher would inevitably begin to talk about the students with emphasis on their differences, their specialness, and their individual development. The descriptions were usually full and detailed, often revealing some deep sensitivity to the special vulnerabilities or harsh experiences of a student.

In an advanced course in comparative literature, ten students and their teacher sit around a large oval table, their bodies bent forward in animated exchange. They are wrestling with uncovering the plot in a very complicated play, Pirandello's *Six Characters in Search of an Author*, and this requires patience and tenacity. During the discussion, there are no raised hands; no one is taking notes. Together they try to penetrate the confusing narrative. The teacher leads the exchange with a mellow voice and a gentle style. He does not seem to be bothered by the aggressive voices of the handful of girls who dominate the discussion, neither does he seek to draw out the silent, reticent students. Occasionally he calls on a quiet student who answers without embarrassment. When they finally reach a moment of clarity and understanding, there is an explosion of laughter that seems to signal relief. But the teacher warns them that there is more to come: "We have only managed to unscramble the *little* story . . . you have to tolerate the uncertainty . . . your wish for closure won't be satisfied." In the last several minutes of class, the teacher assigns roles to the students and they begin to read the dialogue unself-consciously. His casting choices appear to be calculated to bring out hidden qualities in students. A subdued, motionless boy gets the part of a confident, aggressive character. And a comely Black girl is asked to be the ingenue. "You know what that is?" asks the teacher mischievously. "Yes," replies the girl, "Someone who pretends to be more innocent than she is."

After class, the teacher is "high" on the "yeasty" exchange and immediately tells them the stories of his "friends." He begins with the "boy who said nothing" and offers interpretations of his silence:

Jason is a very disturbed kid who is barely keeping his head above water. He is a brilliant, published poet, but he has only been able to complete one course in his last several semesters. A group of concerned teachers and counselors have tried to find ways of supporting him. A poet on the faculty has been reading his work and giving him critical feedback; others have sought to encourage his talents in productions of plays and poetry readings. "We recognize his genius and his vulnerability—both need to be protected."

Pamela, the girl who has dominated the class discussion, stands out in her tight-fitting, low-cut leotard top, her bright purple knickers, and her long, blond hair pulled to the side. The teacher, whose fondness for her is apparent, tells me that she is bright and capable. "Given a couple of chances to rewrite her pieces, she is compelling and strong." From a recently affluent Irish family on Boston's South Shore, she shows vestiges of her family's culture and history. "Pamela works hard and plays hard," smiles the teacher. "She has intensity and flair . . . a fancy dresser, *very* interested in the male athletes."

Janine, the comely Black girl, is the daughter of a professional, upper middle-class family in Milton. "She's a brilliant writer and a sensitive and tough-minded person," admires the teacher. Occasionally, she uses her writing as a way to explore issues of identity and cultural connection. Recently, she wrote a "complicated and rich" story that used her father as the central character. The story "took its own shape . . . gathered it own momentum," and emerged as a tale of a man with vivid imperfections. Janine was disturbed by the story's negative turn and worried "that she was not honoring her father, not being fair to him or revealing his strengths." She brought her concerns to the teacher, who helped her distinguish between a story's narrative and a biography and reinforced the creative, risk-taking turns in her writing. When Janine finally read her story to the class, her peers responded with admiration and awe—impressed by her talents and the resolution of her personal struggle.

The teacher offers ten vivid descriptions of the ten students who sat around the table. Although he seems enlivened by this particular collection of people and feels a special affection for these seniors whom he has known for several years, it is clear that these are not highly unusual relationships for him. Neither is he unusual in his knowledge of students' lives. A history teacher, who enjoys his reputation as a cynic and tough guy, banters with students during the class discussion but gives serious attention to their intellectual and emotional development. He, too, can recite the problems and prospects faced by each member of his European history class; tell me the colleges to which they applied and their reasons for deciding on the one of their choice; and give plausible reasons for why certain students need harsh criticism from him while others need solace and comfort.

The humanistic approach is not merely a matter of style or even depth of understanding. Milton also attempts to design a curriculum that will reflect this value stance. A good example of the explicit curricular design is a ninth-grade required course, "Movement and Mime," co-taught by Bradley, an intense young man who some colleagues describe as "brilliant," and Jasmine, a dramatic woman who was trained in the Martha Graham technique. This course is a collaborative tour de force. When I ask the male teacher why it is taught at Milton, he says slightly flippantly, "To get kids through early adolescence," and then adds in more serious tones, "To help with self-image issues, physicality, poise, confidence, release . . . and of course to teach something about drama, mime, and dance." The curricular purpose is closely linked to the humanistic tradition and Bradley and Jasmine see clear connections between the substance and pedagogy of their course and the intellectual psychic demands of academic life at Milton.

At 8:30, directly following the morning assembly, twenty-five fourteen year-olds gather in their tights and T-shirts in a large, open room on the second floor of Ware Hall. On two sides of the room there are tall windows that let the sunlight and fresh air in. The square space, designed as a studio, has free-standing dance bars against the walls and is empty of furniture except for a few stray chairs, an old grand piano, and a stereo system that plays an eclectic assortment of music. Before class the students gather in small groups, some in animated conversation, others in a waiting pose. When they see me walk in, some try to find ways of covering up their exposed bodies. One girl stretches her T-shirt towards her knees and exclaims, "Oh, how embarrassing, a visitor . . . I *hate* to wear these things!" After the initial awkwardness, they seem to forget my presence and become fully involved in the activities. The teachers, Jasmine and Bradley, are wearing the same uniform as their students. Their posture of confidence and poise seems to reflect what they hope their charges will learn—a comfort with their physical selves, an unself-consciousness about movement and expression.

This course meets once a week but lasts through a double class period. For almost two hours, there is focused action with moods and tempos swinging from contemplative and mellow to fast and peripatetic. The hard-working teachers guide the boys and girls through shifting tempos and extraordinary transformations. Their approach is firm, disciplined, and carefully orchestrated. When tension builds, they provide occasions for release with screaming and laugher. When students begin to "mess around" the teachers insist that they regain their composure and focus. During most of the exercises, students are not allowed to talk. When they chatter to one another a teacher bellows, "No talking! You are mute."

With easy jazz playing on the stereo, the class begins with Bradley directing student in stretching movements. "I want to hear some post-vacation cracking. . . .

Take an inventory of your body. . . . When you hear your name, use the music and make three stretching movements around the room. . . . Wake up, it's morning and it's school! . . . Really stretch, use the music, use the sun coming out, use the fresh air . . . make everything bigger." As the boys and girls stretch slowly, deliberately, in and out of body shapes, Bradley walks around the room getting different angles on the movement. Jasmine, who stands by the stereo, watches intently and makes comments to individual students passing by.

Suddenly the music shifts to a rhythmic, pulsating beat and the atmosphere becomes charged. Bradley develops a fantasy and the students respond with excitement. "There is something chasing you! There are obstacles in front of you, leap over them! There is a high place to get away, go! Keep running! Fight it, get away from it!" Bodies are being hurled across the floor, faces are frightened and intense, hands are extended like protective claws as students enter the fantasy. There is no self-conscious laughter or distracting embarrassment. "Run across an open field! Use everything but your hands to get it away from you! Freeze! You won! Relax."

Students fall out on the floor panting from exhaustion, but the hard-driving teachers offer no break before the next activity. Within less than a minute, the music has returned to calming, melodic sounds and the students are standing in seven straight lines following Jasmine's lead in smooth exercises. "Smile, it's Wednesday," she says. Then they arch their backs and look upward as she says, "Kiss the ceiling . . . keep stretching, flatten your tummy . . . with nice long arms reach. . . ."

As soon as the quiet, disciplined mood has settled in, there is another abrupt shift. As Jasmine plays the drums, Bradley directs the students to join hands and make a circle. "This is called a tangle. I'll pick a leader . . . move slowly, move considerately until everyone is in a knot. . . . This is called Massachusetts politics," he jokes. As students become increasingly wound up with one another, Bradley warns, "*No* talking . . . use your eyes to communicate, be aware, use your face to send messages. . . . It's getting there. . . . Freeze . . . that's excellent." All twenty-five bodies are huddled in a tight knot and they now face the much harder task of getting unwound. The drum beats insistently, slowly. The disentanglement is slow, difficult, and laborious. Occasionally there are flares of frustration, giggling or talking, and the teachers demand silence. Ten minutes later, the snake emerges into a single circle and there is great relief and clapping. Compliments from Bradley follow. "That has taken as long as half an hour in other classes and it only took you ten minutes. . . . See how smart you are!"

The class continues to work through increasingly complicated and subtle activities that stress collaboration, creativity, discipline, and balance. By the end of the first hour, they are building six-person statues that symbolize "a pizza, a ladder, a balloon, a skyscraper." With their weight supporting one another, and one foot off the floor, the groups struggle to establish form and equilibrium. As they hold their shapes for ten seconds, Bradley says, "I want to see something in your *face* that says 'skyscraper' too."

After an hour of observation, I leave feeling exhausted yet exhilarated. I am impressed by the focused energy, intensity of action, clarity of purpose, and the coordination of goals between the teachers. Later on, when I ask Jasmine how the Movement/Mime course became part of the curriculum, she says slyly, "By pushing very hard." The ninth-grade co-educational course is always co-taught by a man and a woman and it follows a required sequence of movement courses beginning in the seventh grade. By now most faculty seem to be convinced of the course's value to the productivity, self-image, and development of students at Milton and have great regard for the creative energies of the instructors. But Jasmine believes the courses have another important ripple effect on the life of the school. They help to erode some of the stereotypic views of boys and girls. The insistence upon the unisex uniform of tights and T-shirts tends to obscure the severe sex differentiations to which fourteen year-olds often cling. Also, the collaborative teaching of a man and woman is an important symbol of the strength and grace of males and females. "We are deliberately bucking the preppy culture and preppy advising," smiles Jasmine.

Not only is the curriculum at Milton shaped by humanistic approaches to education, but the pedagogical processes are often inspired by those same values. Jessica Locke, a sensitive and thoughtful art teacher, talks earnestly about how she uses art as a medium for helping students discover their strengths and express their intellectual and aesthetic creativity. A serious practicing artist, Locke sees strong connections between what she asks of herself as a painter and the pedagogical craft of working with students. We talk together in the large painting studio, surrounded by the drawings, collages, and sketches of her students. Some of the work looks primitive and awkward, other pieces are inspired and technically impressive, but Locke points to the examples of a developing style, an emerging self-confidence in her students. Her voice is soft and intense as she searches for ways to articulate her deep and complicated feelings about art and learning:

> "In my teaching I want to compel and provoke students to reveal themselves. . . . Through art, I can help them become conscious of their personalities . . . help them see that their lives are patterns like their art.
> "I don't care if any of my students become artists . . . I want to know that they have an imagination . . . can express themselves with an intangible, creative idea and see the connections between visual and verbal expression.
> "The whole experience of teaching has been very humbling. . . . *They* teach me. . . . In one class I have with thirteen students, I have learned an enormous amount about my own capacity for expression. They are just great. All of them are superstars . . . but when I gave them a difficult assignment, they did not attend to it seriously. I was angered by their complacency . . . and yelled and screamed at them about standards and expecta-

tions. In that angry moment I felt a new freedom. In being able to rant and rave I let them know I was a human being with feelings . . . *we* were human beings."

Jessica Locke's words are strikingly emotional (she describes herself as a "very dramatic person"), and express the fervor of one who has recently become committed to hard-won values. But the essence of her ruminations are compatible with Milton's holistic approach to education, with the tender loving care that has surrounded generations of students.

Even in the most bureaucratic corners of the school, there is evidence of this humanistic ideology. A faculty member, proud of the philosophical consistencies, says, "You will find this sense of care for the individual even in our scheduling of courses. . . . I think we are the only school that still uses a hand-built schedule. It is not computerized. The kids make their course selections first and the schedule is designed to meet *their* needs. Ninety-eight percent of the kids get their first choices of courses. It is amazing!"

With the faculty expressing such a clear consensus of views on the values of an individualistic, holistic approach to education, I anticipated some voices of dissent. I did not hear any vigorous disagreement. Rather, I heard murmurings of concern about the inevitable distortions of the basic philosophical stance. When does individualism threaten the cohesion of community life? When does the humanistic approach reduce standards of intellectual excellence? When does a unitary philosophical approach diminish opportunities for diversity of style, temperament, and pedagogy? Among some faculty and students these questions were asked not to discredit the humanistic orientation, but to underscore the need for a critical perspective, balance, and an open mind in sustaining a healthy educational community.

Susan Kagan, a student leader with unusual sensitivity and bold ideas, pointed to the strengths and distortions of the humanistic approach. In referring to the power of individualism, Susan described her experiences on the Discipline Committee; one of three school-wide committees that represent students, faculty, and the administration. When a major disciplinary problem is too "serious to be handled" by the principals for girls or boys, it comes before the Discipline Committee. In an effort to protect all the persons involved, the procedures for committee action are very explicit and impersonal, but the regard of the student is highly personal. When a student is brought before the committee for review, he or she is joined by the appropriate principal, the student advisor, and any teacher who might be involved. Before the hearing, the accused student writes a statement about what he or she has done. After the statement is read by the committee, the paper is burned, and the student appears before it to explain the incident in his own words. After questioning by the committee, the accused leaves the room and the committee deliberates. In its deliberations, the committee follows clear guidelines that refer to degrees of punishment for various offenses.

Susan offers several examples of the latitude and personal focus of committee decisions. "Drug or alcohol offenses could lead to suspension for one week, probation for the rest of the year, or an expulsion from school . . . depending upon your previous record." A senior who was recently caught cheating on a math test was only given a week's suspension because he had a reputation for "being very honest and had no previous record." Plagerism is considered one of "the most serious offenses." There has not been a case in recent memory, but punishments are extremely severe. When they enter Milton, all students must sign a contract saying they will not plagerize, and they are informed of the serious consequences if they disobey. By contrast, "Whereabouts," an offense that occurs when students neglect to sign out of the dormitories or give a faulty destination, is considered much less onerous. In these cases, the committee puts the students on "Close Bounds," and they are not allowed to go off campus. "We try to make the punishment fit the crime," says Susan confidently. However, even with explicit and visible procedures and punishments, she describes the process as "incredibly time consuming, taxing, and tiring . . . but it is personal. . . . It matches one of the main purposes of Milton . . . to be humane and individualistic."

Sitting on committees with faculty has given Susan Kagan a rare window on adult perspectives, deliberations, and interactions. She remembers being surprised by their sense of fairness and caring, but even more by their lack of cynicism. "The faculty are super and very liberal . . . I was amazed by their idealism." Susan admires these rare qualities but points to the excesses of empathy and liberalism. The excesses are not limited to committee deliberations; they are embedded in the wider community's regard for student life.

In describing the tendency towards "overindulgence" at Milton, Susan tells the story of a "very prominent" student who had a long history of serious offenses and drug abuse. Despite his numerous transgressions, he was a seductive force, "a very idealistic, very enthusiastic, and very charismatic person . . . when he wasn't stoned." At the end of last year, he came before the committee with a major disciplinary charge. In responding to the charge, he lied about the incident. "At that moment, he should have been *immediately* expelled," says Susan unsympathetically. Instead, he was allowed to return this year and assume a leadership position in the school. Susan is still confused by the faculty's reluctance to take action, but recognizes the clear signals that her peers received when his visible abuse went unpunished. "He was close to killing himself, very self-destructive, and his charismatic behavior gained him a large following . . . it was a danger to all of us . . . maybe they were afraid of angering his following!" she laments.

Certainly, Susan's single story of overindulgence does not match the many tales she tells of the powerful attractions of the humanistic approach at Milton. She recounts the story of excess in order to underscore the possibilities of "things going wrong even with the best intentions"; the vulnerabilities of an approach that relies so heavily on individualistic interpretations and empathetic regard.

A few faculty echo Susan's concern for the fuzzy boundaries between love and overindulgence. One teacher, who describes herself as a strident, convinced humanistic educator, says that it is important to distinguish between the uncomplicated love of being a teacher and the very complicated love of being a parent. The former relationship allows teachers to be clear and decisive in their actions, to be unambivalent about the dangers of egocentrism and self-indulgence, and to not worry about losing the affections of their students. With a smile, she says, "It is *work* to love my twelve year-old kid, very complicated, very energy consuming . . . but teaching allows a detached kind of love. I am not plugged in in the same way. . . . I will not be hurt if they don't come to class . . . and this allows me the freedom to be clear."

Another teacher, who taught for several years at a more traditional boarding school, worries about the negative effects of indulgence on student motivation and achievement. He does not admire the narrow conservatism and harshness of his former school, but neither does he support "the permissiveness" of Milton. "Milton is supposed to be a humane place . . . that is good to a certain extent but it can be problematic. . . . It can lead to fuzziness, to mediocrity." He ponders out loud, "I don't know whether Milton tends to attract soft kids or whether it supports kids in being soft," and then tells me about a "coddled senior girl" who is beautiful, fragile, and lazy. "No one dares to confront her. They're afraid to be too harsh because she'll break out crying . . . so she has been allowed to do nothing challenging for four years."

Although I am certain that some students go unchallenged and that Milton's humanistic approach permits the excesses of abusive individuals, I observed no evidence of encouraged overindulgence. Rather, I witnessed the subtle combinations of caring and criticism. After establishing a tone of trust, teachers did not seem reluctant to be discerning and judgmental. In an advanced drama class, I witnessed this union of support and empathy joined with tough scrutiny and criticism.

The drama teacher is working with seven of her best students. Sitting or lying on the carpeted floor of the drama studio, they exchange ideas about the preparations for the upcoming arts weekend. With only "two weeks and two days" left before the event, the teacher openly expresses her anxiety about fleeting time: "We have a lot of exploring, experimenting . . . that is what frightens me . . . so much to do before the play gets set." Then, a bit concerned that she has transmitted her anxiety to the students, she recovers, "Theater is a matter of faith . . . it will work out." With new optimism, for most of the class the students and teacher wrestle with the technical and aesthetic dimensions of the plays they have written for the occasion.

Fifteen minutes before the end of class, the teacher asks the students to rehearse one of the pieces, and within seconds they emerge as totally transformed characters. Holding their scripts, they move about the room in vigorous motion, saying their lines with confidence and flair. With her face cupped in her hands, the teacher watches intently, silently. Occasionally her face explodes into laughter, followed by the serious, watchful gaze. At the conclusion of the short piece, the students fall on the rug, exhausted. Their faces wait for the director's response. Without seeming defensive or threatened, they anticipate her disapproval. "We know, it has been a *very* long vacation . . . we're rusty," says a nervous voice. "Yes, it's been a long vacation," the teacher agrees, "and that is okay for getting back into it for the first time . . . but I see two problems that may be emerging. One, I see your old clichés reappearing. . . . I want you to explore it, but don't bring in those stylized clichés . . . look for meaning in it . . . certain thoughts go together . . . find the shape and form of this work. Two, something that is happening that I *really* don't like . . . there is some kind of competitive thing going on among you. It is as if you are saying, 'I'll top this.' . . . This is not true of your work in general and I want to stop it before it becomes habit." A couple of students offer mild rebuttals, but the tone is one of recognition and acceptance. The exchanges in class have offered wonderful examples of trust and criticism, empathy, and the pursuit of excellence.

ACHIEVEMENT AND STRESS

Most faculty and administrators at Milton emphasize the high quality of academic life and the dramatic shift in the school's image as a serious intellectual community. When I ask him to recount the strengths of Milton, the headmaster says straightforwardly, "On all the traditional indicators of success, we are *super*. There are just a dozen schools in the whole country that could register as high as we do on all of the conventional criteria of success and achievement." Franklin Jones, director of admissions, who has a Ph.D. from Harvard in English, is primarily responsible for projecting and selling Milton's image. He reduces the comparisons from the field of twelve that Jerry Pieh cites to the "real competitors" that Milton "loses kids to": Andover, Exeter, St. Paul's, and Groton. But even in contrast to the stiffest competition, Jones claims that Milton "looks very good." He points to the great changes in the intellectual standards and social class biases of Milton since he arrived in 1974. "Milton is a *totally* different school now. Ten years ago it used to be haughtier than Andover, more concerned with social status issues . . . now it is focused on the quality of teaching and learning . . . and that is now excellent." An English teacher, who once taught at Andover and arrived at Milton fourteen years ago, also sees transformations in the "academic clout" of the place. He still believes that the Andover students tend to be brainier and more aggressively intellectual, but finds that in the last few years his classes at Milton have become increasingly high powered. "I now have several students who could easily match the Andover kids."

Students tend to emphasize the rigor and intensity of academic life at Milton. Almost every student I talked with spoke of feeling intimidated by the intellectual expectations and academic pressures when they first arrived at Milton, then slowly gaining some feelings of confidence and stamina during the first couple of years. A very successful senior who will enter Yale next fall described the struggles of adjusting to life at Milton: "The first year I came here, I hated it . . . I am a really conscientious person and I soon developed an identity crisis here. There were so many people who seemed so intelligent. . . . The teachers appeared to be so professional . . . and more interested in working with older kids . . . and I found the school work overwhelming." By the middle of the second year, her peers no longer seemed so extraordinary, the teachers seemed less distant and awesome, and she began to get good grades in her school work. Her emerging academic self-confidence was reinforced by involvement and rewards in numerous extracurricular activities. Now an articulate and forceful advocate for Milton, she says, "Most people like it at Milton. I've noticed that those people who do not seem to be interested in academics are nevertheless very intelligent and involved in interesting things. *Everyone* finds something to be involved in . . . and not just things to look good on their college applications."

The senior pauses for a moment and remembers the exceptions to her proud proclamations of involvement and excellence. Pointing, as many others have, to the "Butt Room Crowd," she says, "They are a very defensive group." The "Butt Room" is a room reserved on campus for juniors and seniors who wish to smoke. The reputation of the frequent inhabiters of this room encompasses more than smoking habits. I am told "they wear sloppy clothes, look like the old sixties' Bohemians, are often into drugs, have a lot of personal problems, are disillusioned and bitter against the world. . . . The group serves as their refuge." Everyone who identifies the Butt Room Crowd describes them as a fringe group, an impotent minority, and a group whose problems originate from sources other than the school—primarily the brutal combinations of family indulgence and neglect. A proclaimed member of the Butt Room Crowd mistakes me for a talent scout from New York. A rock guitarist, who hopes one day to be discovered and make it big, he approaches me with questions about "the big-city scene." Although he is disappointed that I am into "academic stuff," he is gracious enough to talk about his peripheral, lonely life at Milton, his wish to leave, and his passion for music. Never once does he blame his problems on the school. Wearily he says, "Listen, I just don't fit . . . it's not their fault."

The many references to the Butt Room Crowd strike me as a way of underscoring the generally positive and productive experience of most students at Milton. By pointing to the clearly deviant pattern, people can identify the normal range. There is no attempt to hide the existence of this fringe element (at one point, Pieh is worried that I am getting an overly positive view of student life and asks, "Have you visited the Butt Room?"); only a wish to note that it is a circumscribed, small group of disaffected students.

The almost universal theme among students centers on demands for achievement and the stresses they engender. Many recognize that the demands have multiple origins: family ("My parents are paying all this money and I've *got* to do well"); teachers ("They expect a lot from us and won't settle for mediocre work"); and self ("I can't tell whether the pressure is coming from outside or inside"). Some claim that the emphasis on high standards stands in opposition to the humanistic orientation that shapes the school's philosophical stance; that the competition to achieve distorts opportunities for collaboration, creativity, and empathy for peers. These sentiments are voiced most vigorously by seniors, who have just endured the grueling application process for college. In a senior American literature course, the students talked about the tough academic demands, the relentless work, and the competitive atmosphere at Milton. Their voices revealed a mixture of sensitivity, bitterness, and nostalgia for lost time, lost creativity, and lost innocence. Their criticisms were certainly fueled by the aggressive and outspoken stance of the teacher, who opened the discussion by saying, "Milton is an excellent school . . . but I worry about the character of education. I worry that people get channeled, lose their creative spunk . . . also I worry that Milton awards brash, aggressive types, and at the same time does not reinforce the more contemplative, shy types." Without further provocation, the seniors distilled their years of experience at Milton into a litany of criticisms.

TED: There is the problem of getting into a narrow pattern at Milton. If you learn to do something technically well you are often destroying creative initiative. . . . Maybe these are the incoherent parts of education.

AMY: Milton is simply a college-prep school. But they mean a *certain* college. You must learn *certain* things, get a *settled* job, become an *important* person, on top of everything . . . then you'll send your children to a prep school . . . and they will have prep school friends.

CARLA: When I came here as a freshman, I was intimidated by all the other talented people. I withdrew from everyone, everything. The teachers do not encourage you in finding your own creative expression enough.

JENNIFER: Last year I came—as a junior—from a public school in Vermont. I could just feel my creativity being crushed by all the worries of college applications, by worries about what my mom and dad would think. . . . but a strange thing happened. The insistence that I put things together for exams made me feel more and more competent. Exams turned out to be a wonderful, satisfying, confidence-building experience.

LAURA: Milton puts too much emphasis on the amount of information, the quantity rather than the quality. . . . There is no time to play around with ideas . . . I don't remember *anything* I learned in "U.S. History."

AMY: There is so much stress on achievement. You are told a special formula and if you fit the formula, you'll get into college.

SUSAN: The formula does seem like a game . . . but the game is not just played at Milton . . . it's society's game. You have to learn the strategies for getting into college and we're lucky they teach them so well here.

AMY: Yes, but you can get a good education at lots of places. You don't have to go to Harvard or Yale!

DAVE: Maybe that's a human nature . . . to want to achieve and to want public acclaim.

TED: Still, I think there is too much emphasis on product and too little on the process of learning.

SUSAN: I think there needs to be more opportunity for applying what we learn to real world issues. Sometimes the things we learn feel so irrelevant.

AMY: But at Milton, you almost have to rationalize reading the newspaper. 'Cause if you're reading the paper, you're obviously not doing your homework.

TED: That's right, you don't get a grade for being worldly or sophisticated, for reading the newspaper.

The conversation takes other related twists and turns without the teacher's intervention or direction. As I listen, I am struck by the negative tone, but I am also impressed by the vivid and articulate expressiveness, by the questioning spirit. Most of the students seem to understand the multiple forces at work here. They recognize that Milton is part of a wider imperative; that sometimes grueling work leads to feelings of confidence; that some qualities that they see in themselves and their peers are part of "human nature," not necessarily institutionally imposed. Also, I recognize that as seniors already accepted at college, they can finally feel safe offering blazing assaults on their school. (Perhaps their angry words will help them separate from a place to which they have grown very attached, however ambivalently.) As we leave the classroom, a wistful senior confirms my suspicions. "The kids in Milton don't take many risks. This is the first year I've dared to disagree . . . or maybe I *forgot* how to take risks as college loomed large. I do remember having fun my sophomore year."

In an elective course in English literature, I witness the spirit of adventure and spark of enthusiasm that the senior girl had nostalgically recalled. For sophomores, the course offers a chronological study of literature from Chaucer to the early seventeenth century with a special emphasis on Chaucer and Shakespeare. Carol Gregory, who teaches it, is considered by her colleagues to be a gifted, inspired, and experienced teacher. Some admiring faculty describe her as one of Milton's "stars." Younger teachers often speak of her as a powerful mentor, and others recognize her influences as an educational leader. With fourteen sophomores gathered around a large oval table, she leads the class in a vigorous, adventurous discussion about the form and cultural purposes of early ballads. The tone is both playful and intensely serious. There is none of the cynicism and disappointment expressed by the seniors as their younger peers reveal their uninhibited pleasure in exploring the historical mysteries.

> With an almost maternal style, Gregory begins enthusiastically, "One of the things that has transformed our world is canned music." She has their attention. In this early period "when did people sing?" The responses are spontaneous and immediate. "For religious purposes . . . at festivals . . . at feasts . . . in the fields." "What are the oldest forms of singing?" asks Gregory. "Lullabies," offers a girl. "Religious incantation," responds a boy. "But what came first, the community or the personal thing?" In chorus, several students reply, "The community thing." These introductory exchanges are followed by a short historical description of ballads as an aesthetic and cultural form. But Gregory's monologue quickly shifts back to an explanatory dialogue with students.

GREGORY: If you think of them as old, what culture do ballads remind you of?

DANIEL: Primitive culture.

GREGORY: What does that conjure up in your mind?

DANIEL: Maybe primitive is a bad word. I really mean simple.

GREGORY: Primitive is a good word. It has grown to have a pejorative connotation . . . but it is a fine word that refers to things which have their roots way back.

On this gray, rainy day the discussion feels surprisingly lively as students tell each other mysterious tales that are inspired by ancient recollections. The teacher moves easily from witty, humorous interludes to clear, focused questioning when she says in a stage whisper, "Tell me a few mysterious things . . . we are groping our way towards magical beliefs . . . what is our relationship to the magical, the bizarre, the supernatural . . . we are attracted and compelled by it . . . we desire to believe it." "Yes," agrees Aaron, "and we also want to control it, to feel in charge." From a discussion of the psychic uses of magic, the conversation shifts to the primitive forms of communicating.

GREGORY: Repetition is a powerful way of communicating. Why is repetition so deeply embedded in language?

MARY: Maybe it relieves stress . . . or maybe it helps us understand the message better.

"Yes," exclaims Gregory as she launches into a precise and funny imitation of two ladies on their front stoop gossiping with their sharp Cockney accents. The ladies keep repeating their stories to one another. Gregory's Cockney drama, theatrical and convincing, is in sharp contrast to her usual, highly educated British speech and the students laugh with great pleasure. "You can hear a certain rhythm in these ladies' talk . . . what is the satisfaction in repetition?

ROBERT: It is a sort of comfort. You know what to expect.

GREGORY: In ancient, oral traditions you look for pattern, repetition, supernatural, dark colors . . . what else do you look for?

STEVEN: Exaggeration!

The class concludes on a rising crescendo as Gregory and her students, in chorus, read a ballad. "Let's see if we can make it swing. . . . Really belt it out!" demands Gregory before she launches into the dramatic reading. Her lines are followed by the students' repeated refrain, "In Christ receive thy soul." As the ballad unfolds, the voices capture a rhythmic spirit, the tones darken, and the students seem to journey back in time. As she leaves the classroom, a girl with a glazed expression exclaims, "I feel I'm in a trance!"

Although she has orchestrated this adventure and provided the students with information, intrigue, and catharsis, Gregory speaks modestly about her work. "The kids are real eager beavers. I feel so lucky!" she exclaims as she turns to welcome the students arriving for her next class.

Some of the fifteen-year-old energy and enthusiasm appears to be diminished by the time students reach the last semester of their senior year. By many twelfth graders' accounts, they begin to feel the intrusions of the real world, the narrowing effects of competition and achievement,

292

and they know they must buckle down and "play the game." The nurturing, encompassing culture of Milton enjoyed by the sophomores no longer protects seniors from the anticipations of a tougher world beyond school boundaries. By their senior year, students are fully preoccupied with getting into college—not merely a good college, but an elite, prestigious school. The pressures begin during the spring of their junior year and impose a tone and structure on school life that is often overwhelming.

At Milton, 99 percent of the students apply to four-year colleges. Usually around ten or twelve seniors defer admissions; some reapply to new schools because they have not been accepted at the college of their choice; others move on to postgraduate schools hoping to improve their academic record for future admission; and a tiny percentage decide to work or travel abroad for a few years. Of the 170 seniors who apply, usually 30 percent are accepted for early admission and do not have to endure the anxious wait for April acceptance letters. Those 70 percent who have not received early admission tend to apply to an average of six colleges, and many are accepted by their first choice.

The Milton catalogue prominently displays a listing of the numbers of students who matriculated at various colleges from 1975–81. It is a most impressive batting average and offers visible evidence of Milton's success. An admissions officer tells me that it is the first page parents of prospective applicants to Milton turn to when perusing the catalogue. They must be satisfied to find that Harvard, Princeton, Dartmouth, Yale, and Brown head the list of colleges with, respectively, 97, 47, 42, 39, and 38 Milton graduates. Large numbers of students also enter the University of Pennsylvania, University of Vermont, Tufts, Williams, Duke, Vassar, and Wesleyan. The list of colleges often attended by Milton graduates names no "losers"—no schools that would cause ambitious parents embarrassment. Sprinkled throughout the list are smaller, excellent schools like Reed, Swarthmore, Bryn Mawr, Carlton, and Sarah Lawrence, that often attract discerning students who want a fine education "without the ivy league hoopla."

The impressive college statistics are not accidental. They reflect, of course, the institutional reputation and fine education at Milton, but also a very careful, calculated college advising process. Steve Cox, director of college counselling, is referred to by many of his colleagues as "the best college counselor in the country." A clean-cut, handsome man in his late thirties, he exudes the civility and poise of his preppy past: St. George's School, Middlesex, and Harvard. After teaching for five years at St. Paul's School, he moved to Milton to work in the college counseling office and has enjoyed the philosophy, tone, and eclecticism of the less isolated environment of Milton. As Cox describes his role and the counselling program, one is aware of his deep knowledge of private school cultures, his keen understanding of adolescent psychology, and his administrative and organizational strengths. All of these talents combine with a classic style that is both warm and sophisticated, both revealing and appropriately discreet.

"The model" used by Milton's college counselors was developed several years ago by Cox's predecessor, a woman with innovative ideas about the sequence, pacing, and form of a carefully designed counselling process. The model, now firmly in place, is improved upon each year and now works like a well-oiled machine. Cox and his colleague, who counsel 170 girls and boys through the college application process, claim that the ratio of students to advisor is the best among private schools and allows them to combine individual meetings with small and large group forums. The process begins in the spring of the junior year with students and their parents individually completing an "elaborate" questionnaire about their goals and expectations of college. This initial inquiry is followed by three individual meetings with students. The first two meetings are designed to "get to know the students as people, to see them as prospective candidates, and to lessen their inhibitions." In these sessions, the counselors purposefully avoid reference to specific colleges. They do approach the broad issues of student values, goals, preferences, talents, and styles. Cox uses these meetings "like mock interviews," as he gets a good sense of how they will perform in an actual college interview. The third individual meeting with students focuses directly on specific choices. Cox describes this encounter as the "most difficult" meeting because he feels responsible for being "both conservative and candid" in his remarks, and students are often unrealistic and overly optimistic about their chances. He must balance his piercing realism with efforts to build self-confidence in students and this is usually a subtle task. Usually Milton students need to "broaden their horizons," look beyond the Eastern elite schools, add realistic supplements to their original list of choices, and consider "the match" between person and institution.

In addition to the individual sessions, the counselors organize small group meetings that focus on particular skills or alternative perspectives related to college applications. For example, in small group meetings counselors discuss strategies of testing, consider the size of the college as an important indicator of institutional life and culture, and teach students how to read a college catalogue. The psychological counselors are invited to offer a few seminars on negotiating the pressures and emotional stresses of the application process, and there are small group sessions on role playing, essay writing, and interviewing. Each of these pieces of information, counsel, and practice are designed to follow a logical building sequence, culminating in a student's successful entry into college.

The procedure consumes an enormous amount of the time and energy of counselors, teachers, advisors, and students. By the time I arrive at Milton in early April, many seniors have been happily accepted into college, while others are still waiting to hear from their first choice. All seem to be worn down and weary, only half-attending to the last several weeks of school. A senior, who has not read her history assignment and can only giggle when she does not know how to respond to the teacher's question, explains her casual response: "We're all seniors. We've received our acceptances and couldn't care less. . . . We deserve a rest!"

Despite the vigorous structure he has created, Steve Cox gets his greatest pleasure from the invisible victories. "My personal triumph is getting a weaker kid into a school that is good for *him*." At the same time, he is well aware that his work will be judged solely on the numbers of graduates who attend the prestigious schools. Parents and alumni are wholly preoccupied with admittance rates to Harvard, Yale, and Princeton. Thankfully, Cox has devised a system that insures overall successful results and that satisfies most parents. Even with this security he admits, "More than anything, I am threatened by the irrational, angry parent."

DIVERSITY AND COMMUNITY

A secondary theme at Milton centers on building a diverse community. It is secondary in the sense that people actually mention the goal of diversity after they proclaim the values of individuality. Headmaster Pieh is fond of referring to a "diversity of talents," a natural extension of reinforcing the individual strengths of each person. Most faculty use the concept of diversity to refer to the changing image of Milton. They point to the "haughty, aristocractic, upper-class" students and teachers who inhabited the school in recent history, and the "dramatic" transition to a more heterogeneous community. Class barriers have been largely removed and Milton now draws a smattering of working-class students, a large group from the middle and upper middle-classes, and a strong presence of alumni children from affluent families. People admit a lingering edge of privilege and the imprint of elitism, but compared to earlier times, they claim that Milton has opened its doors very wide.

One old-timer claims that the biggest shift towards diversity has come in the faculty. She remembers a time, twenty years ago, when 60 percent of the faculty were Harvard graduates who "had private incomes, large trust funds, and summer homes in Maine." The rest of the faculty were "sprinkled among Yale and Princeton . . . with an occasional Williams type." The atmosphere was one of privilege and dignified affluence. Although the past two decades have brought an increasingly varied faculty, she credits Pieh with taking a leadership role in this area. In his search for new faculty, he purposely looks for variations in educational backgrounds, life experiences, and socioeconomic origins.

When I ask this long-time observer about the presence of minorities on the faculty, she questions me abruptly, "What do you mean minority?" Before I can answer, she refers to the diversity of perspectives and styles on the Milton faculty. "You see, nothing is very obvious anymore. We have a range of voices and costumes. . . . In fact, no minority exists. We have a whole bunch of eccentric people on the faculty." Soon realizing that I was asking about minorities in the racial, ethnic, and religious sense, she struggles a bit self-consciously with remembering the percentages. "I think there are about two or three Asians, some Greek and Spanish-speaking teachers, and lots and lots of Jewish faculty—maybe 15 to 20 percent . . . there are two Black faculty, a man and a woman" (actually, there is only one—the Black woman resigned from the faculty last year). Then, slightly defensively, she explains, "You know, recruiting Blacks is very hard. If they are good, they can go anywhere. If they are not good, we don't want them."

The shift in the social class origins of teachers has meant that greater attention has had to be paid to faculty salaries and perquisites. It used to be that the "dollar-a-year men" had only a trivial interest in their tiny income derived from teaching. Now most faculty must live on their salaries, and salary decisions attract much more concern and interest. A teacher who has been at Milton almost twenty-five years observes that teachers' contracts "used to be very gentlemanly, now they have become more professional . . . it still would be seen as very amateurish by the outside world." Once again, most faculty point to Jerry Pieh's good efforts in raising faculty salaries "to a very respectable level compared to other private schools," and applaud him for putting the school on a solid financial base. As with most private schools, there is no tenure system at Milton. Teachers receive a contract letter in March for the following year.

296

I heard no complaints from faculty about the short-term, informal contracts, only appreciation for the "generous and fair" salaries and a single
comment about "the minor degree of anxiety" that accompanies contract
letters. "But if some people are not going to be asked to come back, they
know well ahead of time. It is handled as humanely as possible," one
observer remarked.

Although I saw several gentlemen on the faculty who matched my
stereotype of understated privilege and subtle elitism, I noticed wide
variations in faculty style, dress, and demeanor that seemed to reflect
their myriad origins. The listing of faculty in the back of Milton's catalogue includes their educational backgrounds and credentials. Although
less dominated by Harvard roots, one is still impressed by the generous
number of Ph.D.'s sprinkled throughout the faculty and by the excellence
of the institutions most of them attended: Columbia, University of London, Dartmouth, Harvard, Middlebury, Mount Holyoke, Oxford, and
Tufts. The credentials are impressive but many tell autobiographical stories that do not match the experiences of their private school charges.
Some come from public school origins and still cling to an outsider's
perspective on private schools. A few speak about the value of having
worked their way through college and see great differences between
themselves and their more privileged colleagues.

The earlier familial and educational experience of faculty may bear
some relation to their views of Milton's attractions and seductions. Unlike many more geographically isolated boarding schools, Milton's faculty do not all orient inward toward the school community. Others feel
deeply connected to school life and rarely venture into nearby Boston or
beyond. One such person claims he would never survive as a civilian,
recognizes the "streak of dependency" in his temperament, and claims
that the increasing crime rates in Boston make the city uninhabitable. His
deep connections to Milton, however, express feelings of ambivalence. In
the same breath, he speaks about loving Milton and feeling trapped
there. Other faculty have developed a way to have "the best of both
worlds," to experience "the safety and security of Milton and enjoy venturing forth to seek other adventures and friendships." A young woman
who shares this dual perspective offers a mild criticism of Milton's parochialism: "I don't think that there is enough acknowledgment of people's
needs to be separate. . . . You have to be distant enough to be able to
bring new energy to the school." A third group of faculty treat Milton as
a day school and leave each afternoon to return to the real world. One of
these teachers was a product of boarding schools and wants to escape
"the claustrophobic tendencies" in his adult life. In order to live a full

and productive life now, he feels he must leave Milton and avoid the paternalistic seductions. At the same time, he recognizes the losses of maintaining a distance. He always feels slightly peripheral to school life, never in touch with the central core. "I really don't have any close friends here," he admits sadly.

These diverse orientations toward community life seem to reduce the tendencies towards uniformity and conformity often found in private boarding schools. But these very same qualities of variation make it more difficult for some faculty to feel "connected to a larger whole." Says one woman who experiences a vague loneliness at Milton: "Each person exists here as an island . . . there is no sense of community or common purpose . . . maybe that is partly regional. It seems to be a phenomenon of the Northeast."

There are few visible signs of racial or ethnic diversity on the faculty. The presence of Lloyd Mays, the sole Black faculty member, can only be interpreted as tokenism. A dignified, thoughtful teacher of Spanish, Mays arrived three years ago after eleven years on the faculty at St. George's School in Rhode Island. A native of Jamaica, he immigrated to Canada in the late sixties and moved "south of the border" when he found that his training in Spanish and Latin was not very relevant to educational priorities in Ontario. Mays came to St. George's "during the peak of the Black Revolution" and was seen as both a traitor and a role model by the very small group of minority students. They needed him as a source of identification but they were also convinced that he was "selling out" by coming to this predominantly white, elite boarding school. Despite the antagonistic images of his role ("I felt a bit like a martyr"), Mays tried hard to advocate for minority students, to serve as interpreter of their special needs, and to protect them from subtle forms of racism. Throughout his tenure at St. George's, he also pressed for additional minority faculty without success. "But the minute I left, suddenly a minority person appeared," says Mays sharply. "You see, if the token is there, all efforts stop for additional hiring."

Because of his token experience at St. George's, the transition to life at Milton was not difficult for Mays. It is not that Mays is any more accepting of the isolation or unique responsibilities of tokenism at Milton; it is that he is more practiced in the posture and strategies of adjustment. In addition, the ideology and rhetoric of the 1980s are strikingly different from the 1960s, and he no longer feels victimized by the negative assaults of radicalized minority students as he did a decade ago. But Mays still faults Milton for its lack of vigilance in pursuing minority faculty. He is genuinely puzzled by Milton's tradition of risk-taking which somehow excludes a commitment to faculty diversity. "They are not as prepared to take risks with minority faculty. . . . In other ways, the school is ready to experiment and be innovative and I find that exciting about this place."

When Mays comments on his visible and unique status on the faculty, he seems less concerned with his own experiences of isolation and separateness and more worried about the effects of his tokenism on the perspective and behavior of minority students. "Without more role models, they can feel terribly lost," he laments. Minority students need a combination of support, realism, and confrontation from their teachers, and majority faculty rarely are sensitive to these special needs. Explains Mays: "Most minority kids come from totally different environments, and their advisors have to be sympathetic and sensitive to the contradictions they are facing in coming to Milton . . . but they must be both sensitive and demanding . . . they must help students face realities." Mays's voice is neither bitter nor resigned. He sees much room for improvement, but he also has observed positive changes in the last ten years. "There has been lots of trial and error and we've made lots of mistakes. . . . In the early seventies, minority kids were the victims of a double standard, treated with kid gloves . . . never any demands." Now there is the emerging recognition that they "are different," but must be honored with the "same expectations." The seeming paradox is elusive and difficult to translate into behavior, but Mays feels it is the only way to create a truly pluralistic community.

Lloyd Mays mainly focuses his comments on the need for more minority faculty at Milton, and the need for changes in how minority students are regarded and treated by their advisors and teachers. He sees these as interlocking problems. Many other faculty, also concerned about diversity among students, feel embarrassed by the low numbers of minority students. Franklin Jones, director of admissions, feels this problem most pointedly and has "worried a lot about how to increase the percentages." He is not proud, neither is he defensive, about the 7 percent minority presence that includes Blacks, Hispanics, and Asians. His comments to me focus on the Black students, the source of his greatest concern; and he begins by making a surprising assertion, "I would think it would be easier for Blacks to live in Milton than in other boarding schools because of its urban flavor." But he is immediately reminded of the hostile wider environment. With his North Carolina southern accent, Jones forcefully reminds me, "Yankees are so provincial. . . . This is not a welcoming environment . . . how do you think it feels for a Black parent to see on the front page of the *Globe* a picture of the Tall Ships and then banners saying 'Kill Niggers.' . . . It's a scary place for a minority family to send a kid!"

Jones tells a story to drive home his point. In the mid-seventies, David, an able, but shy Black boy arrived from Atlanta. The son of a policeman, he had attended public elementary school. His parents were frightened by the newspaper headlines of racism in Boston, but were eager for their son to get a first-class education. Their apprehensions, heightened by hundreds of miles of distance from their son, caused them to make unrealistic demands upon him. "His mother forbade him to set foot off campus," remembers Jones. The inhibitions and loneliness soon became unbearable for David and he left Milton after a year.

Jones offers other tales of blatant racism, parental fears, student isolation, and retreat. He does not cite the subtle forms of stereotyping and bias within Milton alluded to by Mays, but focuses instead on the vulgarities and ironies of a city known as the "cradle of liberty" and the ripple effects felt by Milton inhabitants. With slight optimism, he tells me about a recent meeting called for minority parents at Milton, the first event of its kind. The discussion was candid and charged as they shared their experiences. There were resentments expressed, for instance, about a study skills course set up especially for minority students. Many felt that this seemingly benign gesture reflected racist assumptions about the academic competence of their children and did not recognize the wide variations among them. By the end of the meeting, the parents had decided to take a first step designed to provide mutual support and solace. Each minority boarder was to be assigned to a minority day student's family for the year. It was hoped that the host family would provide a sense of home away from home, a place of safety beyond the campus, and a source of perspective and identification for the student.

A faculty member who is "deeply concerned" about the small numbers of minority students at Milton says, "In the late sixties and early seventies we had 9 percent minorities and now we have 7 percent . . . and those kids really take their lumps . . . many come and leave after the first two years." In trying to figure out the drop in numbers in recent years, he says hesitantly, "I think at some point there were tradeoffs—perhaps not consciously made—and Milton decided to concentrate on admitting working-class whites. . . . You know they are a minority at Milton . . . and as a result Milton began to take fewer Blacks and Hispanics."

Several faculty rehearse the casualties and disappointments of minority student careers at Milton. I hear about the low-income, Puerto Rican kid from New York who came as a ninth grader and had a very marginal year. He had great troubles academically and felt socially ostracized by his peers. His hostility was expressed in the abuse of school property and mischievous pranks against fellow students. Among other things, he charged hundreds of dollars in telephone calls to another student and was finally expelled. A sympathetic faculty member recognizes the clash of cultures and the lack of academic preparation, but faults the boy's parents for not offering him "direction and discipline . . . or being committed to his staying and producing." I hear another story of an energetic, charismatic Black girl "who took the place by storm" when she first arrived as a ninth-grader. She was an incredible actress, spent most of her time involved in dramatic productions, and neglected her other studies. Her academic struggles were heightened by the financial difficulties her working-class family was having paying for even the small costs beyond her generous scholarship. "Her parents did not understand the value of a Milton education . . . and didn't provide the needed encouragement and support," claims one of her close advisors.

One hears other tales of defeat at Milton. Certainly, privileged majority students occasionally get into academic or disciplinary trouble. But a great number of the stories of failure that I hear describe students from minority backgrounds, primarily from lower-class or working-class origins. As a matter of fact, many students and faculty point to the fine successes of Black students from professional, upper middle-class backgrounds. Catherine, a White senior going to Yale, tells me proudly that two Blacks in her class just won National Merit Scholarships. "They are just amazing, such super kids!" she exclaims. William, a tall, quiet light-skinned Black boy will go to Harvard next year. The son of a doctor who lives a few miles down the road from Milton, no one is surprised by his achievement or his decision to go to nearby Harvard. His English teacher would like to push him beyond his safe and "overly cautious" tendencies and wishes he had made a "more creative choice . . . and not followed the typical pattern." Another teacher makes a similar mild complaint of upper middle-class minority success. He tells me excitedly that the next student body president of Milton may be Black. In the morning assembly, a Black boy was one of three candidates who made campaign speeches and "he was head and shoulders above" his competitors. "He was the archetype preppy!" the teacher recalls with amazement; his voice mixing surprise with disappointment.

Most observers would agree that the tiny proportion of minority students inevitably leads to distorted perceptions. In the classes where minorities are present, there is most often only one, and their singular status heightens their visibility. "Most of the time I stick out like a sore thumb," says one dark-skinned girl matter of factly. Another middle-class Black girl, used to moving in a predominantly White world, claims that "there are not enough Black kids to make a group. We're scattered in all directions and there is no center." A third claims that when they sit together in the dining room "everyone says *we* are segregating ourselves off from other folks." Their remarks reflect feelings of high visibility and intense scrutiny. They also point to how difficult it is for them to find a comfortable place in community life. Those who accommodate fully to the language, style, and manner of their privileged white counterparts are regarded by some as bourgeois assimilationists; and those who attempt to shape some sort of minority group are viewed by many as separatists. There are simply too few of them to create diversity at Milton. There is not the critical mass. A sensitive White student, saddened by the departure of a Black friend, says, "There are just not enough of them to make it natural."

THE CRITICAL EDGE

Several minority students speak of their discomfort to me, as well as their moments of success and accommodation. In their minds, unease and pleasure are not necessarily incompatible experiences. Although I suspect that minority and majority students have qualitatively different experiences at Milton, this dualism is also expressed by majority students who are both applauding and critical of their school. The point is that there are degrees of comfort and adaptation to life at Milton, but the overriding impression is that it is a place where few feel comfortable. This lack of calm satisfaction and complacency is not to be regarded as a negative sign. It is almost a symbol of pride. Comfort might lead to a deadly lethargy, and people at Milton seem perpetually poised for discussion, questioning, and criticism. Most do not seem to tire of debate, but seem enlivened by the spirit of inquiry. The school is alternately described as "confused", "yeasty", "lively", "complaining", and "questioning" by its inhabitants. Despite the fact that students may complain of the regimentation and narrowing aspects of academic pursuit, their voices are lively with complaint and criticism. Some teachers appear to actively encourage tough criticism, even irreverence.

It is among faculty that I experienced the most active debate, sharp differences in perspective, and intense feelings. The divergences do not appear to reduce to factionalism or small group frictions, but to a variety of strongly expressed views. It is easy to see individual faces and hear voices in the large faculty because they rarely appear as a monolithic group. Everyone is not noisy or argumentative, but everyone I spoke to had an opinion, often one that was in sharp contrast with what they perceived to be general group beliefs. Although the headmaster sometimes has difficulty negotiating the troubled waters and orchestrating the many voices, he strongly believes in individual expression and diversity of opinions and is willing to risk the potential chaos.

For a stranger, the "yeasty" exchanges can often be heard as divisiveness, even hostility, and the complaining can be heard as deep dissatisfaction. But the longer one listens, the more one recognizes the legitimacy granted to expressing conflict and publicly examining divergent beliefs. Occasionally, the arguments sound almost playful. Many faculty warn me not to take the sharp exchanges "too seriously" even as they continue to voice their intense feelings. "We always behave as if our lives were on the line!" smiles an old-timer who claims it is an environment of "exaggeration." Milton seems all the more intense in contrast to other elite private schools that tend to have a more settled, unruffled façade.

Some believe that Milton's critical stance is related to the persistent idealism of faculty and administrators. With idealistic notions of what might be, the present, worldly scene will inevitably feel unsatisfying. A few students, used to the cynicism of their parents and imperfections of the wider world, are actually surprised by the idealistic goals of their teachers. Says one incredulously, "They want us to be real human beings in an inhuman world." A skilled and successful English teacher conveys the spirit of idealism and criticism as she contemplates the joys and disappointments of Milton. She begins by saying, "Milton is a fabulous school. . . . I teach a writing workshop for ninth graders and I try to say to the kids that writing is like a Rubik's cube, a puzzle. . . . It is a very exciting and illuminating process." She ends by saying, "Underlying my uneasiness is a great malaise. This notion of fitting things into forms, be it teaching ninth graders one lesson and giving them all the same assignment for the same night, or getting my students to think in terms of form for their writing to be coherent and convincing, or seeing students channeled through a series of courses and into college, this molding process depresses me more than ever. I know it has to go on . . . but still, in some students, I see such acquiescence. Why? Because they are dutiful, good, deferential students—all the things society and teachers taught them to be. What is frightening is the way students wonderfully, ingenuously proceed in this educative process. I wish there were more skepticism. I wish there were a greater sense of teachers doing service for students, instead of having students do what we want."

A sharp observer of Milton's history claims that the idealism has been strongly underscored by Jerry Pieh and his family. Though Lucy Pieh has staunchly resisted the traditional, stereotypic role of a headmaster's wife, she has had "a subtle and substantive influence on life here." Another faculty member refers to the Pieh family imprint: "The Piehs have lived out the idealism. . . . People honor and admire them as private individuals. Their life has been a model for the rest of the community."

It is not only idealism that leads to a "complaining" place, or even the pursuit of high standards. It is also, I think, the choice to create an institution that is "not an either/or, but a both/and" school. Finding a way to integrate boys and girls, boarders and day students, urban and suburban images; while still trying to preserve the integrity and goodness of each is a difficult, and maybe impossible challenge. The attempt to do everything, and do it well, almost invites imperfection and disappointment. But Milton continues to try, and try very hard, to achieve the synthesis.

The integration of realms means more than the rearrangements of structure and process. It rests on the clear examination and articulation of values. The history of girl/boy divisions, for instance, is a history of contrary values. Bringing these two schools together is like seeking an integration of moral perspectives. Risking oversimplification, one sees in the girl's school the dominating values of nurturance, privacy, and family, and in the boy's school the strong themes of competition, hierarchy, and success. A utopian synthesis of these two perspectives would incorporate the strengths of both and help students learn when to use the skills and strategies of each tradition. But Milton is not utopia.

In a girls' assembly, Mrs. Emmet, an alumna of Milton, looked straight into the storm and warned her audience of young women not to lose touch with their "feminine principles." In a talk entitled "Keeping Faith With Family," this elegant and dignified woman in her seventies; this author, environmentalist, mother, and grandmother, spoke forcefully about the strong and resilient female qualities that must not be lost in the pursuit of equality with males. Mrs. Emmet had been one of two young women in her Milton graduating class to go on to college ("a joker in the cards"), and began by recognizing the endless choices open to today's female graduates. "There is no occupation not open to you, including being a Supreme Court Justice . . . most prejudice, stereotypes, and restrictions have been removed."

With a soft but determined voice, Mrs. Emmet continued, "It is important not to lose touch with feminine nature. There are fundamental differences in the psychic natures of men and women, and a woman must maintain a connection to the roots of her feminine nature . . . I don't mean feminine wiles, but I mean feminine principles—a dynamic force, energy used in action. . . . Women have the feeling tendencies—not sentimental or soft—qualities of understanding, sympathy, and compassion. These qualities are found in both sexes, but they are more intrinsic to women. . . . The feminine nature is needed desperately at this point in history when there is a suicidal drive of the masculine. The western industrial world is the masculine world gone berserk; aggressive, given to excess. . . . But history is full of matriarchy. Women have made a huge contribution to cultural history. . . . The female, by nature, is homemaker, preserver. . . . Women, by nature, are conservationists."

The applause following Mrs. Emmet's talk was polite, but not enthusiastic. Many girls were offended by what they interpreted as classically "sexist and reactionary" comments about the woman's place. A large, imposing senior had rage in her voice, "Do you believe that women are, by nature, homemakers? Do you believe in non-sexist child raising? Do you think it might be early conditioning that causes these so-called female qualities? . . . Do you think the battle is won when there is not one boy in this audience? They were invited to come, but they'd rather lie out on the grass in the sun. . . . They see this as trivial!"

In the midst of the heated ideological debate, a junior stood to make a more personal statement. "I think men suffer from being strong and aggressive, but I think the world is turning. I know boys at Milton who remind me of my father . . . they have a soft, gentle side. . . . Aren't they being hurt also?" Her question hung in the air.

The dialogue, charged and spirited, reflected the vivid tensions of value and morality at Milton: the tensions between feminine and masculine perspectives, between historical and contemporary views, between achievement and nurturance, between nature and technology. These opposing themes, always to be struggled with and never to be resolved, create the energy and vitality of Milton, but also the persistent feelings of incompleteness and unease.

I remember again the first words uttered by the teacher with the furrowed brow during my initial visit to speak at Milton: "I think of my work as play . . . a great adventure," and I recognize the pleasure of his discomfort. Education, as adventure, will never feel complete or wholly satisfying. There will always be the gnawing imperfections. And then I remember seeing Janet Malcolm's *Psychoanalysis: The Impossible Profession* on Milton's library shelf and recall the quotation that begins her book.

It almost looks as if analysis were the third of those "impossible" professions in which one can be sure beforehand of achieving unsatisfying results. The other two, which have been known much longer, are education and government.

—Sigmund Freud
"Analysis Terminable and Interminable" (1937)

PART FOUR

GROUP PORTRAIT

VII

On Goodness in
High Schools

THE IMPERFECTIONS OF GOODNESS

The search for "good" schools is elusive and disappointing if by goodness we mean something close to perfection. These portraits of good schools reveal imperfections, uncertainties, and vulnerabilities in each of them. In fact, one could argue that a consciousness about imperfections, and the willingness to admit them and search for their origins and solutions is one of the important ingredients of goodness in schools.

This orientation towards imperfection was most vividly expressed in Milton Academy, where the philosophical ideals of humanism invited tough self-criticism, persistent complaints, and nagging disappointments. Among students, faculty, and administrators there was a clear recognition of the unevenness and weaknesses of their school. Criticism was legitimized, even encouraged. The stark visibility of the institutional vulnerabilities was related, I think, to a deeply rooted tolerance for conflict, idealism, and to feelings of security. In trying to press toward idealistic goals, there were always disappointments concerning the present realities. Headmaster Peih, for example, saw the strengths and vulnerabilities of Milton as the "flip sides of the same coin." The individualistic orientation and collective authority of Milton offered opportunities for power, autonomy, and initiative to students and teachers, but it also permitted criticism and abuse from members who attacked the non-authoritarian, decentralized structure. The "house of cards" was fragile and vulnerable to those who did not believe in it or who sought to undo it, but allowed an openness and flexibility that would be impossible if the pyramid were firmly and rigidly glued together.

Not only did teachers, administrators, and students at Milton recognize imperfections and offer open criticisms, some even seemed to enjoy the lack of certainty, the impending chaos, and the "exaggerated" environment. More than tolerating the rough edges, they delighted in facing them openly and squarely. Certainly there was a range of tolerance for confronting imperfections at Milton. Some people seemed to welcome the "yeasty" exchanges while others grew impatient with the conflicts and confusion. But, in general, the school community saw goodness, frustration, and criticism as compatible responses. In fact, they believed that goodness was only possible if the imperfections were made visible and open for inspection.

Although less inviting of conflict than Milton, Brookline people also spoke of goodness as being inextricably linked with self-criticism. While recognizing their school's exemplary qualities, they also pointed to its vulnerabilities. For example, teachers often referred to the high-powered, achieving, largely upper middle-class students who inhabited the Honors courses and spoke proudly of their abilities. At the same time, most admitted the degrading, divisive qualities of ability grouping and the disproportionate numbers of lower-class and minority students in the bottom levels. Without defensiveness, Bob McCarthy, the headmaster, pointed to the "two totally separate schools" at Brookline—one an elite academy, the other a tough environment dominated by disaffected students turned off from learning. Facing the persistent inequalities and stark differences was a critical part of McCarthy's agenda. It required a clear articulation of the problem and a shift in images of goodness. "People used to say diversity was a weakness," he said firmly and optimistically. "Now we are saying diversity is a strength. This is an important shift in orientation for faculty, students, and the community." At Brookline, then, goodness was not only enmeshed with a recognition of imperfections, but it was also related to changing perceptions of what is good— shifting ideals of excellence.

Being less secure in its identity and less certain of its emerging strengths than Brookline or Milton, the George Washington Carver High School sought to create an invincible image, free of imperfections. The shiny, slick vision portrayed by Principal Hogans, displayed in the slide show, and enacted in the graduation ceremonies did not match the difficult and changing realities underneath. It was in the dissonance between image and reality, in the denial of the many visible signs of weakness, that Carver was most vulnerable to defeat. Hogans, recognizing the need for motivation and inspiration of students and faculty, presented an idealized picture that he hoped would galvanize their energies. To the wider world, he offered overly optimistic and smooth images in order to shift long-entrenched public perceptions and inspire generous gifts. The focus on images, though understandable, drew attention away from the substance of education and the interior of the institution. In an attempt to portray goodness, the imperfections tended to be ignored, denied, or camouflaged. Hogans, who often talked about "selling the product" and "projecting the model," must have felt he could not afford to admit the weaknesses of Carver for fear of losing the momentum of change. Once having managed to "disturb the inertia," he did not want to risk being pulled back down into the mire. He had to keep moving outward and upward. Recognizing the vulnerabilities would have required contemplation, a deliberative process which might have undone all he had accomplished. At Carver, the denial of imperfections was a signal of vulnerability, just as the recognition of more subtle weaknesses at Milton was a sign of confidence and strength.

This more modest orientation towards goodness does not rest on absolute or discrete qualities of excellence and perfection, but on views of institutions that anticipate change, conflict, and imperfection. The search for good schools has often seemed to be marked by a standard much like the societal expectations attached to good mothers: enduring qualities of nurturance, kindness, stimulation, and stability. Inevitably, this search finds no winners. No mothers can match these idealized pictures and the vast majority must be labeled inadequate. But if one recognizes, as many scholars and lay people now do, that mothers (no matter how tender and talented) are uneven in their mothering, that their goodness has inevitable flaws, then one finds a great many more "good mothers." D. W. Winnicott, a British psychoanalyst, calls them "good enough" mothers— thus removing the absolutist standard and admitting human frailty and vulnerability as integral to worthiness.[1]

In many ways I believe that this more generous view should also apply to perceptions of schools. The search should be for "good enough" schools—not meant to imply minimal standards of talent and competence, but rather to suggest a view that welcomes change and anticipates imperfection. I would underscore, once again, that I am not arguing for lower standards or reduced quality. I am urging a definition of good schools that sees them whole, changing, and imperfect. It is in articulating and confronting each of these dimensions that one moves closer and closer to the institutional supports of good education.

The reference to conscious change as a central quality of good schools points to another aspect of goodness underscored in these portraits: the staged quality of goodness. It is clear that these six schools are not equally good; neither do they judge themselves by the same standards. St. Paul's, confident, secure, and privileged, can focus on the subtleties of excellence. Assured that the vast majority of their graduates will move on to prestigious colleges and universities, the faculty do not worry much about skills preparation for the college boards, how to perform during college interviews, or teaching the social graces and nuances of elite university culture. Those behaviors are firmly embedded in the everyday life of St. Paul's. For many students, they have been reinforced by generations of family heritage. The appropriate attitudes seep through the students' pores without deliberate effort. For the most part, then, St. Paul's can concentrate on the finer points of education: the art of criticism, the skills of analysis, the aesthetics of writing. All of these become part of the institutional definition of goodness.

Highland Park, less secure in its abundance, less certain of its goals, carefully counts the heads of those who go on to prestigious Eastern schools and memorizes the number of National Merit scholars graduating each year. There is great pressure from parents for their children to succeed academically, and counselors and teachers work to counteract the harsh and grueling demands. In Highland Park, the standards of goodness are primarily limited to the group most likely to succeed—the affluent, largely Jewish community—and to their success in being admitted to colleges of status. Competition and hierarchy are accepted by many as inevitable by-products of the drive to achieve. There are winners and losers. The standards of excellence are applied to winners.

In Atlanta, teachers at George Washington Carver High School hope that their students will become industrious, hard-working citizens. School people focus on the measurable, visible indices of progress: steady attendance rates, fewer disciplinary problems, a decline in acts of vandalism to property, and more jobs filled upon graduation. On each of these indices, Carver has made great strides under Hogans's leadership. The standards of goodness also include the more psychosocial, less measurable qualities of civility, poise, and ambition. Carver still lags behind many other Atlanta high schools on indices that reflect the substance of education, curricular design and structure, and pedagogical processes. There are a few shining examples of competent and inspired teachers who battle the educational malaise, and a great many faculty who deeply believe in motivating and supporting the talents of their students, working hard at building strong self-images in them. But the school has a long way to go before it could claim that most students were receiving a good education. Looking back at the chaos, disintegration, and negligence before Hogans, one is impressed with the great progress that has been made in four years. The qualities of goodness reflect the impressive changes, the progress from terrible to much better, an improving school.

These more minimal standards of goodness I would envision as a first stage of movement towards higher goals. Order and decorum are required *before* the deliberative acts of criticism and contemplation. Regular attendance is required before any teaching can be done. It is not that we would be content if Carver's educational standards never reached any higher, or if faculty felt satisfied with orderliness, cleanliness, and passivity among students. But we must recognize, it seems to me, that institutional invigoration and restoration is a slow, cumbersome process; that present judgments must include a view of historical precedents; and that there are jagged stages of institutional development.

Not only has the search for good schools been absolutist in quality, it has also been encumbered by the negative tones of social science inquiry—the tendency for researchers to uncover malignancies rather than health. This temptation was evident in the *Daedalus* deliberations on secondary schools, but is a far more pervasive phenomenon. It is almost as if there is a cynical, complaining edge to much of social science investigation that begins by asking what is missing, wrong, or incomplete, rather than asking what is happening, or even what is good. Understandably, most social observers feel compelled to inquire about pressing social problems rather than document healthy and workable environments. Their social consciences turn them toward issues of survival, pain, and struggle. Why waste their wisdom on thriving people and prosperous institutions?

I support the quest for solving "real" problems of human struggle and pain, and I know that my work has been largely inspired by these fundamental concerns. I do not object, therefore, to heightened concern for profound, rather than trivial problems. My skepticism lies in the more subtle emphasis of the literature—an emphasis that points towards weakness rather than strength, uniformity rather than diversity of standards, undermining rather than supporting the subjects of inquiry. What impact does this have on the investigation of schools? It seems to me that it has led to an exaggeration of the negative elements of schooling, undermined the spirit and energy of school people, and limited our understanding of the myriad ways in which schools might be organized and structured. At this point, I am not squabbling with the serious intentions of researchers, their systematic methods or their sense of responsibility, but I am complaining about the subtle assumptions of weakness and wrongdoing that undergirds much of their work.

This responsible scholarship on schooling has been additionally fueled by the journalistic, muckraking accounts of writers who have made angry assaults on schools as oppressive, imprisoning environments. Most of these passionate attacks on schools appeared in the late sixties and early seventies and echoed the liberal rhetoric and radical chic of that period. Many of the charges of abuse, neglect, and incompetence leveled at teachers and administrators were warranted and needed to be disclosed to a large audience; but the attacks were also myopic and misinformed. They victimized people who were themselves caught in an impossibly unresponsive and uncaring system, who themselves felt victimized. But more important, the angry accounts lacked empathy and rarely searched for the origins of weakness and abuse. In *Death At An Early Age*, for example, Jonathan Kozol made headlines revealing the atrocities of a ghetto school in Boston. He spent a year teaching his young Black charges, moving from optimism and innocence to guarded realism and anger. After getting out of the cauldron and removing himself from the implications of guilt, he turned on his former colleagues and charged them with being empty, disenchanted, and stupid. The anger at the children's wasted youth and the assaults on the teachers' characters and spirit were fully justified. The arrogance and biting cynicism of Kozol, however, was dysfunctional and added fuel to the already smoldering school battles.[2]

The combined impact of the subtle negativisms of social science investigations and the flagrant attacks of muckrakers over the last few decades has produced a cultural attitude towards schools which assumes their inadequacies and denies evidence of goodness. This pessimism and cynicism has had a peculiarly American cast.[3] The persistent complaints seem to reflect a powerful combination of romanticism, nostalgia, and feelings of loss for a simpler time when values were clear; when children were well behaved; when family and schools agreed on educational values and priorities; when the themes of honor, respect, and loyalty directed human interaction. In comparison to this idealized retrospective view, the contemporary realities of school seem nothing short of catastrophic. David K. Cohen, in a powerful essay entitled "Loss As A Theme of Social Policy," talks about the ways in which our grief over a lost community frames our views of today's chaos.[4] We envision an idealized past of homogeneous and firmly entrenched values, and the contemporary conflict over competing moral systems appears threatening. We envision a time long ago when communities and neighborhoods were glued together by mutual exchange, deeply felt gratitude, and common interests, making today's transient city blocks and urban anonymity appear profoundly troublesome.[5]

However, the romanticism and idealization of the past is most vividly felt when we look back at schooling. Rural and small town images flood our minds; pictures of earnest, healthy children sitting dutifully in a spare classroom; big students attending to the small ones. The teacher, a revered and dedicated figure, lovingly and firmly dispenses knowledge, and the conscientious children, hungry for learning, respond thoughtfully to the teacher's bidding. These romantic pictures, that many Americans continue to refer to when they look at today's schools, produce feelings of great disappointment and disenchantment.

Today's high schools, in particular, seem farthest away from this idealized past. They appear grotesque in their permissiveness and impending chaos. The large, unruly adolescents appear threatening, and their swiftly changing, faddish preoccupations are baffling to their parents' conservative eyes. It is simply difficult for parents and the community to see them as "good." They are seen as scary and incomprehensible, or dull and boring. Rarely can adults look beyond their comparisons with idealized visions of a more simple and orderly world, beyond the mannerly high school scenes that they remember, beyond the often trivial swings of adolescent fashion and habit, to see the good inside the institutions adolescents inhabit.[6]

After years of doing research in schools for very young children, I recall these vague feelings of threat and disappointment when I began visiting high schools. I was struck by how physically large the students were, how I was sometimes confused about who was teacher and who was student. Boys with men's voices, bearded faces, and huge, bulky frames filled the hallways with their large movements. Girls, with their painted faces, pseudo-sophisticated styles, lady's gossip, and casual swagger seemed to be so different from the pleated skirts, bobby socks, and ponytails that I remembered from my high school days. At first I was shocked by the children in adult frames, afraid of their groupiness, and saw the lingering dangers just below the surface of tenuous order. As I became increasingly accustomed to their presence, their habits, their rituals, I began to see the vulnerabilities and uncertainties of adolescents, rather than be preoccupied with the symbols of maturity and power. In a strange way, I began to be reminded of my own adolescence and saw great similarities between my high school days and the contemporary scene. But before I could explore and document "the good" in these high schools, I had to move inside them, grow accustomed to today's scene, and learn the difference between my own inhibitions and fears and the real warnings of danger. Perceptions of today's high schools, therefore, are plagued by romanticized remembrances of "the old days" and anxiety about the menacing stage of adolescence. Both of these responses tend to distort society's view of high schools and support the general tendency to view them as other than good.

PERMEABLE BOUNDARIES AND INSTITUTIONAL CONTROL

The standards by which schools define their goodness are derived from internal and external sources, from past and present realities, and from projected future goals. One is struck by how much more control private schools have over definitions and standards of goodness than their public school counterparts. In St. Paul's, for example, there is a sustained continuity of values and standards that is relatively detached from the mercurial changes in the wider society; it is a continuity that is internally defined. Surrounded by acres of magnificent woods and lakes and secluded in the hills of New Hampshire, it feels faraway from the harsh realities faced by most public secondary schools. The focus is inward and backward. Movement towards the future is guided by strong and deeply rooted historical precedents, ingrained habits, and practiced traditions. The precedents are fiercely defended by alumni who want the school to remain as they remember it, old and dedicated faculty who proudly carry the mantle of traditionalism, and the rector who sees the subtle interactions of historical certainty and adventurous approaches to the future. It is not that St. Paul's merely resists change and blindly defends traditionalism, but that it views history as a solid bedrock, an anchor in a shifting and turbulent sea.

In addition, St. Paul's faces changes with a clear consciousness and great control over the choices it creates. The changes are deliberate, calculated, and balanced against the enduring habits. Ten years ago, for example, St. Paul's became coeducational, a major change in the population and self-perception of the institution. Certainly, there are ample examples of lingering sexism. Women faculty are few and experience the subtle discrimination of tokenism. But one is more impressed with the thorough integration of boys and girls, the multiple leadership roles girls play in the life of the school, and the easy, comfortable relationships that seem to develop between the sexes. Although the decision to become coeducational represented a critical and potentially disruptive change in school culture, the planning was carefully executed, the choice was self-imposed, and the negotiations were internally controlled.

Highland Park offers an example of a largely reactive institution with standards imposed from the outside. One is immediately aware of the school's permeable boundaries and sees the ways in which internal structures and goals reflect shifts in societal trends. The control of standards largely originates within the immediate community, which receives and interprets messages from the wider society. The waves of change reverberate within the school and administrators and faculty are often put in the position of trying to resist the shifts, negotiate a middle ground, or offer alternative views. The principal describes his role as largely reactive. Poised between the often opposed constituencies of parents and teachers, he acts as an interpreter and negotiator, and not as a visionary or initiating leader. He remarks sadly that the school is no longer at the moral center of the community; that it has become a "satellite" in the lives of students. The "real world" defines what is important and the school lags closely behind or it risks obsolescence.

The curriculum and academic structure of Highland Park, for example, have closely followed the trends of progressivism and liberalism that dominated social attitudes during the late 1960s and 1970s, and reverted back to the conservatism that resurfaced in the early 1980s. When feminist rhetoric was at its height, it was not uncommon to see boys in the home economics and interior design courses and many girls clamoring for courses in auto repair and industrial arts. Now the traditional sex-related patterns have been largely re-established and the increased competition, rigid status hierarchies, and return to subjects that will "pay off" echo the resurgence of conservative attitudes abroad in society. An old-timer on the Highland Park faculty, who has watched the shifting trends for almost three decades, refuses to become invested in the newest wrinkle. She wishes the school leadership would take a firmer, more conscious position on the school's intellectual goals and the moral values that guide them, and looks with sympathy at her younger colleagues who ride the waves of change not knowing where the tide will land.

Brookline, faced with many of the same shifts in standards and morality as Highland Park, has responded differently. Certainly it experiences similar societal reverberations within its walls, but it has also taken a more deliberate, initiating stance in relation to them. In the mid-to-late 1970s, the increased diversity of the student body caused factionalism, divisiveness, and eruptions of violence in the school. A counselor speaks of these harsh encounters as distinct echoes of the racial strife in the wider Boston community. Under the new leadership of Bob McCarthy, school violence was no longer tolerated. First, McCarthy helped his teachers express their long-suppressed rage at the inappropriate student behavior; second, there were immediate and harsh punishments handed down to all of the aggressors; and third, the school began to look upon "the problem" of diversity as a rich resource. The battle against factionalism is not won. The shifts in consciousness are elusive and difficult to implant in community life. Everyone continues to speak of the stark divisions among racial and ethnic groups; but now those students who manage to move across the boundaries tend to be perceived as strong and unthreatened. There is a clear admiration for their risk taking and their versatility. The social worker who once saw the school as an echo of the inequalities and injustices of the community, now says it serves as an asylum for many; a place of safety from violence; a place to learn different patterns of behavior; a place to take risks.

Headmaster McCarthy's attempts at restructuring patterns of authority in Brookline High are also aimed at undoing behaviors and attitudes learned in the wider world and marking the distinctions between school and society. Adolescents are offered a piece of the power in exchange for responsible action. It is an uphill battle. Many students prefer a more passive, reactive role and resist the demands of responsibility and authority; others are suspicious of bargaining with any adult and do not trust McCarthy's rhetoric. But the school's efforts are conscious and deliberate, designed to counteract the cultural, ideological sweeps of contemporary society and make clear decisions about philosophical goals and moral codes.

In these three examples we see great variations in the ways in which boundaries are drawn between the school and the community. St. Paul's high standards, goals, and values are most protected from societal imperatives, most preciously guarded, and most thoroughly ingrained. They are chosen and defended. Highland Park mirrors the societal shifts, sometimes offering resistance but rarely initiating conscious counter plans. Brookline lies somewhere between these approaches to the outside world. Its walls are not impenetrable, but neither are they invisible. Brookline has permeable boundaries that provide intercourse with and separation from society. Attempts are made to defend the school from the severity of societal intrusions, define educational goals and standards through internal consensus, and build resilient intellectual and moral structures.

Kennedy High School resembles Brookline in its conscious and deliberate attempts to define boundaries between inside and out. Bob Mastruzzi recognizes the need to be knowledgeable about the social, economic, and cultural patterns of the surrounding community; the need to have a heightened visibility in the neighborhood; and the need to be a keen observer of and participant in the political networks of the borough, city, and state. His role as "community leader" is designed to assure Kennedy's survival in a skeptical, sometimes hostile, community. Without his devoted community work, Mastruzzi fears the school would face politically debilitating negativism from neighborhood forces. But Mastruzzi does not merely reach out and embrace the community, he also articulates the strong contrasts between neighborhood values and priorities and those that guide the school. It is not that he capitulates to community pressure. Rather, he sees his role as interpreter and negotiator of the dissonant strains that emerge in the school-community interface. Sometimes he must engage in calculated, but intense, battles where the differences flare into heated conflicts. He was ready and willing to fight when he believed the Marblehead residents in the nearby working-class neighborhood did not adhere to the negotiated settlement both parties had reached.

However, Mastruzzi's concern with defining workable boundaries is not limited to establishing relationships with the wider community. He is at least as preoccupied with negotiating the bureaucratic terrain of the New York City school system. There are layers of administrators and decision makers in the central office whose priorities and regulations affect the internal life of Kennedy. These external requirements are felt most vividly by the principal and assistant principals, who must find effective and legal adaptations of the prescribed law. Once again, Mastruzzi does not passively conform to the regulations of the "central authorities." He tries to balance the school's need for autonomy and the system's need for uniform standards. He distinguishes between the spirit and the letter of the law, sometimes ignoring the latter when the literal interpretation is a poor match for his school's needs. He also serves as a "buffer" against the persistent intrusions of the wider system in order to offer his faculty and staff the greatest possible freedom and initiative.[7]

Institutional control is a great deal easier for schools with abundant resources, non-public funding, and historical stability. It is not only that private schools tend to be more protected from societal trends, divergent community demands, and broader bureaucratic imperatives; they are also more likely to have the advantage of the material and psychological resources of certainty. In many ways, these six schools seem to exist in different worlds. The inequalities are dramatic, the societal injustices flagrant. One has feelings of moral outrage as one makes the transition from the lush, green 1,700 acres of St. Paul's to the dusty streets of the Carver Homes where the median income is less than $4,000 a year. How could we possibly expect a parity of educational standards between these point-edly different environments? Of course, St. Paul's enjoys more control, more precision, more subtlety. Of course, life at St. Paul's is smoother and more aesthetic.

Yet despite the extreme material contrasts, there are ways in which each institution searches for control and coherence. Gaining control seems to be linked to the development of a visible and explicit ideology. Without the buffers of land and wealth, Carver must fashion a strong ideological message. It is not a surprising message. Even with the newly contrived rhetoric of "interfacing" and "networking" used by Dr. Ho-gans, the ideological appeal is hauntingly similar to the messages given to many Carver student ancestors. Several generations ago, for example, Booker T. Washington, one of Hogans's heroes, spoke forcefully to young Black men and women about opportunities for advancement in a White man's world. He urged them to be mannerly, civilized, patient, and en-during; not rebellious, headstrong, or critical. They were told of the dan-gers of disruption and warned about acting "uppity" or arrogant. Al-though they were encouraged in their patience, these Black ancestors recognized the profound injustices, the doors that would be closed to them even if they behaved admirably. Industriousness was the only way to move ahead and ascend the ladders of status, but Black folks recog-nized that the system was ultimately rigged.

Carver's idelogical stance, enthusiastically articulated by Hogans, echoes these early admonitions—be good, be clean, be mannerly, and have a great deal of faith. Recognize the rigged race but run as hard as you can to win. School is the training ground for learning skills and civility, for learning to lose gracefully, and for trying again in the face of defeat. Education is the key to a strong sense of self-esteem, to personal and collective power. Hogans's rhetoric, old as the hills and steeped in cultural metaphors and allusions, strikes a responsive chord in the com-munity and serves as a rallying cry for institution building. His ideologi-cal message is reinforced by the opportunities Hogans creates for the immediate gratification of success and profit and to the connections he reinforces between education and religion. When Carver students, in their gleaming white Explorer jackets, cross the railroad tracks and enter the places of money and power in downtown Atlanta, their eyes are open to new life possibilities. Hogans tells them their dreams can come true. The work programs at Carver provide the daily experiences of industry, punctuality, and poise; and the immediate rewards that keep them involved in school.

The connections to church and religion, though less clearly etched, underscore the fervor attached to education by generations of powerless, illiterate people. The superintendent of Atlanta uses spiritual metaphors when he urges parents and students to join the "community of believers."[8] Carver faculty and administrators reinforce the religious messages and link them to themes of self-discipline, community building, and hard work at school. Hogans's rhetoric is culturally connected, clearly articulated, and visibly executed in student programs, assemblies, and reward ceremonies. The ideology is legible and energizing to school cohesion.

One sees a similar enthusiasm and ideological clarity at Milton Academy. Humanism and holistic medicine are broad labels that refer to a responsiveness to individual differences, to a diversity of talent, and to the integration of mind, body, and spirit in educational pursuits. Headmaster Pieh offers a subtle and complex message about providing a productive and nurturant ethos that will value individual needs; the registrar develops a hand-built schedule so that students can receive their first choices of courses, and teachers know the life stories and personal dilemmas of each of their students. Underneath the New England restraint of Milton, there is a muted passion for humanism. Students talk about the special quality of relationships it provides ("They want us to be more humane than human beings in the real world"), teachers worry over the boundaries between loving attention and indulgence, and the director of admissions offers it as the primary appeal of Milton, a distinct difference from the harsh, masculine qualities of Exeter. Although Carver and Milton preach different ideologies, what is important here is the rigorous commitment to a visible ideological perspective. It provides cohesion within the community and a measure of control against the oscillating intrusions from the larger society.

Highland Park lacks this clear and resounding ideological stance. The educational vision shifts with the times as Principal Benson and his teachers listen for the beat of change and seek to be adaptive. Although the superb record of college admissions provides institutional pride, it does not replace the need for a strong ideological vision. Rather than creating institutional cohesion, the quest for success engenders harsh competition among students. The persistent complaints from many students that they feel lost and alone is in part a statement about the missing ideological roots. Without a common bond, without a clear purpose, the school fails to encompass them and does not take psychological hold on their energies. The director of counselling at Highland Park observes students reaching out to one another through a haze of drugs in order to reduce feelings of isolation and dislocation. Drugs are the great "leveler," providing a false sense of connection and lessening the nagging pain. A minority of students are spared the loneliness and only a few can articulate "the problem," but it is visible to the stranger who misses "the school spirit."

Ideological fervor is an important ingredient of utopian communities. Distant from the realities of the world and separated from societal institutions, these communities can sustain distinct value structures and reward systems. In his book *Asylums*, Erving Goffman makes a distinction between "total institutions" that do not allow for any intercourse with the outer world and organizations that require only a part of a person's time, energy, and commitment. In order to sustain themselves, however, all institutions must have what Goffman calls "encompassing tendencies" that wrap their members up in a web of identification and affiliation, that inspire loyalty.[9]

Schools must find way of inspiring devotion and loyalty in teachers and students, of marking the boundaries between inside and outside, of taking a psychological hold on their members. Some schools explicitly mark their territories and offer clear rules of delineation. Parochial schools, for instance, are more encompassing than public schools because they vigorously resist the intrusions of the outer world and frame their rituals and habits to purposefully contrast with the ordinary life of their students. Parents who choose to send their children to parochial schools support the values and ideological stance of the teachers and the clear separation between school life and community norms.[10] Quaker schools often mark the transition from outside to inside school by several minutes of silence and reflection at the beginning of the school day. After the noise, energy, and stress of getting to school, students must collect themselves and be still and silent. Those moments separate them from non-school life and prepare them to be encompassed by the school's culture.

Although I am not urging schools to become utopian communities or total institutions, I do believe that good schools balance the pulls of connection to community against the contrary forces of separation from it. Administrators at Kennedy vividly portray their roles as a "balancing act." They walk the treacherous "tightrope" between closed and open doors, between autonomy and symbiosis. Schools need to provide asylum for adolescents from the rugged demands of outside life at the same time that they must always be interactive with it. The interaction is essential. Without the connection to life beyond school, most students would find the school's rituals empty. It is this connection that motivates them.

For Carver students, it is a clear exchange. "I'll commit myself to school for the promise of a job . . . otherwise forget it," says a junior who describes himself as "super-realistic." Milton Academy symbolizes the attempts at balance between separation and connection in its public relations material. The catalogue cover pictures the quiet, suburban campus with the city looming in the background. The director of admissions speaks enthusiastically about the meshing of utopian idealism and big-city realities. The day students arrive each morning and "bring the world with them." The seniors speak about the clash between the school's humanitarian spirit and the grueling requirements of college admissions. The protection and solace good schools offer may come from the precious abundance of land, wealth, and history, but they may also be partly approached through ideological clarity and a clear vision of institutional values.

FEMININE AND MASCULINE QUALITIES OF LEADERSHIP

The people most responsible for defining the school's vision and articulating the ideological stance are the principals and headmasters of these schools. They are the voice, the mouthpiece of the institution, and it is their job to communicate with the various constituencies. Their personal image is inextricably linked to the public persona of the institution.

The literature on effective schools tends to agree on at least one point—that an essential ingredient of good schools is strong, consistent, and inspired leadership.[11] The tone and culture of schools is said to be defined by the vision and purposeful action of the principal. He is said to be the person who must inspire the commitment and energies of his faculty; the respect, if not the admiration of his students; and the trust of the parents. He sits on the boundaries between school and community; must negotiate with the superintendent and school board; must protect teachers from external intrusions and harrasment; and must be the public imagemaker and spokesman for the school.[12] In high schools the principals are disproportionately male, and the images and metaphors that spring to mind are stereotypically masculine. One thinks of the military, protecting the flanks, guarding the fortress, defining the territory. The posture is often seen as defensive, the style clear, rational, and focused.

323

One imagines the perfect principal will exhibit an economy of thought and action, impeccable judgment, and a balanced fairness. Decisions should not be obscured by prejudice or emotion. One rarely thinks about the principal as a person with needs for support, counsel, and nurturance. Somehow he stands alone, unencumbered by the normal human frailties. He is bigger than life.

The military image of steely objectivity, rationality, and erect posture intersects with another compelling prototype: principal as coach and former jock. Certainly, in every school system there have been ample examples of football coaches rising to prominence as popular male mentors, community heroes, and finally no-nonsense principals. The coach image offers a different set of male metaphors. Rather than emphasizing the impeccable judgment and cold rationality of the military man, the coach-principal is known for his brawn, masculine physicality, brute energy, and enthusiasm. He is expected to use the same powers of motivation and drive he used as a coach to inspire faculty and students; and his talents are likely to be focused on building team spirit, loyalty, and devotion. This charisma and force are often derived from his former stature as a sports figure in the community. Some people can even remember the old days when he was a tough young athlete with a lot of hustle and muscles gleaming with sweat. Few high school principals match this caricature, but the images of effective leaders are partly shaped by these exaggerated male images.

A third, softer image often associated with the role and person of the principal envisions him as father figure: benign, stern, and all-knowing. The father is seen as the great protector of his large and loyal family. He will offer guidance, security, and protection in exchange for unquestioned loyalty and approval. He will exude what Richard Sennett refers to as "paternalistic authority"—an authority which assumes the leader knows what is best for his followers. His wisdom, experience, and lofty status put him in a position high above petty turmoil; and his "children" will be spared from the harsh realities of the world if they submit fully, listen intently, and follow in line.[13]

In each of these dominant principal images, authority is centralized; power is hierarchically arranged with the principal poised at the top of a steep pyramid; the metaphors are strikingly masculine; and personal characteristics combine with institutional role to produce a bigger than life-size figure. And in each of these images the principal stands alone, without support and guidance from others. To admit the need for support or comfort would be to express weakness, softness, and femininity.

The military, jock, father caricatures of the principal reflect exaggerated, anachronistic perspectives on the role and the man. Yet the expectations and views of high school leaders continue to be influenced by the caricatures. When school leaders diverge too far from the ingrained images, their followers often feel threatened, distrustful, and unsafe. A deputy of Brookline's principal talked about the discomfort many faculty feel with Headmaster McCarthy's attempts to be an "ordinary person." They want him to express the superiority, infallibility, and distance of a classic headmaster. They worry about who is sailing the ship, navigating the course, and protecting them from disaster. In Milton, some reluctant faculty complain about the broad distribution of power. They accuse Headmaster Pieh of being afraid to make decisions, get frustrated with the inefficiency of collective action, and are wary of the masking of an enormous amount of informal power. The single complaint about Mastruzzi's inspired leadership at Kennedy is his persistent attempts to encourage broad-based participation among his staff. Mastruzzi recognizes the potential inefficiencies of collective decision making and is willing to endure them in exchange for the positive gains of building commitment within his faculty. Yet his admirers and critics alike tend to interpret these actions as weakness, his "one tragic flaw", his inability "to say no" and act decisively.[14]

In all of the schools I visited, the leaders, all male, did cast a long shadow and did match some of the stereotypic images of principals. They were all primarily responsible for defining the public image of the school, establishing relationships with parents, creating networks with the surrounding community, and inspiring the commitment of teachers. Beyond these duties, they defined their roles and relationships very differently, and exhibited dramatically contrasting styles. Their styles reflected their character, temperament, and individual inclinations as well as the demands and dynamics of the institution. Despite the great variations among them, perceptions of the six principals were partially shaped by the three caricatures discussed above. For example, Mastruzzi, former coach at De Witt Clinton High, felt a strong identification with his colleagues in Kennedy's physical education department, exuded a powerful physicality, and used a language laced with sports metaphors. One of his favorite pastimes was to stand at his office window proudly gazing down on the athletic fields below. He particularly liked to watch poor city kids learning sports like tennis and soccer, formerly the exclusive province of upper-class youngsters. There was a lot of "the coach" still left in Principal Mastruzzi.

Principal Hogans, with the brawn and toughness of an ex-football player and the dominating paternalism of a "Big Daddy," combined the coach and father images. His constant references to "being part of the team," to "hustling hard," and to "benching" those who didn't play hard and tough were vividly reminiscent of the jock world in which he had risen into prominence. His regard of teachers as childlike and submissive matched the father-principal role. He would keep teachers in line through strict rules, firm regulations, and hard punishments. He would nourish them through their bellies (not their heads or hearts) by feeding them a good, southern-style breakfast every morning.

With great restraint and subtlety, the rector at St. Paul's also reinforced fatherly relationships with faculty and students. His image combined a benign, autocratic style that felt both protective and frightening to all of those below him. The vision of consummate poise and serenity seemed even loftier than most father-figures. Male rationality and precision marked his approach and made his cover almost impenetrable. The title "Rector" means "ruler" and his fatherly leadership had the qualities of distance and cool dominance that match the imperial stance. Many of the older faculty appreciated the protection and security of the classic father, while some of the younger faculty quietly resisted the childlike urges it encouraged. Feeling great respect for the calm and efficient leadership the rector provided, they wanted to break out of the suffocating restraints of his autocratic directives. Theirs was a position of great ambivalence—one that has distinct analogies in family life. They enjoyed the rector's clearly powerful position when it provided protection and solace, but when it felt limiting to their autonomy and adulthood, they quietly resented the inhibitions.

Principal Benson at Highland Park represented an imperfect example of leader as military man. Certainly his style was softer and he worked very hard at "keeping a low profile," but he did exude the polish, rationality, and steely toughness of a military leader and saw his role in territorial terms. That is, he sat on the uncomfortable boundaries between parents and teachers, acting as buffer, interpreter, and negotiator. He received commands from his superior, the superintendent, and he acted smoothly and decisively. The weariness that he spoke of seemed to stem from the endless demands of defining and defending territories, and his attempts at rationality in the face of passionate battles waged by parents on behalf of their children.

Although in the examples of Kennedy, Carver, St. Paul's, and Highland Park one sees evidence of the imprint of exaggerated masculine stereotypes, I am struck by how each of the four leaders has adapted the stereotype to match the setting and his needs. There is an uncanny match between personal temperament, leadership style, and school culture. For example, the abundance and stability of St. Paul's permitted a subtle, cool leadership, almost understated in its character. Whereas the newly emerging, fast-building Carver High School required the visible charisma of Dr. Hogans—aggressive, undaunted, relentless—combining a profound commitment to Black youth and community and some measure of personal ambition. Both Hogans and Oates are visible leaders who cut clear figures, but part of their effectiveness lies in the adaptation and matching of leadership style and institutional life. One cannot imagine their changing places with one another. Hogans would be too brash and colorful for the restrained and cultured environment of St. Paul's and Bill Oates would be overwhelmed by the neediness and vulnerabilities of Carver. Each would feel uncomfortable and lost in the other's environment.

Looking at the match between institutional life and leadership style alters somewhat the view of dominance etched by the three caricatures of principal. Coach-principals are unlikely to take hold or wield power in a school that resists being molded into a team. Fatherly principals must be supported by teachers and students who are willing to respond with the impulses and associations of a big family. If we recognize that, in order to be effective, leaders must pick up cues from institutional culture, then the spotlight on power shifts. Leadership is never wholly unidirectional, even when there is stark asymmetry of power between leaders and followers. There are always elements of interaction, even symbiosis, between the leaders and the organization. If the match is unworkable, if the leader totally resists or ignores deeply ingrained institutional imperatives, then he will not be effective.

The three caricatures of principal are further altered by examining the leaders' perceptions of their own needs. The caricatures picture a man standing strong and alone without support or guidance from others, without the need for personal relationships or intimacy. However, the portraits reveal contrary patterns of self-perception even in the instances where the leaders more closely match the caricatures. Rather than standing alone, it appears that these principals and headmasters recognize the need for intimacy and support as essential ingredients of effective leadership. They seem to need an intimate colleague, one whom they trust implicitly, whom they turn to for advice and counsel, and from whom they welcome criticism. At St. Paul's, this intimate colleague seems to be the historical figure of Rector—the deeply ingrained traditions of the office that offer guidance and shape to Bill Oates's actions and decisions. He can look backward to well-established rituals and practices, to the imprint of time, for help in guiding him forward.

The principals of Highland Park, Kennedy, and Carver cannot count on the historical imprint. Carver looks towards the future, trying to bury the ugly past and all of its images of failure and low status. Each day offers promise and hope, but Hogans must be a pioneer who carves out new territory and shapes new relationships. Hogans braves the new terrain with Mr. James, the tall, slender, impeccable vice-principal. Through their walkie-talkies, they are wired together and immediately in touch with each other's moves and decisions. James's partnership serves Hogans in several critical ways. First, James mimics his boss's style, commitments, and ideological stance. He idolizes Hogans and wants to follow in his big footsteps. From James's mouth come proclamations and proposals that echo Hogans's words, and even his demanding, uncompromising stance duplicates the behavioral patterns of his hero. Not only does James reproduce Hogans, he also complements him and does the things that elude the heavy hand of the principal. Hogans provides the big picture, the grand plan, and James figures out the details. Hogans develops the vision and James takes care of the mundane, technical aspects. A third way in which James's partnership serves Hogans is that it allows for expression, spontaneity, and playfulness between them. After maintaining tough male fronts all day they can relax, tell stories, laugh, and rib one another behind the scenes; each knowing that their private selves will never be revealed by the other. The backstage behavior makes the daily public images possible. Hogans does not stand alone. His power is fueled by relationship rather than independence.

There are similar deep bonds between Principal Benson and Vice-Principal Peteccia at Highland Park. Only here, we find vivid contrasts in style, temperament, and areas of competence. For almost twenty years they have been loyal and affectionate partners. Benson is smooth and urbane, Peteccia rough and provincial. Benson focuses on school policies, curriculum development, and sustaining an institutional identity while Peteccia "works in the trenches," keeping the peace and fighting chaos. Each one views the other's job as essential but personally abhorrent or incompatible with his own temperamental inclinations. Neither would trade places with the other and neither could do without the other. At Kennedy High, Mastruzzi's relationship with his assistant principal, Arnold Herzog, resembles the Benson-Peteccia match. They, too, are opposites with complementary temperaments and skills. Not only do they express contrasting styles, but Herzog's identity as the "bad guy" allows Mastruzzi to shine as the "good guy." A perceptive observer recognizes the compelling dynamic of image making that works to produce effective leadership. "They complement each other completely . . . Bob could not be seen as good if Arnie wasn't seen as bad." Once again, we find a professional marriage in a place where we might have assumed a solitary position. Once again, the relationship of intimacy and trust seems critical to the expression of strong and consistent leadership.

To some extent, the three caricatures of principal are reshaped and redefined by close scrutiny of leaders in action. These leaders seemed to require intimacy and support, not distant solitude.[15] The expression of their authority was shaped by the interaction of personal style and institutional culture. In reality, they are less stereotypically male than the caricatures drawn of them; and they reveal many tendencies more in keeping with the feminine principles of relationship—a sensitivity to the cultural forms already embedded in the institutions, a need for expression of feelings with trusted intimates, and authority partly shaped by a dependence on relationships.[16]

In Milton and Brookline, there are more conscious and vivid departures from the male caricatures of principal. The departures are framed in explicit, ideological terms and defined by the temperamental inclinations of their leaders. The original mandate of Milton Academy was to provide tender, loving care to the offspring of affluent families who had difficulty adapting to the tone and pedagogy of local public schools. The historical mandate has survived eight decades of institutional change and become thoroughly integrated into the ideological orientation of humanism. When an observer tries to probe the meanings that faculty and staff attach to themes of humanism, many will make contrasts with other private schools that exude maleness. Exeter is like a "boot camp," a "cold nest" compared to Milton, which seeks to respond to the individual needs of students and view them in all their myriad dimensions. Exeter will not tolerate students who do not measure up to the tough academic standards and military rigor, while Milton welcomes divergent student styles and is attentive to the interaction of psychosocial and intellectual dimensions. "It is a softer, more giving environment," says one male faculty member. In the contrasts with the male dimensions of competitive private schools, Milton's qualities are strikingly feminine in tone and perspective.

Not only is the school's culture shaped by the original mandate of tender, loving care, it is also sustained by the vital dialectic between the values and morality that have guided the girls' and boys' schools. The classic male tendencies of competition, hierarchy, and ambition are challenged by the traditional female qualities of nurturance and affiliation as faculty and administrators struggle with institutional integration. The clash of male and female cultures is palpable and provides much of the institutional energy and impending divisiveness. Unlike many schools that have recently become coeducational, both the male and female roots of Milton were part of the original school and have taken a firm hold on the institution's values, norms, and rituals. Several faculty point to the few "powerful grande dames," the female veterans who have great influence on the life of the school. They are committed to the "utopian values" and "feminine principles" that were deeply etched in the girls' school and are influential advocates of those perspectives. In addition to their substantial political clout, they are revered teachers who have "educational power." In observing one of these grande dames at work, I witnessed the resourcefulness, excitement, and skill to which her peers referred as well as the maternal quality of her interactions with students.

The leadership of Milton's headmaster matches the dominant themes of the school. His style and educational ideals seem to be sympathetic to and reinforcing of the humanistic goals. It is Headmaster Pieh who describes "holistic medicine" as the appropriate metaphor for the values that frame institutional life. His talk is interspersed with the softer language of "ethos," "process," "personal space," "relationships." When I ask him about the most difficult challenge of his work as a headmaster, he describes the "personal struggle" of combining family commitments and work demands, the ways in which Milton business sometimes robs his wife and children of his time and "erodes the family's private space." The struggle to find a balance between the spheres of work and love seems to echo the contemporary challenge faced by most working women and an increasing number of working men who see themselves as central to family nurturance. The conscious recognition of the need for work and family integration and balance is a powerful message from an institutional leader, and is clearly divergent from the exaggerated masculinity of the principal caricatures.

Jerry Pieh commits himself even more deeply to female tendencies in his explicit views of authority and in his decisions about the priorities of his work. When I ask him to describe a "typical day," he offers a detailed review of the activities and duties that have consumed the day of our meeting. It is a day that begins at 6:00 A.M. with a three-mile run and ends at 11:00 P.M. after an evening meeting of a museum's board of directors on which he sits. It is a strenuous day of high visibility, rapid interactions, and abrupt changes of pace. What is striking to me, however, is how much of Pieh's time is devoted to motherly attention toward his staff. On the day of our lengthy conversation, he has seen one faculty member at 9:00 in the morning and another at 10:00. The first meeting

Pieh described as a "constructive, positive, building conversation" in which Pieh and the faculty member were talking about a way to expand the latter's job in order "to use more of his person." The second meeting was "a raw and difficult conversation with a faculty member in a state of real crisis." After the optimism of the 9:00 meeting, the 10:00 session demanded the sympathy, support, and clarity of Pieh, who finally had to ask the teacher to leave the school. Pieh estimates he spends one-third of his time on fund-raising, one-sixth on administrative routine, and half on what he describes as "people problems."[17] Fifty percent of his self-described duties require the maternal energies of nurturance, patience, and attention to emotion.

As he reflects on the priorities of his leadership, Pieh admits that his behavior is grounded more in stylistic, temperamental qualities than in an intentional philosophical stance. "Style first, then philosophy . . . I want to set a tone that is permeating the environment. . . . It is not so much a campaign or a clear philosophical view. I want my actions to speak." His clearest ideological statement focuses on his views of authority. He pointedly resists "paternalistic authority" and refuses to play the "Big Daddy" role. Such ultimate and narrow authority would not only be antithetical to his personal style but also undermine the humanistic orientation of Milton. Pieh makes explicit attempts at encouraging collective authority, group decision making, and a dispersion of power and responsibility. In broadening the circles of power, people are confronted with a decision-making system that is less efficient and less clearly defined, an authority structure which is less visible, and the potential for greater conflict and dispute among themselves. Many faculty resist the collective structure—its inefficiencies and ambiguities—and fight for the classic, pyramidal arrangements of power. But Pieh believes the advantages far outweigh the disadvantages. With collective authority, there is a consonance between educational ideology and political process; there is an integration of leadership style and power negotiations; and there is the opportunity for Pieh to express both the female and male dimensions of his character. He may occasionally experience "the loneliness of making an unpopular decision," but it is unlikely that he will stand alone and above his colleagues and experience the extreme isolation of the caricatured principal.

At Brookline High, Headmaster McCarthy is even more outspoken on destroying the traditional, pyramidal arrangements of power. He says boldly, "They can take *all* the power for all I care," and he is trying to develop a school-wide structure that will give administrators, teachers, staff, and students a way to participate in real decision making and experience the duality of power *and* responsibility. His enthusiasm and determination for changes in authority patterns are heightened by his wish to undo the exaggerated hierarchical structure of his predecessor, Mr. Lombardi. The former headmaster was a stereotype of the "Big Daddy"—autocratic, charismatic, uncompromising, and paternalistic. For many faculty, McCarthy's predecessor engendered feelings of protection and safety, and in most of them he inspired affection and gratitude. The great majority of faculty now recognize that his dominating and theatrical style could no longer withstand the complex and diverse problems the school faced. His simple, autocratic approach was too uncomplicated for the worldly realities that surfaced in the final years of his reign. In pioneering a new form of leadership, McCarthy was faced with powerful past images of a super-masculine predecessor and found it necessary to develop explicitly contrary patterns. Everyone noticed the difference as they described the "visible, definitive, and uncompromising" qualities of Lombardi and the "invisible, contemplative, and ambiguous" dimensions of McCarthy. His primary deputies, the housemasters, spoke of the male metaphors linked to their roles during Lombardi's reign ("We were his lieutenants"), and the transformations under McCarthy ("He wants us to give the job our personal imprint and take all the responsibility for running the houses").

What is interesting here is not merely the vivid contrasts in leadership and the transition from exaggerated masculine images to a more diverse and reflective style, but also the recognition on McCarthy's part that a more complicated institution demanded the integration of male and female tendencies. The increased diversity of the student population, the echoes of racial strife in the wider community, the shifting cultural values and norms, the conflicting messages from the various parent groups all combined to create an intensely complex scene—one that could not be deciphered or understood by any single person. The caricatures of principal were simply unworkable in this environment. In order to meet the difficult challenges, McCarthy recognized the need for multiple perspectives and dispersed responsibility. He also seemed to recognize the need for a style that was subtle, patient, and improvisational; one that would focus on building relationships as the bedrock of problem solution; one that centered on interactional processes as well as explicit goals. In essence McCarthy recognized that, in order to be effective, his leadership needed to encompass a heavy dose of feminine principles. Standing bravely and alone in glowing masculinity would assure his demise. Reaching out for guidance and support from colleagues, and spending time nurturing relationships that would complement his authority, would be more likely to lead towards a productive and responsive school setting.[18]

In all of these portraits of good schools, leadership is given a non-stereotyped definition. The three powerful caricatures of principals do not match these leaders in action. Certainly, we see evidence of the stereotyped imprint. Hogans exudes the raw masculinity of the coach and the paternalism of the father-principal. Mastruzzi cheers on the sidelines like a determined, enthusiastic coach. Oates seems comfortably positioned as an imperial father figure. Yet in all cases, the masculine images have been somewhat transformed and the arrangements of power have been adjusted. In the most compelling cases, the leaders have consciously sought to feminize their style and have been aware of the necessity of motherly interactions with colleagues and staff. In one case, the heightened male style seemed unresponsive to the new demands of the school culture and wider community; in another, it was antagonistic with long-held principles of educational ideology. But even in the schools where the leaders have not expressed a clearly articulated divergence from male caricatures, we find that the leaders express a need for partnership and nurturance. They do not want to go it alone. Part of the goodness of these schools, I think, has to do with the redefinition of leadership. In all cases, the caricatures are empty and misleading. The people and the context demand a reshaping of anachronistic patterns. The redefinition includes softer images that are based on nurturance given and received by the leader; based on relationships and affiliations as central dimensions of the exercise of power; and based on a subtle integration of personal qualities traditionally attached to male and female images.

TEACHER AUTONOMY AND ADULTHOOD

Just as the principals in these portraits are seen as more complex and less dominant than their caricatures, so too are teachers recognized as bolder and more forceful than their stereotypes would imply. In all six schools, I was struck by the centrality and dominance of teachers and by the careful attention given to their needs. To varying degrees, the teachers in these schools are recognized as the critical educational authorities; the ones who will guide the learning, growth, and development of students most closely. Their intimacy with students and the immediacy of their involvement with the substance of schooling puts them in a privileged and special position. In addition, school leaders, who are more distant from the daily interactions, must depend upon teachers as major interpreters of student behavior and values. They are positioned at the core of education. They give shape to what is taught, how it is taught, and in what context it is transmitted. In turn, their behavior is most directly shaped by the responses and initiations of students. Teachers experience the quality and pace of human interaction and the shifts in mood and tempo during class sessions. It is their closeness to students and their direct engagement in the educational process that make teachers the primary adult actors in schools and the critical shapers of institutional goodness.

The high regard for teachers and their work expressed in the six high schools I visited marked them as different from a great many schools where teachers are typically cast in low positions in the school's hierarchy, and not treated with respectful regard. In the worst schools, teachers are demeaned and infantilized by administrators who view them as custodians, guardians, or uninspired technicians. In less grotesque settings, teachers are left alone with little adult interaction and minimal attention is given to their needs for support, reward, and criticism.[19]

The careless or negligent attitudes towards teachers within a large proportion of schools are reinforced by negative and distorted cultural views of them. On the one hand, they are expected to be extraordinary human beings with boundless energy, generosity, and commitment to their pupils. Their work is supposed to consume their lives and they are expected to be more dedicated than most mortals. These idealized images of teachers are often interchangeable with expectations of the clergy; that they be clean, pure, devoted, and otherworldly. On the other hand, teachers are seen as lowly, uninspired, and boring people who are unfit to do anything requiring talent and ingenuity. Lacking substance and resourcefulness, they are relegated to teaching. Teachers usually recognize that they do not match these extreme, opposing stereotypes, but they often feel threatened and defensive about the molds into which they are placed. These contrary cultural views, often held simultaneously, are experienced by teachers who receive mixed and sharp messages from parents and the community. In the same moment, they are idealized and abused.[20] The cultural perceptions are shaped by passion. Parents feel protective of and deeply identified with their children while their views of professional caretakers are highly charged and often unrealistic.[21] Certainly, there are many teachers who are dull and stupid, even malicious, and they deserve harsh criticism. But there are also competent and capable teachers whose work is subtly undermined by denigrating messages from the wider community.

A central theme of the good schools I visited was the consistent, realistic messages given to teachers and the non-stereotyped views of them. Teachers were not expected to be superhuman, neither were they regarded as people of meager talent and low status. In some sense, the schools sought to buffer the mixed societal perspectives by building an intentional context that supported and rewarded teachers' work. Each school developed different ways of expressing kind and consistent regard. The theme of nurturance became a central metaphor.

The public schools, in particular, were faced with the difficult challenge of providing inspiration in a time of severe retrenchment. With budget cut-backs, public school closings, and an exodus to private and parochial schools, public schools faced the pressing problem of rejuvenating an unmoving teacher staff. Weary and uninspired tenured teachers can drag a school down, and with no new blood there are few opportunities for the challenge and criticism that used to be voiced by uncompromising and optimistic novice teachers.

Principal Benson, at Highland Park, described the static conditions as the single most difficult dilemma that will be faced by his system in the 1980s. Ten years ago, Benson remembers hiring thirty to forty new teachers a year. Now he struggles to get rid of "deadwood," fills the rare vacancy with two part-time teachers, and searches for innovative strategies to encourage teacher growth and challenge. Now, more than ever, Benson worries about providing an environment for teacher satisfaction and renewal. In Highland Park, teachers seem to be nurtured by what many refer to as "a sense of professionalism" that combines relatively high status in the community, autonomy and respect, creature comforts, and an association with a school of fine reputation. Every teacher I spoke to expressed their appreciation for the many rewards Highland Park offered and compared their good fortune to schools in neighboring towns with equally affluent populations, but with a less respectful and benign view of their teachers. First, Highland Park teachers were most thankful for being recognized as intellectuals whose responsibility it was to define and shape the curriculum. In concert with colleagues, teachers were expected to develop the intellectual substance of their courses and decide on their appropriate sequencing in the student's career. There were few directions sent down from above, and many teachers spoke of the rejuvenating quality of intellectual discovery that their autonomy permitted. In the best cases, students could witness the teacher's intellectual adventure and become a part of the improvisational effort.

335

Second, Highland Park teachers were given the freedom to express their own personal style in their work. Benson believed that staff homogeneity was deadly, so he encouraged individuality among teachers and permitted idiosyncrasies to flourish. Even those teachers whose style and behavior were somewhat controversial received his protection. He believed the nonconformist behavior added spice and vigor to the school, and he hoped the controversies engendered by stylistic conflict would disrupt the institutional inertia that he saw looming on the horizon.

The protection and benign regard teachers received from the administration were reinforced by the generally positive feedback faculty received from the community. Parents applauded their fine work, expressed most vividly in the statistics of college attendance rates and admissions into prestigious universities. When individual parents were disappointed by their child's school career, Benson sought to protect teachers from their harsh assaults. Teachers appreciated the safety of their position and they certainly enjoyed the warm glow of community approval. However, a few observed that protection and safety encouraged a subtly dangerous complacency among them.[22] Their professional and personal growth required a less secure environment with more structures designed for direct, piercing criticism.

Benson interpreted teacher nurturance, therefore, as providing autonomy, protection, and support for individuality among them. Similar themes were present at Brookline where teachers were regarded as intellectuals, where diversity among them was encouraged, and where they were asked to take a responsible role in the authority structure of the school. Only in Brookline was there an even stronger emphasis on teachers as "academics" and a great admiration for teaching as a craft. When teachers talked about their work, they would frequently refer to the intellectual puzzles they were trying to unravel or their search for the appropriate pedagogical strategies that would meet the diverse needs of students.

A teacher, applauded by her colleagues as one of the "stars" on the Brookline faculty, told me about the struggle she was having getting the students in her advanced writing class past their defensive, secretive posturing with one another. After trying various strategies to encourage spontaneity and expressiveness in their writing, she decided to read them a very personal letter she had written to three dear friends after the death of a fourth friend. The letter, composed in the middle of the night, was unguarded, revealing, and painful. The teacher hoped her own openness would inspire similar responses in her students. In deciding whether to use this personal piece as a pedagogical tool she struggled with herself, tried to anticipate the possible repercussions, and reflected on her motives. Was she being overly seductive by revealing so much of her person? Could she tolerate making herself so vulnerable? Would her students abuse her intentions? Would it destroy the needed separations between teacher and students? In the end, at the last minute, the teacher decided against reading the letter in class. "My gut told me it wasn't right," she said with lingering ambivalence. What is important here is not the way she resolved this educational dilemma, but the intellectual and psychological journey this teacher traveled and her perceptions of herself as a resourceful and responsible actor. The school culture supported this teacher in her personal adventure by its generous appreciation of her ruminative, unorthodox style, and through the criticisms of a few close colleagues.[23]

With less clarity and force, I saw this resourcefulness in other Brookline teachers who were working hard on developing an innovative curriculum using primary historical documents; who were teaching interdisciplinary courses that sought to provide different angles on a single phenomenon; who were trying to teach complex ideas to students who were regarded as less academically capable. I also saw resourcefulness among Brookline teachers in their combined criticism and support of the school. Many expressed concern for issues beyond their immediate purview and traced the connections between larger cultural and institutional forces and life in their classrooms. One of the housemasters, a former English teacher, showed me a piece he had written for the *New York Times* Op Ed page. It was a sensitive, witty essay on the recent cultural and educational trends that he felt encouraged student conservatism and dimished the risk taking so crucial for inspired learning.

In Brookline, therefore, teachers are nurtured by the substance of their work, by their collective reputation as a spirited faculty, by colleague support and criticism, and by moving beyond the myopic view of classroom life to consider the larger institutional culture and its interaction with the wider community. They are encouraged in their autonomy, creativity, and excellence. "Star" teachers are bigger than life and offer models for their colleagues. Rather than the usual envy and competitiveness that often surfaces within teaching faculties, star teachers are applauded at Brookline.

In Milton Academy, teachers are also viewed as thinkers and pedagogues. Most have been trained in elite universities and a substantial proportion have advanced degrees from prestigious graduate schools. They exude a self confidence about their intellect that is rare among high school teachers. Within the faculty there are striking differences in teacher style, an unusual concern for the philosophical issues that shape educational matters, and an expressed need for intellectual invigoration. Here, too, the great teachers are given much acclaim. But in addition, at Milton, teachers are offered numerous opportunities for renewal and exchange through guest lectures, seminars, and workshops. This year, there was a monthly series on the personal and professional development of teachers given by veteran faculty who traced their own life histories. These faculty forums are enhanced by the general spirit of criticism and reflection at Milton. With the legitimation of conflict and criticism, faculty exchanges can move beyond polite encounters.

In somewhat different ways, Highland Park, Brookline, and Milton nurture teachers by offering them autonomy and support; by regarding them as thinkers; by providing opportunities for colleague exchange and criticism; and by offering an association with schools of fine reputation. The reputation protectively cloaks teachers and provides a measure of community good will and trust.

Carver High, in Atlanta, interprets teacher nurturance differently. In interesting ways, Dr. Hogans does the opposite of his principal peers, encouraging docility, discipline, and respect from his teachers. He begins by offering a very literal definition of nurturance. "I feed the faculty hot breakfast every morning . . . grits, eggs, bacon . . . the whole thing." In addition, he relieves them of the onerous responsibilities of hall patrol and keeps faculty meetings to a minimum. Rather than increasing teacher responsibility, he believes that teacher satisfaction will come with decreased institutional commitments.

Hogans makes much of the privileges and honor that teachers receive at Carver, but focuses most of his energies on creating conformity among them. He feels the rigorous discipline and control of teachers must follow the years of casual, irresponsible behavior permitted by the former administration. Quite literally, Hogans treats his faculty like he treats his students—emphasizing rules, directives, and discipline, and not tolerating deviations from standard procedures. He chafes at their less malleable responses. For Hogans, teachers must be directed from above, prodded into uniformity, and indulged through tangible rewards. Those who have witnessed the chaos of earlier years and lived through the transition in leadership at Carver are not all appreciative of Hogan's autocratic style. Many cringe at his uncompromising directives. But most faculty seem to recognize the protection and certainty that order brings and appreciate the positive image of their school that has begun to emerge.

The interpretations of nurturance in Highland Park, Brookline, and

Milton seem linked to views of teachers that support their adulthood. The power disparities between administrators and teachers are purposefully diminished, and their special role as educational authorities is emphasized. At Carver, teacher nourishment is interpreted as a paternalistic gesture. In exchange for their discipline and loyalty, teachers are given food, a slightly reduced work load, and an ordered environment in which to work. The power disparities between leader and followers are exaggerated, and teachers are sometimes made to feel like children.

Some Carver teachers feel that the enforced discipline is antagonistic to intellectual creativity and the development of inspired pedagogy. One teacher, a published poet and writer of short stories, quietly complained to me about the dulling effects of teacher "infantilization." When she first started teaching at Carver, she was initially enthusiastic about trying to find an integration between her writing and her teaching. Slowly, the oppressive culture began to erode her spirit of adventure and undermine her attempts at the integration of her worlds. The creative impulse simply could not survive the harsh and uncompromising structure. She and her students have managed to produce a small collection of poems and drawings, but she is dispirited and feels unsupported in her work.

To his credit, Hogans is aware that the substance of education has remained largely unaddressed at Carver. He knows that good educational practices will require more than a structured environment. But he does not seem fully aware of the debilitating effects of the enforced order on many teachers, nor does he recognize that educational sparks will only be lighted when there is heat in the intimate and complicated relationships between teachers and students.[24] Teachers must feel inspired and committed to educational goals in order to be in a position to light the fire in students. Finally, it seems to me that teachers are energized not by diminished responsibility, but through greater substantive participation in the structures and processes of education. They may feel gratitude at being relieved of the menial, custodial tasks that consume too much of their time, but that should not be confused with their wish for less real work. Teachers want to move towards central positions of educational responsibility. The want to feel part of something larger than themselves or their classrooms, and their participation must include substantive matters that make a difference to institutional life. Deprived of this wide angle on school culture, deprived of colleaguial interactions, teachers grow dull.[25]

At Kennedy, Mastruzzi recognizes the critical interaction between broad-based participation and teacher commitment to school life. He stresses the dynamic mutuality between responsibility and power, between freedom and initiative. Within the heavy constraints of the board of education and teachers' union regulations, Mastruzzi and his deputies try to carve out space for the teachers' independent actions. They encourage teachers to express their intellectual creativity through developing electives; and inspired faculty members are rewarded by "ego stroking" and generous praise. Not only does Mastruzzi encourage initiative among his teachers, he also gives them room to make mistakes. When they make great efforts and fumble, he is quick to be critical and discerning, but usually helps them try to diagnose the problem and encourages them to try again. One faculty member, who had "created a disaster" and was permitted a "second chance," referred to Mastruzzi's "forgiving" nature. "He's a generous man. He sees failure as an opportunity for change."

But the principal's bountiful patience and generosity are not merely gifts. They are part of an exchange; he expects something in return. Says one admirer, "He gives with his full heart," but he also expects a "fair exchange." Almost everyone I spoke to at Kennedy marveled at their inability to resist Mastruzzi's requests and claimed they had never worked so hard in all of their professional careers. Some have begun to understand the source of their renewed energy despite advancing age. "He never says 'no' to us, and he expects that we will never say 'no' to him." It is a dignified adult barter where both parties seem to recognize what they must relinquish in order to gain something more valuable. For many teachers, more work and increased responsibility buys them more power and autonomy. For Mastruzzi, less imperial control and more dispersion of power buys him increased faculty commitment and loyalty. Said a relatively new and young Kennedy teacher, "All the other signals (from the union and from the board of education) make me feel less than adult. Mastruzzi's signals honor my maturity."

St. Paul's teachers seemed poised between adulthood and childhood. In many respects, they receive the most elaborate rewards—stipends for university study, travel fellowships, generous sabbatical leaves, and invigorating visits from experts in their fields. They also receive great gain from being identified with an institution of high prestige. They feel like the chosen ones and that, in itself, provides important reinforcement. Despite the abundant rewards, the rhythm and structure of school life make enormous demands on their time, energy, and good will. The elements of St. Paul's that approach Goffman's prototype of a "total institution" also require boundless commitment from the faculty. In their myriad roles as surrogate parents, confidantes, teachers, coaches, and friends to students, they must be expansive, generous, and all-giving. In essence, they must be super-adults. In the constant presence of students there are almost no opportunities for letting down their hair, letting go of their emotions, or expressing their weariness.

The totality of commitment is further amplified by St. Paul's isolation from the real world. The setting is idyllic *and* seductive. It gets harder and harder to leave. A teacher who frequently leaves St. Paul's to go to professional meetings in order not to "grow stale and empty," claims that there are some faculty members who have not traveled the ninety miles to Boston in fifteen years. The isolation, often self-imposed, encourages tendencies contrary to adulthood, qualities of dependence and parochialism. The dependent responses are reinforced by the faculty's place in the school's structure. The rector's unquestionable dominance and benign power underscores their relative powerlessness and reinforces the child-like impulses. Rarely do old faculty complain of combining these adult/ child roles. The practices are so deeply ingrained that they do not feel them as contrary pulls. But newer faculty sometimes admit to the difficulties in balancing the themes of dependence and autonomy and shifting from childlike submission to mature authority in relation to students.

In all of these schools, therefore, teachers are seen as the central actors in the educational process. Their satisfaction is critical to the tone and smooth functioning of the school. Their nurturance is critical to the nurturance of students. Each school interprets teacher rewards differently, but all of them search for a balance between the expression of teacher autonomy, initiative, and adulthood on the one hand, and the requirements of conformity, discipline, and commitments to school life on the other. The balance schools are able to achieve reflects their leadership style, established authority structures, institutional ideology and priorities, and the particular collection of teachers—their competence, ambitions, vitality, and good will. It would be misleading to suggest that good schools automatically emerge when they effectively balance teacher autonomy and interdependence, reinforce teacher intellect and innovation, and offer opportunities for teacher participation in broad-based school structures. I believe all of these institutional qualities, in various proportions, support the work of teachers. Good schools are ultimately dependent on good teachers—smart and inspired people, people who have something to teach. Increasing the independence of a lazy and uninspired teacher will merely encourage greater malaise in him or her. Increasing the opportunities for real participation of irresponsible faculty would be an empty ritual. But increasing autonomy, reward, stimulation, and the adult regard of teachers who are generally competent, or even gifted, will enhance their effectiveness as pedagogues and critical members of the school community. Highland Park, St. Paul's, Brookline, Kennedy, and Milton have more than their share of able teachers and fewer poor teachers than most schools their size. Carver is beginning to attract more confident teachers now that the school is gaining a better reputation. In addition, these schools have visible, charismatic teachers— "stars," "grande dames," "mensches"—who act as important catalysts for their peers and who serve as critical symbols of excellence. There is a chemistry of proportions—a few "duds," many able teachers, and a few stars. In order to achieve goodness, therefore, schools must collect mostly good teachers and treat them like chosen people.

THE FEARLESS AND EMPATHETIC REGARD OF STUDENTS

One reason to encourage adulthood and autonomy in high school teachers is so that they will be able to have mature and giving relationships with their adolescent charges. If teachers are infantilized, or if they feel caught between adult and child roles, then it will be difficult for them to establish consistent and unambiguous relationships with students. Adolescence is a time of great vulnerability and turbulence; and high school students need secure and mature attention from adults, a firm regard that offers consistent support, realism, and certainty.

One of the most striking qualities of these good schools is their consistent, unswerving attitudes towards students. The first impression is that teachers are not afraid of their students. Ordinary adults often seem frightened by adolescents, fearing both their power and their vulnerability. They are apprehensive about, and do not understand, the broad emotional sweeps that send adolescents from vitality and joy into deep moments of sadness, or the sweeps that swiftly carry them from childish impulses to mature adult behavior. It is hard to know whether the adult images of adolescents are superficial overlays of a vulnerable child or the beginning progression towards maturity. Adult fears of adolescents stem partially from not knowing them, or not even knowing how to get to know them. Adolescents seem to be our culture's greatest puzzle and uncertainty inspires fear.[26]

So a compelling dimension of good high schools is the fearless regard of adolescents. It is not that some teachers do not feel threatened by eruptions of violence, or do not wisely protect themselves from physical assaults, but rather that most good high school teachers seem to be unafraid of these young people who tend to baffle and offend the rest of us.

The easy rapport between students and teachers is immediately apparent in public settings where large numbers of students tend to congregate in groups—in the cafeteria, outside the gym, on territorial steps and entrances to the school building. To the visitor, these crowds of adult-sized people can feel ominous. Teachers pass through them or around them without the need to avoid, intervene, or interact with the students. Sometimes they will offer a humorous comment, or prod the group to move out of the way of traffic, or try to talk to an individual student who has been eluding them for days. But as these teachers move through the crowds, they seem unself-conscious and mostly unafraid.

During the elections for Town Meeting representatives at Brookline High, five hundred students from of each of four houses packed into the school auditorium, student lounges, and cafeterias. None of the rooms could comfortably hold the volume of people. In the meeting I observed, bodies were pressed close with students on the floor, on chairs, on the tops of tables, on widow sills, everywhere. The situation seemed to invite chaos and disruption. Yet slowly, order descended on the room and the housemaster welcomed the assembled crowd. As students settled in, teachers were available but not dominant. They helped to direct people to empty spaces and strategically scattered themselves throughout the crowd, but in no way did they seem to be policing the room; their interactions were non-adversarial.

In Carver, I observed similar comfort and fearlessness among many teachers. I stood talking with a young Black male faculty member at the bottom of the stairwell. Suddenly a cacophonous sound echoed down the stairs, noises of students shrieking and bodies connecting. It was hard for us to tell if the cries were ones of desperation or excitement. The teacher and I chased up the stairs to locate the scene and heard the sounds of sneakers racing ahead of us and out of sight. We had lost them. A large grin covered the teacher's face, "And the beat goes on. . . . " he said, as he shrugged his shoulders. His expression had first registered alarm, then concern, and finally humor when he recognized the adolescent mischief. Judging the incident to be trivial, he felt no need to punish the youngsters or to catch them in their wrongdoing. His face seemed to say, "That's the way adolescents are—give them room."

The fearlessness of teachers is revealed in face-to-face, personal encounters as well. When an angry, distraught Highland Park senior lashed out at her favorite teacher with screams of rage, "This is the stupidest course I've ever taken . . . real junk!" I was alarmed at her anger and worried that the outburst might spread among other students. The blond, attractive teacher, standing the same size as her student, met her without flinching, first with a question about the girl's motives, "Are you saying that because you haven't done the work?," then with an attempt to reach out to her, "Talk to me. If not today, then tomorrow." There are numerous examples of these charged personal encounters between teachers and students. They are scattered among the daily experiences of adults and adolescents in high schools. The teachers seem to be better able than most adults not to respond with fear or hurt, but with an attempt to understand. The Highland Park teacher did not experience the incident as a personal assault and she was not embarrassed by my witnessing the scene. By way of explanation she told me the family story of the girl, a tale of extreme parental pressure and manipulation. The teacher was determined not to reproduce the parent-daughter relationship in her encounters with the student.

What I am calling fearlessness in teachers should not be interpreted as careless abandon on their part. Neither is it an expression of naiveté or innocence. They feel appropriately threatened by real danger. I would not even argue that their fearlessness comes from a greater personal confidence and certainty in them. I think it reflects their intimate and deep knowledge of adolescence as a developmental period; their understanding of individual students; and the strong authority structures within which they work. I was constantly amazed by teachers' understanding, diagnosis, and quick interpretations of adolescent needs. The interpretations were rarely made explicit or clearly articulated. They seemed almost intuitive to the observer. But when I asked teachers why they had acted in a certain way or made a specific decision, they tended to have ready responses that recognized the adolescent view and perspective. Their decisions to act combined a sensitivity to the student's individual character and history and an understanding of the developmental tendencies associated with adolescence. The same behavior expressed by different students might receive very different reactions from the teacher. A mischievous act by one student might bring a smile to the face of the teacher while another student would receive a harsh reprimand for the same behavior. Attention to individual differences gets interpreted through an awareness of the range and character of adolescence.

One finds striking evidence of the teacher's familiarity with individual and group phenomena in the humor that passes between teachers and students, and in the ease with which they can move from serious to funny moments. It is in the humor that subtle understandings of adolescents are expressed. The metaphors, illusions, and preoccupations of adolescents fuel the jokes that evoke laughter on all sides. The observer may miss the joke entirely, or may be made to feel like an outsider listening to a foreign language. But teachers, who know their students, usually know how to make them laugh and know how to respond to their attempts at humor.

At Milton Academy, I watched an English teacher show these elements of knowing as he struggled with his students to uncover the tangled plot of "Six Characters in Search of an Author." He gave guidance, not dominance, to the charged discussion. He pushed hard for clear thinking and careful analysis. When the students finally unlocked the plot's code, their serious and intense faces exploded into laughter. The teacher roared in glee as well. When he assigned parts for them to read, the play's characters intersected in interesting ways with the students' personalities, and the odd matches caused surprise and pleasure. The teacher knew his students, liked them, and felt their pain. He knew them as part of a "breed" of adolescents and could anticipate the range of possible developmental turns. He also knew each one—their families, their styles, and their dreams.

The deep understandings teachers display I refer to as "empathy"; the ability to place oneself in another's position and vicariously experience what he is feeling and thinking. The empathetic stance is a crucial ingredient of successful interactions between teachers and students. Empathy is not adversarial; it does not accentuate distinctions of power; and it seems to be an expression of fearlessness. By empathy I do not mean something sentimental and soft. As a matter of fact, the empathetic regard of students is often communicated through tough teacher criticism, admonitions, and even punishment.

Teacher fearlessness not only comes from deep understandings of students, it also derives from an institutional authority that supports their individual encounters with students. The most explicit and visible signs of strong institutional authority are seen in the schools' responses to violence and other disciplinary matters.[27] In all the schools I visited, there were clear codes of behavior and great attention paid to law and order. Acts of violence were quickly diluted and swiftly punished. In Carver, Hogans was primarily concerned with establishing a safe environment and making the strict rules visible and clear to students and teachers. After coming to Brookline, McCarthy's first administrative move was to express outrage at the frequent eruptions of violence; insist that parents come to witness student punishments; and develop a disciplinary committee that would respond immediately to acts of transgression. And in

345

Highland Park, Mr. Petaccia, the vice-principal in charge of discipline, became a legendary figure whose job it was "to keep the peace." Petaccia's rules were consistent, his punishments swift and impeccably fair, and he engendered both fear and admiration. Students and teachers were threatened by his power, but appreciated the feelings of order and safety he produced. Good schools are safe environments. Adults do not merely react to the random eruptions of violence, they seek to create a visible order that will help to prevent chaos. Said the Brookline principal, "I want the disciplinary committee to become like the judicial branch of government . . . with the same kind of stature, rationality, and philosophical stance."

Beyond the explicit disciplinary codes, therefore, the social organization of good schools is based on a clear authority[28]—what Yves Simon refers to as "the rightful use of power to create the means of coordination of action."[29] Not to be confused with authoritarianism, "authority" refers to the relationships and intercourse required to sustain a coherent institution. As authority becomes increasingly "legible" and dispersed, the opportunities for individual participation and responsibility increase.[30] Brookline provides a striking example of a leader and his colleagues who are attempting to reorder old hierarchies of power that appear unworkable and replace them with structures that encourage collective action and coordinated responsibility. This broad-based concern for how a school will function as a collective, and how authority will be expressed and interpreted, is more subtle than explicit behaviorial codes, but just as important to goodness in schools. With clear and consistent authority relations, teachers feel supported in their individual efforts to build empathetic relationships with students. This bedrock of authority provides an institutional coherence that is often expressed in teacher fearlessness.

The six portraits in this book illustrate the countless ways in which administrators, teachers, and students combine to form a community. Both adults and adolescents seem to need to feel a part of a larger network of relationships and want to feel identified with and protected by a caring institution. A good school community is defined by clear authority and a vivid ideological stance. Both separate the school from the wider society, marking internal and external territories.

People are more likely to feel a sense of community in small institutions. The scale is important to members' feelings of belonging, visibility, and effectiveness. With a population of five hundred, students at St. Paul's seemed deeply committed to the school and identified with institutional goals and values. In Milton, larger by a couple of hundred, most students felt the encompassing power of the school's strong educational ideology. They could clearly articulate the tenuous balance between individual expression and collective responsibility, the subject of much public dialogue. In Highland Park and Brookline, both schools with more than 2,000 students, it was difficult for students to feel a sense of belonging and visibility. In both places, several students spoke of a faceless quality, and a disconnection with the school that many attributed to its size. "I don't know how to enter the circle. I'm always on the outside," said an attractive sophomore whose family had moved to town a year ago. A teacher who had been at Brookline for more than a decade complained, "I can walk through these halls all day and not see anyone I know."

In Kennedy High, almost two and a half times the size of Highland Park or Brookline, a visitor feels overwhelmed by the crowds and uneasy in the midst of the body crunch in the halls between class periods. Many students refer to the huge scale of the school, but usually follow immediately with a comment on how the size permits variety in course offerings, extra-curricular activities, and student groups. The feelings of anonymity seem to be diminished by the personal encounters in classrooms. Students claim that they are known by their teachers, even if the rest of the population is a blur. The teachers in turn seem to feel a special responsibility for keeping the connections alive beyond the walls of the classroom. In the halls, cordial greetings between teachers and students continue the dialogue begun in class; and when a student is misbehaving in the halls, the teacher who knows him is likely to intervene—her scope of responsibility extending beyond the classroom. "When I see her, I straighten up," says a boy with a mischievous smile. "She thinks I'm a good kid and I want her to keep on thinking I'm a good kid . . . not see me messing up."

Strong evidence of many students' feelings of belonging at Kennedy are reflected in the conversations they occasionally initiate with teachers and administrators about broad institutional concerns. Two junior girls approach Mastruzzi in the hall and politely inquire about the pending decision on who will be hired as the gymnastics coach. The girls have met some of the candidates and they want to express their preference for one of them. With earnestness and candor, they try to win Mastruzzi over to their position. "He's really the best. He's a great teacher and a great coach . . . and we would really rally behind him. Please, Mr. Mastruzzi, consider it . . . and get back to us." The principal promises to inquire of the A.P. of physical education, learn more about the various candidates, and return to the students with a progress report. Another example of student concern for school matters: A boy enters the principal's office at the end of the day and finds Mastruzzi sitting in the outer office talking to some of his staff. "Mr. Mastruzzi," he says with urgency, "I thought of a great idea about how we can keep the halls clean—get some of those candy wrappers and stuff off the floor." Noting Mastruzzi's interest, he continues, "We could put a few big barrels on every floor . . . you know, so kids could drop their trash in them." The principal, who has told me of his frustration with the debris that students carelessly discard in the hall-ways, warmly thanks the boy for his suggestion and promises to "give if a try." The initiations of students seem to reflect their sense of belonging, their view that their individual actions make a difference to the life of the school, and their sense of being visible and accounted for.

The massive student body, however, does inhibit individual encoun-ters and institutional responsiveness in some corners of the school, par-ticularly in the places where students need focused, personal attention. Despite the heroic and gifted efforts of many counselors in the guidance office, for example, a caseload of 400 students prohibits the individual interactions needed for good academic planning and clinical work. The college counselling office, with one full-time faculty member and a cou-ple of part-time people, cannot possibly do an adequate job of serving the needs of the 60 percent of the senior class that goes on to college each year. The office must rely on large meetings, bulletin board announce-ments, and Xeroxed handouts in order to dispense the critical information for college application procedures. "You feel invisible!" complains a dis-gusted senior who is fortunate enough to have knowledgeable, highly educated parents to whom he can turn for advice and counsel. "I'm to-tally lost," says a shy girl whose parents never finished high school and look to her college career as their great ambition. "I don't know where to begin."

Encompassing institutions must also be encompassable, and large schools need to find ways of creating smaller communities within them—places of attachment for subgroups of students. In Brookline, the house system has not been successful in building smaller communities among students. Although housemasters often become important sources of identification and leave their personal imprint on their houses, most students view houses as bureaucratic structures designed to accomplish administrative duties. They are not seen as homes or places of asylum. On the other hand, the alternative school within Brookline High ("The School Within a School") that chooses its one hundred students, feels very much like a community. "This feels more like home than home!" claims one enthusiastic junior. In SWS, students feel visible, even special, up in the cozy fourth-floor corner of the big building, and constantly refer to the contrary themes of the "Downstairs School" as a way of defining the boundaries of their own space.

In Highland Park, students search for pockets of safety in the small communities that surround charismatic teachers or special student activities. The staff of the newspaper and yearbook, with its own crowded and busy rooms, feel an esprit de corps that grows out of their collaborative work, sense of fraternity, and high status as a student organization. The devoted followers of the drama teacher also feel tightly and intimately bound together by their love for their guru and her craft. However, many students of Highland Park can't find a niche and feel excluded from the central life of the school. They yearn to belong to something that will take hold of them and demand their loyalty and affiliation. When people talk about "school spirit," I think they are referring to the combined elements of ideology, authority, and community that engender responses of loyalty, belonging, and responsibility in the membership.

A final way of judging institutional goodness for students is to observe the regard and treatment of the weakest members. In each of these portraits, we see a strong institutional concern for saving lost souls and helping students who are most vulnerable. In Highland Park, there is an elaborate system for monitoring the movements of all students and immediately tracking down those who are late, absent, or deviant. The broad scrutiny has yielded a daily attendance rate of 93 percent but it has also served as an effective way of spotting problems early. Those students who need help are quickly responded to with appropriate educational and psychological supports. The expert staff of counselors works closely with the faculty and builds networks with hospitals and psychotherapists in the wider community. In Brookline, there are similar efforts at coordinated, prophylactic measures. In addition, the counselling staff is aided by three social workers who "work the underside of the school" and "have no fear." Their territories extend far beyond school boundaries as they go to bars, police stations, tenements, sports events, and courthouses to retrieve students in trouble. One of the social workers is known for cruising the streets of Brookline on Saturday nights as he looks for his most fragile charges and hopes to save them from further destruction. "I'm eclectic," he says matter of factly. "I'll do anything that works."

In all of the other schools I visited, there are vivid examples of this care and concern for the weakest members. The care may be expressed by feats of mercy and love on the part of faculty and counselors. It may also be revealed in their recognition of the limits of their ability to help in defining the tenuous boundaries between a therapeutic and an educational community. But more than these acts of incredible love for the weak, I will remember the general attitudes of respect and good will towards all students in these good schools. In every case, adults interacted with adolescents in ways that underscored their strength and power. Occasionally I heard faculty voice words of discouragement, frustration, and even outrage to one another about difficulties they were having with students. But even the backstage conversations in the faculty rooms were not abusive of them. Teachers did not use students as targets of their own rage or projections of their own weaknesses. There must have been at least a few angry teachers who purposefully victimized students. But I either missed seeing them, or their negative behavior was muted by the critical regard of their peers. Good schools are places where students are seen as people worthy of respect.

STUDENT VALUES AND VIEWS

Good high schools provide safe and regulated environments for building student-teacher relationships. Rules and behavioral codes are the most explicit and visible symbols of order and structure, but the inhabitants' feelings of security also spring from an authority defined by relationships, by coordinated interactions among members. A strong sense of authority is reinforced by an explicit ideological vision, a clear articulation of the purposes and goals of education. Ideology, authority, and order combine to produce a coherent institution that supports human interaction and growth. These institutional frameworks and structures are critical for adolescents, whose uncertainty and vulnerability call for external boundary setting. In their abrupt shifts from childishness to maturity, they need settings that are rooted in tradition, that will give them clear signals of certainty and continuity.

The abrupt psychic transformations experienced by adolescents should not be interpreted as a reflection of their unorthodox and spontaneous natures. Quite the contrary. These cycles from adulthood to childhood occur against the backdrop of heightened conservatism. Adolescence is not a time of diminished inhibitions and greater risk-taking despite some behavior that seems to point to abandon and reckless release. It is a time of great uncertainty and conservatism, and the expression of the former seems to demand the inhibitions of the latter. Adolescents want clear structures that will order their periods of disorientation. They want visible rules that will keep them from hurting themselves and others. They want relationships with faculty that underscore the teachers' adulthood. In other words, students do not want adults to behave like peers or buddies. They want to be able to distinguish between their friends and their mentors. The need for underscoring differences in power, knowledge, and perspective between adults and adolescents in high schools does not mean that relationships between students and teachers cannot be intense and deep. It means that close relationships are rarely formed when adults assume the style of teenagers. Adolescents tend to distrust adult attempts at peer-like friendships. They want and need adults who will behave with maturity and confidence; who will define the traditions and standards of the institution; who will reach out to them, but not try to join their fragile and changing world.[31]

The students at Carver, for example, welcomed the structure and order imposed by Dr. Hogans. The soar in attendance rates partly reflected the students' comfort in the safe and conservative environment. Before Hogans, the disorder and institutional chaos invited student restlessness and violence and did not provide an environment in which adolescents could thrive. They stayed away from school in great numbers, perhaps not wanting to risk the dangers or not seeing a clear distinction between the violence in their community and the chaos in school. The lack of distinction made school less appealing. The rigid and visible structures imposed by Hogans now sometimes feel inhibiting to students. Many complain about pleasures that are denied in the strict environment. But the complaints are often interspersed with expressions of comfort and relief. It feels right that there are behaviors which are not allowed. It assures students that they will be protected, that people care, that adults perceive the world differently, that they are not more powerful than their teachers. These assurances of adult tradition and order inevitably inspire adolescent criticism, but they also appeal to the profound conservatism of students, who often recognize their own vulnerability. Said one worldly young woman of fourteen, a freshman at Carver, "Listen, I have to fend for myself on the streets. When I'm here [at school] I want to relax and let them take care of me." A perceptive young man put it another way. "The best teachers around here are the strictest ones. They act like grownups." For students, who in their other lives may have to take on adult roles prematurely, Carver becomes an asylum for expressing childlike impulses; for letting go of the brittle façade. It is also a place that appeals to their conservative tendencies. Both in structure and in ideological stance, the school emphasizes the certainty of tradition and the promise of a future.

Yet even in more privileged environments, students express their conservatism and their wish for adult clarity and maturity. In Milton Academy, for instance, the faculty's humanistic stance sometimes felt dangerously close to permissiveness. Students enjoyed the individualized, caring attention of their teachers, but many worried when this individualization seemed to relax the clear institutional structures. When a student council leader flagrantly broke the rules by smoking marijuana in public and coming to meetings "high as a kite," the faculty's lenient and non-specific response offended and worried many students. Despite the boy's great popularity and charisma, his peers feared the flaunting of rules. In not quickly and decisively issuing punishment, some students thought the adults were not performing their mature and conservative function. Said one strong student critic, "The teachers' attempts to 'understand' were perverse. He was doing stuff that endangered the whole community and they should have hammered him down hard!" Often surprised at the faculty's "idealism," Milton students search for faculty definition of structure and regulation. The order is less clear in a humanistic environment and students sometimes ask for it to be made more visible. The sensitivity and caring of Milton's ideological stance appeal to adolescents who "want to be known as a person not a number," but the less rigid structures engender some feelings of threat and fear among them.

Adolescent conservatism is not only expressed in their wish to have ordered schools and clear distinctions between teacher and student roles; it is also seen in their "groupiness" and factionalism. Adolescence is a time of heightened affiliation and identification with peers, and the conservative choice usually points towards finding friends who mirror one's attributes and behaviors. In all the high schools I visited, I was struck by the rigid definition of student groups and their internal homogeneity. Of course, there were the expected divisions of race, class, ethnicity, and religion that separated students and shaped territories. But within each of these more obvious divisions, there were smaller groupings that reflected more refined similarities. Everyone at Brookline pointed to the cafeteria as the place to witness "the natural" groupings among students. The distinctions of Black, White, and Asian were visible markers of group identification. A more discerning eye could pick out the Irish Catholic kids from High Point, the working-class enclave in Brookline, and distinguish them from the upper middle-class Jewish students. In this case, the divisions of religion, ethnicity, and class seemed to be more harshly drawn than the more obvious categories of race. But one had to sit and talk with students in the cafeteria, not merely observe seating patterns, in order to experience the depth of student conservatism and the important indicators of friendship choice.

Many students, for example, spoke of the divisions between the "indigenous" upper middle-class Brookline Blacks, and the "interlopers" from inner-city Boston. Social class was a powerful divider and close friendships between these groups were rare. Foreign-born Blacks from West Africa or South America also spoke about feeling excluded from the inner circle of Black-American cliques. There are also experiential dividers. Students point to the Black "jocks" and their similarity in dress and style to the White jocks. Their preoccupation with athletics becomes more powerful than racial affiliation. This group identification tends to be seasonal and shifts when football fades into basketball season. A different configuration emerges and many athletes may return to their old racial or ethnic groups in the off season.

A Brookline teacher, aware of the heightened factionalism among students, claims that SWS students (the School Within a School, the small alternative school within Brookline High) "are the most victimized of any group at the school." Their exclusion reflects both the envy and ridicule of their peers. Many "downstairs" students seem to be jealous of the special attentions, rituals, and territories reserved for SWS members and feel slightly threatened by the unorthodox character of their small environment. When SWS began twelve years ago, it tended to attract the "fringe element" and its students were quickly labeled the "freaks." Now there are great variations in habit and behavior among the SWS students, but they continue to be perceived as long-haired hippies. The point is that adolescents partly express their conservatism in safe choices of friends; that the choices are often based on categories of interest and style as well as connected to boundaries of race, class, and religion; and that old perceptions of groups can linger long after the membership of the group has shifted.

Of course, students are expressing more than conservatism in their choices of intimates. They are usually rehearsing long-established attitudes and values perpetuated by their families and reinforced over the years. Their choices echo the prejudice and bias of their parents. But these stereotypes usually appear in exaggerated form in high schools. In many cases, prejudice and conservatism combine to produce rigid factionalism, separations that appear vivid and powerful. In Highland Park, the divisions among the working class Italians and the upper middle-class Jewish students reinforce their differences. Many people describe the defensiveness and physicality of the Italians who feel as if the school is not giving them "a fair shake," and the aggressiveness and sense of entitlement expressed by the Jews who feel as if their superior position is earned by their hard and persistent efforts. The group stereotyping reflects prejudice in the broader Highland Park community, but brought inside the school it is reinforced by adolescent conservatism and aggression and expressed in territoriality and occasional eruptions of violence.

There is an inevitable tension, therefore, in the adolescent conservatism and efforts towards diversity in high schools. One would, of course, expect intergroup frictions and strains within a community that was largely segregated by class and race. One would anticipate echoes of societal divisions within schools. However, it seems to me that the divisions are not merely expressed in high schools, but tend to be accentuated by adolescents who need to feel safely surrounded by like-minded, like-acting people with similar physical attributes. This conservatism and groupiness stands as a tough challenge for schools that are seeking to undo prejudicial views and discriminatory acts among their students. They must work extra hard to rearrange "natural" patterns and point out other dimensions that students might group themselves around. Brookline administrators and faculty recognize both the needed safety and asylum of tight groups, and the divisiveness and mutual distortions they engender. The new ideology of pluralism articulated by Headmaster McCarthy tries to address the positive and negative faces of group formation. The ideology asserts the richness and strength of diversity. Diversity requires a rootedness in one's group and a reaching out beyond its borders. It means that the collective strength one gains from group affiliation can be used to fuel the building of new relationships. Like the articulation of most ideological visions, the behavior of people lags far behind, but shifts have been visible. Now divisions and fear among groups in Brookline High appear *less* exaggerated than in the broader community, and students who take the risk of reaching across boundaries tend to be admired by their peers rather than ostracized by them.

The group identification among students at Kennedy High did not have the qualities of rigidity and hostility that I observed in Highland Park and Brookline. Rather than seeing an exaggeration of factionalism when community perceptions were transported inside the school, I witnessed the opposite. As distinctly different groups arrived at Kennedy from West Harlem, Upper Manhattan, and various parts of Riverdale, I sensed an easing of the barriers derived from community affiliation. Certainly Blacks, Hispanics, working-class Irish, and upper middle-class Jews tended to "hang out together" and form within-group friendships. But these alliances rarely degenerated into divisiveness or harsh confrontations between groups. Adults and adolescents offered any number of theories about the unusual calm that had settled over Kennedy. The most convincing analyses pointed to the workable proportions of racial and ethnic groups, the non-prejudicial behaviors of teachers, and the explicit "humanitarian" ideology voiced (and acted upon) by most adults. Since its opening ten years ago, the ratios of Blacks to Browns to Whites have remained relatively stable. With 40 percent Hispanic, 35 percent Black, and 23 percent White, no one group seems to fear the dominance of another. (The Asians, with 2 percent of the population, are a distinct minority. But their "quiet, unobtrusive, and studious manner and their group solidarity seem to protect them from the usual assaults of tokenism.") When students come together in classes, they rarely group themselves according to racial or ethnic categories, and teachers appear to be surprisingly fair about broadly and evenly distributing attention, criticism, and praise. This evenhandedness is reinforced by Mastruzzi's forceful stance, "I don't have a prejudiced bone in my body," and echoed by teachers who were attracted to Kennedy partly because of its heterogeneity. Many claim "a good teacher can teach anyone." Kennedy, therefore, is unusual in its relatively open and undefended interactions among student groups. Adolescents "hang together" with their "own kind" but seem to reach out to others without fear or inhibition.

Adolescents in high schools not only tend to seek comfort by close affiliation with selected peers, they also search out special adults with whom they form close relationships. The high school experience can be totally transformed by a vital relationship with a special adult. It can abruptly turn from being a foreign and ungiving environment to being one of enticement when a student connects with a special person. These relationships are best described as "magical matches," when chemistries coincide to produce a bond. A young Black girl at Milton told of a surprising match with her tough and critical history teacher. "He bugged me until I would talk and I knew he wanted to know *me*." Before their mutual discovery, she had felt adrift and alone at Milton, "But when my hate for him turned to trust," the school became a safe place. In every school I visited, several students spoke of developing these bonds that were highly individualized and mutual, and very different from the generalized affection of a kind and popular teacher. A lanky, awkward senior at Carver told me how it felt when, in his sophomore year, an English teacher described his writing as "poetic." "I couldn't believe what she was saying . . . so I asked her to say it again." Everyday he finds a way of stopping by her room, even if it is just for a brief greeting. She traces him through the day, knows most of the details of his life, and gets "a rare pleasure" from their relationship.

Many fortunate students, therefore, seem to attach themselves to schools through a profound affection for an individual teacher. This charged and important relationship can transform the high school experience for a student and send him off in new directions. Beyond these intimate associations, students thrive in schools where adults behave in mature and confident ways and do not mimic the behaviors of their charges. Peer groups provide contrasting relationships of intimacy and dependence. They serve as powerful sources of judgment and criticism but also as places of refuge and solace. Good schools balance the pulls of peer group affiliation with adult perspectives on the world. Students seem to rely on adult maturity to balance the adolescent vulnerabilities. The attachments students create with one another and with the school's adults are partly a reflection of their heightened conservatism, their search for roots and structure in their fragile and shifting world.

Against this developmental backdrop of conservatism and vulnerability, teachers and students engage in educational exchanges. With all of the stark and visible psychological and social drama, it is sometimes difficult to discern intellectual matters. In high schools teachers, administrators, and students often seem to be preoccupied with apprehending "the culture" and tone of school, with creating and preserving a livable environment, with reducing the student factionalism. Even in good high schools where truancy, violence, and drug traffic may not be major threats, attention to the substance and processes of intellectual exchange do not seem to be in the forefront of most people's minds.

There are several explanations for this seeming neglect of academic substance. One is that the adults recognize, probably correctly, that the school culture is critical to adolescents' readiness to pursue curricular matters. Adolescents are perceptive, social animals with very sensitive antennae that pick up signs of threat and danger. Unless the school environment feels safe and secure, they will not be able to focus on matters of the mind. If teachers do not recognize the psychological and social distractions, the argument goes, they will never be able to guide the students towards the academic agenda.

A second reason for the seeming focus away from intellectual substance is that high schools always seem poised towards the future. There appears to be at least as much attention given to where students are headed as is to their present status. Teachers and students face outward, looking to the future rather than the present.[32] That external view encourages a greater emphasis on positioning and competition for slots in society beyond school, for places in prestigious colleges, or for jobs in a tight and unyielding market. Poised towards the future, students are more likely to focus on getting there, and teachers become their reluctant (or enthusiastic) sponsors. This future orientation can be distracting to the mastering of educational dialogue in high schools.

A final source of distraction from intellectual matters in high schools lies in their multiple, often confused, purposes. The thickness of most high school catalogues points to their institutional ambiguity and competing agendas.[33] Oftentimes little thought is given to the values and substance that should provide the core of the curriculum. Instead, the courses expand in response to shifting cultural priorities and the special faddish interests of the inhabitants, producing a vast smorgasbord of offerings that rarely have a coherent base. The 188 pages of the Brookline catalogue, for example, are filled with over 500 course descriptions listed under 15 departments. Oldtimers on the faculty worry about the proliferation of courses and the thoughtless expansion of options. More, they observe, does not necessarily mean better.

At Kennedy, they discovered that less was better. In 1972, the school offered a wildly chaotic curriculum with course offerings that responded to the faddish and eclectic interests of students and faculty, but lacked intellectual substance and coherence. After enduring the fragmentation and turmoil produced by the seemingly endless choices, a few years later the course offerings were drastically reduced and academic rationales were developed for the inclusion of courses. Kennedy now has a highly structured curriculum with many requirements and few electives. The catalogue is substantially thinner and more easily decipherable by students.

The incoherence of the great array of courses in most high schools is reinforced by the various paths taken by students. Whether schools describe themselves as "tracked," "ability-grouped," "leveled," or "streamed," large public schools are often serving three or four quite separate groups who want different things from the school. The academic or Honors-track students want careful preparation for the intellectual demands of college. The vocational-track students hope to learn marketable skills that will translate into a job as soon as they leave high school. The middle range of students, with a less definable path, want respectable but untaxing courses that will assure entry into two-year colleges or modest four-year schools, as well as some experience with hands-on, reality-based job experiences. Responding to the wishes and needs of each group is extremely difficult, particularly since their interests are often in competition with one another.

Their different needs are accentuated by the persistent inequalities felt by students, particularly those on the bottom rungs. Typically, the fast-track academic students receive more than their share of glory and status in high schools. They tend to attract the attention of the most inspired and creative teachers, and their ambitious image shapes the external perceptions of the school. In Highland Park, for example, Italian parents complain that the best faculty teach the Honors courses full of bright Jewish students, that their children are rarely encouraged in the academic direction, and that the school culture gives subtle and explicit messages of exclusion to their offspring. Since the prosperous and ambitious image of the school is defined by its highly successful academic students and by the proportion going on to elite Eastern universities, the working-class Italian students not only feel unfairly treated, they also feel invisible.

One sees similar tensions in the emerging divisions between "vocational training" and "comprehensive education" at Carver High. Principal Hogans wants to broaden the horizons of Carver students, as well as elevate the pedestrian image of the school, by creating a broad-based curriculum. Historically, vocational education had been the singular mission of Carver and there was little ambivalence among the faculty about their role as job trainers. With twenty-four shops that include auto mechanics, horticulture, child care, and dry-cleaning, students were trained in specific skills by practitioners of the craft. Some of the shops produced confident and competent graduates, but they usually left Carver with little or no intellectual training and skills that might soon be unnecessary due to technological innovations. Critics also charged that the vocational training was vastly inefficient and wasteful of student energy. Skills that might be quickly learned in apprenticeship positions on actual work sites were practiced over periods of several months in school shops.

When Hogans arrived at Carver, he did not intend to get rid of the vocational shops or to denigrate the importance of manual skills. He often points to the essential and potentially lucrative work of carpenters and electricians and reminds listeners of teachers and social workers who are unemployed because of a shrinking job market. He also recognizes that the one solid attraction of Carver for students is the promise it offers for immediate skills and future jobs. But Hogans seems aware of the ways in which vocational students might be cheated by narrow training and short-sighted solutions, and many faculty are convinced that academic work must be emphasized even for students who see it as irrelevant to their lives.

To complicate things further, the academic side of Carver is embryonic, uncertain, and uneven. Not only is intellectual training resisted by many students, it also seems to be out of reach for many teachers who have not yet figured out how to teach academic subjects to "slow learners" who are "fighting you all the way." A biology teacher, admired by her colleagues as a strong teacher, faces the challenge with realism and optimism. A large and imposing woman dressed in a white lab coat, she cajoles, criticizes, pushes, and prods students to engage the material, always insisting upon civility, manners, and poise. When a boy becomes slightly belligerent because he has received a disappointing grade on a homework assignment, she is tough, "Darryl, you are wasting all of our time. How dare you drag us all down with you!" But later sympathetic: "I can understand your frustration. This is hard work." Through all of these attempts at maintaining an ordered environment, the focus is on biology. Concepts and definitions are introduced, explained, and practiced. However, few of her colleagues have the same patience and stamina. In many classes, academic lessons tend to get lost in the barrage of disciplinary exchanges, students quickly get turned-off, and faculty grow weary of trying to teach through the chaos.

The chaos is broader than individual disruptions between unruly students and stale or disheartened teachers. The chaos is partly defined by the myriad agendas to which Carver is trying to attend and by the adult uncertainty regarding their students' futures. Some perceptive faculty recognize the tensions between the historically defined vocational training and the more ambiguous, broader goals of a "comprehensive education." But few understand what the latter would entail in terms of actual rearrangements in the curricular structure and interactions with students. The old habits of perception and expectation are firmly embedded at Carver and it is difficult to foresee the institutional and personal changes that would be necessary to create a new school culture. Such institutional confusion arises out of attempts to embrace loftier but less clear goals and to replace choice and options for a singular path.

Although there are great differences in the levels of instruction and intellectual content among the various tracks at Kennedy High, there appears to be a universal concern for civility, order, and structure across all ability levels. Certainly, most teachers claim their preference for teaching bright and inspired students and voice some frustration about the slow and laborious pace required in the remedial courses. But I saw no diminution of effort on the teachers' part and certainly no explicit hostility or disdain for the less capable students.

Beyond the emphasis on civility and form at all levels, at Kennedy there is an ideological commitment that tends to encompass all students rather than exclude or enhance certain groups. The image and reputation of the school does not seem to rest on the high-achieving, academic stars, although people are proud of their accomplishments. There is, instead, a broadly expressed concern for producing good "human beings," people who will grow up to be "good parents and neighbors." Everyone, no matter what their I.Q., is considered a promising candidate for good citizenship. Mastruzzi is outspoken on the issue of charity, learning to give generously to others, reaching out to others in greater need. Each year his address to the graduating seniors revolves around this point and he reiterates the theme in his everyday expectations of student behavior. To some extent, the ideology of charity imbues the daily encounters of teachers and students and begins to erode the barriers between the privileged and less privileged, between the intellectually talented and those less academically capable. "Kennedy doesn't undo social class distinctions," claims a proud teacher, "but it does challenge the social pyramid."

Private schools, rarely faced with a diverse range of students or the often conflicting demands of parent and community groups, are better able to focus on academic and curricular matters. Private schools are likely to choose relatively homogeneous student populations to whom they can successfully offer a streamlined, focused curriculum. The vast majority of students come from backgrounds of affluence and privilege, and their high school careers usually follow several years of superior preparatory training in elementary school. In most private schools, diversity is limited to token groups of working-class and minority students, but the proportions remain small enough so that the homogeneous culture is largely unchallenged. It is expected that the unusual students, not the curriculum or pedagogy, will have to be transformed. Said one Black girl at St. Paul's, "We have to do all of the stretching and changing. They will always remain the same whether we're here or not."

The private school's mandate from parents is vividly clear. The talented faculty and school reputation are supposed to combine to produce impressive college entrance statistics. When parents visit the admission office with prospective freshmen, they want to be assured that their child will have a good chance of entering Harvard, Yale, or Princeton in four years. The college counselors are rarely judged by their success in deftly guiding students through the admissions hurdles or coming up with subtle and unusual matches between a particular student and an appropriate college; rather, they are evaluated on the basis of the proportion of graduates admitted to prestigious colleges and universities. This singular focus permits private schools to concentrate on building a circumscribed and coherent curriculum. Milton's catalogue, with thirty-six pages describing the curriculum, looks thin compared to its public school counter-parts. For each department listed, the course offerings are preceded by a faculty statement about the goals of their curriculum. The statements combine intellectual rationale with philosophical ideals and reflect faculty conversation and consensus.

Paradoxically, the more serious attention given to the curriculums in many private schools invites a more playful educational atmosphere. By playful I do not mean frivolous or trivial. I mean that educational exchanges tend to be more spontaneous and less bound by functionalism, that teachers and students are able to attend to the present without constant reference to the future. I mean playful in the sense of students being encouraged to play with ideas, turn them on their sides, consider them from several angles. Teachers and students, engaged in an exciting intellectual adventure, can suspend time and live fully in the existential present without considering the immediate relevance of what they are learning. They can pause long enough to consider the logic and aesthetics of an argument; they can be captured by the pursuit of truth rather than focus exclusively on searching for the right answer. Certainly, such intellectual play is both rare and fleeting in any environment. It requires a creative and challenging teacher, a trusting and relaxed relationship among students, and a direct engagement with the material. Play is unlikely to occur in a highly competitive or combative environment because it requires the collaboration and elaboration of ideas, one building upon the other. Play is unlikely to occur in a classroom where teachers are dominant and powerful and students passive and accommodating. And play is unlikely to be found in schools where students are worried about their own survival. It requires abundance, certainty, and the assurance of a future.

I saw examples of intellectual play among teachers and students in most of the schools I visited, but it was a more common genre in the prestigious private schools. At St. Paul's, I recall a senior course in human personality where the teachers and students engaged in a searching dialogue about the impact of Freudian theory on Western views of the individual psyche. The teacher, with a furrowed brow and a halting voice, struggled with students to clarify the shifts in psychological theory. He refused to bring premature closure to the discussion or provide facile answers to difficult and complex problems. He looked for good and interesting questions rather than right answers. His last words to students before the close of class: "The struggle—I'm happy in it!" I recall vivid playfulness in a course in English literature at Milton Academy. The teacher led fourteen sophomores gathered around an oval table through an adventurous discussion about the cultural purposes of early ballads. She probed their fantasies of "primitive" culture, explored the power of repetition in language, and led them in a choral reading of a classic ballad. There were moments of serious and critical exchange followed by eruptions of laughter and release. When the bell sounded to end the class period, the students were shocked back into the present. For fifty minutes, they had been in a time capsule.

Of course, we would expect more opportunities for intellectual play at places like Milton and St. Paul's. First, these schools tend to attract more than their share of confident and inspired teachers. Second, the relatively homogeneous student body consists of adolescents who feel confident of their place in society's future. They do not know the specific path they will take, neither are they absolutely certain that they will be admitted to the college of their choice. Yet their affluence and family status assures them of a solid place in a projected future. These assurances permit them to attend to the present, protect them from premature adulthood, and encourage the playful dimensions of education.

By contrast, students at Carver have none of the assurances of Milton students. All around them they see destruction and poverty and few examples of people who have been able to climb out of the mire. They are aware of the stacked deck, the rigged race, and the discriminatory institutions that will inhibit their movement upward. Without promises in the future or abundance in their present, Carver students become preoccupied with defining the future and want to see visible signs of connection between school work and job openings. For many, high school will be their final school experience; therefore, they must prove their adequacy and fight for position before they leave. A large group of students, deciding that the chances are too slim and the prizes too few, have opted out a long time ago and seem to be marking time in high school. They are without hope or energy. They are what one teacher described as "dead weight." But for those with lingering hope, school becomes the functional link to a better life. These students, who view school as a vehicle for mobility, tend to count on its utilitarian role and want teachers to provide the necessary skills. "I have no time to play!" exclaimed a determined junior girl. "My mom would kill me if I messed up. This is my chance to make it!" By play, she was meaning "the messing around" that gets you in trouble and distracts you from your studies. However, it is also true that her gritty pursuit allowed no room for intellectual play.

In more affluent communities we see some of the same narrowly focused and uninspired paths to student achievement. In Highland Park, for example, the great majority of students come from privileged backgrounds. More than 85 percent of the graduating seniors continue on to further education after graduation from high school and their school prides itself on being able to successfully compete with fancy private academies on most standards of excellence. Despite the community's abundance and the students' bright futures, the primary complaint of administrators and teachers points to the brutal competition and stress within the student body—the kind of striving and anxiety that makes intellectual play very rare. Teachers who try to get students to be adventurous and uninhibited in their exchange of ideas feel stifled by the competitive atmosphere, and blame parents for creating the debilitating tension. Complains one teacher who is constantly frustrated by the competitive tone, "If we could take the students way from their parents, they might find the pure joys of education . . . but as long as the parents need to gain status through their kid's achievements, education will be brutal and boring." The drama teacher at Highland Park creates an asylum for students; a place of refuge from the large, competitive school; a place she calls "the magic space filled with all our ghosts." She reinforces and rewards values that are explicity counter to community themes, and rails against the town's "materialism and subtle violence." Drama provides the vehicle for spontaneity and expression, a direct contrast to the calculating ambition of the outside world.

Even though Carver and Highland Park students are headed towards very different futures and are surrounded by strikingly contrasting life styles, they are similar in that their preoccupation with the future beyond school distracts them from intellectual adventures in the present. In both cases, the perspectives of parents work against educational exploration. Poor parents are likely to warn their children to be good, mannerly, and submissive—admonitions that realistically respond to the institutional constraints they will face. The upwardly striving parents of Highland Park are likely to compel their offspring to be aggressively ambitious and cautious. In both cases, the educational exchanges get distorted and rigidified. These are not surprising or dysfunctional behaviors, but they tend to limit the scope of dialogue between teachers and students, making school less adventurous and fun. There are persistent complaints from students that school is no fun. In the town of Highland Park, the graffiti on the railroad viaduct reflects even greater doom. "This town is no fun anymore," it says in big sprawling letters.

In Brookline, a school with a more diverse student population, the various perspectives on school work are vividly apparent. By and large, the divisions among racial and social class groups are reinforced by the school's grouping practices. The working-class Black students who travel from Boston are disproportionately represented in the lowest rungs and the upper middle-class Jewish students dominate the Honors and Advanced Placement courses. Despite the fact that movement among the levels is possible, it is not common practice and the slight shifts occur across close boundaries. A bright student who is feeling overwhelmed by Advanced Placement biology may transfer to the Honors section after consultation with her counselor and approval of her parents. But rarely do students take the giant leap from Basics to Honors history, for example. Occasionally a Black student appears in Honors physics or a working-class Irish student is found in an advanced writing class, but their appearances are very unusual.

Basic level courses look very different from Honors courses not only in the skin color and origins of their inhabitants, but also in the students' orientation towards intellectual work.

In a writers workshop for Basic level students, an inspired teacher recognizes the very limited skill of her students, but strives to engage them in an intellectual adventure. She resists their laziness and complaints and urges them to find out what they think.

On beautiful signs with elegant calligraphy, she projects the message of intellectual play. A purple and magenta sign hangs over the blackboard, "Write what you know about, care about, and can communicate." Another poster, in turquoise and green, suggests, "When you write, don't put a tuxedo on your brain." The first ten minutes of each class are devoted to journal writing. Students can write whatever they want, but it must be their own work. Over the course of the year, journal entries tend to become more personal and less guarded; and it becomes less difficult for students to sit still, focus their attention, and enjoy the ritual of writing.

On the morning I visit, the topic for the day also reinforces intellectual exploration. The teacher hands out a paper with three questions printed on it, and says, "Would you write your opinion on each of those questions. Do not state facts, offer opinions." After several minutes of writing, each question is discussed out loud. The exchanges often seem aimless and chaotic, but the teacher insists that they not give up. "Don't wait for someone else to think. Think it yourself," she exclaims when they grow lazy or fearful of exposing their inadequacies. Out of a very confused discussion, the teacher discovers order. She underscores three reasons why they have had trouble offering an opinion on the second question ("Why are there so many divorces?"). First, they have not had firsthand experience; second, it is difficult to know what other people are really feeling; and third, there are too many variables to be able to pinpoint the cause. The homework assignment for the next day is to "Rewrite the question so it is answerable."

I am exhausted by just watching the stamina and perseverance of this teacher and surprised when she says to me brightly, "I think that went well . . . better than it does a lot of the time." My look of puzzlement inspires further explanation from her. "You see, this is the lowest class, the lowest of the low . . . and if I see any shimmering signs of thinking, I view that as progress." Although most of the fourteen students come from lower- and working-class backgrounds, their faces show diverse origins. Four Black boys, all tall and lanky, are star basketball players and terrible readers. Gregory writes at a second-grade level and this is the first time Willie has been allowed in a regular English course. Tom Soon, a twenty year-old Chinese student, is illiterate in Chinese and English and judged to be slightly retarded. Sandra and Betty are "school-haters" who have missed more than half of each school year. Both from middle-class white families, they share a passion for horses. Jake, an exuberant working-class Irish kid, comes from a famous family of football players. He says "I'm here to play ball, man!" Roberto, a Puerto Rican, is chronically late and broodingly silent. The day I visited he had a "big breakthrough" and spoke for the first time in class. A Russian girl is dressed in tight blue jeans and a sweater with a plunging neckline. She toys with her gold chains and stares off into space for most of the class. One girl's absence from class is a welcome relief for the teacher. "I call her my roller-skating queen because she zooms in on skates. I think she is involved in soft pornography, possibly prostitution."

This class is worlds apart from the English course inhabited by the more privileged and skilled Brookline students. There are vast differences in academic competence, but more subtle contrasts in orientation. Despite the fact that the teacher urges and rewards adventurous inquiry, the students seem focused on the utility of their learning. "Why do we have to know that?" is a frequent question. "I already know enough to get by," is the defensive reasoning.

Occasionally working-class students, by dint of hard work and extraordinary achievements, enter the enclaves of their upper middle-class peers and receive Honors instruction. In essence, they enter an environment of greater rigor, but also a setting of enhanced certainty and abundance. With privilege and certainty comes the opportunity for intellectual play. To the working-class student who has strived mightily to gain a loftier place, the intellectual play may seem threatening and absurd. With such high stakes, how can he dare to test out alternative propositions? He must search out the right answer. How can he spin out fantasies of adventurous projects? He must take the sure and straight path. Teachers occasionally notice the grinding conservatism of the token working-class students and may recognize their inability to totally immerse themselves in the classroom culture. Admonished by parents to behave and achieve, they may be too focused to notice the playful exchanges. Socialized to respond to teacher power with submissiveness, they rarely challenge the authority of intellectual claims. Alone in a largely upper middle-class environment, they may feel constrained by the heightened visibility of their tokenism and feel excluded from subtle nuances. In a classroom that encourages intellectual play, they are inhibited from full participation. They know they are diligent and smart. Their grades prove it. But they feel different—less secure, less spontaneous, and less entitled than their more privileged peers.[34]

In an Honors writing course, a Brookline teacher finds it difficult to inspire creativity and "irreverence" in all her students. She fights their inhibitions and conservatism. "They are too thoroughly socialized for my taste," she admits with a mischievous smile. But it is the working-class students, very few in number, whom she finds most cautious and guarded. Even when their writing is fluid and their spelling impecable, "They won't let it flow . . . even though their stories are probably far more interesting." Even when the less advantaged students move up within the hierarchy in schools, they rarely enter the same environment as their peers. Arriving with different attitudes towards adult authority, different views of educational utility, and the awkward moves of a stranger, poor and working-class students may cross class lines in school but they rarely fully arrive.

It would be misleading to claim that the great majority of children from privileged families enter into educational settings with creativity and the spirit of adventure; that they are unaffected by the narrowing effects of job and status pursuits. As a matter of fact, administrators and teachers in all the schools I visited were alarmed at the increasingly utilitarian view of education by all their students. From all backgrounds, students seemed more concerned with the learning of specific technologies that will equip them for work, college, and beyond. "There is a premature narrowing," claims a Brookline history teacher. "It reaches all the way down to the high school level. . . . The other day a freshman girl asked me 'What courses do I need to get admitted to law school?' . . . and that's eight years away!" A Milton English teacher in her late thirties talked about "an ironic reversal of roles" between adults and young people. "When I was an adolescent my parents were always blaming me for my idealism and telling me to be practical. Today, I find myself telling kids to be less practical and less conservative. I'm still the idealist." Across all social groups, then, adolescents are feeling the effects of a tight job market and making cautious and narrow choices. In this environment, there is less opportunity for teacher-student creativity and resourcefulness. But in those rare instances where intellectual adventure thrives, privileged students are more likely to be the advantaged participants.

Intellectual play is rare but very visible. The pleasure of inspired exchange is obvious to any visitor of high school classrooms. In courses where there is intellectual adventure, discipline is rarely a problem and time does not drag. Students appear alert, engaged, and responsive. A "star" teacher at Brookline says almost innocently, "I've been here twelve years and never had a problem with discipline." A colleague listening to our conversation interprets her statement. "You see, she seduces those kids into learning and they get lost in the ideas and forget about their teenage complaints." In a United States history course for Honors seniors, students are re-enacting the First Continental Congress, role playing the prominent political figures of the time. In order to be persuasive in their roles, they must incorporate the historical and political themes that shaped the debate. Their drama is being videotaped for "Parents' Night" the following week. Although some students are more theatrical and articulate than others, everyone participates in the dialogue, either as aggressive protagonists or eager listeners. The time speeds by and there are groans when the debate must stop because it is time for them to move on to their next class.

At Kennedy, I saw intellectual play in an early morning Latin class primarily inhabited by Black and Hispanic students. The teacher, an intense and dynamic Italian with a lingering, musical accent, made the rehearsal of vocabulary and the lessons on conjugation feel like an adventure. The pace was accelerated, the praise plentiful, and the pedagogical "tricks" numerous. At 8:00 A.M., there were no yawns. Most students showed intense interest, hands were waving in the air as they clamored to speak, and smiles of satisfaction spread on their faces when the smooth and quick exchanges began to feel like a well-oiled machine.

Intellectual play can provide the spark of education for adolescents. It is a habit that requires stimulation, practice, and a safe and abundant environment. In contrast to the adventures of intellectual engagement, high school students seem to yearn for a direct and functional engagement with the real world. For many this translates into trying to find work within or outside of school. In my visits to schools, I was impressed by the large proportion of students who are working after school. None of the schools had gathered exact statistics on the number of students with after-school jobs, but faculty spoke about the noticeable change in tone that the "job exodus" has created. In Highland Park, for example, the principal observed that in the last several years jobs have sapped the psychic and physical energies of students and relegated school to a "satellite" position. Most of these students do not even claim to need the money; rather, they seem to be searching for feelings of productivity and competence as well as visible and tangible rewards. Many aspects of school seem to work against the competence and stature that students feel they gain from their jobs. A Brookline student spoke about the surge of energy that comes at 3:00 when he is about to depart for his job at the local McDonald's. "Suddenly I feel like I could take on the world . . . I'm ready."

Many of the same sentiments are expressed by students who are actively involved in producing a school play, working on the school newspaper, or practicing on the swim team. Those activities offer students the opportunity to join with others in a common goal, work on skills whose development makes a difference, and experience the rewards of applause, acclaim, or their words in print. The Carver students, whose work is often necessary for survival, can also feel the satisfaction of contributing to the welfare of their families. "When I make money, I feel big!" exclaimed a small sophomore with a large grin.

For many students, high school stands uncomfortably between intellectual play and real work, and the no man's land stretching between them tends not to be very appealing. Adolescents are inspired by the immediacy and practicality of work and the adventure and intrigue of intellectual play. One requires tenacity and responsibility; the other invites imagination, analysis and fantasy. Both reward different aspects of their being. Good high schools try to respond to the inevitable tensions that these adolescent needs produce and seek to create environments that will connect their students to the wider world and protect them from it. Said one Kennedy senior forcefully, "I like this school. It's going to prepare me for the real world, but in the meantime I can figure out who I am and what I think."

Afterword: The Passion
of Portraiture

Portraiture is a genre whose methods are shaped by empirical and aesthetic dimensions, whose descriptions are often penetrating and personal, whose goals include generous and tough scrutiny. It is a sensitive kind of work that requires the perceptivity and skill of a practiced observer and the empathy and care of a clinician. Throughout this research, I was continually struck by the power of human encounter and its effects on the quality of my work. For generations, anthropologists have written about the struggles of objectivity and the problems of establishing a balance between empathetic regard and over-identification with the subjects of their research. Ethnographers entering a new culture have tried to find the appropriate ratios between being a participant and an observer, fearing that the engrossing and intimate dimensions of the former might distort their role as researcher, and that the distance of the latter might make their subjects untrusting and uncomfortable. Throughout the anthropologist's sojourn in the field, the ratios of participant to observer usually shift over time, reflecting the researcher's adaptation to the setting, the subjects' feelings of trust, and the strategies and tools required for the inquiry. Some of the shifts are conscious, purposely designed to accomplish certain research goals. Others are not under the researcher's control. They often remain unconscious and are defined by contextual and interpersonal forces beyond one's awareness. Often they are only recognized in retrospect, when there is time for contemplation and reflection on one's actions.

In various ways, all researchers who do field work that requires personal contact with subjects in their natural habitat face the challenges, dilemmas, and opportunities of human encounter and struggle with problems of distance and intimacy. Classical anthropologists, who have tended to study foreign, "simple" societies and spend long periods of time in the field, have been most self-conscious and reflective about these issues of adaptation and investigation. Their field notes have recorded their fumbling attempts, their awkwardness, their naiveté as well as their exhilaration at finally making a breakthrough, their excitement at finally understanding the meaning of a ritual. But even those researchers, whose forays into the field are brief, usually become aware of the interventionist quality of their work, the ways in which they have disturbed the environment, and the ways in which personal exchange is a key ingredient of their successful work.

So it was with me as I collected the data for these portraits. From the moment I sought entry into these schools until many months after I crafted the chapters, I was concerned about the personal aspects of this work. It is not only that qualitative research uses "the person" as the research tool, the perceiver, the selector, the interpreter, and that one must always guard against the distortions of bias and prejudice; it is also that one's personal style, temperament, and modes of interaction are central ingredients of successful work. Phenomenologists often refer to the "inter-subjectivity" required in qualitative inquiry—the need to experience and reflect upon one's own feelings in order to successfully identify with another's perspective. Empathetic regard, therefore, is key to good data collection. The researcher must relate to a person before she collects the data and if an impasse develops in the first instance, the empirical work will not be able to proceed. These are old understandings recognized by generations of committed field workers, rituals and rules that are easier to talk about than do well.

In my prior work I have confronted these issues, struggled with them, and found workable but imperfect solutions. What was striking about the portraiture work was my growing awareness of the heightened quality of these dilemmas. The interpersonal aspects of the work were somewhat exaggerated by the relatively short periods of time I spent in the field and by the exploratory methods I was using that allowed little reference to established rules and traditions. Without the elaborate rituals of entry and greeting behavior that characterize long-term field research, much depended on quick, intuitive work, on intense and focused exchanges. Without having the generous, elastic time in which to make contact, build rapport, and develop trust, my interactions with people were more dependent on my ability to seize the moment and take personal risks. Rather than using the patient, receptive approaches that had characterized my earlier work, I was aware of an increased purposefulness and assertiveness on my part. Interestingly, I noticed no evidence of people shrinking back from my more forceful pursuits. In fact, I observed the opposite phenomenon. People seemed to rise to the occasion, responding with intensity and thoughtfulness. They appeared to feel supported and invigorated by the focused attention.

During the interviews, several respondents used words loaded with affect when they described the experience of human encounter. "I feel honored by your interest. You really seem to care," said a senior member of the St. Paul's faculty. "It's like you bring the sunshine," smiled a Puerto Rican girl at Kennedy. "Your attention bathes me in light," said an art teacher with a whimsical style. There was passion in these moments, connections made at deeply personal levels. These respondents were experiencing the glow I had felt when, at eight years old, my seventy year-old friend had drawn me in charcoal. The experience of full and caring attention superseded any concern for how I might be perceived and rendered on paper.

Beyond the emotional content of these encounters, the interviewers' responses to my probing inquiries often referred to the knowledge gained through self-reflection. For the first time, many of them were being asked to reflect upon and think critically about their work, their values, and their goals; and as they talked out loud, they discovered how they felt. Frequently people would say, "I never knew I felt that way," or "That idea just seemed to sneak up on me." Or when I would return the following day, someone would search me out to tell me of thoughts inspired by our conversation of the day before. Sometimes people would refer to the momentary confusions or disorientation that our exchanges had inspired. Claimed a young teacher at Carver High, "You destroyed the balance. I thought I had it all in place." A young English teacher, who was struggling over a decision to leave teaching, wrote me a long, passionate letter after our hour-long conversation.

> Naturally, talking with you managed to stir up the settled silt in my mind—about teaching, leaving teaching, and power. I thought I'd take the liberty to restate or enlarge on some of my viewpoints. First the more pressing—these days, I am practically childishly exuberant to be leaving teaching—though the school thinks I may come back and I am prepared to eat those words—. You asked me why. On paper, I can see my response much better and see if it's right. I'm tired of being in front of a class. I'm tired of having expectant student eyes upon me, waiting for my kick-off before they return the ball.

371

Afterword: The Passion of Portraiture

> I'm tired of calling the plays, though this year more than any other I have tried to be a game-player and less the quarterback, if you'll excuse the extended metaphor. I'm tired of having to read everything with teaching it on my mind. Being academic, in that respect, deadens literature for me— ach!—. When I sit down to write myself, I find the immediate need to label what I'm doing—another English teacher offshoot that seems more inhibiting at this time in my life than productive.

Her letter continued with an exploration of her personal and institutional power, her ideological and philosophical views on curriculum and pedagogy, and her notions about success and failure in a professional career. She ended her missive graciously: "Clearly you have inspired me and filled me with energy. I wish you the very, very best."

Whether people are energized, enhanced, disoriented, or made more critical because of the researcher's presence and inquiry, it is important to be cognizant of the interventionist quality of this work and assume responsibility for establishing the boundaries of interaction and exchange. After spending several days in one school, the principal drove me to the airport. His eyes searched my face as we bid farewell. "I'm not going to make any great speeches," he said haltingly, "but I just want to say that your visit to our school had a tremendous impact on me. It was the high point of my professional career." Such proclamations, generously and openly expressed, were not unusual during my school visits, and they would often shock me into recognizing the power and personal dimensions of this work.

To some extent, my previous research had helped me anticipate the emotionally consuming aspects of portraiture, the struggles to find a balance between investigator and confidante. But never before had I so directly confronted the responses and responsibilities that accompany the research aftermath. Never before had I been brought face to face with the power and pain of portraiture. Certainly, in my past research, I had coped with the ethical and empirical dilemmas of the public exposure of research subjects; worried about the appropriate role for subjects to play in manuscript review; weighed the merits of collaboration with subjects; and struggled with reconciling the divergent perspectives of actor and observer. I discovered that portraiture, with its deeply personal imprint, invited a heightened concern from research subjects. Their responses to the portraits were vividly reminiscent of my reactions to the painting done of me several years ago when the artist worked "from the inside out." I had been shocked by the artist's portrayal and at first denied its resemblance to me. I complained about the way I had been rendered— the details of my features, the weary stance, and the passivity in my eyes.

372

But even as I denied the portrait's resemblance to my person, I recognized the profound likenesses. The artist had captured my essence, qualities that often remained hidden from view, dimensions that I rarely allowed myself to see. The artist had also captured more than a moment in time. With her piercing gaze she had seen my ancestors and anticipated my future. The scrutiny was threatening. The view of my interior brought denial *and* revelation.

So it was with these high school portraits. The three pieces that originally appeared in *Daedalus* were first read by the school people after their publication. By prior agreement with the schools involved, the editor had not offered the portraits' subjects the chance for pre-publication review. When I negotiated entry with the second wave of schools, I promised the headmasters and principals that they would be given the opportunity to read the pieces immediately after I finished writing them, before I released them to a broader audience. Despite the fact that the leaders of all six schools expressed confidence and pride in their schools and seemed unthreatened by my intrusions or scrutiny, the arrival of the manuscript brought them great trepidation. One headmaster described the "painful" process of reading the "Lightfoot piece": "I received it on Tuesday and couldn't stand to read it immediately and buried it in my briefcase underneath all the trivial paperwork. I waited until Friday night . . . after the family was all in bed. I closed the door to the den, found a comfortable chair, opened up a can of beer and drank it down . . . only then did I turn to the report. I read the first chapter, went and got another beer . . . read the second chapter, another . . . and so on." The beer was the needed lubricant. Another headmaster received the portrait during the middle of the summer. He took it with him to his summer home and read it over several times. "It was the oddest thing, each time it got harder *and* easier to take. All at the same time, I wanted to say 'this is absolutely true . . . and this is wrong.' It was like an emotional seesaw of acceptance and denial." The other school people who spoke about their responses to the pieces were not as reflective or open about the impact of the written word. Yet all of them expressed the trepidation that accompanied their first reading of the manuscript, the "terror" of public scrutiny and criticism, and the combination of denial and recognition. Everyone expressed surprise at the vividly personal character of the pieces. "I didn't expect so many adjectives," said a Milton teacher. "You know, usually research does a good job of masking reality. There is some comfort in that. Your work takes the mask off and that's very hard," claimed a Brookline teacher.

Occasionally, the denial and turmoil lasted a long time and only turned to recognition months later. The portrait of one of the schools published in *Daedalus* caused some furor among the faculty and students when it first appeared in print. I was initially baffled because I felt the piece was laudatory and would have reassured and pleased its readers. According to the reports of some insiders, responses ranged from complete denial (one faculty member put up a public sign denying that I had ever talked to him and claiming that my references to his views were totally false), to expressed differences in perspective, to disputes over details. The headmaster, a wise, confident, and powerful figure, calmed the turbulent seas by commenting on his own responses to the "Lightfoot piece." He admitted to his faculty that parts of the portrait were difficult and painful to read, that he did not share all of my views, and that an observer's perspective is potentially useful precisely because it rarely corresponds fully to the views of inhabitants. He also told them that part of the pain they were experiencing reflected the discomforts associated with the uncovering of truths.

At the same time that many of the school's faculty were upset by the portrait, I received several letters from alumni who all commented on the "authenticity" and "candor" of the piece, who expressed pride in their alma mater's openness to scrutiny and criticism. The dissonance between faculty denials and alumni confirmations was striking. More than a year later, when some of the dust had settled, I began to receive missives from a few faculty who thanked me for my "honesty." One commented that my "diagnosis" had begun to challenge some of their most entrenched collective assumptions. "At first we wanted to use your piece to fuel our fires. Now some of us use it to fuel our thoughts," claimed another teacher with surprise in his voice.

The second wave of portraits was read and reviewed by the headmasters and principals before publication. In each case, when I sent them the manuscripts, I said I was eager to hear their reactions and I also asked them to correct any factual errors they found in the piece. I concluded by offering my great thanks for their generosity and helpfulness, saying that I would be glad to discuss the portrait with them or members of their faculty if they thought it would be appropriate and useful. The principals were to decide on the strategies they would use in distributing the document to their colleagues.

In one case, the headmaster interpreted my letter as an invitation for "dialogue." When the two of us met to discuss the portrait, he began by praising the work—its life and perceptivity—and then worried out loud about a few sections that he felt were overly harsh and potentially hurtful to individuals. He also pointed out a few factual errors. I felt no compunction about correcting the errors or softening the sharp edge of several of my words. These changes amounted to minor adjustments in a few paragraphs. Most of our two-hour conversation was spent discussing interpretative sections where the headmaster expressed concern about "imbalances" in the manuscript and the "discomfort" and "awkwardness" that might be caused to individuals. These were milder worries that tended to focus on issues about which faculty and administrators felt particularly vulnerable. In a few cases, the headmaster suggested that selected individuals be allowed to review and revise excerpts of the portrait. In no case did he claim that the interpretations were untrue or even unfair. He worried, instead, about the response of his colleagues to portrayals that might reveal them in a way they rarely were seen by the school community. The headmaster admitted that he was expressing his "cautious self" at the same time he recognized that the power of the piece lay in its "sharpness."

This conversation was both difficult and instructive for me. I began to recognize that I had given the headmaster mixed messages when I asked him for his responses to the portrait. I had not been clear whether I was inviting his input and collaboration, or whether I really wanted him to simply comment on a finished document. Certainly neither extreme seemed feasible, but the wide range of possible interactions presented us with a broad and treacherous terrain. In a letter written several days after our meeting, I tried to clear up my ambiguous signals:

> After thinking long and hard about the way we planned to proceed with the review of the manuscript, I began to feel that I needed to clarify my views and correct some misperceptions I might have created. As you know, I am eager to have members of your faculty read and respond to the piece. I value their insights and comments and I would hope that my work might serve as a catalyst for internal conversation and self-criticism at your school. I do distinguish, however, between wanting their response and making changes and revisions on the basis of their suggestions. As you said initially this is my piece, reflecting my perceptions, and it must maintain the coherence and integrity that I have tried to bring to it.
>
> This is very personal work, both for the researcher and the school, and inevitably it creates feelings of exposure and vulnerability on all sides. It is also a kind of work that tends to more fully reveal the interests and preoccupations of the researcher. The work loses its power and honesty, I feel, if it becomes a consensus document. If a collection of people, other than the author, have veto power, it loses the edge of criticism (in its best sense) that makes it useful to you and your colleagues, to researchers, and to other schools that may be coping with many of the same complex issues. As the researcher/author, I have carefully combed through the data, searched my soul on many questions of interpretation, and take full responsibility for my

observations. I feel I have substantial evidence (not all of it included in the final document) for most of my views. But given that I bring a "stranger's" external view, I would anticipate contrary opinions from others who necessarily will have different perspectives. I could not, in good conscience, respond to each of these contrasting perceptions.

The response to my letter was immediate and gracious. The headmaster seemed relieved by the clarity of my statement and convinced that "tampering would render the study lifeless and useless."

In another school, the portrait became an opportunity for self-criticism and reflection among the faculty. The headmaster used it as the basis for a staff development day and commented, "It is a live document.... You talk about things we see but don't want to notice . . . it will be a valuable vehicle for institutional growth." To the foundation that had funded the study, the headmaster wrote appreciatively:

> It has been several weeks since Sara Lawrence Lightfoot submitted her marvelous portrait of this school to me. It has been read by over 20 staff members here, including the superintendent of schools. It provides a candid picture, a freeze frame of the school. We all agree the portrayal is incredibly perceptive in its ability to capture and highlight the great and deep strengths of this institution that are allowing it to respond to the challenges of a changing urban school in the 1980s. The vision many of us have of the school for the year 2000 has become a bit less hazy because of Sara's study. We are grateful for this aid to our ongoing work.
>
> I am aware of the legitimate concern many people in foundations have regarding the impact of their productivity. Let me assure you that in this case "The Lightfoot Report" will be used to energize us. We are currently planning a series of faculty meetings centering upon its content. We plan to use the document to help us continue the stressful task of moving this school and community through changing times and diminished resources.
>
> The report delineates the diversity of our student body. It praises the strengths of our teachers, and it describes the difficult transitional period the school is moving through. But what we like most about the report is that it tries to tell the truth. Some would say that truth-telling is always good teaching, but not always good administration. We would say that we must tell our community the truth about the schools. Otherwise, they will be unable to understand how difficult it is to obtain such elusive objectives as solid achievement and demonstrated competence in the High School of the '80s.

Typically, researchers who have worked "in the field," have stressed the difficulties and challenges of entry, adaptation, and encounter before and during data collection. They have spoken about the need for empathy, sensitivity, and humility in relation to subjects and underscored some of the ethical problems that arise when researchers make decisions solely based on expedience, pragmatics, or "pure" empiricism. Rarely have researchers referred to the aftermath of their work; to the subjects' responses to their efforts as a deliberate part of the research enterprise. Rarely do they see method as extending beyond the crafting of the manuscript.

Through this work I have learned several lessons about the challenges and opportunities that face a researcher engaged in portraiture. One is that the investigator must be conscious of the affective dimensions of this work. By this I am not merely saying that investigators should be aware of the biases that plague their perceptions and try to counter those by the pursuit of contrary evidence. I am also saying that the human encounter, central to the process of data collection, is the opportunity for reflection on and expression of ideas *and* emotion; and researchers must be ready to deal with the empirical *and* clinical dimensions of their work. Portraiture is a highly interactive research form, and the interactions proceed at many levels of human experience.

Because the exchanges between the researcher and subjects can be highly charged, it is important that the researcher not incorporate all the myriad responses as part of his or her self-image. The potent reactions, be they positive or negative, must be listened to attentively, but not taken at face value by the portraitist or used as evidence of his or her goodness or maliciousness. The investigator needs to find a way to hear the responses without feeling devastated by harsh criticism or expanded by high praise. If the portraitist incorporates all of the charged reactions and is vulnerable to all the cycles of emotion, it will inevitably lead to distortions of perception, to the compromising of descriptive powers. Portraiture is essentially a descriptive and interpretive task. It demands generous and benign regard as well as tough criticism. Both require that the researcher not be swayed by responses, but must find an unswerving, confident position that listens and accepts, but is not controlled, enhanced, or diminished by others' perceptions and judgments.

Second, the portraitist should give careful attention to the research aftermath and see it as within the boundaries of the methodological domain. The researcher's "exit," with all of its ritualized, negotiated elements, must be viewed with the same kind of judicious concern as the "entry" into the field. The exit is not only a highly charged, negotiated process, it is also based on dynamics peculiar to the setting. Each negotiation will be shaped by institutional and interpersonal forces that are situationally determined. In this study, each headmaster and his faculty experienced my leaving differently and dealt differently with my request that they review and respond to the manuscript.

Third, there seem to be anticipative stages of reaction that people experience when they read the portraits. The first response reflects the "terror" of exposure and the pain of visibility, no matter whether the words are praising or critical. The second stage seems to combine the elements of denial and recognition. At the same time, people experience the paradoxical sensation of denying that the piece represents them and recognizing that it is profoundly true. The third stage comes after what one teacher called "the healing of time." The subjects have gained some distance and perspective which allows them to embrace the praise and confront the criticism. It is a stage in which the portrait can become a tool of institutional diagnosis—the opportunity for self-criticism, reflection, and conscious change.

Finally, the social scientist engaged in portraiture should recognize the potential impact of the work on individuals and institutions. Portraits are not static documents or exclusive texts that are directed towards a small circle of academic colleagues. They directly touch the actors in the portrait and may speak more broadly to a diverse range of people concerned about the issues and ideas expressed in the piece. The personal dimension of the portraits and their literary, aesthetic qualities create symbols and images that people can connect with, offer figures with whom readers can identify, and ground complex ideas in the everyday realities of organizational life. This textured form may serve as a catalyst for change within an institution. It may become an organizational text that invites response and criticism from its inhabitants. The external, wide-angle view of the portraitist may contrast sharply with the various perspectives of insiders. But the dissonant strains provide opportunities for examining the power of roles, perspectives, and values in school life. Used in this way, social science portraiture may play a critical role in shaping educational practice and inspiring organizational change.

NOTES

Origins: Art and Science

1. This fault-finding regarding schools is not new. America has a long history of disappointment and disapproval concerning schools and the historical complaints have haunting echoes today. Discipline in schools, for example, has always been a primary concern of the American public. In *The Social Ideas of American Educators* (Patterson, New Jersey: Littlefield, Adams & Co., 1963), Merle Curti examines early school reports. "In 1837, some three hundred teachers were driven out of their schools (in Massachusetts) by unruly and riotous pupils over whom, in spite of the prevalent use of the whip, they were unable to keep any semblance of order." For other accounts of the long-standing disapproval of schools, see Harry S. Broudy, *The Real World of the Public Schools* (New York: Harcourt, Brace, Jovanovich, 1972), and Edward Eggleston, *The Hoosier School-Master* (New York: Hill & Wang, 1957. Originally published 1871).

2. In *Teacher in America* (Boston: Little, Brown & Co., 1945) Jacques Barzun described the exaggerated hopes for schooling in America. Many of these extravagant expectations are still held by contemporary Americans almost forty years later. "Sociologists and the general public continue to expect the public schools to generate a classless society, do away with racial prejudice, improve table manners, make happy marriages, reverse the national habit of smoking, prepare trained workers for the professions, and produce patriotic and religious citizens who are at the same time critical and independent thinkers."

3. Research on "effective schools" has begun to focus on the organizational characteristics of schools that correlate with high student achievement. Recent studies of effective schools include: Michael Rutter et al., *Fifteen Thousand Hours* (Cambridge: Harvard University Press, 1979); Ronald Edmonds, "Some Schools Work and More Can," *Social Policy*, 1979; G. Weber, *Inner City Children Can Be Taught To Read*, Occasional Paper No. 18 (Washington, D.C.: Council for Public Education, 1971); G.R. Austin, "Exemplary Schools and the Search for Effectiveness," *Educational Leadership* 37 (1979): 10–14; W.B. Brookover et al., *Elementary School Social Environments and Achievement* (East Lansing: Michigan State University, College of Urban Development, 1973); J.B. Wellish et al., "School Management and Organization in Successful Schools," *Sociology of Education* 51 (1978): 211–226. In 1959, James Conant wrote *The American High School Today* (New York: McGraw Hill), an exceptional book for its time. In a broad-based study of fifty-five high schools in eighteen states, Conant was the first to attempt a description of school characteristics that support and encourage student achievement. The heart of his book consists of twenty-one carefully detailed recommendations for high schools seeking to improve their instructional program.

4. My notion of social science "portraiture" was greatly influenced by the work of three scholars who come from different disciplinary backgrounds, but share an interest in the interpretive character of social inquiry, the integration of art and science, and the use of personal knowledge and interpersonal exchange in qualitative research. See Clifford Geertz, *The Interpretation of Culture* (New York: Basic Books, 1973); Michael Polanyi, *Personal Knowledge: Towards A Post-Critical Philosophy* (Chicago: The University of Chicago Press, 1958); and Elliot Eisner, *Educating Artistic Vision*, (New York: Macmillan, 1972); Elliot Eisner, *The Educational Imagination: On the Design and Evaluation of School Programs*, (New York: Macmillan, 1979).

5. For examples of the ways in which I have used these various methodological strategies in longitudinal, descriptive research see: Sara Lawrence Lightfoot, "An Ethnographic Study of the Status Structure of the Classroom" (Ph.D. diss., Harvard University, Graduate

Notes

School of Education, 1972); "Politics and Reasoning: Through the Eyes of Teachers and Children," *Harvard Educational Review* 43 (May 1973): 197–244. Also see Jean Carew and Sara Lawrence Lightfoot, *Beyond Bias: Perspectives on Classrooms* (Cambridge: Harvard University Press, 1979).

6. In *Personal Knowledge*, Michael Polanyi argues that there is the "personal participation" of the knower in all acts of understanding. He rejects the ideal of scientific detachment and claims this false ideal has had a destructive influence on social scientists' description and comprehension of social reality. In *Culture, Behavior, and Personality*, Second Edition, (Chicago: Aldine, 1981), Robert Levine compares "person-centered ethnography" with "traditional ethnography." One of the dimensions of the former that distinguishes it from the latter is the recognition of the centrality of the investigative relationship—that biographical information collected in the field is inevitably filtered through the relationship between field worker and biographical subject, reflecting the personalities of both and the nature of their interaction and that this process deserves explicit examination and publication. (pp. 291–293).

7. In "On the Difference Between Scientific and Artistic Approaches to Qualitative Research," *Educational Researcher*, April 1981, pp. 5–9, Elliot Eisner makes a similar point when he refers to contrasting criteria for appraisal used by scientists and artists. The scientist worries about whether the conclusions are supported by evidence, and whether the methods used to collect the evidence did not bias the conclusions. Validity in the arts, on the other hand, is "the product of the persuasiveness of personal vision. . . . What one seeks is illumination and penetration" (p. 6).

8. Both the artist and the social scientist attempt to get close to life. But neither art nor science can present total reality; so the reader/viewer/audience must be satisfied with the selection and composition of social reality. When scientists or artists carefully choose dimensions on which they will focus, however, they hope to convey something about the broader experience or terrain. Within the particular resides the general. For an insightful discussion of the historical connections between fiction and social science, see Morroe Berger, *Real and Imagined Worlds: The Novel and Social Science* (Cambridge: Harvard University Press, 1977). Berger underscores the selectivity and attempts at coherence in both realms. "In selecting aspects of 'all life' to put into a novel, the writer is imposing some sort of order upon jumbled experience, even if he claims to be portraying the very chaos of experience" (p. 3). Also see John Berger, *Ways of Seeing* (New York: Penguin Books, 1973), for an intriguing analysis of perception, selection, and composition. In "Blurred Genres: The Refiguration of Social Thought," *American Scholar* 49 (Spring 1980): 165–179, Clifford Geertz applauds the genre-mixing between the social sciences and humanities, and claims that the analogies drawn from the humanities are coming to play the kind of role in sociological understanding that analogies drawn from crafts and technology have long played in physical understanding. Geertz argues that the erosion of boundaries between social science and art will expand the conventions of interpretations available to explore human behavior and experience. Much earlier, John Dewey made a similar observation in his book *Art as Experience.* (New York: Capricon, 1959).

9. This is a common strategy among ethnographers who rarely enter the field with a clearly prescribed research design or have narrowly focused research questions. For good descriptions of the in-field process of research design, see: William Foote Whyte, *Street Corner Society*, Revised Edition (Chicago: University of Chicago Press, 1955); Joseph Howell, *Hard Living on Clay Street* (New York: Anchor Books, 1973); Elliot Liebow, *Tally's Corner: A Study of Street Corner Men* (Boston: Little, Brown, & Co., 1967); Carol Stack, *All Our Kin* (New York: Harper & Row, 1974).

10. In *The Interpretation of Culture*, Clifford Geertz speaks about the need to recognize the highly interpretive character of ethnographic work at the same time as one makes every effort to be systematic, disciplined, and detailed in descriptions of social reality. Geertz likens the interpretation of culture to the playing of a Beethoven quartet—there are many ways to interpret the music without losing its distinctiveness or making it unrecognizable as a particular Beethoven quartet (p. 11). Skill, training, and talent are required, but creativity and imagination are equally essential for a successful performance.

11. Clifford Geertz argues that cultural analysis is intrinsically incomplete. The unfinished quality of the work becomes increasingly apparent as one's knowledge of and sophistication about the culture grows. "It is a strange science whose most telling assertions are its

most tremulously based, in which to get somewhere with the matter at hand is to intensify the suspicion, both your own and that of others, that you are not quite getting it right" (p. 29).

12. Prior research has tended to concentrate on global descriptions of school organizations and student outcomes. The literature on effective schools, for example, has treated the school as a "black box" and failed to explain how school structures and processes influence teaching and learning in the classroom. These studies offer no view of the within-school processes that have proximal effects on student achievement. For good, critical reviews of the "black box" literature see: S.T. Bossert, *Instructional Management Program Plan* (San Francisco: Far West Laboratory for Educational Research and Development, March 1981); K. Duckworth, *Linking Educational Policy and Management with Student Achievement* (Eugene, Oregon: Center for Educational Policy and Management, 1981); Hugh Mehan, *Learning Lessons* (Cambridge: Harvard University Press, 1979).

13. The decision to use the school inhabitants' definition of "good" marks a significant departure from most of the literature on school effects in which researchers have tended to assert their judgments of school success. It is important to distinguish between outside experts' views on goodness and the perspectives of insiders because they often contrast sharply with one another. Researchers' judgments of effective schools, for example, often do not correspond to practitioners' subjective appraisals. See: W. J. Tikunoff et al., *Success Indicators and Consequences for Limited English-Language Proficient Students* (San Francisco: Far West Laboratory for Educational Research and Development, 1981). The authors found that school people and their constituencies assess school effectiveness in a variety of domains including the expression of organizational, social, and emotional objectives. Measures of effectiveness that focus exclusively on instruction do not reflect the complex mixture of dimensions by which practitioners judge their environment. Also see: J. A. Frechtling, "Alternative Methods for Determining Effectiveness: Convergence and Divergence" (Paper presented at the Annual Meeting of the American Educational Research Association, New York, March 1982.).

14. Past research has defined school effectiveness narrowly as instructional effectiveness and measured this construct using standardized achievement tests. For examples, see: G. Weber, *Inner City Children Can Be Taught to Read*; W. B. Brookover et al., *Elementary School Social Environments and Achievement*; R. Edmonds, "Effective Schools for the Urban Poor," *Educational Leadership* 37 (October 1979): 15–24. But organizational health is a multi-dimensional construct that requires a much more complicated view of institutional ingredients. Research on organizational behavior suggests that factors such as leadership, expectations, and effectiveness are related by a pattern of simultaneous causation that defies simple description See: O. Grusky, "Managerial Succession and Organizational Effectiveness," *American Journal of Sociology* 69 (1963); L. W. Porter and E. E. Lawler, *Managerial Attitudes and Performance* (Homewood, Illinois: Richard D. Irwin, 1968). The authors suggest that research should be designed to correspond with this complexity.

15. In *Fifteen Thousand Hours*, Michael Rutter et al., use the term "ethos" to refer to the subtle and complex combination of dimensions that cannot be disentangled for discrete, quantitative measurement and analysis, but which have an enormous impact on the vigor and cohesion of the school.

16. Here I express the typical concerns of classical anthropologists and other qualitative researchers who are interested in describing the *processes* of social exchange and human encounter, and for examining the *actors'* views and interpretations of social discourse, behavior, and events. For good accounts of the methodological strategies of qualitative inquiry and the values that guide them see: P. Pelto, *Anthropological Research: The Structure of Inquiry* (New York: Harper & Row, 1970); D. Hymes, *Reinventing Anthropology* (New York: Vintage Books, Random House, 1974); B. G. Glaser and A. L. Strauss, *The Discovery of Grounded Theory: Strategies for Qualitative Research* (Chicago: Aldine, 1967); H. S. Becker, *Sociological Work: Method and Substance* (Chicago: Aldine, 1970); Robert Levine, "Knowledge and Fallibility in Anthropological Field Research," *Scientific Inquiry and the Social Sciences*, eds., M. Brewer and B. Collins (San Francisco: Jossey-Bass, 1981).

17. For a compelling discussion of context as an essential resource for understanding human behavior see: Elliot Mishler, "Meaning In Context: Is There Any Other Kind?" *Harvard Educational Review*, 49 (February 1979) 1–19.

18. A primary characteristic of portraiture is the attention to detailed and subtle

description; to what Clifford Geertz calls "very densely textured facts" (p. 28). The rendering of details is displayed in order to point to larger cultural themes. "Small facts will speak to large issues" (Geertz, *The Interpretation of Culture*, p. 23).

NOTES: Chapter VII

1. D. W. Winnicott, *The Maturational Processes and Facilitating Environments* (London: Hogarth Press and The Institute of Psychoanalysis, 1965), pp. 145–146.

2. Jonathan Kozol, *Death At an Early Age* (Boston: Houghton Mifflin Co., 1967). Other examples of this genre include: Ivan Illich, *Deschooling Society* (New York: Harper and Row, 1970); Jules Farber, *The Student As Nigger* (New York: Pocket Books, 1970); Edgar Friedenberg, *Coming of Age in America* (New York: Vintage Books, Random House, 1963); Paul Goodman, *Growing Up Absurd* (New York: Random House, 1960).

3. There is, for example, more evidence of optimism in British studies of education and schooling. *Fifteen Thousand Hours* (Cambridge: Harvard University Press, 1979) by English social scientists Michael Rutter et al., has received a great deal of attention in the United States partly because it offers a positive view of effective schools and identifies those institutional variables that correlate with high student achievement. A less well-known British study, *Ten Good Schools: A Secondary School Inquiry* by Her Majesty's Inspectorate of Schools (London: H.M.S.O., 1977) is even more unusual in its pursuit of goodness.

4. David K. Cohen, "Loss As A Theme in Social Policy," *Harvard Educational Review* 46 (1976).

5. In *What Schools Can Do* (New York: Liveright Publishing Co., 1976), pp. 108–129, Joseph Featherstone points to the retrospective distortions of families, communities, and schools in early America. He warns social scientists not to get stuck in the "History of Amnesia," curiously repressing or forgetting the complexities of history. Other social historians and sociologists who provide important correctives to romanticized visions of the American past include: William Goode, *World Revolutions and Family Patterns* (New York: Free Press, 1963); John Demos, "Demography and Psychology in the Historical Study of Family Life: A Personal Report," *Household and Family in the Past*, ed. Peter Laslett (New York: Cambridge University Press, 1972); Tamara Haraven, "Urbanization and the Malleable Household," *Family and Kin in Urban Communities 1700–1930* (New York: Franklin Watts, 1977); Tamara Haraven, "Family Time and Historical Time," in *The Family*, eds. Tamara Haraven, Alice Rossi, and Jerome Kagan (New York: W. W. Norton & Co., 1978); Mary Jo Bane, *Here to Stay* (New York: Basic Books, 1976).

6. In "The Failure of High Schools and The Progress of Education," *Daedalus* 110 (Summer 1981): 69–90; David K. Cohen and Barbara Neufeld offer another reason for society's negative view of high schools. With the dramatic changes in the high school population over the past eighty years (that is, high schools graduated 6 percent of seventeen year olds in 1900; 30 percent in 1930; 59 percent in 1950; and 75 percent in 1979), they have become more diverse and inclusive social institutions. It has become harder to impose academic rigor or maintain discipline when the schools can no longer be selective and when students arrive with such diverse backgrounds, needs, and expectations. When today's adults recall the more orderly, serious high schools of their youth, or remember their parents' reminiscences about school, it is likely that they are referring to institutions that served a more elite and privileged population. Also see Martin Trow "The Second Transformation of American Education" *International Journal of Comparative Sociology* 2 (1961): 144–165; for a historical account of shifts in the ways the American public has judged the standards and opportunities of secondary education..

7. In "The Character of Education and the Education of Character," *Daedalus* 110 (Summer 1981): 135–150; Gerald Grant criticizes the vast changes that have occurred since the turn of the century in the locus of authority of American public schooling. He draws an analogy between various forms of authority and avocados, cantaloupes, and watermelons. Before 1900, public schools were like avocados; the center of authority was in the school, a large seed surrounded by a community and a very thin skin of federal and state control. (Grant argues that this continues to be the case for private schools.) In the 1950s, schools

became like cantaloupes; the core gave up control to community pressures and federal regulations. Finally, schools evolved into watermelons, thick rinds of federal directives, mushy community involvement, and the seeds scattered all about in "loosely coupled" organizations. Authority was transferred out of schools, away from teachers, parents, and community and into the state and federal government.

8. Alonzo Crim, "A Community of Believers," *Daedalus* 110 (Fall 1981): 145–162.

9. Erving Goffman, *Asylums: Essays on the Social Situation of Mental Patients and Other Inmates* (New York: Anchor Books, Doubleday, Inc., 1961), pp. 1–124.

10. In *High School Achievement* (New York: Basic Books, 1982), James Coleman et al., underscore the rigorous discipline of parochial schools and point to the sharp contrast with the standards of behavior required in their public school counterparts. Clearly their emphasis on discipline is one of many explicit attempts to impose standards that are in many ways contrary to contemporary societal norms and values, that emphasize the boundaries between inside school and outside life.

11. See W. B. Brookover and L. W. Lezotte, *Changes in School Characteristics Coincident with Changes in Student Achievement* (East Lansing: Michigan State University, College of Urban Development, 1979); R. Edmonds,"Effective Schools for the Urban Poor," *Educational Leadership* 37 (October 1979): 15–24; M. Rutter et al., *Fifteen Thousand Hours*; G. Weber, *Inner City Children Can Be Taught to Read: Four Successful Schools*, Occasional Paper No. 18 (Washington, D.C.: Council for Basic Education, 1971). According to this literature, the other characteristics that appear to define the differences between effective and less effective schools include: a safe and orderly environment; a clear and focused school mission; a climate of high expectations; the opportunity to learn with a high percentage of student time engaged in well-planned intellectual activities; the frequent monitoring of student progress; and good home-school relations.

12. In "High School Principal: Man in the Middle," *Daedalus* 110 (Summer 1981): 105–118; Gordon McAndrew vividly describes the multiple demands made on the high school principal and the many constituencies to whom he must relate and between whom he must negotiate. Also see H. Wolcott, *The Man in the Principal's Office: An Ethnography* (New York: Holt, Rinehart, and Winston, 1973).

13. Richard Sennett, *Authority* (New York: Alfred A. Knopf, 1980), chapter 2.

14. See Howard Becker, "The Teacher in the Authority System of the Public School," *Complex Organizations: A Sociological Reader*, ed. Amitai Etzioni (New York: Holt, Rinehart, and Winston, 1961), pp. 243–251. The author claims that teachers make an implicit bargain with their superiors. In exchange for their loyalty and commitment to the institution, they expect the principal to protect them from the external intrusions of parents and community. Part of the teachers' concern about administrative attempts to share power may be related to their fears that they will not be able to as effectively bargain for protection from threatening outside forces. For interesting discussions about teacher apprehensions concerning the rearrangements of authority and power in school see Seymour Sarason, *The Culture of School and the Problem of Change* (Boston: Allyn & Bacon, 1971); and Willard Waller, *Sociology of Teaching* (New York: John Wiley & Sons, 1932).

15. In *The Effective Principal: Perspectives on School Leadership* (Boston: Allyn & Bacon, 1980), Arthur Blumberg and William Greenfield claim that isolation is one of the greatest threats that haunt school principals. This threat is exaggerated by the orchestrating role the principal must play and by the broad scope of his responsibilities. In the six high schools in which I observed, all the principals made determined efforts to reduce the isolation by forming collaborative partnerships with trusted colleagues.

16. For insightful discussions of some of the differences in the meanings women and men tend to attach to relationships, intimacy, and dependence see Carol Gilligan, *In A Different Voice* (Cambridge: Harvard University Press, 1981); and Jean Baker Miller, *Toward A New Psychology of Women* (Boston: Beacon Press, 1976).

17. A central aspect of dealing with "people problems" is what Erving Goffman describes as "face work"; the intensity of one-on-one dialogue; the multiple, often mixed, messages conveyed in conversation; and the face-saving rites of social intercourse. What complicates it further is that these exchanges are highly individualized and idiosyncratic. They change in substance and form depending on whom the actors are. See Erving Goffman, *Interaction Ritual: Essays on Face-To-Face Behavior* (Garden City, N.J.: Anchor Books, 1967).

Notes

18. In "Authority in Education," *Harvard Educational Review* 40, (August 1970): 385–410; Kenneth Benne presents a model of "Anthropogogical Authority," which is defined by diminished power distinctions, reciprocal relationships, and the dialectic between power and responsibility. It is a dynamic, not a static, conception of authority. Benne's "Anthropogogical Authority" resembles Principal McCarthy's ideal of institutional transformation.

19. For an extensive discussion and analysis of the socio-cultural and economic factors that contribute to the low status of teachers see Dan Lortie, *School Teacher* (Chicago: University of Chicago Press, 1975); Gertrude McPherson, *Small Town Teacher* (Cambridge: Harvard University Press, 1972); and Myron Brenton, *What's Happened to Teacher?* (New York: Avon Books, 1970).

20. For an in-depth description of the contrary cultural images and their impact on teacher self-perception see Sara Lawrence Lightfoot, *Worlds Apart: Relationships Between Families and Schools* (New York: Basic Books, 1978), chapter 2; and Sara Lawrence Lightfoot, "The Lives of Teachers," *Handbook of Teaching and Policy*, ed. Lee Sullivan (New York: Longman, 1983).

21. In *Sociology of Teaching*, Willard Waller gives an interesting analysis of the origins of adult passion. He claims that adult perceptions of teachers are extensions of childlike fantasies and images. The issue of dominance and subordination, for example, that shapes the nature of relationships between teachers and students in school, is unconsciously repeated by adults unable to escape the deeply rooted childhood conceptions. Parents are likely to approach their child's teacher with the same fears and inhibitions that they felt when they approached their own teacher thirty years earlier.

22. In "Authority System of the School and Innovativeness: Their Reciprocal Relationships" (Paper presented at the meeting of the Annual Conference of the Canadian Sociology and Anthropology Association, St. Johns, Newfoundland, June 1971); M. Fullan and W. Spady argue that teachers who are systems loyalists, who are wholly dependent on their "positional authority," look to the principal to protect them from the intrusions of parents and community. The reciprocal loyalties among the teachers and principal create a static, closed institution that resists innovations and change and discourages development and growth in teachers.

23. The opportunity for teachers to express their "selves" through their work contrasts sharply with the general societal expectation that teachers should strictly conform to the neutralized role expectations of "the teacher." The rigid and static role teachers are expected to play is inhibiting to their work and deadens their motivation and spirit. For analyses of the relationship between societal and institutional restrictions and teacher expression and development see Dan Lortie, *Schoolteacher*; Willard Waller, *The Sociology of Teaching*; Gertrude McPherson, *Small Town Teacher*; Mary Haywood Metz, *Classrooms and Corridors* (Berkley: University of California Press, 1978); Frederic W. Terrien, "The Occupational Role of Teachers," *Journal of Education Sociology* 29 (1955): 14–20; and J. W. Getzels and E. G. Guba, "The Structure of Roles and Role Conflict in the Teaching Situation," *Journal of Educational Sociology* 29 (1955): 30–40.

24. See Jean Carew and Sara Lawrence Lightfoot, *Beyond Bias: Perspective on Classrooms* (Cambridge: Harvard University Press, 1979); and Philip Jackson, *Life In Classrooms* (New York: Holt, Rinehart, & Winston, 1968); for descriptions of the rewards teachers receive through the intimate, individualized, idiosyncratic relationships that they establish with students. Responding to individual needs and watching the progress of individual children is especially exciting within the context of group experiences in the classroom.

25. One of the dominate complaints of teachers focuses on the isolation of classroom life, the meager opportunities for adult interaction and colleague support. Behind closed doors, they are asked to perform a complex and demanding job alone, without companionship and supportive criticism, and their lack of adult contact gives them a distorted view of their own power and maturity. See Seymour Sarason, *The Culture of School and the Problem of Change*; Dan Lortie, *Schoolteacher*; and Robert Dreeben, *The Nature of Teaching* (Glenview, Ill.: Scott, Foresman, 1970).

26. Although various theorists offer a range of interpretations concerning the psychodynamic, social, and cultural dimensions of adolescent development, they all point to the special vulnerabilities and instability of that period. See, for example, Peter Blos, "The Second Individual Process of Adolescence," *Psychoanalytic Study of the Child* 22 (1967); Peter Blos, *On Adolescence: A Psychoanalytic Interpretation* (New York: The Free Press,

Notes

1962); Peter Blos, *The Adolescent Passage* (New York: International Universities Press, 1979); Erik Erikson, *Identity, Youth, and Crisis* (New York: W. W. Norton & Co., 1968); Anna Freud, "Adolescence," *Psychoanalytic Study of the Child* 13 (1958); Jerome Kegan and Robert Coles, eds., *12 to 16, Early Adolescence* (New York: W. W. Norton & Co., 1971); James Coleman et al., *Youth: Transition to Adulthood* (Report, U.S. President's Science Advisory Committee—Panel on Youth) (Chicago: University of Chicago Press, 1974); James Coleman et al. "Identity in Adolescence: Present and Future Self-Concepts" *Journal of Youth and Adolescence* 6 (1977): 63–75.

27. The literature on effective schools points to the positive correlation between consistent and firm school discipline and high student achievement. See Michael Rutter et al., *Fifteen Thousand Hours*; Ronald Edmonds, "Some Schools Work and More Can," *Social Policy* 9 (March/April 1979) 28–32; W. B. Brookover et al., *Elementary School Social Environments and Achievement*; E. H. Ogden et al., "A Study of Strategies To Increase Student Achievement in Low Achieving Schools" (Paper presented at the annual meeting of the American Educational Research Association, New York, March 1982). In *High School Achievement*, James Coleman et al,. contrast the rigorous disciplinary standards of the parochial schools they studied with the relatively lax and inconsistent standards of the public schools. The authors claim that the greater discipline of parochial schools contributes to the higher achievement of their students.

28. In "Authority in Education," Kenneth Benne distinguishes between "authority of rules" and "anthropogogical authority." The first refers to prescriptive forms and explicit, institutional regulations; the second to a more consensual, reciprocal, dynamic form of exchange among the institution's inhabitants.

29. Yves Simon, *The Nature and Functions of Authority* (Milwaukee: Marquette University Press, 1948), p. 6.

30. See Richard Sennett, *Authority*, chapter 5, "Visible, Legible Authority."

31. Informative accounts of the developmental transformations experienced by adolescents and their changing relations with peers and adults include: Erik Erikson, *Youth, Identity, and Crisis*; Peter Blos, "The Second Individuation Process of Adolescence"; Anna Freud, "Adolescence"; S. Dragastin and G. Elder, *Adolescence in the Life Cycle* (Washington, D.C.: Hemisphere Publishing Corp., 1975); Lawrence Kohlberg and Carol Gilligan, "The Adolescent as a Philosopher: The Discovery of the Self in a Post-Conventional World," *Daedalus* 100 (Fall 1971): 1051-1086; Patricia Meyer Spacks, *The Adolescent Idea* (New York: Basic Books, 1981).

32. In "The Failure of High Schools and the Progress of Education," David Cohen and Barbara Neufeld argue that as soon as high school became a common achievement open to the masses, the more privileged members of society sought to maintain their advantage by sending their children on to college. "Upward expansion protects competitive advantages for those who can purchase more schooling, but it also reduces the value of the soon to be universally held lower diploma" (p. 73). The reduced value of high school forces students and teachers to take the present less seriously and focus their attentions on the more selective options of future education. Also see Edward A. Krug, *The Shaping of the American High School* (New York; Harper & Row, 1964) for a description of changes in high school curriculums and pedagogy and how those relate to opportunities in the work force.

33. In "Literacy: A Goal for Secondary Schools," *Daedalus* 110 (Summer 1981): 119–134; Patricia Albjerg Graham criticizes the unfocused, incoherent character of most high school curriculums today. She strongly urges that high schools refocus their efforts on developing "literacy" in all of their students. She defines literacy as the ability "to read, to communicate, to compute, to make judgments, and to take actions resulting from them" (p. 119). As a way of giving perspective to the current distress regarding literacy, Daniel P. Resnick and Lauren B. Resnick in "The Nature of Literacy: An Historical Exploration" *Harvard Educational Review;* 47 (August 1977): 370–385, trace the historical changes in the meaning of literacy. The perceptions of incoherence in today's curriculum may reflect higher expectations of an expanded population. "The old tried and true approaches . . . were designed neither to achieve the literacy standard sought today nor to assure successful literacy for everyone. . . . early dropping out and selective promotion were in fact used to escape problems that must now be addressed through a pedagogy adequate to today's aspirations" (p. 385).

34. In *Hunger of Memory* (Boston: David Godine, 1982), Richard Rodriguez gives a

poignant and passionate account of his journey from the warm intimacy of his working-class Mexican family to the distant, dispassionate, and judgmental American school classroom. He describes the inhibitions, cautiousness, and fear that he experienced in school surrounded by more privileged Anglo children. An excellent student, Rodriguez perfectly imitated the good, mannerly child; never daring to take the risks his peers allowed themselves, rarely daring to ask a question; never daring to think or speak critically. Also see Richard Sennett and Jonathan Cobb, *The Hidden Injuries of Class* (New York: Alfred A. Knopf, 1972) for an interesting examination of the pain and ambivalence experienced by many of those who have become recently upwardly mobile and the caution and awkwardness that often defines their behavior.

BIBLIOGRAPHY

The Good High School: Portraits of Character and Culture

AUSTIN, G. R. "Exemplary Schools and the Search for Effectiveness." *Educational Leadership* 37 (1979); 10–14.

BANE, Mary Jo. *Here to Stay.* New York: Basic Books, 1976.

BARZUN, Jacques. *The Teacher in America.* Boston: Little Brown & Co., 1945.

BECKER, Howard. *Sociological Work: Method and Substance.* Chicago: Aldine, 1970.

BECKER, Howard. "The Teacher in the Authority System of the Public School." *Complex Organizations: A Sociological Reader*, pp. 243–251. Edited by Amitai Etzioni. New York: Holt, Rinehart, & Winston, 1961.

BENNE, Kenneth. "Authority in Education." *Harvard Educational Review* 40 (August 1970): 385–410.

BERGER, John. *Ways of Seeing.* New York: Pelican Books, 1973.

BERGER, Morroe. *Real and Imagined Worlds.* Cambridge: Harvard University Press, 1977.

BLOS, Peter. *The Adolescent Passage.* New York: International Universities Press, 1979.

BLOS, Peter. *On Adolescence: A Psychoanalytic Interpretation.* New York: The Free Press, 1962.

BLOS, Peter. "The Second Individuation Process of Adolescence." *Psychoanalytic Study of the Child* 22 (1967).

BLUMBERG, Arthur and Greenfield, William. *The Effective Principal: Perspectives on School Leadership.* Boston: Allyn & Bacon, 1980.

BOSSERT, Steven T.; Dwyer, David C.; Rowan, Brian; and Lee, Ginny V. "The Instructional Management Role of the Principal." *Educational Administration Quarterly* 18 (Summer 1982): 34–64.

BRENTON, Myron. *What's Happened to Teacher?* New York: Avon Books, 1970.

BROOKOVER, W. B.; Gigliotti, R. J.; Henderson, R. P.; and Schneider, J. M. *Elementary School Social Environments and Achievement.* East Lansing: Michigan State University, College of Urban Development, 1973.

BROOKOVER, W. B., and Lezotte, L. W. *Changes in School Characteristics Coincident With Changes in Student Achievement.* East Lansing: Michigan State University, College of Urban Development, 1979.

BROUDY, Harry S. *The Real World of the Public Schools.* New York: Harcourt, Brace, Jovanovich, 1972.

CAREW, Jean V., and Lightfoot, Sara Lawrence. *Beyond Bias: Perspectives on Classrooms.* Cambridge: Harvard University Press, 1979.

COHEN, David K. "Loss As A Theme in Social Policy." *Harvard Educational Review* 46 (1976): 108–129.

COHEN, David K., and Neufeld, Barbara. "The Failure of High Schools and the Progress of Education." *Daedalus* 110 (Summer 1981): 69–90.

COLEMAN, James et al. *High School Achievement.* New York: Basic Books, 1982.

COLEMAN, James et al. "Identity in Adolescence: Present and Future Self-Concepts." *Journal of Youth and Adolescence.* 6 (1977): 63–75.

COLEMAN, James et al. *Youth: Transition to Adulthood* (Report, U.S. President's Science Advisory Committee—Panel on Youth) (Chicago: University of Chicago Press, 1974).

COMER, James T. *School Power.* New York: The Free Press, 1981.

CONANT, James Bryant. *American High School Today.* New York: McGraw-Hill, 1959.

CRIM, Alonzo. "A Community of Believers." *Daedalus* 110 (Fall 1981): 145–162.

Bibliography

CURTI, Merle. "The Social Ideas of American Educators. Patterson, New Jersey: Littlefield, Adams, 1963.

DEMOS, John. "Demography and Psychology in the Historical Study of Family Life: A Personal Report." Household and Family in the Past. Edited by P. Laslett. New York: Cambridge University Press, 1972.

DEWEY, John Art as Experience. New York: Capricon, 1959,

DRAGASTIN, S., and Elder, G. Adolescence in the Life Cycle. Washington, D.C.: Hemisphere Publishing Corp., 1975.

DREEBEN, Robert. The Nature of Teaching. Glenview, Ill.: Scott, Foresman, 1970.

DUCKWORTH, Kenneth. Linking Educational Policy and Management With Student Achievement. Eugene, Ore.: Center for Educational Policy and Management, 1981.

EDMONDS, Ronald. "Effective Schools For the Urban Poor." Educational Leadership 37 (October 1979): 15–24.

EDMONDS, Ronald. "Some Schools Work and More Can." Social Policy (March/April 1979): 28–32.

EGGLESTON, Edward. The Hoosier School-Master. New York: Hill & Wang, 1957. Originally published 1871.

EISNER, Elliot W. "The Arts of Knowing and the Tasks of Teaching." John Dewey Lecture presented at the Laboratory School of the University of Chicago, May 1976.

EISNER, Elliott W. Educating Artistic Vision, New York: Macmillian, 1972.

EISNER, Elliott W. The Educational Imagination: On the Design and Evaluation of School Programs, New York: Macmillan, 1979.

EISNER, Elliott W. "On the Difference Between Scientific and Artistic Approaches to Qualitative Research." Educational Researcher (April 1981): 5–9.

ERIKSON, Erik H. Identity, Youth and Crisis. New York: W. W. Norton & Co., 1968.

FARBER, Jerry. The Student As Nigger: Essays and Stories. New York: Pocket Books, 1970.

FEATHERSTONE, Joseph. What Schools Can Do. New York: Liveright Publishing Corp., 1976.

FRECHTLING, J. A. "Alternative Methods for Determining Effectiveness: Convergence and Divergence." Paper presented at the Annual Meeting of the American Educational Research Association, March 1982, New York.

FREUD, Anna. "Adolescence." Psychoanalytic Study of the Child 13 (1958).

FRIEDENBERG, Edgar. Coming of Age in America. New York: Vintage Books, Random House, 1963.

FULLAN, M. and Spady, W. "The Authority System of the School and Innovativeness: Their Reciprocal Relationship." Paper presented to the Annual Conference of the Canadian Sociology and Anthropology Association, June 1971, at St. Johns, Newfoundland.

GEERTZ, Clifford. "Blurred Genres: The Refiguration of Social Thought," American scholar 49 (Spring 1980).

GEERTZ, Clifford. The Interpretation of Cultures. New York: Basic Books, 1973.

GETZELS, J. W. and E. G. Guba. "The Structure of Roles and Role Conflict in the Teaching Situation," Journal of Educational Sociology 29 (1955) 30–40.

GILLIGAN, Carol. In A Different Voice. Cambridge: Harvard University Press, 1982.

GLASER, B. G. and Strauss, A. L. The Discovery of Grounded Theory: Strategies For Qualitative Research. Chicago: Aldine, 1967.

GOFFMAN, Erving. Asylums. New York: Doubleday, Anchor Books, 1961.

GOFFMAN, Erving. Interaction Ritual: Essays on Face-to-Face Behavior. Garden City, N.Y.: Anchor Books, 1967.

GOODMAN, Paul. Growing Up Absurd: Problems of Youth in the Organized System. New York: Random House, 1960.

GRAHAM, Patricia Albjerg. "Literacy: A Goal for Secondary Schools," Daedalus 110 (Summer 1981) 119–134.

GRANT, Gerald. "The Character of Education and the Education of Character," Daedalus 110 (Summer 1981) 135–150.

GRUSKY, O. "Managerial Succession and Organizational Effectiveness," American Journal of Sociology 69 (1963).

HARAVEN, Tamara. "Family Time and Historical Time." The Family, edited by Tamara Havaven, Alice Rossi, and Jerome Kagan. New York: W. W. Norton & Co., 1978.

HARAVEN, Tamara. "Urbanization and the Malleable Household." Family and Kin in Urban Communities 1700-1930. New York: Franklin Watts, 1977.

388

H.M.I.S.—Her Majesty's Inspectorate of Schools. *Ten Good Schools: A Secondary School Inquiry.* London: HMSO, 1977.

HOWELL, Joseph. *Hard Living on Clay Street.* New York: Doubleday, Anchor Books, 1973.

HYMES, D. *Reinventing Anthropology.* New York: Random House, 1974.

ILLICH, Ivan. *Deschooling Society.* New York: Harper & Row, 1970.

JACKSON, Philip W. *Life in Classrooms.* New York: Holt, Rinehard & Winston, 1968.

KAGAN, Jerome and Coles, Robert, eds. *12 to 16, Early Adolescence.* New York: W. W. Norton & Co., 1971.

KOHLBERG, Lawrence and Gilligan, Carol. "The Adolescent as a Philosopher: the Discovery of the Self in a Post-Conventional World." *Daedalus* 100 (Fall 1971) 1051–1086.

KOZOL, Jonathan. *Death at an Early Age.* Boston: Houghton Mifflin Co., 1967.

KRUG, Edward A. *The Shaping of the American High School.* New York: Harper & Row, 1964.

LEVINE, Robert. *Culture, Behavior, and Personality.* 2nd rev. ed. Chicago: Aldine, 1981.

LEVINE, Robert. "Knowledge and Fallibility in Anthropological Field Research." *Scientific Inquiry and the Social Sciences,* edited by M. Brewer and B. Collins, chapter 7. San Francisco: Jossey-Bass, 1981.

LIEBOW, Elliot. *Tally's Corner: A Study of Street Corner Men.* Boston: Little, Brown & Co., 1967.

LIGHTFOOT, Sara Lawrence. "An Ethnographic Study of the Status Structure of the Classroom." Doctoral dissertation, Harvard University, 1972.

LIGHTFOOT, Sara Lawrence. "The Lives of Teachers." *Handbook of Teaching and Policy,* edited by Lee Shulman. New York: Longman, 1983.

LIGHTFOOT, Sara Lawrence. "Politics and Reasoning: Through the Eyes of Teachers and Children." *Harvard Educational Review* 43 (May 1973).

LIGHTFOOT, Sara Lawrence. *Worlds Apart: Relationships Between Families and Schools.* New York: Basic Books, 1978.

LORTIE, Dan C. *Schoolteacher: A Sociological Study.* Chicago: University of Chicago Press, 1975.

McANDREW, Gordon. "The High School Principal: Man in the Middle." *Daedalus* 110 (Summer 1981): 105–118.

McPHERSON, Gertrude. *Small Town Teacher.* Cambridge: Harvard University Press, 1972.

MEHEN, Hugh. *Learning Lessons.* Cambridge: Harvard University Press, 1979.

METZ, Mary H. *Classrooms and Corridors: The Crisis of Authority in Desegregated Secondary Schools.* Berkeley: University of California Press, 1978.

MILLER, Jean Baker. *Toward a New Psychology of Women.* Boston: Beacon Press, 1976.

MISCHLER, Elliot. "Meaning in Context." *Harvard Educational Review* 49 (February 1979).

OGDEN, E. H., et al. "A Study of Strategies to Increase Student Achievement in Low Achieving Schools." Paper presented at the Annual Meeting of the American Educational Research Association, March 1982, New York.

PELTO, Pertti J. *Anthropological Research: The Structure of Inquiry.* New York: Harper & Row, 1970.

PESHKIN, Alan. *Growing Up American: Schooling and the Survival of Community.* Chicago: University of Chicago Press, 1978.

POLANYI, Michael. *Personal Knowledge.* Chicago: University of Chicago Press, 1958.

PORTER, L. W. and Lawler, E. E. *Managerial Attitudes and Performance.* Homewood, Ill.: Richard D. Irwin, 1968.

RESNICK, Daniel P., and Lauren B. Resnick. "The Nature of Literacy: An Historical Exploration" *Harvard Educational Review* 47, no. 3 (August 1977): 370–385.

RODRIGUEZ, Richard. *Hunger of Memory: The Education of Richard Rodriguez.* Boston: David Godine, 1982.

ROWAN, Brian; Bossert, Steven T.; and Dwyer, David C. "Research on Effective Schools: A Cautionary Note." San Francisco: Far West Laboratory for Educational Research and Development, 1982.

RUTTER, Michael; Maughan, B.; Mortimore, P.; and Ouston, J. *Fifteen Thousand Hours: Secondary Schools and Their Effects on Children.* Cambridge: Harvard University Press, 1979.

SARASON, Seymour. *The Culture of School and the Problem of Change.* Boston: Allyn & Bacon, 1971.

SENNETT, Richard. *Authority.* New York: Alfred A. Knopf, 1980.

Bibliography

SENNETT, Richard and Cobb, Jonathan. *The Hidden Injuries of Class*. New York: Alfred A. Knopf, 1972.

SIMON, Yves. *The Nature and Function of Authority*. Milwaukee: Marquette University Press, 1948.

SPACKS, Patricia Meyer. *The Adolescent Idea*. New York: Basic Books, 1981.

STACK, Carol. *All Our Kin*. New York: Harper & Row, 1974.

TERRIEN, Frederic. "The Occupational Role of Teachers." *Journal of Educational Sociology* 29 (1955): 14–20.

TIKUNOFF, W. J. et al. *Part I of the Study Report. Volume II: Success Indicators and Consequences for Limited English-Language Proficient Students in the SBIF Study*. San Francisco: Far West Laboratory for Educational Research and Development, 1981.

TROW, Martin. "The Second Transformation of American Secondary Education." *International Journal of Comparative Sociology* 2 (1961): 144–165.

TYACK, David and Hansot, Elisabeth. "Conflict and Consensus in American Public Education." *Daedalus* 110 (Summer 1981): 1–26.

WALLER, Willard. *The Sociology of Teaching*. New York: John Wiley & Sons, 1932.

WEBER, George. *Inner-city Children Can Be Taught to Read: Four Successful Schools*. Occasional Paper No. 18. Washington, D.C.: Council for Basic Education, 1971.

WELLISCH, Jean B.; MacQueen, A. H.; Carriere, R. A.; and Duck, G. A. "School Management and Organization in Successful Schools." *Sociology of Education* 51 (1978): 211–226.

WHYTE, William Foote. *Street Corner Society: The Social Structure of an Italian Slum*. Rev. ed. Chicago: University of Chicago Press, 1955.

WINNICOTT, Donald Woods. *The Maturational Process and Facilitating Environments*. London: Hogarth Press and The Institute of Psychoanalysis, 1965.

WOLCOTT, Harry. *The Man in the Principal's Office: An Ethnography*. New York: Holt, Rinehart, & Winston, 1973.

INDEX

Index

Index